T0366219

DATA ENVELOPMENT ANALYSIS

Using the neoclassical theory of production economics as the analytical framework, this book provides a unified and easily comprehensible, yet fairly rigorous, exposition of the core literature on data envelopment analysis (DEA) for readers based in different disciplines. The various DEA models are developed as nonparametric alternatives to the econometric models. Apart from the standard fare consisting of the basic input- and output-oriented DEA models formulated by Charnes, Cooper, and Rhodes and Banker, Charnes, and Cooper, the book covers more recent developments, such as the directional distance function, free disposal hull (FDH) analysis, nonradial measures of efficiency, multiplier bounds, mergers and breakup of firms, and measurement of productivity change through the Malmquist total factor productivity index. The chapter on efficiency measurement using market prices provides the critical link between DEA and the neoclassical theory of a competitive firm. The book also covers several forms of stochastic DEA in detail.

Subhash C. Ray has served on the faculty in the Department of Economics at the University of Connecticut, Storrs, since 1982. Before moving to the United States, he taught economics at graduate and undergraduate levels at the University of Kalyani in West Bengal, India. Professor Ray has held visiting faculty positions at the Indian Statistical Institute, Calcutta; University of Sydney; and the University of Alicante, Spain. During the fall semester of the academic year 2000–2001, he was a Fulbright Visiting Lecturer at the Indian Institutes of Management, Calcutta and Ahmedabad, where he offered seminar courses on DEA.

Professor Ray's research has been published in major professional journals including *American Economic Review; Management Science; The Economic Journal; European Journal of Operational Research; Journal of Productivity Analysis; American Journal of Agricultural Economics; Journal of Money, Credit, and Banking; Journal of Banking and Finance; International Journal of Systems Science; Journal of Forecasting; International Journal of Forecasting*; and *Journal of Quantitative Economics*. He served as one of the guest editors of a special issue of *Journal of Productivity Analysis* honoring William Cooper. Professor Ray coauthored *Applied Econometrics: Problems with Data Sets* in 1992 with William F. Lott.

Data Envelopment Analysis

Theory and Techniques for Economics and Operations Research

SUBHASH C. RAY

University of Connecticut

CAMBRIDGE
UNIVERSITY PRESS

CAMBRIDGE
UNIVERSITY PRESS

32 Avenue of the Americas, New York NY 10013-2473, USA

Cambridge University Press is part of the University of Cambridge.

It furthers the University's mission by disseminating knowledge in the pursuit of
education, learning and research at the highest international levels of excellence.

www.cambridge.org
Information on this title: www.cambridge.org/9780521802567

© Subhash C. Ray 2004

First published 2004

A catalogue record for this publication is available from the British Library

Library of Congress Cataloguing in Publication data
Ray, Subhash C.
Data envelopment analysis : theory and techniques for economics
and operations research / Subhash C. Ray.
p.   cm.
Includes bibliographical references and index.
ISBN 0-521-80256-3
1. Data envelopment analysis.   2. Production (Economic theory).   I. Title.
HA31.38.R39   2004
338.4′5′01 – dc22   2003061673

ISBN 978-0-521-80256-7 Hardback
ISBN 978-1-107-40526-4 Paperback

For Shipra, who has cheerfully given up many precious evenings and weekends that rightfully belonged to her in order to make it possible for me to complete this book.

Contents

Preface

Researchers from diverse fields ranging from economics to accounting, information management, and operational research use Data Envelopment Analysis (DEA) to measure technical efficiency of firms (often called Decision-Making Units [DMUs]). Scholars from the different disciplines, in general, approach the question of measuring efficiency from different perspectives. Often, an operations research analyst is primarily interested in the solution algorithm of an inequality-constrained optimization problem but is less careful in defining the inputs and outputs. At times, the input variables may include both the number of workers and wage expenses even though, under the implicit assumption of competitive wages, they are broadly proportional to one another. Similarly, sometimes both sales revenue and profits earned are defined as outputs, even though profit maximization is the implicit objective of the firm. Clearly, the efficiency measure derived from an optimization model becomes more meaningful when the choice variables and the constraints correspond to an explicitly conceptualized theory of firm behavior. At the other end of the spectrum, there are numerous empirical applications in economics where some DEA model is employed to evaluate efficiency without careful attention to the appropriateness of the specific version of DEA for the production technology and the implicit objective of the firm. For the applied researcher, a clear understanding of the differences between the various DEA models is absolutely necessary for a proper interpretation of the results.

My principal research interest in production economics has convinced me over the years that one must treat the production technology and the objectives of firm behavior under the constraints specified as fundamental to any analysis of efficiency and, just as in econometric modeling one estimates a frontier production, cost, or profit function for measuring efficiency, in much the same way one has to specify the appropriate DEA model in order to obtain a proper measure of the efficiency of a firm. Thus, the neoclassical model of production economics, in its primal–dual forms, is the basic analytical framework of this book as it provides the economic rationale of the various DEA models.

The principal objective of this book is to provide a unified and easily comprehensible yet fairly rigorous exposition of the essential features of the core literature on DEA for the interested readers coming from different disciplines. The standard concepts of technical, scale, and cost efficiency are first explained using simple parametric functional forms. Subsequently, the various DEA models are developed as nonparametric alternatives to the parametric models. This should be particularly helpful for the average economist more familiar with parametrically specified production, cost, or profit functions. At the same time, various numerical examples of the parametric models have been included for the benefit of the reader whose principal background is in operations research or management science, even though such examples may appear superfluous to readers familiar with neoclassical production economics.

Apart from the standard fare consisting of the basic input- and output-oriented DEA models formulated by Charnes, Cooper, and Rhodes (CCR) and Banker, Charnes, and Cooper (BCC), the book includes detailed coverage of more recent developments like the directional distance function, free disposal hull (FDH) analysis, nonradial measures of efficiency, multiplier bounds, merger and breakup of firms, and measurement of productivity change through the Malmquist total factor productivity index. The chapter on efficiency measurement using market prices provides the critical link between DEA and the neoclassical theory of a competitive firm. In the chapter on nonparametric approaches to production analysis, a number of models that complement DEA are presented to establish the common intellectual lineage of these two approaches – one coming from economics and the other from operations research. Similarly, for the interested reader, a detailed discussion of Shephard's distance function is provided in an appendix to Chapter 2. Finally, several forms of stochastic DEA are discussed in detail.

This book is designed to provide the theoretical and methodological background that would enable interested readers to formulate the relevant DEA model for the specific problem under investigation. The emphasis is on setting up the appropriate linear programming models in the primal–dual forms. Although, for most types of models, sample computer programs in SAS are provided as examples, it is expected that readers will either write their own programs for any software that serves their purpose or get a skilled programmer to translate the DEA optimization problems that they formulate into a set of computer commands.

I have personally been interested in DEA as an analytical tool in production economics right from its inception into the literature. In 1978, while I was a graduate student at the University of California, Santa Barbara, Llad Phillips, who was teaching a course in Labor Economics, introduced me to the neoclassical theory of duality in production. Shortly thereafter, Jati Sengupta brought to my attention a paper by CCR published in the *European Journal of Operational Research* on measurement of technical efficiency using a new method called Data Envelopment Analysis (DEA). Later, in 1979, I joined Phillips and one of his past Ph.D. students, Manuel Olave, from INCAE, Managua, Nicaragua, as a research assistant for their project on measuring the productive efficiency of primary health care and family planning centers in Costa Rica and Guatemala. My own contribution to the study was to complement their Translog cost function analysis with the new approach of DEA. The data set included various manpower hours (physicians, nursing, and other personnel) for inputs and different types of cases treated (like maternity, family planning, and others) for outputs. The units observed were health care facilities from different regions categorized as urban, rural, or tribal (Indian), and observations were recorded for different semesters over years. In our first application, based on our intuition from production economics, we used the regional characteristics as ordered categorical variables, thereby anticipating a subsequent development in the literature. Similarly, we conceptualized nonregressive technical change and constructed a series of sequential frontiers for the chronologically ordered time periods. Looking back, ours must have been one of the earlier applications of DEA, which has remained unrecognized in the chronology of the literature. This is explained largely by the fact that during the subsequent political turmoil in Nicaragua, I lost contact with Manuel Olave and, over the years, the project report slipped into oblivion. Over the decade that followed, my interest in productivity analysis deepened and I continued to work on DEA just by myself with little intellectual discourse with anyone else. This led to two papers that appeared in *Socio-Economic Planning Sciences* and *Management Science*, respectively. Finally, in 1991, I presented a paper in the DEA stream of the EURO-TIMS Meetings held in Aachen, Germany. My first exposure to the community of researchers working on productivity and efficiency analysis was a most exciting and intellectually rewarding experience. It was at this meeting that I first met some of the leading scholars in the field such as Bill Cooper, Knox Lovell, and Rolf Färe. Thereafter, I became a regular participant in the Productivity Workshops held in the United States and in Europe in alternate years. Interaction with fellow researchers at these meetings has greatly contributed to the development of this book. I am particularly grateful to Knox Lovell, who at various times has been a very constructive critic of my work. At a different level, Bill Cooper has always been a source of inspiration and encouragement for me. Subal Kumbhakar, a long-time friend and a leading exponent of the stochastic frontier analysis, has always been an open-minded listener to my ideas and has judged the essence of any research idea from the broad perspective of neoclassical production economics rather than through the narrow lenses of a methodologist of a particular conviction. Steve Miller, who was a colleague for nearly two decades here at the University of Connecticut, has patiently read and offered valuable comments on much of what I have written on DEA and efficiency measurement, including several of the earlier chapters of this book.

Over the years, my own graduate students at the University of Connecticut, many of whom have been my coauthors, also have often helped me to clear up confusions about different aspects of DEA in particular and neoclassical duality theory in general through many perceptive questions they have raised in my research seminar course. In particular, Evangelia Desli and Kankana Mukherjee have continued to offer valuable comments and suggestions on all of my papers – even when they were not coauthors. Two of my current graduate students, Anasua Bhattacharya and Yanna Wu, helped me by drawing the figures in Microsoft Word.

Finally, a Fulbright Lecturer award in the fall of 2000 offered an opportunity to teach DEA for a month at the Indian Institute of Management, Calcutta, and for the next three months at the Indian Institute of Management, Ahmedabad, and allowed me to organize the lectures around the planned chapters of this book. The doctoral students at these two institutions attending my lectures helped me to improve the exposition of the topics covered in the chapters.

Special thanks go to Scott Parris, economics editor of Cambridge University Press at New York, for his enthusiastic support and encouragement. Although I alone bear responsibility for whatever is presented in this book, the body of literature dealt with is the contribution of a host of outstanding scholars from economics, management science, and operations research. If the book helps to bridge the gap between different strands within the literature, it will have served its purpose.

1

Introduction and Overview

1.1 Data Envelopment Analysis and Economics

Data Envelopment Analysis (DEA) is a nonparametric method of measuring the efficiency of a decision-making unit (DMU) such as a firm or a public-sector agency, first introduced into the Operations Research (OR) literature by Charnes, Cooper, and Rhodes (CCR) (*European Journal of Operational Research* [EJOR], 1978). The original CCR model was applicable only to technologies characterized by constant returns to scale globally. In what turned out to be a major breakthrough, Banker, Charnes, and Cooper (BCC) (*Management Science*, 1984) extended the CCR model to accommodate technologies that exhibit variable returns to scale. In subsequent years, methodological contributions from a large number of researchers accumulated into a significant volume of literature around the CCR–BCC models, and the generic approach of DEA emerged as a valid alternative to regression analysis for efficiency measurement. The rapid pace of dissemination of DEA as an acceptable method of efficiency analysis can be inferred from the fact that Seiford (1994) in his DEA bibliography lists no fewer than 472 published articles and accepted Ph.D. dissertations even as early as 1992. In a more recent bibliography, Tavares (2002) includes 3,183 items from 2,152 different authors. Indeed, at the present moment, an Internet search for DEA produces no fewer than 12,700 entries! Parallel development of computer software for solving the DEA linear programming (LP) problems made it considerably easier to use DEA in practical applications. Apart from the LP procedures within general-purpose packages like SAS and SHAZAM, specialized packages like Integrated Data Envelopment System (IDEAS) and Data Envelopment Analysis Program (DEAP) eliminate the need to solve one LP at a time for each set of DMUs being evaluated. As a result, applying DEA to measure efficiency using a large data set has become quite routine. Unlike in Management Science where DEA became virtually an instant success, in economics, however, its welcome has been far less enthusiastic. There are three principal reasons for skepticism about DEA on the part of economists.

First, DEA is a nonparametric method; no production, cost, or profit function is estimated from the data. This precludes evaluating marginal products, partial elasticities, marginal costs, or elasticities of substitution from a fitted model. As a result, one cannot derive the usual conclusions about the technology, which are possible from a parametric functional form.

Second, DEA employs LP instead of the familiar least squares regression analysis. Whereas a basic course in econometrics centered around the classical linear model is an essential ingredient of virtually every graduate program in economics, familiarity with LP can by no means be taken for granted. In text-book economics, constraints in standard optimization problems are typically assumed to be binding and Lagrange multipliers are almost always positive. An average economist feels uncomfortable with shadow prices that become zero at the slightest perturbation of the parameters.

Finally, and most important of all, being nonstatistical in nature, the LP solution of a DEA problem produces no standard errors and leaves no room for hypothesis testing. In DEA, any deviation from the frontier is treated as inefficiency and there is no provision for random shocks. By contrast, the far more popular stochastic frontier model explicitly allows the frontier to move up or down because of random shocks. Additionally, a parametric frontier yields elasticities and other measures about the technology useful for marginal analysis.

Of the three, the first two concerns can be easily addressed. Despite its relatively recent appearance in the OR literature, the intellectual roots of DEA in economics can be traced all the way back to the early 1950s. In the aftermath of World War II, LP came to be recognized as a powerful tool for economic analysis. The papers in the Cowles Commission monograph, *Activity Analysis of Production and Resource Allocation*, edited by Koopmans (1951), recognized the commonality between existence of nonnegative prices and quantities in a Walras–Cassel economy and the mathematical programming problem of optimizing an objective function subject to a set of linear inequality constraints. Koopmans (1951) defined a point in the commodity space as efficient whenever an increase in the net output of one good can be achieved only at the cost of a decrease in the net output of another good. In view of its obvious similarity with the condition for Pareto optimality, this definition is known as the Pareto–Koopmans condition of technical efficiency. In the same year, Debreu

(1951) defined the "coefficient of resource utilization" as a measure of technical efficiency for the economy as a whole, and any deviation of this measure from unity was interpreted as a deadweight loss suffered by the society due to inefficient utilization of resources.

Farrell (1957) made a path-breaking contribution by constructing a LP model using actual input–output data of a sample of firms, the solution of which yields a numerical measure of the technical efficiency of an individual firm in the sample. In fact, Farrell's technical efficiency is the same as the distance function proposed earlier by Shephard (1953). Apart from providing a measure of technical efficiency, Farrell also identified allocative efficiency as another component of overall economic efficiency.

Linear Programming and Economic Analysis by Dorfman, Samuelson, and Solow (DOSSO) (1958) brought together the three branches of linear economic analysis – game theory, input–output analysis, and LP – under a single roof. At this point, LP came to be accepted as a computational method for measuring efficiency in different kinds of economic decision-making problems.

Farrell recognized that a function fitted by the ordinary least squares regression could not serve as a production frontier because, by construction, observed points would lie on both sides of the fitted function. He addressed this problem by taking a nonparametric approach and approximated the underlying production possibility set by the convex hull of a cone containing the observed input–output bundles. Farrell's approach was further refined by a group of agricultural economists at the University of California, Berkeley (see the papers by Boles, Bressler, Brown, Seitz, and Sitorus in a symposium volume of the Western Farm Economic Association published in 1967). In fact, a paper by Seitz subsequently appeared in *Journal of Political Economy,* one of the most prestigious and mainstream journals in economics.

Aigner and Chu (1968) retained a parametric specification of a production frontier but constrained the observed data points to lie below the function. They proposed using mathematical programming (either linear or quadratic) to fit the specified function as close to the data as possible. In a subsequent extension of this approach, Timmer (1971) allowed a small number of the observed data points to lie above the frontier in an attempt to accommodate chance variation in the data.

In a parallel strand in the literature, Afriat (1972) and Hanoch and Rothschild (1972) proposed a variety of tests of consistency of the observed data with technical and economic efficiency. One could, for example, ask whether a sample of observed input–output quantities was technically efficient.

Similarly, when input price data were also available, one could ask whether the observed firms were choosing input bundles that minimized cost. One would, of course, need to specify the technology to answer these questions. Further, the answer would depend on what form of the production technology was specified. What Afriat and Hanoch and Rothschild investigated was whether there was *any* production technology satisfying a minimum number of regularity conditions like (weak) monotonicity and convexity with reference to which the observed data could be regarded as efficient. Like Farrell (1957), they also took a nonparametric approach and used LP to perform the various tests. Although these regularity tests were designed for screening individual data points prior to fitting a production, cost, or profit function econometrically, the degree of violation of the underlying regularity conditions at an individual data point often yields a measure of efficiency of the relevant firm. Diewert and Parkan (1983) further extended the literature on nonparametric tests of regularity conditions using LP. Varian (1984) offered a battery of nonparametric tests of various properties of the technology ranging from constant returns to scale to subadditivity. Moreover, he formalized the nonparametric tests of optimizing behavior as *Weak Axiom of Cost Minimization* (WACM) and *Weak Axiom of Profit Maximization* (WAPM). More recently, Banker and Maindiratta (1988) followed up on Varian to decompose profit efficiency into a technical and an allocative component and defined upper and lower bounds on each component.

It is clear that DEA fits easily into a long tradition of nonparametric analysis of efficiency using LP in economics. In fact, in the very same year when the CCR paper appeared in *EJOR*, Färe and Lovell (1978) published a paper in *Journal of Economic Theory* in which a LP model is specified for measurement of nonradial Pareto–Koopmans efficiency.

The problem with the nonstatistical nature of DEA is much more fundamental. In fact, the lack of sampling properties of the technical efficiency of a firm obtained by solving a mathematical programming problem was recognized as a limitation of this procedure virtually right from the start. Winsten (1957), in his discussion of Farrell's paper, speculated that the frontier relationship between inputs and output would be parallel to but above the average relationship. This evidently anticipated the so-called corrected ordinary least squares (COLS) procedure that adjusts the intercept for estimating a deterministic production frontier (see Richmond [1974]; Greene [1980]) by two decades. Similarly, the production frontier was conceptualized as stochastic by Sturrock (1957), another discussant of Farrell's paper, who pointed out that the output producible from an input bundle would be subject to chance variations beyond the control of the firm and argued against using "freakishly good" results to define 100 percent efficiency.

Lack of standard errors of the DEA efficiency measures stems from the fact that the stochastic properties of inequality-constrained estimators are not well established in the econometric literature. Even in a simple two-variable linear regression with a nonnegativity constraint on the slope coefficient, the sampling distribution of the constrained estimator is a discrete–continuous type and the estimator is biased (see Theil [1971], pp. 353–4). Naturally, for a DEA model with multiple inequality constraints, the problem is far more complex and a simple solution is unlikely in the near future. At this point in time, however, there are several different lines of research underway to address this problem.

First, Banker (1993) conceptualized a convex and monotonic nonparametric frontier with a one-sided disturbance term and showed that the DEA estimator converges in distribution to the maximum likelihood estimators. He also specified F tests for hypothesis testing. Subsequently, Banker and Maindiratta (1992) introduced an additional two-sided component in the composite error term and proposed an estimation procedure of the nonparametric frontier by DEA.

Second, several researchers (e.g., Land, Lovell, and Thore [1993]) have applied chance-constrained programming allowing the inequality constraints to be violated only with a prespecified low probability.

Third, a line of research initiated by Simar (1992) and Simar and Wilson (1998, 2000) combines bootstrapping with DEA to generate empirical distributions of the efficiency measures of individual firms. This has generated a lot of interest in the profession and one may expect the standard DEA software to incorporate the bootstrapping option in the near future.

Finally, in a related but somewhat different approach, Park and Simar (1994) and Kniep and Simar (1996) have employed semiparametric and nonparametric estimation techniques to derive the statistical distribution of the efficiency estimates.

1.2 Motivation for This Book

At present, an overwhelming majority of practitioners remain content with merely feeding the data into the specialized DEA packages without much thought about whether the LP model solved is really appropriate for the problem under investigation. The more enterprising and committed researcher has to struggle through the difficult articles (many of which appeared in OR journals) in order to understand the theoretical underpinnings of the various types of LP models that one has to solve for measuring efficiency. The principal objective of this book is to deal comprehensively with DEA for efficiency measurement in an expository fashion for economists. At the same time, it seeks to provide the economic theory behind the various DEA models for the benefit of an OR/management science (MS) analyst unfamiliar with neoclassical production theory. The book by Färe, Grosskopf, and Lovell (FGL) (1994) does provide a rigorous and systematic discussion of efficiency measurement using nonparametric LP-based methods. But their persistent use of set theoretic analysis intimidates the average reader. On the other hand, the more recent book by Coelli, Rao, and Battese (1998) is, as the authors acknowledge, designed to provide a lower level bridge to the more advanced books on performance measurement.

By far the most significant book on DEA in the MS/OR strand of the literature is the recent publication by Cooper, Seiford, and Tone (2000). The authors carefully develop the different DEA models and cover in meticulous detail various mathematical corollaries that follow from the important theorems. As such, it is essential reading for one who wants to pursue the technical aspects of DEA. Designed primarily for the OR analyst, however, it understandably lacks the production economic insights behind the various models.

The present volume is designed to fill a gap in the literature by systematically relating various kinds of DEA models to specific concepts and issues relating to productivity and efficiency in economics. It may be viewed as a somewhat "higher level" bridge to the more advanced material and is meant primarily for readers who want to learn about the economic theoretical foundations of DEA at an intuitive level without sacrificing rigor entirely. This background should enable them to set up their own DEA LP models that best capture the essence of the context under which efficiency is being measured.

The chapters include numerous examples using real-life data from various empirical applications. In most cases, a typical SAS program and the output from the program are included for the benefit of the reader.

1.3 An Overview

The following is a brief outline of the broad topics and themes around which the different chapters have been developed.

**Measurement of Productivity and Technical Efficiency
without Price Data**

Productivity and technical efficiency are two closely related but different measures of performance of a firm. They are equivalent only when the technology exhibits constant returns to scale (CRS). Chapter 2 develops the basic DEA model formulated by CCR for measurement of technical efficiency of individual firms under CRS using observed input–output quantity data. A simple transformation of the variables reduces the CCR ratio model involving a linear fractional functional programming into an equivalent LP problem. An appendix to this chapter includes a discussion of the Shephard distance function and its various properties for the interested reader. The CRS assumption is relaxed in Chapter 3, in which the BCC model applicable to technologies with variable returns to scale is presented. The maximum average productivity attained at the most productive scale size (MPSS) is compared with the average productivity at the actual scale of production to measure scale efficiency. The chapter also presents several alternative ways to determine the nature of returns to scale at an observed point. These two chapters are by far the most important in the entire volume, and a thorough grasp of the material contained in them is essential for a complete understanding of the rest of the chapters.

Chapter 4 presents various extensions to the basic DEA models considered in the earlier chapters. These include (1) the use of the graph hyperbolic distance function and the directional distance function for efficiency measurement, (2) rank ordering firms, all of which are evaluated at 100% efficiency based on DEA models, (3) identifying influential observations in DEA, and (4) a discussion of invariance properties of various DEA models to data transformation. In many situations, there are factors influencing the technical efficiency of a firm that are beyond the control of the producer. These are treated as nondiscretionary variables. One may include these variables within the constraints but not in the objective function of the DEA model. Alternatively, in a two-step procedure, they may be excluded from the DEA in the first stage but specified as independent variables in a second-stage regression model explaining the efficiency scores obtained in the first stage. Chapter 4 also considers the conceptual link between the DEA scores and the subsequent regression model in such a two-step procedure. The reader may skip this chapter at first reading and may choose to return to it at a later stage.

Pareto–Koopmans Technical Efficiency

Pareto–Koopmans technical efficiency is incompatible with unrealized output potential and/or avoidable input waste. Of course, when all outputs and inputs have strictly positive market prices, cost minimization automatically results in a Pareto–Koopmans efficient input bundle and profit maximization results in a similarly efficient input–output bundle. In the absence of market prices, however, one seeks the maximum equiproportionate increase in all outputs or equiproportionate decrease in all inputs. This is known as radial efficiency measurement. Both the CCR and BCC models fall into this category. But such an efficient radial projection of an observed input–output bundle onto the frontier does not necessarily exhaust the potential for expansion in all outputs or potential reduction in all inputs. The projected point may be on a vertical or horizontal segment of an isoquant, where the marginal rate of substitution between inputs equals zero. A different and nonradial model for efficiency measurement was first proposed by Färe and Lovell (1978) and is similar to the invariant additive DEA model.

Chapter 5 considers nonradial projections of observed input–output bundles onto the efficient segment of the frontier where marginal rates of substitution (or transformation) are strictly positive. In such models, outputs and inputs are allowed to change disproportionately.

Efficiency Measurement without Convexity

In DEA, convexity of the production possibility set is a maintained hypothesis. Convexity ensures that when two or more input–output combinations are known to be feasible, any weighted average of the input bundles can produce a similarly weighted average of the corresponding output bundles. In Free Disposal Hull (FDH) analysis, one dispenses with the convexity requirement and retains only the assumption of free disposability of inputs and outputs. FDH analysis relies on dominance relations between observed input–output bundles to measure efficiency. Chapter 6 deals with FDH analysis as an alternative to DEA and shows how FDH results in a more restricted version of the mathematical programming problem in DEA. Although not essential for an overall understanding of DEA, the material presented in this chapter helps the reader to fully appreciate the important role of the convexity assumption.

Slacks, Multiplier Bounds, and Congestion

Presence of input and/or output slacks at the optimal solution of a radial DEA model is an endemic problem. An alternative to the nonradial models considered in Chapter 5 is to ensure *a priori* that no such slacks remain at an optimal solution. The methods of Assurance Region (AR) and Cone Ratio (CR) analysis, described in Chapter 7, focus on the dual of the CCR or BCC model but put bounds on the dual variables. This ensures that the corresponding restriction in the primal problem will hold as equality. As a result, all potential for output gain and input saving is fully realized and Pareto–Koopmans technical efficiency is attained.

Underlying the horizontal or vertical segment of an isoquant or a product transformation curve is the assumption of free or strong disposability of inputs or outputs. Free disposability of inputs, for example, implies that increase in the quantity of any input without any reduction in any other input will not cause a reduction in output. One could simply leave the additional quantity of the particular input idle. In some cases, however, input disposal is costly. In agricultural production, for example, water for irrigation is an input with positive marginal productivity. If, however, excessive rain causes flooding, one needs to use capital and labor for drainage. At this stage, marginal productivity of water has become negative and the isoquant is not horizontal but upward sloping because additional quantities of other inputs are required to neutralize the detrimental effects of excessive irrigation. Along the upward rising segment of the isoquant, in the two-input case, it is possible to increase both inputs (but not only one) without reducing output. This is known as weak disposability of inputs and results in what is described as input congestion. The problem of congestion is also considered in Chapter 7.

Breakup and Merger of Firms
The production technology is super-additive if the output bundles produced individually by two firms can be produced more efficiently together by a single firm. There is an efficiency argument in favor of merger of these two firms. Similarly, in some cases, breaking up an existing firm into a number of smaller firms would improve efficiency. In economics, the question of sub-/super-additivity of the cost function and its implication for the optimal structure of an industry was investigated in detail by Baumol, Panzar, and Willig (1982). Maindiratta's (1990) definition of "size efficiency" applies the same concept in the context of DEA. Chapter 8 deals with the efficiency implications of merger and breakup of firms.

Measurement of Economic Efficiency Using Market Prices
Attaining technical efficiency ensures that a firm produces the maximum output possible from a given input bundle or uses a minimal input quantity to produce a specified output level. But no account is taken of the substitution possibilities between inputs or transformation possibilities between outputs. Full economic efficiency lies in selecting the cost-minimizing input bundle when the output is exogenously determined (e.g., the number of patients treated in a hospital)

and in selecting the profit-maximizing input and output bundles when both are choice variables, as in the case of a business firm. Chapter 9 considers first the cost-minimization problem and then the profit-maximization problem in DEA. Following Farrell, the cost efficiency is decomposed into technical and allocative efficiency factors. Similarly, lost profit due to inefficiency is traced to technical and allocative inefficiency components. Chapter 9 provides the crucial link between DEA and standard neoclassical theory of a competitive firm and plays a key role in the overall development of the volume.

Nonparametric Tests of Optimizing Behavior

Chapter 10 presents some of the major tests for optimizing behavior in producer theory existing in the literature. This chapter considers Varian's Weak Axiom of Cost Minimization and its relation to a number of related procedures. Diewert and Parkan (1983) and Varian (1984) define an outer and an inner approximation to the production possibility set based on the quantity and price information about inputs and outputs of firms in a sample. These yield the lower and upper bounds of various efficiency measures. The material presented here is primarily of a methodological interest and may be skipped by a more empirically motivated reader.

Productivity Change over Time: Malmquist and Fisher Indexes

Caves, Christensen, and Diewert (CCD) (1982) introduced the Malmquist productivity index to measure productivity differences over time. Färe, Grosskopf, Lindgren, and Roos (FGLR) (1992) developed DEA models that measure the Malmquist index. There is a growing literature on decomposition of the Malmquist index into separate factors representing technical change, technical efficiency change, and scale efficiency change. Apart from the Malmquist index, Chapter 11 also shows the measurement and decomposition of the Fisher index using DEA. In light of the increasing popularity of this topic, this chapter is highly recommended even to the average reader.

Stochastic Data Envelopment Analysis

By far the most serious impediment to a wider acceptance of DEA as a valid analytical method in economics is that it is seen as nonstatistical, not distinguishing inefficiency from random shocks. Although a satisfactory resolution of the problem is not at hand, efforts to add a stochastic dimension to DEA have been made along several different lines. Chapter 12 presents Banker's F tests, Chance-Constrained Programming, Varian's statistical test of cost minimization, and bootstrapping for DEA as various major directions of research in this area. Of these, bootstrapping appears to be most promising and is becoming increasingly popular. Chapter 12 is essential reading for every serious reader.

Beyond the standard CCR and BCC DEA models, the choice of topics that are to be included in a standard reference textbook is largely a matter of preference of the author. In the present case, topics that are more directly related to neoclassical production economics have been included. Others, like multi-criterion decision making (MCDM) and goal programming – although by no means less important in the context of DEA – have been excluded. Readers interested in these and other primarily OR/MS aspects of DEA should consult Cooper, Seiford, and Tone (2000) for guidance.

2

Productivity, Efficiency, and Data Envelopment Analysis

2.1 Introduction

Any decision-making problem faced by an economic agent (such as a consumer or a producer) has three basic features. First, there are the variables whose values are chosen by the agent. These are the *choice* or *decision* variables in the problem. Second, there are the restrictions that define the set of feasible values from which to choose. Finally, there is some criterion function that assigns different values to the outcomes from alternative decisions.

In the context of production, the decision-making agent is the firm. The choice variables are the quantities of outputs to be produced as well as the quantities of inputs used. The input–output combination selected by the firm must be technically feasible in the sense that it must be possible to produce the output bundle selected from the associated input bundle. For a commercial firm facing well-defined market prices of inputs and outputs, the profit measured by the difference between revenue and cost serves as the criterion of choice. It is possible, therefore, to rank the alternative feasible input–output combinations in order of the profit that results from them.

When the criterion function has a finite maximum value attainable over the feasible set of the choice variables, this maximum value can be used as a benchmark for evaluating the efficiency of a decision-making agent. The closer the actual profit of a firm is to the maximum attainable, the greater is its efficiency.

It is important to recognize that the scope of decision making defines what can be regarded as choice variables and the criterion function has to be appropriately formulated. For example, in many practical situations, the output produced may be an assigned task that is exogenously determined. The producer then chooses only between alternative input bundles that can produce the targeted output. In this context, efficiency lies in minimizing the cost of production. This is true for many not-for-profit service organizations such as hospitals, schools, or disaster-relief agencies. Even within a for-profit business organization, as one goes down the decision-making hierarchy, the number of choice variables declines. For example, at the lower end of a manufacturing firm is the production foreman on the shop floor, who is typically assigned a specific input bundle and has to manage the workers under his supervision so as to produce the maximum possible output from these inputs. Therefore, at this level, efficiency is to be measured by a comparison of the actual output produced with what is deemed to be maximally possible. For the foreman, input quantities are *nondiscretionary* variables.

The obvious payoff from efficiency measurement is that it provides an objective basis for evaluating the performance of a decision-making agent. The outcome at the highest level of efficiency (e.g., the maximum profit achievable) provides an absolute standard for management by objectives. Further, comparison of efficiency across decision makers at the same level provides a basis for differential rewards. Moreover, one can assess the impact of various institutional or organizational changes by analyzing how they affect efficiency. For example, the economic reforms in Chinese agriculture introduced in the post-Mao era allowed private farming to a limited extent. The farmers' right to appropriate the surplus (at least in part) considerably increased the output quantities produced from the same input bundle. This increase in efficiency provides an economic justification for these reforms.

Any attempt to measure efficiency raises two questions – one conceptual and the other practical. At the conceptual level: *What do we mean by the efficiency of a decision maker?* More specifically, where does inefficiency come from? If the laws of production are interpreted as physical laws, identical sets of inputs *must* produce identical output quantities. Therefore, if the same input bundle results in two different output quantities on two different occasions, it must be true that differences in some other factors relevant for production but not included in the input–output list account for this discrepancy. In agricultural production, for example, the maximum output producible from a given input bundle can vary due to random differences in weather. The stochastic production frontier models allow random shifts in the frontier to accommodate such factors. But even after such accommodation, firms do differ in efficiency. In the spirit of Stigler (1976), one can argue that every observed input–output combination is efficient and any measured inefficiency is due to difference in excluded variables. Thus, if a farmer fails to attain what is considered to be the maximum producible level of output from a given bundle of inputs, it must be due to the fact that he did not either put in the required level of effort or had a lower ability or human capital. Similarly, measured inefficiency of the production supervisor reflects a lower level or quality of managerial input in monitoring efforts of subordinates. Hence, a lower level of efficiency can be ascribed to lower effort, ability, or aptitude.

At the practical level, the benchmark for efficiency measurement depends critically on how the feasible set of input–output bundles is specified. An input–output combination is considered feasible as long as the output quantity does not exceed the value of an estimated function at the specified input quantities. In the absence of any clearly defined engineering formula relating inputs to outputs, this is essentially an empirical issue. A widely applied approach is econometric estimation of a stochastic production frontier. A nonparametric alternative to the econometric approach is provided by the method of Data Envelopment Analysis (DEA), which builds on the pioneering work of Farrell (1957).

At the lowest level of decision making, the objective is to produce the maximum quantity of output from a specific input bundle. The benchmark is determined by the technology itself, and comparison of the actual output produced with the benchmark quantity yields a measure of *technical efficiency*. This is different from *economic efficiency*, in which one compares the profit resulting from the actual input–output bundle with the maximum profit possible. Here, apart from the technology, the market prices of inputs and outputs also play an important role. As will be shown later, technical efficiency is an important component of economic efficiency and a firm cannot achieve full economic efficiency unless it is technically efficient. In this chapter, we focus on technical efficiency and show how DEA can be used to measure it.

2.2 Productivity and Technical Efficiency

Production is an act of transforming inputs into outputs. Because the objective of production is to create value through transformation, outputs are, in general, desirable outcomes. Hence, more output is better. At the same time, inputs are valuable resources with alternative uses. Unspent quantity of any input can be used for producing more of the same output or to produce a different output. The twin objectives of efficient resource utilization by a firm are (1) to produce as much output as possible from a specific quantity of input and, at the same time, (2) to produce a specific quantity of output using as little input as possible.

An input–output combination is a feasible production plan if the output quantity can be produced from the associated input quantity. The technology available to a firm at a given point in time defines which input–output combinations are feasible.

Two concepts commonly used to characterize a firm's resource utilization performance are (1) productivity, and (2) efficiency. These two concepts are often treated as equivalent in the sense that if firm A is more productive than firm B, then it is generally believed that firm A must also be more efficient. This is not always true, however. Although closely related, they are fundamentally different concepts. For one thing, productivity is a descriptive measure of performance. Efficiency, on the other hand, is a normative measure. The difference between the two can be easily understood using an example of two firms from a single-input, single-output industry.

2.3 The Single-Output, Single-Input Technology

Suppose that firm A uses x_A units of the input x to produce y_A units of the output y. Firm B, on the other hand, produces output y_B from input x_B. Then the average productivities of the two firms are

$$AP(A) = \frac{y_A}{x_A} \qquad \text{for firm } A$$

and

$$AP(B) = \frac{y_B}{x_B} \qquad \text{for firm } B$$

If $AP_A > AP_B$, we conclude that firm A is more productive than firm B. We can even measure the productivity index of firm A relative to firm B as

$$\Pi_{A,B} = \frac{AP_A}{AP_B} = \frac{y_A/x_A}{y_B/x_B}.$$

If this productivity index exceeds 1, firm A is more productive than firm B. The higher it goes above unity, the more productive is firm A relative to firm B.

Assuming that $(x_A, y_A) = (16, 3)$ and $(x_B, y_B) = (64, 7)$,

$$AP(A) = \frac{3}{16} \qquad \text{and} \qquad AP(B) = \frac{7}{64}.$$

Thus,

$$\Pi_{A,B} = \frac{12}{7} = 1.7.$$

Hence, firm A is 1.7 times as productive as firm B.

An important point to note is that in the single-output, single-input case, we do not need to know the technology to measure either the absolute or the relative productivity of a firm. In this respect, AP_A or AP_B merely describes the performance of the individual firm without evaluating such performance. Of course, the productivity index does provide a comparison between the firms. Nevertheless, it uses no reference technology for a benchmark.

Now suppose that we do know that the technology is described by the production function

$$y^* = f(x). \tag{2.1}$$

Then, $y_A^* = f(x_A)$ is the maximum output producible from input x_A. Similarly, $y_B^* = f(x_B)$ is the maximum output that can be produced from x_B. We can measure the technical efficiency of a firm by comparing its actual output with the maximum producible quantity from its observed input. This is an *output-oriented* measure of efficiency. For firm A, the output-oriented technical efficiency is

$$TE_O^A = \frac{y_A}{y_A^*} \leq 1. \tag{2.2a}$$

Similarly, for firm B,

$$TE_O^B = \frac{y_B}{y_B^*} \leq 1. \tag{2.2b}$$

If firm A produced the maximum producible output (y_A^*) from input x_A, its average productivity would have been

$$AP^*(A) = \frac{y_A^*}{x_A},$$

whereas at the observed input–output level, its productivity is

$$AP(A) = \frac{y_A}{x_A}.$$

Thus, an alternative characterization of its output-oriented technical efficiency is

$$TE_O^A = \frac{y_A}{y_A^*} = \frac{y_A/x_A}{y_A^*/x_A} = \frac{AP(A)}{AP^*(A)}. \tag{2.3a}$$

Similarly,

$$AP^*(B) = \frac{y_B^*}{x_B}$$

and

$$\mathrm{TE}_O^B = \frac{\mathrm{AP}(B)}{\mathrm{AP}^*(B)}. \tag{2.3b}$$

In this sense, the technical efficiency of a firm is its productivity index relative to a hypothetical firm producing the maximum output possible from the same input quantity that the observed firm is using.

Thus,

$$\mathrm{TE}_O^A = \Pi_{A,A^*} \tag{2.4a}$$

and

$$\mathrm{TE}_O^B = \Pi_{B,B^*}. \tag{2.4b}$$

In Figure 2.1, we measure input x along the horizontal axis and output y up the vertical axis. Points P_A and P_B represent the input–output bundles of firms A and B, respectively. Average productivity of A is equal to the slope of the line OP_A. Similarly, the slope of OP_B measures the average productivity of B. Because the input–output combinations of the two firms are actually observed, we know that these two are feasible points.

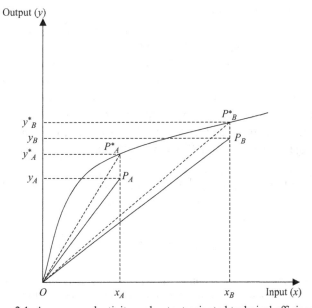

Figure 2.1 Average productivity and output-oriented technical efficiency.

Different information is necessary, as noted previously, to measure productivity and efficiency. First, in order to measure the average productivities of the two firms and to compare their productivities, we do not need to know anything beyond these two points.[1] In particular, we do not need to know what other input–output bundles are feasible. That is, no knowledge of the technology is necessary.

To determine the efficiency of A, we need the point P_A^* showing the maximum output y_A^* producible from A's input quantity x_A. Similarly, point P_B^* provides a benchmark for firm B. Location of these two reference points depends on the functional form and parameters of the production frontier $f(x)$. For firm A,

$$\text{TE}_O^A = \frac{y_A}{y_A^*} = \frac{P_A x_A}{P_A^* x_A} = \frac{\text{slope of } OP_A}{\text{slope of } OP_A^*}.$$

Similarly, for firm B,

$$\text{TE}_O^B = \frac{y_B}{y_B^*} = \frac{P_B x_B}{P_B^* x_B} = \frac{\text{slope of } OP_B}{\text{slope of } OP_B^*}.$$

These ratios are measures of output-oriented technical efficiency. The graph of the production function $y = f(x)$ is the frontier of the production possibility set defined by the underlying technology. Points P_A^* and P_B^* are vertical projections of the points P_A and P_B onto the frontier. In both cases, we hold the observed input bundle unchanged and expand the output level till we reach the frontier. This is known as the output-augmenting or output-oriented approach.

An alternative is the input-saving or *input-oriented* approach. This is shown in Figure 2.2. In this case, the output level (y_A or y_B) remains unchanged and input quantities are reduced proportionately till the frontier is reached. For firm A, the input-oriented projection onto the frontier would be the point P_A^{**}, where output y_A is produced from input x_A^*. Similarly, for firm B, the input-oriented projection is the point P_B^* showing the output level y_B being produced from input x_B^*.

The pair of input-oriented technical efficiency measures for the two firms is as follows:

$$\text{TE}_1^A = \frac{x_A^*}{x_A} \leq 1$$

---

[1] This is true only in the single-output, single-input case. When multiple inputs and/or outputs are involved, we may need to use the technology for aggregation.

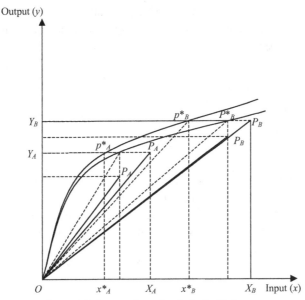

Figure 2.2 Input-oriented technical efficiency.

and

$$\text{TE}_I^B = \frac{x_B^*}{x_B} \leq 1.$$

As before,

$$\text{TE}_I^A = \frac{\text{slope of } OP_A}{\text{slope of } OP_A^*} = \Pi_{A,A^*}$$

and

$$\text{TE}_I^B = \frac{\text{slope of } OP_B}{\text{slope of } OP_B^*} = \Pi_{B,B^*}.$$

In practice, whether the input- or the output-oriented measure is more appropriate would depend on whether input conservation is more important than output augmentation.

Generally, the input- and output-oriented measures of technical efficiency of a firm will be different. The exception is in the case of constant returns to scale (CRS) when both approaches yield the same measure of efficiency. Suppose that the observed input–output combination is (x_0, y_0). Further, the maximum producible output from x_0 is y_0^* whereas the minimum input quantity that can produce y_0 is x_0^*. Thus, both (x_0, y_0^*) and (x_0^*, y_0) are technically efficient points lying on the frontier. For the input- and output-oriented technical efficiency measures to be equal, we need

$$\frac{x_0^*}{x_0} = \frac{y_0}{y_0^*}.$$

This is equivalent to

$$\frac{y_0}{x_0^*} = \frac{y_0^*}{x_0}.$$

Thus, the average productivity at two different points on the frontier remains the same. This, of course, implies CRS.

Before we elaborate on the case of CRS, we note that a firm may be more productive without being more efficient than another firm. Suppose that

$$f(x) = \sqrt{x}.$$

Then,

$$y_A^* = \sqrt{16} = 4 \quad \text{and} \quad y_B^* = \sqrt{64} = 8.$$

Thus,

$$\text{TE}_O^A = \frac{y_A}{y_A^*} = \frac{3}{4}$$

and

$$\text{TE}_O^B = \frac{y_B}{y_B^*} = \frac{7}{8}.$$

Clearly, firm B is more efficient that firm A. At the same time,

$$\text{AP}(A) = \frac{y_A}{x_A} = \frac{3}{16} > \frac{y_B}{x_B} = \frac{7}{64} = \text{AP}(B).$$

Thus, A is more productive without being more efficient than B.

Suppose that firm A actually produces y_A^* rather than y_A from input x_A. In that case, both TE_O^A and TE_I^A are equal to unity. Similarly, if B also produced y_B^* instead of y_B from input x_B, both TE_O^B and TE_I^B would also have been unity. Nevertheless,

$$\text{AP}^*(A) = \frac{y_A^*}{x_A} > \frac{y_B^*}{x_B} = \text{AP}^*(B).$$

In that case, firm A is more productive without being more efficient than firm B.

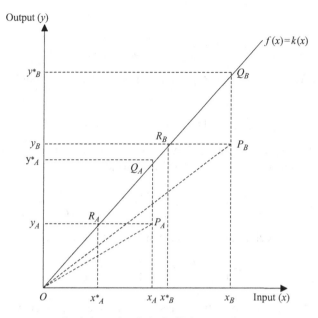

Figure 2.3 Average productivity and technical efficiency under constant returns to scale.

We now consider the case of CRS. For a single-output, single-input technology, the CRS frontier is a ray through the origin as shown in Figure 2.3. Here, the production function is of the form

$$f(x) = kx, \qquad k > 0.$$

Along this frontier (i.e., at every point on this frontier), the average productivity is the constant k.

As before,

$$TE_O^A = \frac{y_A}{y_A^*} = \frac{\text{slope of } OP_A}{\text{slope of } OQ_A}$$

and

$$TE_I^A = \frac{x_A^*}{x_A} = \frac{\text{slope of } OP_A}{\text{slope of } OR_A}.$$

Similarly,

$$TE_O^B = \frac{y_B}{y_B^*} = \frac{\text{slope of } OP_B}{\text{slope of } OQ_B}.$$

and

$$\mathrm{TE}_I^B = \frac{x_B^*}{x_B} = \frac{\text{slope of } OP_B}{\text{slope of } OR_B}.$$

But points R_A, Q_A, R_B, and Q_B are all on the same ray through the origin. Hence,

$$\mathrm{TE}_O^A = \mathrm{TE}_I^A \quad \text{and} \quad \mathrm{TE}_O^B = \mathrm{TE}_I^B.$$

Thus, when the technology exhibits CRS, input- and output-oriented measures of technical efficiency are identical. Further,

$$\frac{\mathrm{TE}_O^A}{\mathrm{TE}_O^B} = \frac{x_A P_A / x_A Q_A}{x_B P_B / x_B Q_B} = \frac{x_A P_A / Ox_A}{x_B P_B / Ox_B} \cdot \frac{Ox_A / x_A Q_A}{Ox_B / x_B Q_B} = \frac{\mathrm{AP}(A)}{\mathrm{AP}(B)}.$$

Hence, when the technology exhibits constant returns to scale,

$$\Pi_{A,B} = \frac{\mathrm{AP}_A}{\mathrm{AP}_B} = \frac{\mathrm{TE}_O^A}{\mathrm{TE}_O^B} = \frac{\mathrm{TE}_I^A}{\mathrm{TE}_I^B}. \tag{2.5}$$

Therefore, higher productivity always implies greater efficiency only under CRS.

2.4 Multiple-Input, Multiple-Output Technology

Once we step outside the simplified world of single-input, single-output production, the concept of average productivity measured by the output–input quantity ratio breaks down. Even in the relatively simple case of one-output, two-input production, we can no longer discuss average productivity in an unequivocal manner.

Assume that firm A uses x_{1A} of input 1 and x_{2A} of input 2 to produce the scalar output y_A. Similarly, firm B produces output y_B using x_{1B} of input 1 and x_{2B} of input 2. Now we have two different sets of average productivities:

$$\mathrm{AP}_A^1 = \frac{y_A}{x_{1A}}, \quad \mathrm{AP}_A^2 = \frac{y_A}{x_{2A}} \qquad \text{for firm } A$$

and

$$\mathrm{AP}_B^1 = \frac{y_B}{x_{1B}}, \quad \mathrm{AP}_B^2 = \frac{y_B}{x_{2B}} \qquad \text{for firm } B.$$

It is inappropriate to treat firm A as more productive than firm B whenever AP_A^1 exceeds AP_B^1 because it is possible that at the same time AP_B^2 exceeds AP_A^2.

A firm's average productivity relative to one input depends on the quantity of the other input as well. Therefore, measuring a firm's productivity relying on a single input disregarding other inputs is wrong. Unfortunately, this was the common practice in the U.S. Bureau of Labor Statistics and other important agencies for many years. Major business economists often compare output per man-hour across regions or over time to study "productivity changes" in manufacturing. But unless one includes the quantities of capital, energy, and other inputs, such productivity measures fail to reflect *total factor productivity*.

In the single-output, multiple-input case, we need to aggregate the individual input quantities into a composite input. We can then measure productivity by the ratio of output quantity to the quantity of this composite input. When multiple outputs are involved, a similar aggregate measure of output is also needed. One practical approach uses market prices of inputs for aggregation. Suppose that r_1 and r_2 are the prices of the two inputs. Then,

$$X_A = r_1 x_{1A} + r_2 x_{2A} \tag{2.6a}$$

and

$$X_B = r_1 x_{1B} + r_2 x_{2B} \tag{2.6b}$$

are the aggregate input quantities for A and B, respectively. In that case,

$$\text{AP}(A) = \frac{y_A}{X_A} = \frac{y_A}{r_1 x_{1A} + r_2 x_{2A}} \tag{2.7a}$$

and

$$\text{AP}(B) = \frac{y_B}{X_B} = \frac{y_B}{r_1 x_{1B} + r_2 x_{2B}}. \tag{2.7b}$$

But, obviously, the aggregate input bundles represent the input costs of the two firms. Thus, a firm's average productivity is merely the inverse of its average cost (AC). That is,

$$\text{AP}(A) = \frac{1}{\text{AC}_A} \quad \text{and} \quad \text{AP}(B) = \frac{1}{\text{AC}_B}.$$

Now suppose that each firm produced two outputs: y_1 and y_2. The output prices are q_1 and q_2, respectively. Then, the aggregate outputs of the two firms are measured as follows:

$$Y_A = q_1 y_{1A} + q_2 y_{2A} \quad \text{for firm } A$$

and

$$Y_B = q_1 y_{1B} + q_2 y_{2B} \quad \text{for firm } B.$$

In that case,

$$\text{AP}_A = \frac{Y_A}{X_A} = \frac{q_1 y_{1A} + q_2 y_{2A}}{r_1 x_{1A} + r_2 x_{2A}} \tag{2.8a}$$

and

$$\text{AP}_B = \frac{Y_B}{X_B} = \frac{q_1 y_{1B} + q_2 y_{2B}}{r_1 x_{1B} + r_2 x_{2B}}. \tag{2.8b}$$

Thus, a firm's average productivity is merely its (gross) rate of return on outlay. The firm with a higher rate of return is deemed to be the more productive one.

Although this approach is simple and appealing from the perspective of a competitive market, input and output prices are not always available. This is especially true in the service sector (such as education, public safety) where prices are seldom available for outputs. Moreover, in the presence of a monopoly, the market prices of inputs or outputs would be distorted. What we prefer, therefore, is a measure of productivity that would not require the use of market prices.

Consider, again, a single-output, multiple-input production technology. Assume further that CRS holds. Let $x_A = (x_{1A}, x_{2A}, \ldots, x_{nA})$ be the (vector) input bundle and y_A the (scalar) output level of firm A. Assume, further, that

$$y^* = f(x)$$

is the production function showing the maximum output (y^*) producible from the input bundle x. Then, the technical efficiency of firm A is

$$\text{TE}_A = \frac{y_A}{y_A^*} = \frac{y_A}{f(x_A)}. \tag{2.9}$$

But, under CRS, $f(x) = \sum_{i=1}^{n} f_i x_i$, where $f_i \equiv \frac{\partial f(x)}{\partial x_i}$. Thus, it is possible to construct the aggregate input quantity as

$$X_A = \sum_{i=1}^{n} f_i(x_A) x_{iA}. \tag{2.10}$$

In this case,

$$\text{AP}(A) = \frac{y_A}{X_A} = \frac{y_A}{f(x_A)}. \tag{2.11}$$

Similarly, for firm B producing output y_B from the input bundle, x_B, $X_B = \sum_{i=1}^{n} f_i(x_B) x_{iB}$.

$$AP(B) = \frac{y_B}{X_B} = \frac{y_B}{f(x_B)}. \tag{2.12}$$

As was pointed out earlier, in this case of CRS, the productivity index of firm B relative to firm A is merely the ratio of their respective technical efficiency levels.

It may be noted that when market prices are actually available, optimizing behavior of competitive firms would result in the prices of individual inputs being equated to the corresponding values of their marginal products. Thus,

$$r_i = q f_i; \quad (i = 1, 2, \ldots, n), \tag{2.13}$$

where r_i is the price of input i and q is the output price. In that case,

$$AP(A) = \frac{q y_A}{\sum_{i=1}^{n} r_i x_{iA}} = \frac{TR_A}{TC_A}, \tag{2.14}$$

where TR_A and TC_A refer to the total revenue and the total cost of firm A. Similarly, for firm B producing output y_B from input x_B,

$$AP(B) = \frac{q y_B}{\sum_{i=1}^{n} r_i x_{iB}} = \frac{TR_B}{TC_B}. \tag{2.15}$$

This, it may be noted, is the *return to the dollar* criterion proposed by Georgescu-Roegen (1951, p. 103).

Of course, one cannot take this approach when market prices are not available. In fact, even when prices exist, they may not be the appropriate weights for aggregation. For example, a firm with higher market power may have higher output prices relative to a firm without market power. In such cases, using actual prices for aggregation will exaggerate productivity or efficiency of the former. When market prices cannot or should not be used, we need to construct *shadow prices* of inputs for aggregation. For a competitive profit-maximizing firm, the price of any input deflated by the output price equals the marginal productivity of the input. Therefore, we can use these marginal productivities as shadow prices. Under CRS, the production function is homogeneous of degree 1 in inputs. Thus, the aggregate input quantities (like X_A and X_B) are also homogeneous of degree 1. It may be noted that unlike the market prices, the shadow prices of inputs are not uniform across firms. Rather, these shadow prices depend on the input bundle at which the marginal productivities are evaluated.

To measure the technical efficiency of any observed input–output bundle, one needs to know the maximum quantity of output that can be produced from the relevant input bundle. One possibility is to explicitly specify a production function. The value of this function at the input level under consideration denotes the maximum producible output quantity. The more common practice is to estimate the parameters of the specified function empirically from a sample of input–output data. The least squares procedure permits observed points to lie above the fitted line and fails to construct a production *frontier*. At the same time, specifying a one-sided distribution of the disturbance term leads to a deterministic frontier, and any deviation from this frontier is interpreted as inefficiency. In a stochastic frontier model[2] one includes a composite error, which is a sum of a one-sided disturbance term representing shortfalls of the actually produced output from the frontier due to inefficiency and a two-sided disturbance term representing upward or downward shifts in the frontier itself due to random factors. For the econometric procedure, one must select a particular functional form (e.g., Cobb–Douglas) out of a number of alternatives. At any input bundle x_0, the value attained by $f(x_0)$ will depend on the functional form chosen. Further, the parameter estimates are also sensitive to the choice of the probability distributions specified for the disturbance terms.

DEA is an alternative nonparametric method of measuring efficiency that uses mathematical programming rather than regression. Here, one circumvents the problem of specifying an explicit form of the production function and makes only a minimum number of assumptions about the underlying technology. Farrell (1957) formulated a linear programming (LP) model to measure the technical efficiency of a firm with reference to a benchmark technology characterized by CRS. This efficiency measure corresponds to the coefficient of resource utilization defined by Debreu (1951) and is the same as Shephard's distance function (1953).

In DEA, we construct a benchmark technology from the observed input–output bundles of the firms in the sample. For this, we make the following general assumptions about the production technology without specifying any functional form. These are fairly weak assumptions and hold for all technologies represented by a quasi-concave and weakly monotonic production function.

---

[2] For a comprehensive exposition of the various models of stochastic frontier production, cost, and profit functions, see Kumbhakar and Lovell (2000).

(A1) All actually observed input–output combinations are feasible. An input–output bundle (x, y) is feasible when the output bundle y can be produced from the input bundle x. Suppose that we have a sample of N firms from an industry producing m outputs from n inputs. Let $x^j = (x_{1j}, x_{2j}, \ldots, x_{nj})$ be the input (vector) of firm j ($j = 1, 2, \ldots, N$) and $y^j = (y_{1j}, y_{2j}, \ldots, y_{mj})$ be its observed output (vector). Then, by (A1) each (x^j, y^j) ($j = 1, 2, \ldots, N$) is a feasible input–output bundle.

(A2) The production possibility set is convex. Consider two feasible input–output bundles (x^A, y^A) and (x^B, y^B). Then, the (weighted) average input–output bundle $(\bar{x}, \bar{y})$, where $\bar{x} = \lambda x^A + (1 - \lambda)x^B$ and $\bar{y} = \lambda y^A + (1 - \lambda)y^B$ for some λ satisfying $0 \leq \lambda \leq 1$, is also feasible.

(A3) Inputs are freely disposable. If (x^0, y^0) is feasible, then for any $x \geq x^0$, (x, y^0) is also feasible.

(A4) Outputs are freely disposable. If (x^0, y^0) is feasible, then for any $y \leq y^0$, (x^0, y) is also feasible.

If additionally we assume that CRS holds,
(A5) If (x, y) is feasible, then for any $k \geq 0$, (kx, ky) is also feasible.

It is possible to empirically construct a production possibility set satisfying assumptions (A1–A5) from the observed data without any explicit specification of a production function. Consider the input–output pair $(\hat{x}, \hat{y})$, where $\hat{x} = \sum_{j=1}^{N} \mu_j x^j, \hat{y} = \sum_{j=1}^{N} \mu_j y^j, \sum_{j=1}^{N} \mu_j = 1$, and $\mu_j \geq 0$ ($j = 1, 2, \ldots, N$). By (A1–A2), $(\hat{x}, \hat{y})$ is feasible. If, additionally, CRS is assumed, $(k\hat{x}, k\hat{y})$ is also a feasible bundle for any $k \geq 0$. Define $\tilde{x} = k\hat{x}$ and $\tilde{y} = k\hat{y}$ for some $k \geq 0$. Next, define $\lambda_j = k\mu_j$. Then, $\lambda_j \geq 0$ and $\sum_{j=1}^{N} \lambda_j = k$. But k is only restricted to be nonnegative. Hence, beyond nonnegativity, there are no additional restrictions on the λ_j's.

Therefore, on the basis of the observed input–output quantities and under the assumptions (A1–A5), we can define the production possibility set or the technology set as follows:

$$T^C = \left\{ (x, y) : x \geq \sum_{j=1}^{N} \lambda_j x^j; \; y \leq \sum_{j=1}^{N} \lambda_j y^j; \; \lambda_j \geq 0; \; (j = 1, 2, \ldots, N) \right\}.$$

(2.16)

Here, the superscript C indicates that the technology is characterized by CRS.

Now consider the output-oriented technical efficiency of firm t producing output y^t from the input bundle x^t. We want to determine what is the maximum output (y^*) producible from the same input bundle x^t. Suppose that ϕ^* is the maximum value of ϕ such that $(x^t, \phi y^t)$ lies within the technology set. Then, $y^* = \phi^* y^t$ and the output-oriented technical efficiency of firm t is

$$\mathrm{TE}_O^t = \mathrm{TE}_O(x^t, y^t) = \frac{1}{\phi^*}. \tag{2.17}$$

The LP problem for measuring the output-oriented technical efficiency is formulated in the following section.

To evaluate the input-oriented technical efficiency of any firm, we examine whether and to what extent it is possible to reduce its input(s) without reducing the output(s). This is quite straightforward when only one input is involved. In the presence of multiple inputs, a relevant question would be whether reducing one input is more important than reducing some other input. When market prices of inputs are not available, one way to circumvent this problem is to look for *equiproportionate* reduction in all inputs. This amounts to scaling down the observed input bundle without altering the input proportions. The input-oriented technical efficiency of firm t is θ^*, where

$$\theta^* = \min \theta : (\theta x^t, y^t) \in T^C. \tag{2.18}$$

Note that $(x^t, \phi^* y^t) \in T^C$. Hence, $(kx^t, k\phi^* y^t) \in T^C$. Setting $k = \frac{1}{\phi^*}$, we get $(\frac{1}{\phi^*} x^t, y^t) \in T^C$. Obviously, under CRS, $\theta^* = \frac{1}{\phi^*}$. That is, the input- and output-oriented technical efficiency measures are identical in this case.

2.5 Data Envelopment Analysis

CCR (1978, 1981) introduced the method of DEA to address the problem of efficiency measurement for decision-making units (DMUs) with multiple inputs and multiple outputs in the absence of market prices. They coined the phrase *decision-making units* to include nonmarket agencies like schools, hospitals, and courts, which produce identifiable and measurable outputs from measurable inputs but generally lack market prices of outputs (and often of some inputs as well). In this book, we regard a *DMU* as synonymous with a *firm*.

Suppose that there are N firms, each producing m outputs from n inputs. Firm t uses the input bundle $x^t = (x_{1t}, x_{2t}, \ldots, x_{nt})$ to produce the output bundle $y^t = (y_{1t}, y_{2t}, \ldots, y_{mt})$. As noted previously, measurement of average productivity requires aggregation of inputs and outputs. However, no prices are available. What we would need in this situation is to use vectors of "shadow" prices of inputs and outputs.

Define $u^t = (u_{1t}, u_{2t}, \ldots, u_{nt})$ as the shadow price vector for inputs and $v^t = (v_{1t}, v_{2t}, \ldots, v_{mt})$ as the shadow price vector for outputs. Using these prices for aggregation, we get a measure of average productivity of firm t as follows:

$$\text{AP}_t = \frac{\sum_{r=1}^{m} v_{rt} y_{rt}}{\sum_{i=1}^{n} u_{it} x_{it}} = \frac{v^{t'} y^t}{u^{t'} x^t} \tag{2.19}$$

Note that the shadow price vectors used for aggregation vary across firms. Two restrictions are imposed, however. First, all of these shadow prices must be nonnegative, although zero prices are admissible for individual inputs and outputs. Second, and more important, the shadow prices have to be such that when aggregated using these prices, no firm's input–output bundle results in average productivity greater than unity. This, of course, also ensures that $\text{AP}_t \leq 1$ for each firm t. These restrictions can be formulated as follows:

$$\text{AP}_j = \frac{v^{t'} y^j}{u^{t'} x^j} = \frac{\sum_{r=1}^{m} v_{rt} y_{rj}}{\sum_{i=1}^{n} u_{it} x_{ij}} \leq 1; \quad (j = 1, 2, \ldots, t, \ldots, N); \tag{2.20}$$

$$u_{it} \geq 0; \quad (i = 1, 2, \ldots, n); \quad v_{rt} \geq 0; \quad (r = 1, 2, \ldots, m).$$

In general, there are many shadow price vectors (u^t, v^t) satisfying these restrictions. From them, we choose one that maximizes AP_t, as defined previously.

This is a linear fractional functional programming problem and is quite difficult to solve as it is. There is, however, a simple solution.[3] Note that neither the objective function (AP_t) nor the constraints is affected if all of the shadow prices are multiplied by a nonnegative scale factor k (>0). Define

$$w_{it} = k u_{it} (i = 1, 2, \ldots, n) \tag{2.21a}$$

and

$$p_{rt} = k v_{rt} (r = 1, 2, \ldots, m). \tag{2.21b}$$

Then, the optimization problem becomes

$$\max \frac{p^{t'} y^t}{w^{t'} x^t}$$

$$\text{s. t.} \quad \frac{p^{t'} y^j}{w^{t'} x^j} \leq 1; \quad (j = 1, 2, \ldots, N); \tag{2.22}$$

$$p^t \geq 0; \quad w^t \geq 0.$$

---

[3] This approach was introduced earlier by Charnes and Cooper (1962).

Now, set

$$k \equiv \frac{1}{\sum\limits_{i=1}^{n} u_{it} x_{it}} \qquad (2.23)$$

Then, $w^{t\prime} x^t = 1$ and the problem becomes

$$\max \sum_{r=1}^{m} p_{rt} y_{rt}$$

$$\text{s. t.} \quad \sum_{r=1}^{m} p_{rt} y_{rj} - \sum_{i=1}^{n} w_{it} x_{ij} \leq 0; \quad (j = 1, 2, \dots, t, \dots, N);$$

$$\sum_{i=1}^{n} w_{it} x_{it} = 1; \qquad (2.24)$$

$$p_{rt} \geq 0; \quad (r = 1, 2, \dots, m):$$

$$w_{it} \geq 0; \quad (i = 1, 2, \dots, n).$$

This is a LP problem and can be solved using the simplex method.

Several important points require emphasis. First, the shadow prices of inputs cause the value of the observed input bundle x^t of the firm under evaluation to equal unity. As a result, the value of the output bundle itself (p^t, y^t) becomes a measure of its average productivity. Second, at prices (p^t, w^t), the observed input–output bundle of no firm in the sample would result in a positive surplus of revenue over cost. If one interpreted the input prices as the imputed values of these scarce resources, then if the prices chosen are such that the imputed value of any input bundle is less than the imputed valuation of the output bundle it produces, clearly the resources are being undervalued and the imputed input prices should be revised upward. Similarly, if the output prices reflect the cost of the inputs drawn away from other uses to produce one unit of the output, then a total imputed value of the output bundle exceeding the total imputed cost of the input bundle used would imply that the output bundle is overvalued. Finally, when CRS are assumed, the efficient production correspondence

$$F(x, y) = 0 \qquad (2.25)$$

is homogeneous of degree zero.

Thus,

$$\sum_i \frac{\partial F}{\partial x_i} x_i + \sum_j \frac{\partial F}{\partial y_j} y_j = 0. \tag{2.26}$$

Further, under competitive profit maximization[4], price of output j is proportional to $\frac{\partial F}{\partial y_j}$ whereas the price of input i is proportional to the negative of $\frac{\partial F}{\partial x_i}$. Hence, when shadow prices are derived from the technology, the imputed profit of the firm is zero.

This constraint applies to every firm including firm t, the one under consideration. As a result, the maximum value of the aggregate output Y_t is unity, implying that

$$\Pi_t = \frac{Y_t}{Y_t^*} = Y_t = p^{t\prime} y^t. \tag{2.27}$$

Thus, the optimal solution of this LP problem yields a measure of the output-oriented technical efficiency of firm t.

For simplicity, consider the two-input, two-output case. Let $y^t = (y_{1t}, y_{2t})$ and $x^t = (x_{1t}, x_{2t})$. Then, the LP problem becomes

$$\max p_{1t} y_{1t} + p_{2t} y_{2t}$$

$$\text{s. t. } p_{1t} y_{11} + p_{2t} y_{21} - w_{1t} x_{11} - w_{2t} x_{21} \le 0;$$

$$p_{1t} y_{12} + p_{2t} y_{22} - w_{1t} x_{21} - w_{2t} x_{22} \le 0;$$

$$\cdots\cdots$$

$$p_{1t} y_{1t} + p_{2t} y_{2t} - w_{1t} x_{1t} - w_{2t} x_{2t} \le 0; \tag{2.28a}$$

$$\cdots\cdots$$

$$p_{1t} y_{1N} + p_{2t} y_{2N} - w_{1t} x_{1N} - w_{2t} x_{2N} \le 0;$$

$$w_{1t} x_{1t} + w_{2t} x_{2t} = 1;$$

$$p_{1t}, p_{2t}, w_{1t}, w_{2t} \ge 0.$$

---

[4] Consider the profit maximization problem $\max \Pi = \sum_j p_j y_j - \sum_i w_i x_i$ subject to the constraint $F(x, y) = 0$. The Lagrangian takes the form

$$L(x, y, \lambda) = \sum_j p_j y_j - \sum_i w_i x_i - \lambda F(x, y)$$

and the first-order conditions for a maximum are

$$p_j = \lambda F_j \quad \text{and} \quad w_i = -\lambda F_i.$$

The dual of this LP is the problem

$$\min \theta$$

$$\text{s. t. } \lambda_1 y_{11} + \lambda_2 y_{12} + \cdots + \lambda_t y_{1t} + \cdots + \lambda_N y_{1N} \geq y_{1t};$$

$$\lambda_1 y_{21} + \lambda_2 y_{22} + \cdots + \lambda_t y_{2t} + \cdots + \lambda_N y_{2N} \geq y_{2t};$$

$$\theta x_{1t} - \lambda_1 x_{11} - \lambda_2 x_{12} - \cdots - \lambda_t x_{1t} - \cdots - \lambda_N x_{1N} \geq 0; \tag{2.28b}$$

$$\theta x_{2t} - \lambda_1 x_{21} - \lambda_2 x_{22} - \cdots - \lambda_t x_{2t} - \cdots - \lambda_N x_{2N} \geq 0;$$

$$\theta \text{ free}, \quad \lambda_j \geq 0, \quad (j = 1, 2, \ldots, N).$$

Define $\phi = \frac{1}{\theta}$ and $\mu_j = \frac{\lambda_j}{\theta}$. Then, minimization of θ is equivalent to maximization of ϕ. In terms of the redefined variables, the LP problem now becomes

$$\max \phi$$

$$\text{s. t. } \sum_{j=1}^{N} \mu_j y_{1j} \geq \phi y_{1t};$$

$$\sum_{j=1}^{N} \mu_j y_{2j} \geq \phi y_{2t};$$

$$\sum_{j=1}^{N} \mu_j x_{1j} < x_{1t};$$

$$\sum_{j=1}^{N} \mu_j x_{2j} \leq x_{2t};$$

$$\phi \text{ free}; \quad \mu_j \geq 0; \quad (j = 1, 2, \ldots, N). \tag{2.29}$$

Thus, clearly $\frac{1}{\phi^*}$ from this problem equals θ^* from the previous problem. Further, by standard duality results, θ^* equals $p^{t*\prime} y^t$.

Example 2.1

Table 2.1. *The hypothetical input and output quantities for six firms.*

Firm	A	B	C	D	E	F
Output 1 (y_1)	4	9	6	8	7	11
Output 2 (y_2)	2	4	3	6	5	8
Input 1 (x_1)	2	7	6	5	8	6
Input 2 (x_2)	3	5	7	8	4	6

To evaluate the technical efficiency of firm C, we solve the following LP problem:

$$\max \phi$$

$$\text{s. t. } 4\lambda_A + 9\lambda_B + 6\lambda_C + 8\lambda_D + 7\lambda_E + 11\lambda_F - 6\phi \geq 0;$$

$$2\lambda_A + 4\lambda_B + 3\lambda_C + 6\lambda_D + 5\lambda_E + 8\lambda_F - 3\phi \geq 0;$$

$$2\lambda_A + 7\lambda_B + 6\lambda_C + 5\lambda_D + 8\lambda_E + 6\lambda_F \leq 6; \qquad (2.30)$$

$$3\lambda_A + 5\lambda_B + 7\lambda_C + 8\lambda_D + 4\lambda_E + 6\lambda_F \leq 7;$$

$$\lambda_A, \lambda_B, \ldots, \lambda_F \geq 0; \quad \phi \text{ free.}$$

Note that the output quantities of firm C appear as coefficients of $-\phi$ in the left-hand sides of the inequalities, whereas its input quantities appear on the right-hand sides of the constraints.

The optimal solution of this problem is

$$\lambda_A^* = 1; \quad \lambda_F^* = 0.667; \quad \lambda_B^* = \lambda_C^* = \lambda_D^* = 0; \quad \phi^* = 1.889.$$

This means that if we construct a reference firm (say C^*) by combining 66.7% of the input–output bundles of firm F with the input–output bundle of firm A, then this new firm would produce 11.33 units of y_1 and 7.33 units of y_2 using 6 units of x_1 and 7 units of x_2. Comparison of this potential output bundle with the actual output levels of firm C reveals that output y_1 can be expanded by a factor of 1.889, while output y_2 can be increased by a factor of 2.444. Note that this new firm does not require more of any input than is actually used by firm C. Thus, it is possible to expand *every output* by at least the factor of 1.889. This is measured by ϕ^* in the optimal solution. Hence, a measure of technical efficiency of firm C is

$$\text{TE}(C) = \frac{1}{1.889} = 0.529.$$

This technical efficiency measure, unfortunately, fails to reflect the full extent of potential increases in all of the outputs individually. In the present case, although y_1 can be increased by only 88.9%, y_2 can be expanded by 144%. Nor does it show any potential reductions in individual inputs that are feasible simultaneously with increases in outputs, although such is not the case here. These LP models yield radial measures of efficiency. Although it is true that for any individual firm, say firm t, the largest output bundle with the same output mix as (y_1^t, y_2^t) that can be produced from the input bundle of firm t is $(\phi^* y_1^*, \phi^* y_2^*)$, it is often possible to expand individual (although not all) outputs by a factor larger than ϕ^*. Similarly, we may not be entirely using up all the individual components of the observed input bundle of the firm under consideration in order to produce the expanded output bundle.

Take another look at (2.29). Suppose that the optimal solution is $(\phi^*; \mu_1^*, \mu_2^*, \ldots, \mu_N^*)$. Define

$$y_{1t}^* = \sum_{j=1}^{N} \mu_j^* y_{1j}; \quad y_{2t}^* = \sum_{j=1}^{N} \mu_j^* y_{2j}; \quad x_{1t}^* = \sum_{j=1}^{N} \mu_j^* x_{1j}; \quad x_{2t}^* = \sum_{j=1}^{N} \mu_j^* x_{2j}.$$

(2.31)

Then, $y_t^* = (y_{1t}^*, y_{2t}^*)$ can be produced from $x_t^* = (x_{1t}^*, x_{2t}^*)$. Note that $y_{1t}^* \geq \phi^* y_{1t}$ and $y_{2t}^* \geq \phi^* y_{2t}$. Similarly, $x_{1t} \geq x_{1t}^*$ and $x_{2t} \geq x_{2t}^*$. Thus,

$$\phi^* = \min \left(\frac{y_{1t}^*}{y_{1t}}, \frac{y_{2t}^*}{y_{2t}} \right).$$

(2.32)

Define the output slack variables $s_1^+ = y_{1t}^* - \phi^* y_{1t}$ and $s_2^+ = y_{2t}^* - \phi^* y_{2t}$. The input slack variables can be similarly defined as $s_1^- = x_{1t} - x_{1t}^*$ and $s_2^- = x_{2t} - x_{2t}^*$. It may be recalled that an input–output bundle (x, y) is regarded as *Pareto efficient* only when (1) it is not possible to increase any output without either reducing some other output or increasing some input, and (2) it is not possible to reduce any input without increasing some other input or reducing some output. Thus, (x_t^*, y_t^*) is *Pareto efficient*, but $(x^t, \phi_t^* y^t)$ is not unless all output and input slacks are equal to zero.

Including appropriate slack variables in the constraints, we get at the optimal solution

$$\sum_{j=1}^{N} \mu_j^* y_{1j} - \phi^* y_{1t} = s_1^{+*} \geq 0;$$

$$\sum_{j=1}^{N} \mu_j^* y_{2j} - \phi^* y_{2t} = s_2^{+*} \geq 0;$$

$$x_{1t} - \sum_{j=1}^{N} \mu_j^* x_{1j} = s_1^{-*} \geq 0;$$

$$x_{2t} - \sum_{j=1}^{N} \mu_j^* x_{2j} = s_2^{-*} \geq 0.$$

(2.33)

Here, (s_1^{+*}, s_2^{+*}) are the output slacks and (s_1^{-*}, s_2^{-*}) are input slacks at the optimal solution. Whenever any output slack is strictly positive, it is possible to expand that particular output by the amount of the output slack even after it has been expanded by a factor ϕ^* (≥ 1). Suppose that in a particular application we get $\phi^* = 1.25$. This means that we can increase both outputs by 25%. In this case, technical efficiency of the firm is 0.80. Now suppose that $s_1^{+*} = 10$. This implies that we can further increase output 1 by 10 units. Hence, 0.80 does not fully reflect the extent of its inefficiency. Moreover, if any one of the input slacks is strictly positive, the implication is that the previous expansion of the output bundle can be achieved while reducing individual inputs at the same time.

In a revision of their original model, CCR (1979) introduced penalties in the objective function for strictly positive input and output slacks. Their revised output-oriented model was

$$\max \ \tilde{\phi} = \phi + \varepsilon(s_1^+ + s_2^+ + s_1^- + s_2^-)$$

$$\text{s. t.} \ \sum_{j=1}^{N} \mu_j y_{1j} - s_1^+ = \phi y_{1t};$$

$$\sum_{j=1}^{N} \mu_j y_{2j} - s_2^+ = \phi y_{2t};$$

$$\sum_{j=1}^{N} \mu_j x_{1j} + s_1^- = x_{1t}; \tag{2.34}$$

$$\sum_{j=1}^{N} \mu_j x_{2j} + s_2^- = x_{2t};$$

$$\mu_j \geq 0 \ (j = 1, 2, \ldots, N); \quad s_1^+, s_2^+, s_1^-, s_2^- \geq 0; \quad \phi \ \text{free.}$$

Here, ε is an infinitesimally small positive number (selected by the researcher). By including input and output slacks in the objective function, we ensure that $\tilde{\phi} > \phi^*$ whenever any slack variable is strictly positive at the optimal solution. Thus, a firm will be rated as fully efficient only when ϕ^* equals 1 and all the slacks are equal to 0 at the optimal solution. Otherwise, its efficiency will be less than unity even when ϕ^* equals 1.

Consider the revised form of the input-oriented model:

$$\min \tilde{\theta} = \theta - \varepsilon(s_1^+ + s_2^+ + s_1^- + s_2^-)$$

$$\text{s. t.} \sum_{j=1}^{N} \mu_j y_{1j} - s_1^+ = y_{1t};$$

$$\sum_{j=1}^{N} \mu_j y_{2j} - s_2^+ = y_{2t};$$

$$\sum_{j=1}^{N} \mu_j x_{1j} + s_1^- = \theta x_{1t};$$

$$\sum_{j=1}^{N} \mu_j x_{2j} + s_2^- = \theta x_{2t};$$

$$\mu_j \geq 0 \ (j = 1, 2, \ldots, N); \quad s_1^+, s_2^+, s_1^-, s_2^- \geq 0; \quad \phi \text{ free.} \quad (2.35a)$$

The dual of this LP problem is

$$\max \ p_{1t} y_{1t} + p_{2t} y_{2t}$$

$$\text{s.t.} \ p_{it} y_{1j} + p_{2t} y_{2j} - w_{1t} x_{1j} - w_{2t} x_{2j} \leq 0; \quad (j = 1, 2, \ldots, N);$$

$$w_{1t} x_{1t} + w_{2t} x_{2t} = 1; \quad (2.35b)$$

$$p_{1t} \geq \varepsilon; \quad p_{2t} \geq \varepsilon; \quad w_{1t} \geq \varepsilon; \quad w_{2t} \geq \varepsilon.$$

The only difference between this problem and its earlier specification is that now we have a lower bound on the shadow prices.

On solving the primal problem, we obtain the input and output bundles

$$x_t^{**} = x^t - s_t^{-*}; \quad y_t^{**} = \phi^* y^t + s_t^{+*}. \quad (2.36)$$

The pair (x_t^{**}, y_t^{**}) is a Pareto efficient production plan.

However, using the optimal value of the objective function from one of the revised models (either $\tilde{\theta}$ or $\tilde{\phi}$) would be problematic. Computationally, $\tilde{\theta}$ and $\frac{1}{\tilde{\phi}}$ will not be exactly equal. Conceptually, inclusion of the slacks in the objective function raises a problem of aggregation because unlike θ or ϕ, the input and output slacks are not unit free.

Finally, the efficiency measure obtained would not be invariant to the numerical value of ε chosen by the analyst.

At present, the overall consensus in the literature is that presence of positive slacks in the optimal solution should be interpreted as merely signifying that the efficient radial projection of (x^t, y^t) is not Pareto efficient. Beyond that, the revised objective function value should not be used to obtain a scalar measure of technical efficiency. One should rather report the slacks separately along with the radial efficiency measure. In a later chapter, we will return to the question of incorporating slacks in a scalar measure of efficiency.

2.6 An Example of Output-Oriented DEA on SAS

Example 2.2 Table 2.2 reports the output and input levels of a sample of 30 electric utilities from Korea. The output is measured by megawatt-hours of power generated. The three inputs are kilowatt-hours of installed capacity, labor (man-years), and fuels (tons of oil equivalent). For the DEA models, the data were rescaled[5] by dividing each input and output variable by its sample mean and multiplying by 1,000. The appropriate LP problem (in SAS) for firm 6 is shown in Exhibit 2A. Note that ϕ is included in the left-hand side of the inequality for the output. The output inequality is of the "greater than or equal to" type. The input inequalities, on the other hand, are of the "less than or equal to" type. Output and input quantities of *all firms* appear on the left-hand sides of the restrictions. The right-hand side includes the quantities of the firm under evaluation (firm 6, in this case).

Exhibit 2B reports the optimal solution of the LP problem specified in Exhibit 2A. The objective function value (1.301866) shows that the quantity of power generated by this firm can be expanded by 30.19%. The output-oriented technical efficiency of firm 6 is 0.768 (which is the inverse of the optimal value of ϕ). In the "variable summary" section, firms 7 and 25 have "activity" greater than 0. Thus, at the optimal solution, only λ_7 and λ_{25} will be strictly positive. The hypothetical comparison unit for firm 6 is a firm that uses 5.262% of the input bundle of firm 7 and 60.527% of the inputs of firm 25 to produce a similar linear combination of the output levels of these two firms. This reference firm would produce 30.19% more of the output compared to the actual performance of firm 6. The negative "reduced cost" associated with any nonbasic firm shows how the objective function would be affected if it entered the basis. The rows identified as OBS_1 through OBS_3 are the input slack variables. Note that there is a positive slack (371.342 units) associated

---

[5] We examine the effect of data transformation on the DEA efficiency score later in Chapter 4.

Table 2.2. *Input–output data for Korean electric utilities*

Firm	Capacity	Labor	Fuel	Output
1	706.70	643.39	648.95	614.66
2	1284.90	1142.20	1101.65	1128.39
3	1027.92	1749.44	531.19	533.52
4	1027.92	1019.30	640.32	611.80
5	1027.92	1033.76	640.41	619.68
6	1027.92	527.72	448.10	404.99
7	2055.85	1048.22	2136.09	2276.89
8	2055.85	1055.45	2140.03	2278.26
9	2055.85	1062.68	2140.18	2172.23
10	51.40	86.75	111.28	71.72
11	51.40	101.21	91.63	73.40
12	51.40	93.98	91.92	73.88
13	51.40	101.21	92.24	73.83
14	1669.35	1612.09	1585.23	1548.44
15	308.38	910.87	344.51	260.83
16	308.38	903.64	344.48	258.85
17	256.98	1178.34	273.29	181.65
18	256.98	1185.57	273.28	179.92
19	1027.92	1366.30	1185.60	1076.19
20	642.45	751.83	699.30	586.16
21	1027.92	838.57	1090.23	959.15
22	1027.92	824.12	1090.26	958.38
23	385.47	1655.46	362.30	278.13
24	865.64	809.66	559.96	660.53
25	906.03	780.74	554.62	673.12
26	256.98	1069.91	221.73	246.69
27	256.98	1033.76	228.01	252.86
28	2878.19	1828.96	3509.60	3708.16
29	2878.19	1821.73	3510.85	3709.64
30	2569.81	1763.90	3352.76	3528.04

Notes: In the original source, capacity is measured in kilowatt-hours, labor in man-years, fuel in tons of oil equivalent, and output in megawatt-hours. In this table, each input or output variable has been scaled by its sample mean and multiplied by 1000.
Source: Table 1 of S. U. Park and J. B. Lesourd, *International Journal of Production Economics*, Vol. 63, 2000, pp. 59–67.

with the capital input (capacity). No slack exists in the labor or fuel inputs, however. This implies that the 30.187% increase in the output can be achieved while reducing the capacity input by the amount of the slack at the same time.

Exhibit: 2A. *Output-oriented DEA LP problem for Firm 6*

Firm	# 1	# 2	# 3	# 4	# 5	# 6	# 7	# 8
capital	706.698	1284.90	1027.92	1027.92	1027.92	1027.92	2055.85	2055.85
labor	643.389	1142.20	1749.44	1019.30	1033.76	527.72	1048.22	1055.45
fuel	648.946	1101.65	531.19	640.32	640.41	448.10	2136.09	2140.03
output	614.660	1128.39	533.52	611.80	619.68	404.99	2276.89	2278.26
objective	0.000	0.00	0.00	0.00	0.00	0.00	0.00	0.00
# 9	# 10	# 11	# 12	# 13	# 14	# 15	# 16	# 17
2055.85	51.396	51.396	51.3962	51.396	1669.35	308.377	308.377	256.98
1062.68	86.749	101.207	93.9782	101.207	1612.09	910.865	903.636	1178.34
2140.18	111.276	91.632	91.9232	92.244	1585.23	344.508	344.483	273.29
2172.23	71.720	73.405	73.8759	73.834	1548.44	260.830	258.852	181.65
0.00	0.000	0.000	0.0000	0.000	0.00	0.000	0.000	0.00
# 18	# 19	# 20	# 21	# 22	# 23	# 24	# 25	# 26
256.98	1027.92	642.452	1027.92	1027.92	385.47	865.640	906.033	256.98
1185.57	1366.30	751.825	838.57	824.12	1655.46	809.658	780.742	1069.91
273.28	1185.60	699.303	1090.23	1090.26	362.30	559.963	554.623	221.73
179.92	1076.19	586.162	959.15	958.38	278.13	660.532	673.120	246.69
0.00	0.00	0.000	0.00	0.00	0.00	0.000	0.000	0.00
# 27	# 28	# 29	# 30	phi	_type_	_rhs_		
256.98	2878.19	2878.19	2569.81	0.000	<=	1027.92		
1033.76	1828.96	1821.73	1763.90	0.000	<=	527.72		
228.01	3509.60	3510.85	3352.76	0.000	<=	448.10		
252.86	3708.16	3709.64	3528.04	−404.985	>=	0.00		
0.00	0.00	0.00	0.00	1.000	max	.		

Exhibit: 2B. *SAS output of output-oriented CCR DEA model for Firm 6: The LP procedure*

Solution Summary	
Objective Value	1.3018661

Variable Summary

Variable Col Name	Status Type	Price	Activity	Reduced Cost
1 COL1	NON-NEG	0	0	−0.319551
2 COL2	NON-NEG	0	0	−0.352614
3 COL3	NON-NEG	0	0	−0.672975
4 COL4	NON-NEG	0	0	−0.455153
5 COL5	NON-NEG	0	0	−0.441649
6 COL6	NON-NEG	0	0	−0.301866
7 COL7	BASIC NON-NEG	0	0.052621	0
8 COL8	NON-NEG	0	0	−0.009117
9 COL9	NON-NEG	0	0	−0.274152

(continued)

		Exhibit: 2B *(continued)*		

Solution Summary

Objective Value			1.3018661	

Variable Summary

Variable Col Name	Status Type	Price	Activity	Reduced Cost
10 COL10	NON-NEG	0	0	−0.128571
11 COL11	NON-NEG	0	0	−0.082295
12 COL12	NON-NEG	0	0	−0.078966
13 COL13	NON-NEG	0	0	−0.082727
14 COL14	NON-NEG	0	0	−0.680701
15 COL15	NON-NEG	0	0	−0.557802
16 COL16	NON-NEG	0	0	−0.559748
17 COL17	NON-NEG	0	0	−0.686168
18 COL18	NON-NEG	0	0	−0.693319
19 COL19	NON-NEG	0	0	−0.775215
20 COL20	NON-NEG	0	0	−0.555766
21 COL21	NON-NEG	0	0	−0.621882
22 COL22	NON-NEG	0	0	−0.618105
23 COL23	NON-NEG	0	0	−0.85466
24 COL24	NON-NEG	0	0	−0.055598
25 COL25	BASIC NON-NEG	0	0.6052773	0
26 COL26	NON-NEG	0	0	−0.35681
27 COL27	NON-NEG	0	0	−0.342487
28 COL28	NON-NEG	0	0	−0.123406
29 COL29	NON-NEG	0	0	−0.119913
30 COL30	NON-NEG	0	0	−0.160087
31 phi	BASIC NON-NEG	1	1.3018661	0
32 _OBS1_	BASIC SLACK	0	371.34196	0
33 _OBS2_	SLACK	0	0	−0.000398
34 _OBS3_	SLACK	0	0	−0.002437
35 _OBS4_	SURPLUS	0	0	−0.002469

Constraint Summary

Constraint Row Name	Type	S/S Col	Rhs	Activity	Dual Activity
1 _OBS1_	LE	32	1027.9237	656.58174	0
2 _OBS2_	LE	33	527.72356	527.72356	0.0003978
3 _OBS3_	LE	34	448.10376	448.10376	0.0024368
4 _OBS4_	GE	35	0	0	−0.002469
5 _OBS5_	OBJECTVE	.	0	1.3018661	.

Finally, the "constraint summary" section shows that the "activity" levels for labor and fuel are equal to the "RHS" value. Thus, these input constraints are binding. The dual activity associated with them are the shadow prices of these inputs. On the other hand, the "activity" level for capacity is 656.582 whereas the "RHS" is 1027.924. This results in the slack of 371.342 units shown earlier.

2.7 Summary

The productivity of a firm is measured by the ratio of the output produced to the input used. We do not always need to know the production technology in order to measure productivity. Efficiency, on the other hand, compares the actual output from a given input with the maximally producible quantity of output. Thus, knowledge of the reference technology is critical for efficiency measurement. In the multiple-input, multiple-output case, individual inputs and outputs need to be suitably aggregated. In the absence of market prices, one can employ the method of DEA, which endogenously generates "shadow prices" of inputs and outputs for aggregation.

Guide to the Literature

Debreu (1951) addressed the question of resource utilization at the aggregate level. Subsequently, Shephard (1953) introduced the Distance function as an alternative characterization of the technology. Farrell (1957) defined technical and allocative efficiency as two separate components of the economic efficiency of a firm and developed the formal LP model for measuring technical efficiency. Introduced by CCR (1978, 1981), the method of DEA generalized Farrell's measure of technical efficiency from the single-output to the multiple-output case. See Førsund and Sarafoglou (2002) for an overview of the developments in the literature subsequent to Farrell's paper that led to the introduction of the DEA methodology.

Charnes, Cooper, Lewin, and Seiford (1994) offer a brief overview of the primal and dual specifications along with a number of extensions of the basic CCR model. They also trace the chronology of development in the literature subsequent to the seminal CCR paper through an interesting flow chart. Ali (1994) offers an in-depth discussion of the computational aspects of DEA in the same volume.

APPENDIX TO CHAPTER 2

The Output-Oriented Shephard Distance Function

Consider some production possibility set

$$T = \{(x, y) : x \text{ can produce } y\}.$$

We assume that T is convex and both outputs and inputs are freely disposable. Now consider some input bundle x and any arbitrary output bundle y. We do not assume that the input–output pair (x, y) is necessarily feasible. Following Shephard (1953), we can define the output-oriented distance function as

$$D_O(x, y) = \min \delta : \left(x, \frac{1}{\delta} y\right) \in T. \tag{2A.1}$$

Thus, it is a mapping from the input–output space to the nonnegative segment of the real line. Note that when $D_O(x, y)$ is greater than unity, the output bundle y cannot be produced from the input bundle x. Only some proportionately scaled-down output bundle will be feasible. On the other hand, if $D_O(x, y)$ is less than unity, then a proportionately expanded output bundle will be feasible. Hence, by free disposability of outputs, the bundle y is also feasible. Thus, an alternative specification of the production possibility set is

$$T = \{(x, y) : D_O(x, y) \le 1\}. \tag{2A.2}$$

Consider the following 2-input, 2-output example. Suppose that the production possibility set is

$$T = \{(x_1, x_2, y_1, y_2) : x_1 + \sqrt{x_1 x_2} \ge \sqrt{y_1 y_2}\}. \tag{2A.3}$$

Then, the output-oriented distance function is

$$D_O(x_1, x_2, y_1, y_2) = \frac{\sqrt{y_1 y_2}}{x_1 + \sqrt{x_1 x_2}}. \tag{2A.4}$$

Whenever $x_1 + \sqrt{x_1 x_2} \ge \sqrt{y_1 y_2}$, (x_1, x_2, y_1, y_2) is a feasible input–output combination. Consider the input bundle $x^0 = (x_{10} = 3, x_{20} = 12)$ and the output bundle $y^0 = (y_{10} = 4, y_{20} = 25)$. For the production possibility set specified previously, this input–output bundle is not feasible. The distance function evaluated at this input–output combination is $D_O = \frac{10}{9}$. The largest output bundle with the same output mix as the bundle y^0 is $y^* = (y_1^* = 3.6, y_2^* = 22.5)$. Note that relative to the bundle y^0, both outputs in the bundle y^* are scaled down by the factor 0.9 (i.e., deflated by the factor $\frac{10}{9}$.) On the other hand, consider the output bundle $\hat{y} = (\hat{y}_1 = 5, \hat{y}_2 = 5)$. Clearly, this output bundle is producible from the input bundle x^0. In fact, the largest feasible output bundle with the same output mix at $\hat{y}$ is $\tilde{y} = (\tilde{y}_1 = 9, \tilde{y}_2 = 9)$. This time the output bundle is scaled up by a factor 1.8 (i.e., deflated by the factor $\frac{5}{9}$.)

It is easy to see that the output-oriented distance function is the inverse of the optimal value of the objective function φ in the output-oriented CCR DEA problem.

Some Properties of the Output-Oriented Distance Function

O1. $D_O(x, y)$ is nondecreasing in y. That is, for any input bundle x, if $y^1 \geq y^0$, then $D_O(x, y^1) \leq D_O(x, y^0)$.

Proof. Let $D_O(x, y^1) = \delta_1$. Then $(x, \frac{1}{\delta_1} y^1) \in T$ and $(x, \frac{1}{\delta} y^1) \notin T$ for any $\delta < \delta_1$. Now, by assumption, $y^1 \geq y^0$ and, therefore, $\frac{1}{\delta_1} y^1 \geq \frac{1}{\delta_1} y^0$. Hence, by free disposability of outputs, $(x, \frac{1}{\delta_1} y^0) \in T$. Define $\bar{y} = \frac{1}{\delta_0} y^0$. Let $D_O(x, \bar{y}) = \bar{\delta}$. Then, by feasibility of $(x, \bar{y})$, $\bar{\delta} \leq 1$. This means, of course, that $(x, \frac{1}{\delta_1 \bar{\delta}} y^0) \in T$. Now consider, $\delta_0 = D_O(x, y^0)$. Clearly, $\delta_0 \leq \delta_1 \bar{\delta} \leq \delta_1$.

O2. $D_O(x, y)$ is nonincreasing in x. That is, for any output bundle y, if $x^1 \geq x^0$, then $D_O(x^1, y) \leq D_O(x^0, y)$.

Proof. Let $D_O(x^0, y) = \delta_0$. Define $\bar{y} = \frac{1}{\delta_0} y$. Then, $(x^0, \bar{y}) \in T$. Now, because $x^1 \geq x^0$, by free disposability of inputs, $(x^1, \bar{y}) \in T$. That is, $(x^1, \frac{1}{\delta_0} y) \in T$. Now, let $D_O(x^1, y) = \delta_1$. Clearly, $\delta_1 \leq \delta_0$.

O3. $D_O(x, y)$ is homogeneous of degree 1 in y. That is, $D_O(x, \alpha y) = \alpha D_O(x, y)$.

Proof. Let $D_O(x, y) = \delta$. That means that δ is the smallest positive real number such that $(x, \frac{1}{\delta} y) \in T$. Now define $\hat{y} = \alpha y$. Let $D_O(x, \hat{y}) = \beta$. This means that, for a given α, β is the smallest real number such that $(x, \frac{\alpha}{\beta} y) \in T$. We need to show that $\beta = \alpha \delta$. Suppose that this is not true and $\beta < \alpha \delta$. That is, $\frac{\beta}{\alpha} < \delta$. But in that case, $D_O(x, y)$ cannot be δ because there exists another real number $\gamma = \frac{\beta}{\alpha}$ smaller than δ such that $(x, \frac{1}{\gamma} y) \in T$. Alternatively, assume that $\beta > \alpha \delta$. But, because the input–output pair $(x, \frac{1}{\delta} y)$ is feasible, so is the input–output pair $(x, \frac{1}{\alpha\delta}\hat{y})$. In that case, $D_O(x, \hat{y})$ cannot be β. Hence, β must be equal to $\alpha\delta$.

O4. $D_O(x, y)$ is convex in y.

Proof. For this, we need to prove that for any $\alpha \in (0, 1)$,

$$D_O(x, \alpha y^1 + (1 - \alpha)y^2) \le \alpha D_O(x, y^1) + (1 - \alpha)D_O(x, y^2).$$

Define $y_*^1 = \alpha y^1$ and $y_*^2 = (1 - \alpha)y^2$. Also, let

$$D_O(x, y_*^1) = \beta_1 \quad \text{and} \quad D_O(x, y_*^2) = \beta_2.$$

By definition, the input–output bundles $(x, \frac{1}{\beta_1}y_*^1)$ and $(x, \frac{1}{\beta_2}y_*^2)$ are both feasible. Hence, by virtue of convexity of the production possibility set, for any $\lambda \in (0, 1)$,

$$\left(\left(x, \lambda \left(\frac{1}{\beta_1}y_*^1\right) + (1 - \lambda)\left(\frac{1}{\beta_2}y_*^2\right)\right)\right) \in T.$$

Select

$$\lambda = \frac{\beta_1}{\beta_1 + \beta_2} \quad \text{so that} \quad (1 - \lambda) = \frac{\beta_2}{\beta_1 + \beta_2}.$$

Then

$$\left(x, \frac{1}{\beta_1 + \beta_2}(y_*^1 + y_*^2)\right) \in T.$$

Therefore,

$$D_O(x, y_*^1 + y_*^2) \le \beta_1 + \beta_2.$$

But because the output-oriented distance function is homogeneous of degree 1 in outputs,

$$\beta_1 = D_O(x, \alpha y^1) = \alpha D_O(x, y^1)$$

and

$$\beta_2 = D_O(x, (1 - \alpha)y^2) = (1 - \alpha)D_O(x, y^2).$$

Thus,

$$D_O\left(x, \alpha y^1 + (1 - \alpha)y^2\right) \le \alpha D_O(x, y^1) + (1 - \alpha)D_O(x, y^2).$$

This concludes the proof.

The Input-Oriented Shephard Distance Function

The input-oriented distance function is

$$D_I(x, y) = \max \mu : \left(\frac{1}{\mu}x, y \right) \in T.$$

The analogous properties of the input-oriented distance function are

I1. $D_I(x, y)$ is nondecreasing in x.

I2. $D_I(x, y)$ is nonincreasing in y.

I3. $D_I(x, y)$ is homogeneous of degree 1 in x.

I4. $D_I(x, y)$ is concave in x.

Proof of these properties is left as an exercise.

3

Variable Returns to Scale: Separating Technical and Scale Efficiencies

3.1 Introduction

The DEA model presented in Chapter 2 measures technical efficiency of a firm relative to a reference technology exhibiting constant returns to scale (CRS) everywhere on the production frontier. This, of course, is rather restrictive because it is unlikely that CRS will hold globally in many realistic cases. As a result, the CCR–DEA model should not be applied in a wide variety of situations. In an important extension of this approach, Banker, Charnes, and Cooper (BCC) (1984) generalized the original DEA model for technologies exhibiting increasing, constant, or diminishing returns to scale at different points on the production frontier.

This chapter develops the DEA linear programming (LP) models that are applicable when the technology does not exhibit constant returns to scale globally. Section 3.2 considers the relation between the scale elasticity and returns to scale. Banker's concept of the *most productive scale size (MPSS)* is described in Section 3.3 followed by a discussion of *scale efficiency* in Section 3.4. The BCC model for measuring technical efficiency is presented in Section 3.5. Three alternative but equivalent approaches to identification of the nature of returns to scale that hold locally at a specific input–output bundle on the frontier are described in Section 3.6. Section 3.7 summarizes the main points in this chapter.

3.2 Returns to Scale

Consider, to start with, a single-output, single-input technology characterized by the production possibility set

$$T = \{(x, y) : y \leq f(x); \ x \geq a\} \tag{3.1}$$

where

$$y^* = f(x) \tag{3.1a}$$

is the production function showing the maximum quantity of output y producible from input x, and a is the minimum input scale below which the production function is not defined. When there is no minimum scale, a equals 0.

At some specific point (x, y) on this production function, the average productivity is

$$\mathrm{AP} = \frac{f(x)}{x}. \tag{3.2}$$

Locally increasing returns to scale holds at this point if a small increase in x results in an increase in AP. Similarly, diminishing returns to scale exist when AP declines with an increase in x. Under constant returns, an increase in x leaves AP unchanged. Thus, $\frac{d\mathrm{AP}}{dx}$ is positive under increasing returns, negative under diminishing returns, and 0 under constant returns. If the production function is differentiable,

$$\frac{d\mathrm{AP}}{dx} = \frac{xf'(x) - f(x)}{x^2} = \frac{f(x)}{x^2}\left[\frac{xf'(x)}{f(x)} - 1\right] \tag{3.3}$$

If average productivity reaches a maximum at a finite level of x, $\frac{d\mathrm{AP}}{dx}$ equals 0 at that point. This, of course, is only the first-order condition for a maximum. But, if the production function is concave (so that $f''(x) < 0$ over the entire range of x), the second-order condition for a maximum is automatically satisfied.

Define

$$\varepsilon = \frac{xf'(x)}{f(x)}. \tag{3.4}$$

Then,

$$\frac{d\mathrm{AP}}{dx} = \frac{f(x)}{x^2}(\varepsilon - 1). \tag{3.4a}$$

Hence,

$\varepsilon > 1$ implies increasing returns to scale,

$\varepsilon = 1$ implies constant returns to scale, and

$\varepsilon < 1$ implies diminishing returns to scale.

Output (*y*)

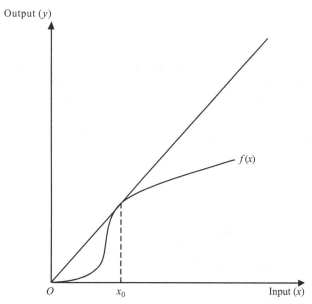

Figure 3.1 Production function under variable return to scale.

Figure 3.1 shows the familiar S-shaped production function representing a single-output, single-input technology exhibiting variable returns to scale. In this case, average productivity increases as the input (x) rises from 0 to x_0. This is the region of increasing returns to scale with $\varepsilon > 1$. Beyond the input level x_0, average productivity falls as x increases and diminishing returns to scale holds. Here, $\varepsilon < 1$. Locally CRS holds at x_0, where $\varepsilon = 1$. This is also the input level where average productivity reaches a maximum.

It may be noted that, in the example shown in Figure 3.1, over the region of increasing returns, the marginal productivity of x is increasing and the production function is convex. Convexity of the production function is not really necessary for the presence of increasing returns. Figure 3.2 shows a single-input, single-output production function with a positive minimum input scale. The production function is globally concave over its entire domain. But increasing returns to scale holds at input levels between x_m and x_0. At x_0, there is locally constant returns, and beyond this input level diminishing returns hold. One critical difference between the two cases is that in Figure 3.1 (unlike Figure 3.2), the production possibility set is not convex.

Consider an efficient input–output combination (x_0, y_0) satisfying

$$y_0 = f(x_0). \tag{3.5}$$

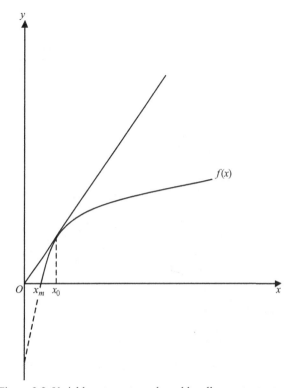

Figure 3.2 Variable returns to scale and locally constant returns.

Let $x_1 = \beta x_0$ and $f(x_1) = y_1$. Further, assume that $y_1 = \alpha y_0$. Thus, $\alpha y_0 = f(\beta x_0)$. Clearly, α will depend on β. Thus,

$$\alpha(\beta) = \max \alpha : (\beta x_0, \alpha y_0) \in T. \tag{3.6}$$

For any efficient pair (x, y),

$$\alpha(\beta)y = f(\beta x). \tag{3.7}$$

Differentiating with respect to β, we have

$$\alpha'(\beta)y = xf'(\beta x). \tag{3.8}$$

Further, at $\beta = 1$,

$$\alpha'(1) = \frac{xf'(x)}{f(x)} = \varepsilon. \tag{3.9}$$

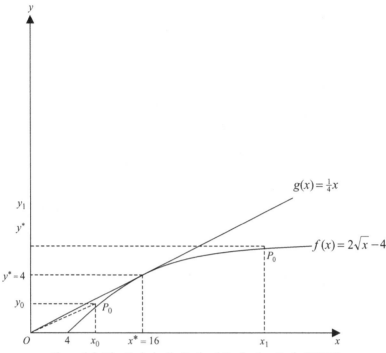

Figure 3.3 The Technically Optimal Production Scale (TOPS).

Thus, at (x, y),

$\alpha'(1) > 1$ implies increasing returns to scale,

$\alpha'(1) = 1$ implies constant returns to scale, and

$\alpha'(1) < 1$ implies diminishing returns to scale.

Consider, for example, the production function

$$f(x) = 2\sqrt{x} - 4; \quad x \geq 4 \tag{3.10}$$

shown in Figure 3.3. For this function,

$$\varepsilon = \frac{\sqrt{x}}{2\sqrt{x} - 4}.$$

For $4 < x < 16$, $\varepsilon > 1$ and AP increases with x signifying increasing returns to scale. At $x = 16$, $\varepsilon = 1$. Here, AP reaches a maximum. Beyond this point, diminishing returns to scale sets in and $\varepsilon < 1$. The input level $x^* = 16$ is of special significance. Because AP is the highest at this level of x, it corresponds to what Frisch (1965) called the *technically optimal scale* of production. The corresponding output level on the frontier is $y^* = 4$.

In the single-input, single-output case, productivity of a firm is easily measured by the ratio of its output and input quantities. When multiple inputs and/or multiple outputs are involved, one must first construct aggregate quantity indexes of outputs and inputs. Productivity can then be measured by the ratio of these quantity indexes of output and input.

Returns to scale characteristics of the technology relate to how productivity changes in the special case involving multiple outputs and multiple inputs, where all the input bundles are proportional to one another and so are all output bundles. For expository advantage, we consider, a single output, two-input production function. Let $x^0 = (x_1^0, x_2^0)$ and $x^1 = (x_1^1, x_2^1)$ be two different input bundles. Further, the input bundles are proportional. Thus, $x^1 = tx^0, t > 0$. Hence, $x_1^1 = tx_1^0$ and $x_2^1 = tx_2^0$. The maximum quantities of output producible from these input bundles are $y_0 = f(x^0)$ and $y_1 = f(x^1)$. In Figure 3.4, the input bundles x^0 and x^1 are shown by the points A^0

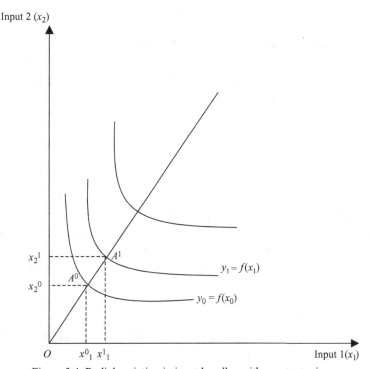

Figure 3.4 Radial variation in input bundles with constant mix.

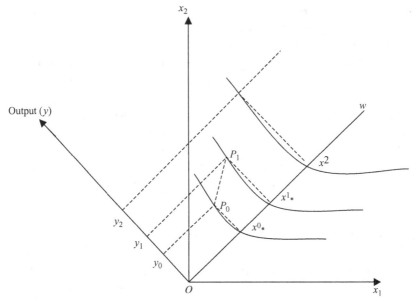

Figure 3.5 Constant input mix and a composite input.

and A^1 on the isoquants for the output levels y^0 and y^1, respectively. Define the input bundle $x^0 = (x_1^0, x_2^0)$ as one unit of a single composite input (say, w). Now consider variations in the scale of this input without any change in the proportion of the constituent inputs. Thus, two units of the input w would correspond to the bundle $(2x_1^0, 2x_2^0)$. By this definition, the bundle $x^1 = (tx_1^0, tx_2^0)$ represents t units of this composite input. Note that the ray from the origin through x^0 (and also x^1 in this case) itself becomes an axis along which we can measure variations in the scale of the constant-mix composite input w.

In Figure 3.5, we modify the diagram shown in Figure 3.4 by introducing a third dimension to show changes in the quantity of the output y, which is assumed to be scalar. The input bundles x_*^0 and x_*^1 produce output quantities y_0 and y_1, respectively. The points P_0 and P_1 in the $y-w$ plane show these input–output pairs. Both points are technically efficient and lie on the production frontier $y = f(w)$.

Figure 3.6 replicates the two-dimensional $(y-w)$ cross section of the three-dimensional diagram shown in Figure 3.5. We have effectively reduced the one-output, two-input case to a single-output, single-input case by considering only input bundles that differ in scale but not in the mix. In Figure 3.6, as in Figure 3.5, points P_0 and P_1 are efficient input–output pairs. The productivity

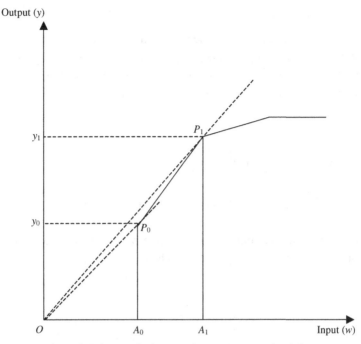

Figure 3.6 Composite input and ray average productivity.

index at P_1 relative to the average productivity at P_0 is the ratio of the slope of the line OP_1 to the slope of the line OP_0. Note that these slopes measure average productivity per unit of the composite input w and are known as *ray average productivities*. By definition, the bundle x^0 measure one unit of w and $x^1 = tx^0$ corresponds to t units of this composite input. Hence, the productivity index is

$$\frac{\text{AP}(x^1)}{\text{AP}(x^0)} = \frac{\frac{P_1 A_1}{O A_1}}{\frac{P_0 A_0}{O A_0}} = \frac{y_1/y_0}{t}. \tag{3.11}$$

This is a ratio of ray average productivities in three dimensions but can be treated as the ratio of average productivities in two dimensions where the composite input is treated like a scalar. Therefore, the foregoing discussion about returns to scale in the context of a single-input, single-output production function can be carried over to this single-output, single-(composite) input case also.

3.3 The Most Productive Scale Size (MPSS)

Starrett (1977) generalized the concept of returns to scale in the context of a multi-output, multi-input technology by focusing on *expansion along a ray*. Suppose that the input bundle $x = (x_1, x_2, \ldots, x_n)$ and the associated output bundle $y = (y_1, y_2, \ldots, y_m)$ are an efficient pair on the transformation function

$$T(x, y) = 0. \tag{3.12}$$

Hence, along the transformation function,

$$\sum_{i=1}^{n} \left(\frac{\partial T}{\partial x_i} x_i \right) \frac{dx_i}{x_i} + \sum_{j=1}^{m} \left(\frac{\partial T}{\partial y_j} y_j \right) \frac{dy_j}{y_j} = 0. \tag{3.13}$$

Suppose that all inputs increase at the same proportionate rate β and, as a result, all outputs increase at the rate α. Then

$$\frac{\alpha}{\beta} = -\frac{\sum_{i=1}^{n} \frac{\partial T}{\partial x_i} x_i}{\sum_{j=1}^{m} \frac{\partial T}{\partial y_j} y_j} \tag{3.14}$$

is a local measure of returns to scale. Starrett defines

$$\text{DIR} = \frac{\alpha}{\beta} - 1 \tag{3.15}$$

as a measure of the degree of increasing returns. Locally increasing, constant, or diminishing returns hold when DIR, respectively, exceeds, equals, or falls below 0. In a dual approach, Panzar and Willig (1977) use a multiple-output, multiple-input dual cost function to derive returns to scale properties of the technology from local scale economies.

Banker (1984) utilizes Frisch's concept of technically optimal production scale to define the MPSS for the multiple-input, multiple-output case. With reference to some production possibility set T, a pair of input and output bundles $(x^0, y^0) \in T$ is an MPSS, if for any (α, β) satisfying $(\beta x^0, \alpha y^0) \in T$, $\frac{\alpha}{\beta} \leq 1$. In the case of a single-output, single-input technology characterized by $T = \{(x, y) : y \leq f(x)\}$, $\frac{df(x)/x}{dx} = 0$ and $xf'(x) = f(x)$ at the MPSS. Thus, CRS holds at the MPSS.

Banker defined the returns-to-scale measure as follows:

$$\rho = \lim_{\beta \to 1} \frac{\alpha(\beta) - 1}{\beta - 1}. \tag{3.16}$$

Because (x^0, y^0) is an MPSS,

$$\frac{\alpha(\beta)}{\beta} \leq 1 \Rightarrow \alpha(\beta) \leq \beta \Rightarrow \alpha(\beta) - 1 \leq \beta - 1. \tag{3.17}$$

Suppose that $\beta < 1$ and $\beta - 1 < 0$.
Then

$$\frac{\alpha(\beta) - 1}{\beta - 1} \geq 1 \tag{3.18}$$

and

$$\lim_{\beta \to 1-\varepsilon} \frac{\alpha(\beta) - 1}{\beta - 1} \geq 1. \tag{3.19}$$

Hence, $\rho \geq 1$ when the input scale is slightly lower than x^0 ($\beta < 1$). Similarly, when the input scale exceeds the MPSS and $\beta > 1$,

$$\lim_{\beta \to 1+\varepsilon} \frac{\alpha(\beta) - 1}{\beta - 1} \leq 1. \tag{3.20}$$

Thus, $\rho \leq 1$ for $\beta > 1$. Finally, if $\lim_{\beta \to 1} \frac{\alpha(\beta)-1}{\beta-1}$ exists, the left-hand and right-hand limits coincide and $\rho = 1$ at the MPSS. Note that by L'Hôpital's rule, $\lim_{\beta \to 1} \frac{\alpha(\beta)-1}{\beta-1} = \alpha'(1)$. Thus, Banker's returns to scale classification coincides with the previous discussion if $y = f(x)$ is a differentiable production function.

3.4 Scale Efficiency

Consider the point (x^*, y^*) on the production function defined previously in (3.10) (see Figure 3.3). The tangent to the production function at this point is the line

$$g(x) = \frac{1}{4}x, \tag{3.21}$$

which is a ray through the origin. Førsund (1997) refers to this as the technically optimal production scale (TOPS) ray. Because $y = g(x)$ is a supporting hyperplane to the set

$$T = \{(x, y) : y \leq f(x); x \geq 4, y \geq 0\}, \tag{3.22}$$

$f(x) \leq g(x)$ over the entire admissible range of x and $f(x) = g(x)$ at $x = 16$. The set

$$G = \{(x, y) : y \leq g(x); x \geq 0, y \geq 0\} \tag{3.23}$$

is the smallest convex cone containing the set T. At all points (x, y) on the TOPS ray, $y = g(x)$, and if these points had been feasible, the average productivity at each of these points would have been

$$AP_{TOPS} = \frac{g(x)}{x}. \tag{3.24}$$

But, as noted previously, at the technically optimal scale x^*, $g(x^*) = f(x^*)$. Hence, AP_{TOPS} equals the maximum average productivity attained at any point on the production function $y^* = f(x)$.

Consider, now, any point (x_0, y_0) on the frontier and compare it with the point (x^*, y^*) where AP attains a maximum. Both are technically efficient points. If either the input or the output quantity is prespecified, it is not possible to increase the average productivity beyond $\frac{y_0}{x_0}$. If the firm could alter *both inputs and outputs*, however, it could move to the point (x^*, y^*), thereby raising the average productivity to its maximum level. Thus, the scale efficiency of the input level (x_0) or the output level (y_0) is

$$SE = \frac{AP(x_0, y_0)}{AP(x^*, y^*)} = \frac{f(x_0)/x_0}{f(x^*)/x^*} \tag{3.25}$$

But, as noted before,

$$\frac{f(x^*)}{x^*} = \frac{g(x)}{x}$$

at every input level x. Hence, scale efficiency can be measured as

$$SE = \frac{f(x)}{g(x)}, \tag{3.26}$$

which is the ratio of the output level on the production frontier and the output on the TOPS ray for the input level x. *No presumption whatsoever exists that the point on the TOPS ray is a feasible input–output combination.* It nevertheless serves as a benchmark for comparing the average productivity at a point on the production frontier, which is feasible, with the maximum average productivity attained at any point on the frontier.

3.5 Measuring Technical Efficiency under Variable Returns to Scale

As in Chapter 2, we hypothesize a production technology with the following properties:

   (i) the production possibility set is convex;
   (ii) inputs are freely disposable; and
   (iii) outputs are freely disposable.

Thus, if (x^0, y^0) and (x^1, y^1) are both feasible input–output bundles, then $(\bar{x}, \bar{y})$ is also a feasible bundle, where $\bar{x} = \lambda x^0 + (1 - \lambda)x^1$ and $\bar{y} = \lambda y^0 + (1 - \lambda)y^1; 0 \leq \lambda \leq 1$. Further, if $(x, y) \in T$, then $(\hat{x}, y) \in T$, when $\hat{x} \geq \hat{x}$, and $(x, \hat{y}) \in T$, when $\hat{y} \leq y$. When a sample of input–output bundles (x^i, y^i) is observed for N firms $(i = 1, 2, \ldots, N)$, we assume, further, that

(iv) $(x^i, y^i) \in T$ for $i = 1, 2, \ldots, N$.

Note that infinitely many production possibility sets exist with properties (i)–(iv). In any practical application, we select the *smallest* of these sets

$$T^V = (x, y) : x \geq \sum_{j=1}^N \lambda_j x^j; \quad y \leq \sum_{j=1}^N \lambda_j y^j; \sum_{j=1}^N \lambda_j = 1;$$

$$\lambda_j \geq 0; \quad (j = 1, 2, \ldots, N). \qquad (3.27)$$

Here, the superscript V identifies variable returns to scale (VRS). Varian (1984) calls it the inner approximation to the underlying technology set.

Construction of a production possibility set from observed data is illustrated for the one-output, one-input case in Figure 3.7. The actual input–output bundle (x^i, y^i) is given by the points P_i for five firms. The area $P_1 P_2 P_3 P_4$ is the convex hull of the points P_1 through P_5. By the convexity assumption, all points in this region represent feasible input–output combinations. Further, by free disposability of inputs, all points to the right of this area are also feasible. Finally, by free disposability of outputs, all points below this enlarged set of points (above the horizontal axis) are also feasible. The broken line $P_0 P_1 P_2 P_3$–*extension* is the frontier of the production possibility set S in this example. This set is known as the *free-disposal convex hull* of the observed bundles.

We can use the benchmark technology set S to measure the technical efficiency of the observation P_5. The input-oriented projection of P_5 is the point A corresponding to the minimum input level (x_5^*) necessary to produce the output level y_5. Thus, the input-oriented technical efficiency of P_5 is

$$\mathrm{TE}_I^V(x_5, y_5) = \frac{x_5^*}{x_5}. \qquad (3.28)$$

Similarly, the output-oriented projection is the point B showing the maximum output (y_5^*) producible from input x_5. The output-oriented technical

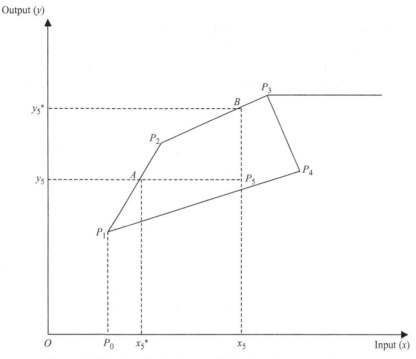

Figure 3.7 The free-disposal convex hull and an inner approximation
of the production possibility set.

efficiency is

$$\mathrm{TE}_O^V(x_5, y_5) = \frac{y_5}{y_5^*}. \tag{3.29}$$

As already noted in Chapter 2, the input- and output-oriented technical efficiency measures will, in general, differ when VRS holds. Note that average
productivity of the input varies along the frontier of the production possibility
set in this case. It initially increases, reaching a maximum at P_2, and declines
with further increase in x.

The input-oriented measure of technical efficiency of any firm t under VRS
requires the solution of the following LP problem due to BCC:

$$\min \theta$$

$$\text{s.t.} \sum_{j=1}^{N} \lambda_j x^j \leq \theta x^t;$$

$$\sum_{j=1}^{N} \lambda_j y^j \geq y^t; \tag{3.30}$$

$$\sum_{j=1}^{N} \lambda_j = 1;$$

$$\lambda_j \geq 0 \ (j = 1, 2, \ldots, N).$$

Let $(\theta^*; \lambda_1^*, \lambda_2^*, \ldots, \lambda_N^*)$ be the optimal solution. Define $x_*^t = \theta^* x^t$. Then (x_*^t, y^t) is the efficient input-oriented radial projection of (x^t, y^t) onto the frontier and

$$\text{TE}_I^V(x^t, y^t) = \theta^*. \tag{3.31}$$

The output-oriented measure of technical efficiency is obtained from the solution of the following program:

$$\max \phi$$

$$\text{s.t.} \ \sum_{j=1}^{N} \lambda_j x^j \leq x^t;$$

$$\sum_{j=1}^{N} \lambda_j y^j \geq \phi y^t; \tag{3.32}$$

$$\sum_{j=1}^{N} \lambda_j = 1;$$

$$\lambda_j \geq 0 \ (j = 1, 2, \ldots, N).$$

Again, define $\phi^* y^t = y_*^t$. Now (x^t, y_*^t) is the efficient output-oriented radial projection of (x^t, y^t) and

$$\text{TE}_O^V(x^t, y^t) = \frac{1}{\phi^*}. \tag{3.33}$$

Example 3.1. Data for input (x) and output (y) are reported for five firms $A, B, C, D,$ and E in Table 3.1.

Under the assumption of VRS, the production frontier is the broken line *KABC-extension* shown in Figure 3.8. But, if CRS is assumed, the production frontier is the ray *OR* passing through the point B which is the MPSS on the VRS frontier. Both A and C are technically efficient under the VRS assumption but not under CRS. Firm B is efficient even when CRS is assumed.

Table 3.1. *Data for input (x) and output (y) for
5 firms A, B, C, D, and E*

Firm	A	B	C	D	E
Input (x)	2	4	6	7	5.5
Output (y)	2	6	8	4	6.5

D and E are both inefficient even under VRS. Consider firm E. Its input-oriented projection onto the VRS frontier is F, where $x_E^*(= 4.5)$ units of the input produce $y_E(= 6.5)$ units of the output. The output-oriented projection, on the other hand, is the point G, where $y_E^* (= 7.5)$ units of the output are produced from $x_E (= 5.5)$ units of the input. Therefore, the input- and output-oriented

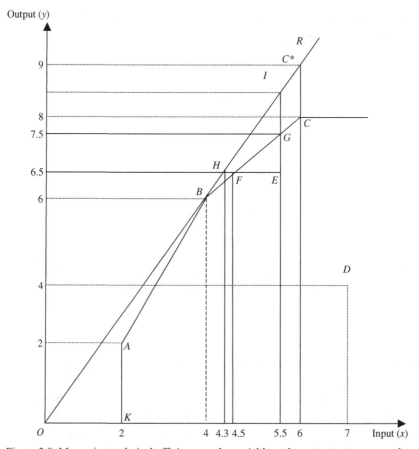

Figure 3.8 Measuring technical efficiency under variable and constant returns to scale.

efficiency levels of firm E under VRS are

$$\text{TE}_I^V(E) = \frac{4.5}{5.5} = \frac{9}{11} \quad \text{and} \quad \text{TE}_O^V(E) = \frac{6.5}{7.5} = \frac{13}{15}, \quad \text{respectively.}$$

On the other hand, the input-oriented projection onto the CRS frontier is the point H, where only $x_E^C (= 4\frac{1}{3})$ units of the input produce the same output. Hence, CRS technical efficiency is

$$\text{TE}^C(E) = \frac{\frac{13}{3}}{\frac{11}{2}} = \frac{26}{33}.$$

The output-oriented projection of E is the point I on the CRS frontier. But comparison of the points E and I yields the same measure of technical efficiency as what is obtained by comparing points E and H.

Firm C, using $x_C (= 6)$ units of the input to produce $y_C (= 8)$ units of the output is located on the VRS frontier. Hence, its technical efficiency (both input- and output-oriented) is 1 under VRS. Its output-oriented projection onto the radial CRS frontier is the point C^* where x_C $(= 6)$ units of the input is shown to produce y_C^* $(= 9)$ units of the output. Thus, the CRS technical efficiency of this firm is

$$\text{TE}^C(C) = \frac{8}{9}.$$

Note that scale efficiency of firm C is the ratio of average productivity at the point C, which is efficient to the maximum average productivity that is attained on the frontier at B. The average productivity at B is the same as the average productivity at C^* (which is not really a feasible point). But comparison of the average productivities at C and at C^* is equivalent to comparing the technical efficiency of the point C to the VRS frontier and a hypothetical CRS frontier shown by the ray through B.

The question of scale efficiency is relevant *only when CRS does not hold.* Therefore, the ray OR does not represent a set of feasible points. The only feasible point on OR is B, because it lies on the VRS frontier. However, because average productivity is constant for all input–output bundles (feasible or not) on the ray OR, we use the point C^* (even though it is not feasible) to measure the average productivity at the point B, which is a feasible point. Thus, the scale efficiency of the point C is simply the ratio of average productivities at C and at B. The scale efficiency of firm C can thus be measured as

$$\text{SE}(C) = \frac{\text{TE}^C(C)}{\text{TE}^V(C)} = \frac{8}{9}.$$

For a point that lies on the VRS frontier, input- and output-oriented scale efficiencies are identical, unlike inefficient points such as E. This is because the input- and output-oriented projections of an inefficient point are two different points on the VRS frontier. Generally, the average productivities at these two points are different. As a result, the input- and output-oriented scale efficiency measures are also different. For firm E, the two measures are

$$SE_I(E) = \frac{TE^C(E)}{TE_I^V(E)} = \frac{(26)/(33)}{(9)/(11)} = \frac{26}{27} \quad \text{and}$$

$$SE_O(E) = \frac{TE^C(E)}{TE_O^V(E)} = \frac{(26)/(33)}{(13)/(15)} = \frac{10}{11}, \quad \text{respectively.}$$

Example 3.2a. Reconsider the input–output bundles from *Example 2.1*. For the input-oriented technical efficiency of firm C under assumption of VRS, we solve the following LP problem:

$$\min \theta$$

$$\text{s.t. } 4\lambda_A + 9\lambda_B + 6\lambda_C + 8\lambda_D + 7\lambda_E + 11\lambda_F \geq 6;$$

$$2\lambda_A + 4\lambda_B + 3\lambda_C + 6\lambda_D + 5\lambda_E + 8\lambda_F \geq 3;$$

$$2\lambda_A + 7\lambda_B + 6\lambda_C + 5\lambda_D + 8\lambda_E + 6\lambda_F - 6\theta \leq 0; \qquad (3.34)$$

$$3\lambda_A + 5\lambda_B + 7\lambda_C + 8\lambda_D + 4\lambda_E + 6\lambda_F - 7\theta \leq 0;$$

$$\lambda_A + \lambda_B + \lambda_C + \lambda_D + \lambda_E + \lambda_F = 1;$$

$$\lambda_A, \lambda_B, \ldots, \lambda_F \geq 0.$$

The optimal solution for this problem is

$$(\theta^* = 0.54955; \lambda_A^* = 0.69369, \lambda_B^* = 0.07207, \lambda_F^* = 0.23423, \lambda_C^* = \lambda_D^* = 0).$$

For the input-oriented measure, the reference firm for C is a weighted average of firms A, B, and F. This reference firm requires 3.29725 units of x_1 and 3.8468 units of x_2. Thus, both inputs can be reduced by a factor of 0.54955. At the same time, output y_2 would increase by 0.55 units whereas y_1 would remain unchanged. The input-oriented technical efficiency is 0.54955. In Chapter 2, the technical efficiency of firm C under CRS was found to be 0.529. Imposition of the additional constraint $(\sum_j \lambda_j = 1)$ has resulted in a higher value of the objective function in this minimization problem for measuring input-oriented technical efficiency.

Example 3.2b. The output-oriented technical efficiency of DMU C is obtained by solving the LP problem:

$$\max \phi$$

$$\text{s.t. } 4\lambda_A + 9\lambda_B + 6\lambda_C + 8\lambda_D + 7\lambda_E + 11\lambda_F - 6\phi \geq 0;$$

$$2\lambda_A + 4\lambda_B + 3\lambda_C + 6\lambda_D + 5\lambda_E + 8\lambda_F - 3\phi \geq 0;$$

$$2\lambda_A + 7\lambda_B + 6\lambda_C + 5\lambda_D + 8\lambda_E + 6\lambda_F \leq 6;$$

$$3\lambda_A + 5\lambda_B + 7\lambda_C + 8\lambda_D + 4\lambda_E + 6\lambda_F \leq 7; \qquad (3.35)$$

$$\lambda_A + \lambda_B + \lambda_C + \lambda_D + \lambda_E + \lambda_F = 1;$$

$$\lambda_A, \lambda_B, \ldots, \lambda_F \geq 0.$$

The optimal solution for this problem is $\phi^* = 1.8333; \lambda_F^* = 1; \lambda_A^* = \lambda_B^* = \lambda_C^* = \lambda_D^* = \lambda_E^* = 0$. Thus, the firm F is the reference firm for C. If C's input bundle were utilized by this reference firm, output y_1 would increase from 6 to 11 (an increase by a factor of 1.8333), while output y_2 would increase from 3 to 8 (by a factor of 2.6666). Further, the quantity of input x_2 would be reduced by 1 unit while input x_1 used would remain unchanged. Thus, $\phi^* = \min(1.8333, 2.3333) = 1.8333$. There is an output slack of 2.5 units in y_2 and an input slack of 1 unit in x_2. The output-oriented technical efficiency of firm C under VRS is

$$\text{TE}_O^V(C) = \frac{1}{1.8333} = 0.54546.$$

Note that this measure differs from the input-oriented efficiency under VRS. The input-oriented scale efficiency of firm C is

$$\text{SE}_I(C) = \frac{\text{TE}_I^C}{\text{TE}_I^V} = \frac{0.529}{0.54995} = 0.9626$$

while the output-oriented scale efficiency is

$$\text{SE}_O(C) = \frac{\text{TE}_O^C}{\text{TE}_O^V} = \frac{0.529}{0.54546} = 0.9698.$$

In *Example 3.1*, we could have directly computed the average productivities at the input- and output-oriented projections and compared them with the average productivity at the MPSS. In that context, measuring the technical efficiency relative to an inappropriate CRS frontier appeared to be an unnecessary exercise. In multiple-input, multiple-output cases (like *Examples 3.2a–3.2b*), average productivity as a ratio of output to input does not have a meaning. We need to compare ray average productivities. The ratio of technical efficiencies under CRS and VRS, respectively, measures the ray average productivity at the efficient projection of an observed input–output bundle onto the VRS frontier relative to the maximum ray average productivity attainable at an MPSS on this frontier.

3.6 Identifying the Nature of Returns to Scale at Any Point on the Frontier

Scale efficiency (SE) falls below unity at any point on the VRS frontier that is not an MPSS. This is true under both increasing and diminishing returns to scale. Thus, SE by itself does not reveal anything about the nature of returns to scale. Three alternative approaches to address this problem are available in the literature.

A Primal Approach
Banker (1984) establishes the relation between an MPSS within a VRS production possibility set and the optimal solution of the CCR DEA problem in the following theorem:

Theorem 1: An input–output bundle (x^t, y^t) is an MPSS if and only if the optimal value of the objective function of a CCR–DEA model equals unity for this input–output combination.

Proof. Consider the data set $\{(x^j, y^j) : j = 1, 2, \ldots, t, \ldots, N\}$. An input-oriented formulation of the CCR–DEA model for (x^t, y^t) is

$$\min \theta$$
$$\text{s.t.} \sum_{j=1}^{N} \lambda_j y^j \geq y^t:$$
$$\sum_{j=1}^{N} \lambda_j x^j \leq \theta x^t; \qquad (3.36)$$
$$\lambda_j \geq 0 \ (j = 1, 2, \ldots, N); \quad \theta \text{ free.}$$

Suppose that the optimal solution for this problem is $(\theta^*; \lambda^*)$. Note that the optimal solution for this CRS problem may not be feasible for the VRS technology, however. We need to show that $\theta^* = 1$ if and only if (x^t, y^t) is an MPSS. Now, assume that (x^t, y^t) is not an MPSS. Then, there exist (α, β) satisfying $\frac{\alpha}{\beta} > 1$ such that $(\beta x^t, \alpha y^t)$ is in the VRS production possibility set. Define $X^t \equiv \beta x^t$ and $Y^t \equiv \alpha y^t$. Because (X^t, Y^t) is feasible under the VRS assumption, there will exist nonnegative weights $\mu_j (j = 1, 2, \ldots, N)$ satisfying

$$\sum_{j=1}^{N} \mu_j x^j \leq X^t; \quad \sum_{j=1}^{N} \mu_j y^j \geq Y^t; \quad \sum_{j=1}^{N} \mu_j = 1; \quad \mu_j \geq 0. \tag{3.37}$$

Let $\lambda_j = \frac{\mu_j}{\alpha}$. Then, $\sum_{j=1}^{N} \lambda_j x^j \leq \frac{X^t}{\alpha} = \frac{\beta}{\alpha} x^t$, and $\sum_{j=1}^{N} \lambda_j y^j \geq \frac{Y^t}{\alpha} = y^t$. Clearly, $\theta = \frac{\beta}{\alpha}$ is a feasible value of the objective function in the CCR–DEA problem. But, because $\frac{\alpha}{\beta} > 1$ by assumption, $\frac{\beta}{\alpha} < 1$ and, in that case, $\theta^* = 1$ cannot be an optimal solution for this minimization problem.

Next, suppose that $\theta^* < 1$ at the optimal solution $(\theta^*; \lambda^*)$ of the CCR–DEA problem. Then, by feasibility, $\sum_{j=1}^{N} \lambda_j^* x^j \leq \theta^* x^t$ and $\sum_{j=1}^{N} \lambda_j^* y^j \geq y^t$. Define $\sum_{j=1}^{N} \lambda_j^* \equiv k^*$ and $\mu_j \equiv \frac{\lambda_j^*}{k^*}$. Then,

$$\sum_{j=1}^{N} \mu_j x^j \leq \frac{\theta_*}{k^*} x^t; \quad \sum_{j=1}^{N} \mu_j y^j \geq \frac{y^t}{k^*}; \quad \sum_{j=1}^{N} \mu_j = 1. \tag{3.38}$$

Thus, $(\frac{\theta^*}{k^*} x^t, \frac{1}{k^*} y^t)$ is in the VRS technology set. Let $\alpha = \frac{1}{k^*}$ and $\beta = \frac{\theta^*}{k^*}$. Then, $(\beta x^t, \alpha y^t)$ is feasible under VRS. But, $\frac{\alpha}{\beta} = \frac{1}{\theta^*} > 1$ if $\theta^* < 1$. In that case, (x^t, y^t) is not an MPSS. *QED.*

An implication of this theorem is that the CRS and VRS frontiers coincide at an MPSS. Three important corollaries of this theorem are

Corollary 1: Firm t is operating under locally CRS if $\sum_{j=1}^{N} \lambda_j^* = 1$ at the optimal solution of the CCR–DEA problem for (x^t, y^t).

Corollary 2: Firm t is operating under locally increasing returns to scale if $\sum_{j=1}^{N} \lambda_j^* < 1$ at the optimal solution of the CCR–DEA problem for (x^t, y^t).

Corollary 3: Firm t is operating under locally diminishing returns to scale if $\sum_{j=1}^{N} \lambda_j^* > 1$ at the optimal solution of the CCR–DEA problem for (x^t, y^t).

The intuition behind *Corollaries 1–3* is easily explained by means of a simple diagram in Figure 3.9 for the single-output, single-input case. Points A, B, C, D, and E show the input–output bundles of five firms in a sample. The VRS frontier is shown by the broken line segment *FABC-extension*. The CRS

Output (*y*)

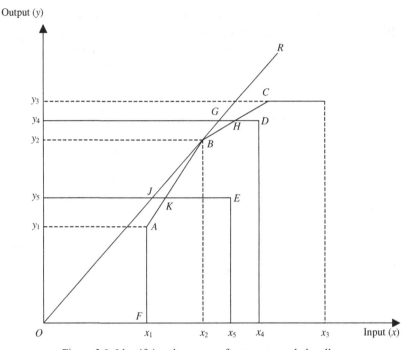

Figure 3.9 Identifying the nature of returns to scale locally.

frontier, on the other hand, is the ray OBR through the origin. Consider point D, where the firm uses input x_4 to produce output y_4. The input-oriented projection of D onto the CRS frontier is the point G, where input $\theta^* x_4$ is used to produce output y_4. Note that point G is not feasible under the VRS assumption. However, the point B on the CRS frontier is feasible under the VRS assumption also. This corresponds to the MPSS at the input–output bundle $(\frac{\theta^*}{k^*} x_4, \frac{1}{k^*} y_4)$. Clearly, when $k^* = \sum_j \lambda_j^* > 1$, the CRS projection $(\theta^* x_4, y_4)$ has to be scaled down to attain the MPSS. In this example, the point G lies to the right of B on the CRS frontier, and the efficient projection of the firm observed at point D onto the VRS frontier is the point H that lies in the region of diminishing returns to scale. Similarly, the efficient input-oriented projection of the point E onto the CRS frontier is point J. One must scale this up (i.e., $k^* < 1$) in order to reach the MPSS at point B. The efficient projection of E onto the VRS frontier is the point K that lies in the region of increasing returns to scale.

One practical problem with this criterion is that there may exist alternative optimal solutions for the CCR–DEA problem where k^* exceeds 1 in some optimal solution but falls short of 1 in another optimal solution for the same problem. Because the solution algorithm terminates whenever an optimal solution is reached, the decision about returns to scale then becomes dependent on which particular optimal solution was reached. We need to qualify the three corollaries as follows:

Corollary 1: Firm *t* is operating under locally increasing returns to scale if $\sum_{j=1}^{N} \lambda_j^* < 1$ at all optimal solutions of the CCR–DEA problem for (x^t, y^t).

Corollary 2: Firm *t* is operating under locally diminishing returns to scale if $\sum_{j=1}^{N} \lambda_j^* > 1$ at all optimal solutions of the CCR–DEA problem for (x^t, y^t).

To implement this revised criterion in practice, we need the following two-step procedure:

Step 1: Solve the CCR–DEA problem and obtain θ^*.

Step 2: Solve the following problem:

$$\max \sum_{j=1}^{N} \lambda_j$$
$$\text{s.t.} \sum_{j=1}^{N} \lambda_j y^j \geq y^t; \qquad (3.39)$$
$$\sum_{j=1}^{N} \lambda_j x^j \leq \theta^* x^t;$$
$$\lambda_j \geq 0 \ (j = 1, 2, \ldots, N).$$

Note that only the λ_j's from the optimal solutions of the Step 1 problem are feasible for the Step 2 problem. Hence, if the optimal value of the objective function Step 2 problem is less than 1, we know that $k^* < 1$ at all optimal solutions of the CCR–BCC problem and, therefore, locally increasing returns holds. To test for diminishing returns, we simply minimize (rather than maximize) the objective function in the Step 2 problem. This time, if the minimum exceeds 1, locally diminishing returns is implied.

A Dual Approach

BCC (1984) offer a different approach to identifying returns to scale at a point on the VRS frontier, which differs in two important respects from the previous approach. First, they focus on the BCC–DEA problem that explicitly assumes VRS. Second, they focus on the dual (rather than the primal) formulation of the problem.

For the VRS input-oriented problem evaluating DMU t with input–output (x^t, y^t), the dual LP problem is

$$\max \sum_{r=1}^{m} u_r y_{rt} - u_0$$

$$\text{s.t.} \quad \sum_{r=1}^{m} u_r y_{rj} - \sum_{i=1}^{n} v_i x_{ij} - u_0 \leq 0; \quad (j = 1, 2, \ldots, N); \qquad (3.40)$$

$$\sum_{i=1}^{m} v_i x_{it} = 1;$$

$$u_r, v_i \geq 0; \quad (r = 1, 2, \ldots, m; \ i = 1, 2, \ldots, n); \quad u_0 \text{ free.}$$

This is equivalent to

$$\max \frac{\sum_{r=1}^{m} u_r y_{rt} - u_0}{\sum_{i=1}^{n} v_i x_{it}}$$

$$\text{s.t.} \quad \frac{\sum_{r=1}^{m} u_r y_{rj} - u_0}{\sum_{i=1}^{n} v_i x_{ij}} \leq 1 : (j = 1, 2, \ldots, N); \qquad (3.41)$$

$$u_r, v_i \geq 0; \quad (r = 1, 2, \ldots, m; \ i = 1, 2, \ldots, n); \quad u_0 \text{ free.}$$

Consider the optimal solution $(u^*; v^*; u_0^*)$. BCC first show that

$$\sum_{r=1}^{m} u_r^* y_r - \sum_{i=1}^{n} v_i^* x_i - u_0^* = 0$$

is a separating hyperplane for the VRS technology set T. Thus,

$$\sum_{r=1}^{m} u_r^* y_{r0} - \sum_{i=1}^{n} v_i^* x_{i0} - u_0^* \leq 0 \quad \text{for any} \quad (x^0, y^0) \in T. \qquad (3.42)$$

For each observation j,

$$\sum_{r=1}^{m} u_r^* y_{rj} - \sum_{i=1}^{n} v_i^* x_{ij} - u_0^* \leq 0. \tag{3.43}$$

Hence,

$$\sum_{r=1}^{m} u_r^* \left(\sum_{j=1}^{N} \lambda_j y_{rj} \right) - \sum_{i=1}^{n} v_i^* \left(\sum_{j=1}^{N} \lambda_j x_{ij} \right) - \left(\sum_{j=1}^{N} \lambda_j \right) u_0^* \leq 0. \tag{3.44}$$

But, if $(x^0, y^0) \in T$, then there exist λ_j's adding up to 1, satisfying

$$x_{i0} \geq \sum_{j=1}^{N} \lambda_j x_{ij} \quad \text{and} \quad y_{r0} \leq \sum_{j=1}^{N} \lambda_j y_{rj}.$$

This means that $\sum_{r=1}^{m} u_r^* y_{r0} - \sum_{i=1}^{n} v_i^* x_{i0} - u_0^* \leq 0$, which proves that it is a separating hyperplane. If, on the other hand, (x^E, y^E) is an efficient projection of (x^t, y^t)

$$\sum_{r=1}^{m} u_r^* y_{rE} - \sum_{i=1}^{n} v_i^* x_{iE} - u_0^* = 0 \tag{3.45}$$

and it is a supporting (or tangent) hyperplane at (x^E, y^E).

Consider the point $Z_\delta = ((1 + \delta)x^E, (1 + \delta)y^E)$ where δ is arbitrarily small in absolute value. Then, locally increasing returns holds at (x^E, y^E) if there exists $\delta^* > 0$ such that

(a) $Z_\delta \in T$ for $\delta^* > \delta > 0$ and
(b) $Z_\delta \notin T$ for $-\delta^* < \delta < 0$.

That is, a small radial increase in scale remains a feasible input–output bundle, but a small radial decrease is not feasible.

CRS holds if

(a) $Z_\delta \in T$ for $|\delta| < \delta^*$ and
(b) $Z_\delta \notin T$ for $|\delta| > \delta^*$.

In this case, a small radial change – either increase or decrease in scale – leaves the resulting input–output bundle feasible.

Locally diminishing returns to scale holds if

(a) $Z_\delta \notin T$ for $\delta^* > \delta > 0$ and
(b) $Z_\delta \in T$ for $-\delta^* < \delta < 0$.

Here, a small reduction in scale leaves the input–output bundle feasible, but a small increase in scale will not be feasible.

Note that because (x^E, y^E) is efficient and lies on the supporting hyperplane,

$$u^*(1+\delta)y^E - v^*(1+\delta)x^E - u_0^* = (1+\delta)[u^*y^E - v^*x^E - u_0^*]$$
$$+ \delta u_0^* = \delta u_0^*. \tag{3.46}$$

Further, when $Z_\delta \in T$, $u^*(1+\delta)y^E - v^*(1+\delta)x^E - u_0^* \le 0$. Thus, $\delta u_0^* \le 0$. Let $\delta > 0$. Then, $Z_\delta \in T$ if $u_0^* < 0$. Hence, in the case of locally increasing returns, the tangent hyperplane has a negative intercept. Similarly, if $u_0^* > 0$, then $Z_\delta \in T$ only if $\delta < 0$. Thus, a positive intercept represents locally diminishing returns. Finally, if u_0^* equals 0, both positive and negative values of δ would be compatible with the feasibility of Z_δ. Thus, in the case of CRS, the tangent hyperplane is a ray through the origin. This compares directly with the simple one-input, one-output case, where the tangent to the production function at an MPSS is a ray through the origin. This is illustrated in Figure 3.10. The VRS frontier is shown by the broken line *KABC-extension*. Point *A* lies in the region of increasing returns to scale on the VRS frontier. The tangent hyperplane through *A* (the line $R_1 R_1$) meets the vertical axis below the origin with a negative intercept. Point *B* is an MPSS where locally CRS holds. The tangent hyperplane through *B* is the ray *OR* through the origin. Point *C* is in the region of diminishing returns. The tangent through $C(R_2 R_2)$ has a positive intercept and meets the vertical axis above the origin.

As in Banker's primal approach, in this dual approach there is also the potential problem of multiple optimal solutions. The following two-step procedure can be adopted in this case:

Step 1: Solve the dual-maximization problem for the BCC–DEA model. Suppose that the optimal value of the objective function is W^*.

Step 2: Now, solve the problem

$$\max u_0$$

$$\text{s.t.} \sum_{r=1}^{m} u_r y_{rj} - \sum_{i=1}^{n} v_i x_{ij} - u_0 \le 0 \, (j = 1, 2, \ldots, N); \tag{3.47}$$

$$\sum_{r=1}^{m} u_r y_{rt} - u_0 = W^*;$$

$$u_r \ge 0; \quad v_i \ge 0; \quad (r = 1, 2, \ldots, m; i = 1, 2, \ldots, n); \quad u_0 \text{ free.}$$

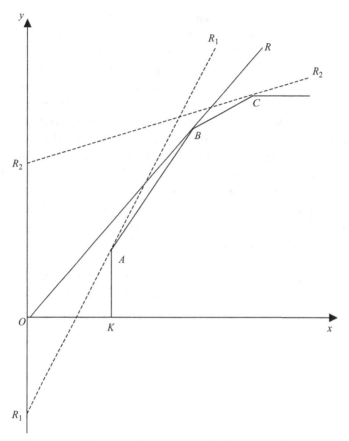

Figure 3.10 Intercepts of the tangent hyperplane to the frontier and local returns to scale.

If the optimal value of the objective function is less than 0, we conclude that u_0 is negative in all of the optimal solutions for the problem in Step 1. Hence, increasing returns holds at this input–output bundle. To test for diminishing returns, we minimize u_0 in Step 2. If the minimum value exceeds zero, diminishing returns to scale is implied.

A Nesting Approach
Färe, Grosskopf, and Lovell (FGL) (1985) exploit the hierarchical relation between the production possibility sets under alternative assumptions about returns to scale.

Under VRS, which allows increasing, constant, or diminishing returns at different points on the frontier, we assume only that convex combinations of actually observed input–output bundles are feasible. Thus, as a first approximation, we treat the convex hull of the observed points as the production possibility set. Further, by free disposability of inputs and outputs, all points in the free disposal convex hull of these points are also considered feasible. Under CRS, all scalar expansions as well as nonnegative radial contractions of feasible input–output bundles are also considered feasible. In that case, the smallest cone containing the free disposal convex hull of the observed bundles, often called the *conical hull*, constitutes the production possibility set.

In between the assumptions of VRS and CRS lies nonincreasing returns to scale (NIRS). When the technology exhibits NIRS, all scalar contractions of observed input–output bundles are feasible; however, scalar expansions of bundles that are feasible under the VRS assumption are not necessarily feasible. The VRS production possibility set is contained in the NIRS production possibility set, which is itself a subset of the CRS production possibility set.

The three different sets are shown in Figure 3.11. Points *A, B, C, D, E,* and *F* show the observed input–output combinations of six firms. As explained

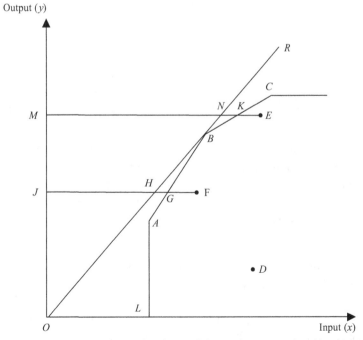

Figure 3.11 VRS, NIRS, and CRS frontiers and the nesting approach to identifying the nature of local returns to scale.

earlier, the broken line *LABC-extension* is the frontier of the production possibility set (T^V) under VRS. Note that points to the left of *LAB* are not considered feasible under VRS. If NIRS holds, however, whenever $(x, y) \in T^V$, (tx, ty) is feasible for $0 \le t \le 1$. This means that whenever any input–output bundle that is feasible under VRS is scaled down, the resulting bundle would be feasible if NIRS holds. The frontier of the production possibility set under NIRS, T^N, is *OBC-extension*. Finally, when CRS holds, the production frontier is the ray *OR* passing through the point *B*, which is an MPSS on the VRS frontier. Note that the NIRS and the CRS frontiers coincide over the range where increasing returns holds along the VRS frontier. On the other hand, the NIRS and VRS frontiers coincide when diminishing returns to scale holds under VRS. At the MPSS (on the VRS frontier), all three frontiers coincide. This extremely useful relation between these frontiers can be utilized to identify the returns to scale characteristics of the technology at any given point.

Consider point *F*, which is an interior point of T^V and is technically inefficient. The input-oriented efficient projection of *F* onto the VRS frontier is *G* and onto the CRS frontier is *H*. This is also the projection onto the NIRS frontier. Thus, the input-oriented technical efficiency of *F* is

$$\text{TE}_I^V(F) = \frac{JG}{JF}, \quad \text{if VRS is assumed, and}$$

$$\text{TE}_I^C(F) = \text{TE}_I^N(F) = \frac{JH}{JF}, \quad \text{if either CRS or NIRS is assumed.}$$

Note that the point *G*, the input-oriented projection of *F*, lies on the increasing returns region of the VRS frontier. Therefore, if $\text{TE}_I^C = \text{TE}_I^N < \text{TE}_I^V$, the input-oriented projection onto the VRS frontier is in the increasing returns to scale region.

Next, consider the point *E*. Its input-oriented projection onto the VRS frontier (which is the same as the projection on the NIRS frontier) is point *K*, but its projection onto the CRS frontier is *N*. For this firm, the input-oriented technical efficiency is

$$\text{TE}_I^V(E) = \text{TE}_I^N(E) = \frac{MK}{ME}, \quad \text{under either VRS or NIRS}$$

and

$$\text{TE}_I^C(E) = \frac{MN}{ME} \quad \text{under CRS.}$$

The input-oriented projection is a point on the region of diminishing returns in the VRS frontier. Thus, when $TE_I^V = TE_I^N > TE_I^C$, diminishing returns hold at the input-oriented projection.

Note two things. First, the assumed technology exhibits VRS. Thus, points outside the VRS frontier are artificial reference points that are not feasible. Second, for some points (e.g., D), the input-oriented projection is in the increasing returns region whereas the output-oriented projection is in the region of diminishing returns on the VRS frontier. For such observations, returns-to-scale characterization depends on the orientation.

To implement this procedure in practice, we need to measure the input- or output-oriented technical efficiency levels using an NIRS frontier as the benchmark. Because every radial contraction of any input–output bundle that is feasible under VRS is feasible under NIRS,

$$T^N = \left\{ (x, y) : x \geq \sum_{j=1}^{N} \lambda_j x^j; y \leq \sum_{j=1}^{N} \lambda_j y^j; \sum_{j=1}^{N} \lambda_j \leq 1; \right.$$

$$\left. \lambda_j \geq 0; (j = 1, 2, \ldots, N) \right\}. \qquad (3.48)$$

Note that under CRS, no restriction is imposed on the sum of the λ_j's. Under VRS, the sum equals unity. Under NIRS, the sum is less than or equal to unity. Thus, the VRS technology set is the most restrictive (the smallest) and the CRS technology set is the least restrictive (largest), whereas the NIRS technology set lies in between.

The following theorem due to BCC (1996) shows that the alternative approaches to returns-to-scale determination are equivalent and will always yield mutually consistent results.

Theorem 2:

(a) There exists a solution for the CCR problem (3.36) with $\sum_j \lambda_j^* = 1$ if and only if $SE = 1$ (i.e., CRS holds).

(b) All alternative optimal solutions of the CCR problem have $\sum_j \lambda_j^* > 1$ if and only if $SE < 1$ and $TE^C < TE^N = TE^V$ (i.e., DRS holds).

(c) All optimal solutions of the CCR problem have $\sum_j \lambda_j^* < 1$ if and only if $SE < 1$ and $TE^C = TE^N < TE^V$ (i.e., IRS holds).

Proof. Part (a): We know from Theorem 1 and Corollary 1(a) that in the case of CRS, $TE^C = 1$ and $\sum_j \lambda_j^* = 1$. Thus, this particular solution is also feasible for the BCC problem resulting in $TE^V = 1$ and $SE = 1$. Conversely, if $SE = 1$, $TE^V = TE^C$. Thus, an optimal solution for the BCC problem is also an optimal solution for the CCR problem. However, because it is a solution for the BCC problem, it must satisfy $\sum_j \lambda_j^* = 1$. For parts (b) and (c), we make use of the following lemma.

Lemma 1: If the CCR problem has two alternative optimal solutions, one with $\sum_j \lambda_j^* > 1$ and another with $\sum_j \lambda_j^* < 1$, then there exists an alternative optimal solution to the CCR problem with $\sum_j \lambda_j^* = 1$.

Proof. Suppose that the first solution is λ_1^* with $\sum_j \lambda_{1j}^* = \alpha_1 > 1$, and the other solution is λ_2^* with $\sum_j \lambda_{2j}^* = \alpha_2 < 1$. Define $\alpha_3 = \frac{\alpha_1 - 1}{\alpha_1 - \alpha_2}$. Next, define $\lambda_3^* = (1 - \alpha_3)\lambda_1^* + \alpha_3\lambda_2^*$. Then, it can be easily verified that λ_3^* provides another optimal solution to the BCC problem. Moreover, $\sum_j \lambda_{3j}^* = (1 - \alpha_3)\alpha_1 + \alpha_3\alpha_2 = 1$.

We now return to the proof of parts (b) and (c) of the theorem. Consider part (c) first. If $\sum_j \lambda_j^* < 1$ at all optimal solutions of the CCR problem, then, by virtue of part (a) of this theorem, $SE < 1$ and $TE^C < TE^V$. But, in this case, these optimal solutions of the CCR problem are all feasible for the NIRS problem. Therefore, $TE^N < TE^V$. On the other hand, when $TE^N < TE^V$, an optimal solution for the NIRS problem is not feasible for the BCC problem. Thus, for all optimal solutions of the NIRS problem, $\sum_j \lambda_j^* < 1$. These are, of course, all feasible solutions for the less restrictive CCR problem. But because $SE < 1$, an optimal solution of the CCR problem with $\sum_j \lambda_j^* = 1$ is ruled out. Further, the lemma rules out solutions with $\sum_j \lambda_j^* > 1$. Hence, if $SE < 1$ and $TE^N < TE^V$, $\sum_j \lambda_j^* < 1$ at all optimal solutions of the CCR problem. This completes the proof of part (c).

Next, consider part (b). If $\sum_j \lambda_j^* > 1$ at all optimal solutions for the CCR problem, then $SE < 1$ by virtue of part (a). Suppose, however, that $TE^N < TE^V$. Let λ_1^* with $\sum_j \lambda_{1j}^* = \alpha_1 > 1$ be a solution for the CCR problem and λ_2^* with $\sum_j \lambda_{2j}^* = \alpha_2 < 1$ be a solution for the NIRS problem. Define, as in the lemma, $\lambda_3^* = (1 - \alpha_3)\lambda_1^* + \alpha_3\lambda_2^*$, where $0 < \alpha_3 = \frac{\alpha_1 - 1}{\alpha_1 - \alpha_2} < 1$. As shown before, $\sum_j \lambda_{3j}^* = 1$. Note that

$$\sum_j \lambda_{3j}^* y^j = \sum_j [(1 - \alpha_3)\lambda_{1j}^* + \alpha_3\lambda_{2j}^*] y^j \geq (1 - \alpha_3)y^t + \alpha_3 y^t = y^t.$$

Similarly,

$$\sum_j \lambda_{3j}^* x^j \leq \sum_j [(1 - \alpha_3)\theta^C + \alpha_3\theta^N]x^t.$$

Hence,

$$\theta^V \leq (1 - \alpha_3)\theta^C + \alpha_3\theta^N < (1 - \alpha_3)\theta^V + \alpha_3\theta^V = \theta^V.$$

This, clearly, is a contradiction. In this case, it is not possible to have $\theta^N < \theta^V$. Therefore, $\theta^N = \theta^V$.

The converse implications for parts (b) and (c) follow immediately because the conditions specified in the theorem are mutually exclusive.

Example 3.3. The input-oriented technical efficiency of DMU C (from *Example 2b*) under NIRS is obtained by solving the problem

$$\min \theta$$

$$\text{s.t. } 4\lambda_A + 9\lambda_B + 6\lambda_C + 8\lambda_D + 7\lambda_E + 11\lambda_F \geq 6;$$

$$2\lambda_A + 4\lambda_B + 3\lambda_C + 6\lambda_D + 5\lambda_E + 8\lambda_F \geq 3;$$

$$2\lambda_A + 7\lambda_B + 6\lambda_C + 5\lambda_D + 8\lambda_E + 6\lambda_F - 6\theta \leq 0; \qquad (3.49)$$

$$3\lambda_A + 5\lambda_B + 7\lambda_C + 8\lambda_D + 4\lambda_E + 6\lambda_F - 7\theta \leq 0;$$

$$\lambda_A + \lambda_B + \lambda_C + \lambda_D + \lambda_E + \lambda_F = 1;$$

$$\lambda_A, \lambda_B, \ldots, \lambda_F \geq 0.$$

Compared to the problem in *Example 3.2a,* here the restriction on the sum of the λs is changed from equality to a "less-than-equal-to" sign.

The SAS program for this problem is as follows.

```
DATA EX3A;
INPUT A B C D E F THETA _TYPE_ $ _RHS_;
CARDS;
4  9  6  8  7  11   0  ≥  6
2  4  3  6  5   8  -0  ≥  3
2  7  6  5  8   6  -6  ≤  0
3  5  7  8  4   6  -7  ≤  0
1  1  1  1  1   1  -0  ≤  1
0  0  0  0  0   0  -1  MIN.
;
PROC LP;
```

Note that in the first two constraints, the output quantities of firm C appear in the right-hand side of the inequality sign and that the input quantities of C appear with a negative sign in the column for THETA. Further, the restriction on the λ_j's is a less-than-equal-to type for this NIRS problem. The optimal solution for this problem is

$$\lambda_A^* = 0.52941; \quad \lambda_F^* = 0.35294; \quad \lambda_B^* = \lambda_C^* = \lambda_D^* = \lambda_E^* = 0; \quad \theta^* = 0.529.$$

Thus, $\mathrm{TE}_I^N(C) = 0.529$. This is also the solution for the CRS model when there is no restriction on the sum of the λ_j's. Therefore, for DMU C, the input-oriented technical efficiency level is higher than the measure obtained under NIRS, which is the same as what we get under the CRS assumption. Hence, we conclude that the input-oriented projection of C falls in the region of increasing returns to scale.

To apply the two-step procedure based on Banker's primal approach, we first scale down the actual input bundle of C by the factor $\theta^*(0.529)$ obtained from the CRS version of the input-oriented DEA model. The resulting values are 3.1765 for input x_1 and 3.7059 for input x_2. The LP problem to be solved in the second step is

$$\max \lambda_A + \lambda_B + \lambda_C + \lambda_D + \lambda_E + \lambda_F$$

$$\text{s.t. } 4\lambda_A + 9\lambda_B + 6\lambda_C + 8\lambda_D + 7\lambda_E + 11\lambda_F \geq 6;$$

$$2\lambda_A + 4\lambda_B + 3\lambda_C + 6\lambda_D + 5\lambda_E + 8\lambda_F \geq 3; \qquad (3.50)$$

$$2\lambda_A + 7\lambda_B + 6\lambda_C + 5\lambda_D + 8\lambda_E + 6\lambda_F \leq 3.1765;$$

$$3\lambda_A + 5\lambda_B + 7\lambda_C + 8\lambda_D + 4\lambda_E + 6\lambda_F \leq 3.7059;$$

$$\lambda_A, \lambda_B, \lambda_C, \lambda_D, \lambda_E, \lambda_F \geq 0.$$

The optimal value of the objective function was 0.8824. This implies that the sum of the λ_j's is less than unity at all optimal solutions of the CCR–DEA problem in Step 1. This confirms that the input-oriented projection of firm C is in the increasing returns to scale region of the VRS frontier.

Example 3.4. We now measure the SE and the nature of returns to scale of firm 6 from the Korean electric utility data set considered earlier in *Example 2.2* in Chapter 2. *Exhibit 3.1* shows the relevant LP problem. Note that there is an additional row called LAMBDA with 1 on the right-hand side for the restriction $\sum_j \lambda_j = 1$. *Exhibit 3.2* shows the optimal solution of the problem. The value of the objective function under VRS is 1.27137, which is

Exhibit: 3.1. *DEA-LP problem for firm #6 under VRS*

Firm	#1	#2	#3	#4	#5	#6	#7	#8
Capital	706.698	1284.90	1027.92	1027.92	1027.92	1027.92	2055.85	2055.85
Labor	643.389	1142.20	1749.44	1019.30	1033.76	527.72	1048.22	1055.45
Fuel	648.946	1101.65	531.19	640.32	640.41	448.10	2136.09	2140.03
Output	614.660	1128.39	533.52	611.80	619.68	404.99	2276.89	2278.26
Lambda	1.000	1.00	1.00	1.00	1.00	1.00	1.00	1.00
Objective	0.000	0.00	0.00	0.00	0.00	0.00	0.00	0.00

#9	#10	#11	#12	#13	#14	#15	#16	#17
2055.85	51.396	51.396	51.3962	51.396	1669.35	308.377	308.377	256.98
1062.68	86.749	101.207	93.9782	101.207	1612.09	910.865	903.636	1178.34
2140.18	111.276	91.632	91.9232	92.244	1585.23	344.508	344.483	273.29
2172.23	71.720	73.405	73.8759	73.834	1548.44	260.830	258.852	181.65
1.00	1.000	1.000	1.0000	1.000	1.00	1.000	1.00	1.00
0.00	0.000	0.000	0.0000	0.000	0.00	0.000	0.000	0.00

#18	#19	#20	#21	#22	#23	#24	#25	#26
256.98	1027.92	642.452	1027.92	1027.92	385.47	865.640	906.033	256.98
1185.57	1366.30	751.825	838.57	824.12	1655.46	809.658	780.742	1069.91
273.28	1185.60	699.303	1090.23	1090.26	362.30	559.963	554.623	221.73
179.92	1076.19	586.162	959.15	958.38	278.13	660.532	673.120	246.69
1.00	1.00	1.000	1.00	1.00	1.00	1.000	1.000	1.00
0.00	0.00	0.000	0.00	0.00	0.00	0.000	0.000	0.00

#27	#28	#29	#30	phi_	_type_	_rhs_
256.98	2878.19	2878.19	2569.81	0.000	<=	1027.92
1033.76	1828.96	1821.73	1763.90	0.000	<=	527.72
228.01	3509.60	3510.85	3352.76	0.000	<=	448.10
252.86	3708.16	3709.64	3528.04	-404.985	>=	0.00
1.00	1.00	1.00	1.00	0.000	=	1.00
0.00	0.00	0.00	0.00	1.000	max	.

lower than the optimal value 1.30187 reported for CRS in *Exhibit 2b* in Chapter 2. Hence, the SE of firm 6 is

$$SE = \frac{1.27137}{1.30187} = 0.97657.$$

This, it should be noted, is a measure of output-oriented SE. The input-oriented VRS technical efficiency of firm 6 would be different leading to a different measure of the SE of the firm. Finally, in order to determine the nature of returns to scale, we solve the DEA problem under the NIRS

Exhibit: 3.2. *Optimal solution of the output-oriented VRS DEA-LP for firm #6*

Solution Summary

Objective Value					1.2713698	

Variable Summary

#	Variable Name	Status	Type	Price	Activity	Reduced Cost
1	#1		NON-NEG	0	0	-0.299656
2	#2		NON-NEG	0	0	-0.387513
3	#3		NON-NEG	0	0	-0.799197
4	#4		NON-NEG	0	0	-0.48423
5	#5		NON-NEG	0	0	-0.4726
6	#6		NON-NEG	0	0	-0.27137
7	#7	BASIC	NON-NEG	0	0.0456371	0
8	#8		NON-NEG	0	0	-0.009969
9	#9		NON-NEG	0	0	-0.275938
10	#10		NON-NEG	0	0	-0.048242
11	#11		NON-NEG	0	0	-0.004273
12	#12	BASIC	NON-NEG	0	0.3861955	0
13	#13		NON-NEG	0	0	-0.004692
14	#14		NON-NEG	0	0	-0.765965
15	#15		NON-NEG	0	0	-0.5793
16	#16		NON-NEG	0	0	-0.580308
17	#17		NON-NEG	0	0	-0.74394
18	#18		NON-NEG	0	0	-0.752029
19	#19		NON-NEG	0	0	-0.837354
20	#20		NON-NEG	0	0	-0.548838
21	#21		NON-NEG	0	0	-0.617631
22	#22		NON-NEG	0	0	-0.611977
23	#23		NON-NEG	0	0	-0.972394
24	#24		NON-NEG	0	0	-0.059233
25	#25	BASIC	NON-NEG	0	0.5681674	0
26	#26		NON-NEG	0	0	-0.401641
27	#27		NON-NEG	0	0	-0.38249
28	#28		NON-NEG	0	0	-0.194577
29	#29		NON-NEG	0	0	-0.190119
30	#30		NON-NEG	0	0	-0.226257
31	phi	BASIC	NON-NEG	1	1.2713698	0
32	_OBS1_	BASIC	SLACK	0	399.47369	0
33	_OBS2_		SLACK	0	0	-0.000528
34	_OBS3_		SLACK	0	0	-0.002415
35	_OBS4_		SURPLUS	0	0	-0.002469

Constraint Summary

Row	Constraint Name	Type	S/S #	RHS	Activity	Dual Activity
1	_OBS1_	LE	32	1027.9237	628.45001	0
2	_OBS2_	LE	33	527.72356	527.72356	0.0005276
3	_OBS3_	LE	34	448.10376	448.10376	0.0024148
4	_OBS4_	GE	35	0	0	-0.002469
5	_OBS5_	EQ	.	1	1	-0.089144
6	_OBS6_	OBJECTVE	.	0	1.2713698	.

assumption. This requires changing the equality restriction in the LAMBDA row to a "less-than-or-equal-to" inequality. The value of the objective function for the NIRS problem is 1.30187, which coincides with the optimal value under the CRS assumption. Thus, for firm 5, $TE^C = TE^N < TE^V$. This implies that the firm is operating in a region of increasing returns to scale.

It would be instructive to verify that the various alternative approaches described herein all lead to the same conclusion about the nature of returns to scale for firm 6. This is left as an exercise for the reader.

3.7 Summary

When the technology allows VRS at different points on the frontier of the production possibility set, the technical efficiency (either input- or output-oriented) of a firm will differ from its SE. Technical efficiency is measured by comparing the (ray) average productivity of a firm with the corresponding average productivity at its input- or output-oriented projection onto the VRS frontier. SE, on the other hand, compares the average productivity at the efficient input- or output-oriented projection with the maximum average productivity attained at the MPSS on the VRS frontier. One can ascertain the returns-to-scale properties at any point on the frontier by looking at the optimal solution of the CCR–DEA problem in either its primal or dual formulation. A third alternative is to compare the technical efficiency levels of a firm measured with reference to a VRS, an NIRS, and a CRS frontier. When the NIRS and CRS measures are equal to one another but differ from the VRS measure, increasing returns to scale holds at the corresponding efficient projection on the VRS frontier. On the other hand, if the VRS and NIRS measures are equal but differ from the CRS measure, diminishing returns to scale holds at the relevant point on the frontier. The three measures coincide only at an MPSS.

Note that in this discussion of SE, VRS is the maintained assumption. The CRS and NIRS frontiers are mere artifacts that permit us to examine different points on the VRS frontier. Further, input or output slacks are not included in the technical efficiency measures. We will return to slacks and nonradial efficiency measures later in Chapter 5.

Guide to the Literature

Farrell and Fieldhouse (1962) recognized the restrictive nature of the CRS assumption underlying the Farrell measure of technical efficiency and proposed an appropriate transformation of the data that would allow nonconstant returns to scale within an activity analysis framework. Førsund and Hjalmarsson (1979) proposed a generalization of the Farrell efficiency measure separating SE from the pure technical efficiency using a parametric production function. Banker (1984) generalized the concept of the *technically optimal production scale* introduced by Frisch (1965) to the multiple-output, multiple-input case. BCC (1984) developed the DEA model for VRS technologies. Although the BCC model has become the standard analytical format in the DEA literature, it may be noted that Byrnes, Färe, and Grosskopf (1984) independently developed a nonparametric model allowing scale inefficiency. Banker and Thrall (1992) derive a number of important results relating to the MPSS. For two excellent surveys of the nonparametric methodology, see Lovell (1993, 1994).

In the parametric literature, the primary interest has been on *scale elasticity* rather than on *scale efficiency*. Ray (1998) extends the earlier approach of Førsund and Hjalmarsson (1979) to measure SE from the more flexible Translog production function.

4

Extensions to the Basic DEA Models

4.1 Introduction

This chapter presents several extensions to the basic DEA models described earlier. Both the CCR and the BCC models are either output- or input-oriented. One has to choose between output expansion and input conservation as the criterion of efficiency. Of course, in the CCR model, output- and input-oriented measures of technical efficiency are identical. This is not true for the BCC model, however. Two alternative technical-efficiency measures considered in this chapter are (a) the graph hyperbolic efficiency described in Section 4.2, and (b) the directional efficiency measure described in Section 4.3. Both of these measures emphasize expanding outputs and contracting inputs simultaneously. The efficiency score computed by DEA permits us to rank-order the performance of inefficient firms. By contrast, the efficient observations are rated equally. Section 4.4 describes how one can rank observations that are all equally rated at 100% efficiency. This section also explains how one can identify influential observations in DEA. The productive performance of any firm is affected by a number of exogenously determined factors over which it has no control. In the DEA literature, such factors are treated as nondiscretionary. Section 4.5 explains how the influence of these nondiscretionary factors can be identified as shifts in the production frontier and provides the rationale for a second-stage regression analysis explaining the variation in DEA efficiency scores in terms of differences in these nondiscretionary factors. In Section 4.6, we consider the effects of transformation of the input and output data on the efficiency measure of a firm obtained from the various DEA models. Section 4.7 summarizes the main points of this chapter.

4.2 Graph Hyperbolic Measure of Efficiency

Consider a single-input, single-output technology defined by the production possibility set

$$T = \{(x, y) : y \leq f(x)\}. \tag{4.1}$$

The set

$$G = \{(x, y) : y = f(x)\} \tag{4.2}$$

is the graph of the technology and any $(x, y) \in G$ is technically efficient. Suppose that a firm uses (scalar) input x_0 to produce (scalar) output y_0. Further, $y_0 < f(x_0)$. Thus, the firm is technically inefficient. As noted in previous chapters, technical efficiency is measured by comparing an observed inefficient point with its projection onto the graph of the efficient frontier.

For an output-oriented projection, we hold the input constant and expand the output to the maximum extent possible. Thus, $(x_0, \phi^* y_0)$ is the relevant bundle on the frontier and the output-oriented technical efficiency of firm is

$$\text{TE}^{\text{OUT}} = \frac{y_0}{y_0^*} = \frac{1}{\phi^*}. \tag{4.3}$$

Similarly, for an input-oriented measure, we consider the two-element bundle

$$(x_0^*, y_0) = (\theta^* x_0, y_0) \in G$$

as the reference point and the input-oriented measure of technical efficiency is

$$\text{TE}^{\text{INP}} = \frac{x_0^*}{x_0} = \theta^*. \tag{4.4}$$

Note that depending on the orientation of the model we either expand output or conserve input but do not do both simultaneously. In Figure 4.1, the point A shows the observed input–output quantities of a firm. Point B vertically above A is its output-oriented projection onto the graph, and the point C is its input-oriented projection. Simultaneous increase in output and reduction in input would lead to some point in the northwest quadrant in the region between C and B on the graph.

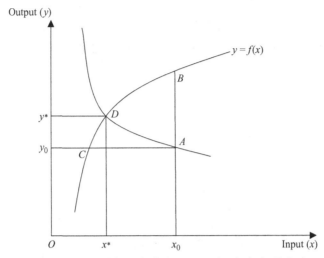

Figure 4.1 The graph hyperbolic measure of technical efficiency.

Now, suppose that we expand the output while contracting the input by the same scale factor. Thus, we seek a point $(x^*, y^*) \in G$ such that

$$y^* = \delta y_0 \quad \text{and} \quad x^* = \frac{1}{\delta} x_0.$$

Relative to this point on the graph, the efficiency of the observed bundle (x_0, y_0) is

$$\text{TE}^{\text{GRAPH}} = \frac{1}{\delta}. \tag{4.5}$$

Note that, by construction, the observed point and its efficient projection on the graph lie on a rectangular hyperbola. Hence, it is called the *graph hyperbolic measure of technical efficiency*.

The following numerical example illustrates the difference between the graph hyperbolic measure of technical efficiency on the one hand and output- or input-oriented measures of technical efficiency on the other.

Suppose that the production possibility set is

$$T = \{(x, y) : y \le f(x) = 6\sqrt{x}\} \tag{4.6}$$

so that the graph of the technology is

$$G = \{(x, y) : y = 6\sqrt{x}\}. \tag{4.6a}$$

Consider, now, the observed input–output bundle

$$(x_0, y_0) = (2, 3).$$

The graph hyperbolic measure can be computed from the equation

$$\delta y_0 = 6\sqrt{\frac{x_0}{\delta}}.$$

Thus, in this example, $\delta = 2$. The efficient hyperbolic projection is $(x^*, y^*) = (1, 6)$, and

$$\text{TE}^{\text{GRAPH}} = 1/2.$$

By contrast, for the output-oriented efficient projection, we solve for ϕ^* from

$$\phi^* y_0 = 6\sqrt{x_0}.$$

Hence, $\phi^* = 2\sqrt{2}$. Therefore, the output-oriented technical efficiency of firm 0 is

$$\frac{1}{2\sqrt{2}} = 0.3536.$$

On the other hand, compared to the input-oriented projection $(\theta^* x_0, y_0)$,

$$\text{TE}^{\text{INP}} = \theta^* = \frac{y_0^2}{36x_0} = \frac{1}{8}.$$

We can easily generalize the graph hyperbolic measure of efficiency to the multiple-output, multiple-input case. Suppose that x^j is the n-element input vector of firm j and y^j is its m-element output vector. Then, the graph hyperbolic measure of its technical efficiency is

$$\text{TE}^{\text{GRAPH}} = \frac{1}{\delta^*}, \tag{4.7a}$$

where

$$\delta^* = \max \delta : \left(\frac{1}{\delta} x^j, \delta y^j\right) \in T. \tag{4.7b}$$

Of course, δ^* will depend on the specification of the production possibility set, T.

Extensions to the Basic DEA Models

We first consider the CRS technology. For the firm 0 – the firm under evaluation – the relevant DEA problem to be solved is

$$\max \delta$$

$$\text{s.t.} \sum_{j=1}^{N} \lambda_j y^j \geq \delta y^0;$$

$$\sum_{j=1}^{N} \lambda_j x^j \leq \frac{1}{\delta} x^0; \tag{4.8}$$

$$\lambda_j \geq 0 \,(j = 1, 2, \ldots, N); \quad \delta \text{ unrestricted.}$$

(Note that there are m inequalities in y^j and n inequalities in x^j.) This, clearly, involves nonlinear inequality restrictions. However, defining the new variables

$$\mu_j = \delta \lambda_j \tag{4.9a}$$

and

$$\phi = \delta^2 \tag{4.9b}$$

we get the transformed problem

$$\max \phi$$

$$\text{s.t.} \sum_{j=1}^{N} \mu_j y^j \geq \phi y^0; \tag{4.10}$$

$$\sum_{j=1}^{N} \mu_j x^j \leq x^0;$$

$$\mu_j \geq 0 \,(j = 1, 2, \ldots, N); \quad \phi \text{ unrestricted.}$$

This is exactly the output-oriented CCR DEA problem. Thus, in the case of CRS, the graph hyperbolic measure of technical efficiency is merely the square root of the output- or input-oriented technical efficiency.

Next, consider the VRS technology. The relevant model now becomes

$$\max \delta$$

$$\text{s.t.} \quad \sum_{j=1}^{N} \lambda_j y^j \geq \delta y^0;$$

$$\sum_{j=1}^{N} \lambda_j x^j \leq \frac{1}{\delta} x^0; \tag{4.11}$$

$$\sum_{j=1}^{N} \lambda_j = 1;$$

$$\lambda_j \geq 0 \, (j = 1, 2, \ldots, N); \quad \delta \text{ unrestricted.}$$

The transformed problem comparable to (4.10) is

$$\max \phi$$

$$\text{s.t.} \quad \sum_{j=1}^{N} \mu_j y^j \geq \phi y^0;$$

$$\sum_{j=1}^{N} \mu_j x^j \leq x^0; \tag{4.12}$$

$$\sum_{j=1}^{N} \mu_j = \sqrt{\phi};$$

$$\phi, \mu_j \geq 0 \, (j = 1, 2, \ldots, N).$$

It should be noted that it remains a nonlinear problem even after the transformation.

One may, however, use a first-order Taylor's series approximation for the nonlinear constraint in the optimization problem in (4.11). Define $f(\delta) = \frac{1}{\delta}$. Then, at $\delta = \delta_0$,

$$f(\delta) \approx f(\delta_0) + f'(\delta_0)(\delta - \delta_0) = \frac{2\delta_0 - \delta}{\delta_0}.$$

Hence, at $\delta_0 = 1$, $f(\delta) \approx 2 - \delta$.

Using this linear approximation, we may replace (4.11) by the linear programming (LP) problem:

$$\max \delta$$

$$\text{s.t.} \quad \sum_{j=1}^{N} \lambda_j y^j \geq \delta y^0;$$

$$\sum_{j=1}^{N} \lambda_j x^j + \delta x^0 \leq 2x^0; \qquad (4.13)$$

$$\sum_{j=1}^{N} \lambda_j = 1;$$

$$\lambda_j \geq 0 \, (j = 1, 2, \ldots, N); \quad \delta \text{ unrestricted.}$$

Exhibit 4.1 shows the DEA LP problem for measuring the graph hyperbolic function (under VRS) for firm #6 from the Korean electrical utilities data set considered previously in Chapter 3. Note that the actual input quantities and the negative of the actual output quantity of the firm under evaluation appear in the column identified as "delta" in the left-hand side of the inequality constraints in the problem. At the same time, entries in the rows for the inputs in the RHS column are twice the input quantities of the firm. Exhibit 4.2 shows the output from the relevant SAS program. The optimal value of "delta" shown in the Variable Summary section (as also in the Objective Value) is 1.11496. This implies that one can expand the output of this firm by 11.496% while *at the same time* reduce all inputs to 89.689% (or less) of their observed levels.

4.3 Technical Efficiency Based on the Directional Distance Function

Chambers, Chung, and Färe (1996) introduced the *directional distance function* based on Luenberger's (1992) *benefit function* to obtain a measure of technical efficiency from the potential for increasing outputs while reducing inputs simultaneously. Consider the pair of input–output vectors (x^0, y^0) and a reference input–output bundle (g^x, g^y). Then, with reference to some production possibility set, T, the directional distance function can be defined as

$$\vec{D}(x^0, y^0; g^x, g^y) = \max \beta : (x^0 + \beta g^x, y^0 + \beta g^y) \in T. \qquad (4.14)$$

Exhibit: 4.1. *DEA LP problem for measuring the graph hyperbolic efficiency of firm #6 from the Korean electrical utilities data*

FIRM	#1	#2	#3	#4	#5
Capital	706.698	1284.90	1027.92	1027.92	1027.92
Labor	643.389	1142.20	1749.44	1019.30	1033.76
Fuel	648.946	1101.65	531.19	640.32	640.41
Output	614.661	1128.39	533.52	611.80	619.68
Lambda	1.000	1.00	1.00	1.00	1.00
Objective	0.000	0.00	0.00	0.00	0.00

#6	#7	#8	#9	#10	#11
1027.92	2055.85	2055.85	2055.85	51.396	51.396
527.72	1048.22	1055.45	1062.68	86.749	101.207
448.10	2136.09	2140.03	2140.18	111.276	91.632
404.99	2276.89	2278.26	2172.23	71.720	73.405
1.00	1.00	1.00	1.00	1.000	1.000
0.00	0.00	0.00	0.00	0.000	0.000

#12	#13	#14	#15	#16	#17
51.3962	51.396	1669.35	308.377	308.377	256.98
93.9782	101.207	1612.09	910.865	903.636	1178.34
91.9232	92.244	1585.23	344.508	344.483	273.29
73.8759	73.834	1548.44	260.830	258.853	181.65
1.0000	1.000	1.00	1.000	1.000	1.00
0.0000	0.000	0.00	0.000	0.000	0.00

#18	#19	#20	#21	#22	#23
256.98	1027.92	642.452	1027.92	1027.92	385.47
1185.57	1366.30	751.825	838.57	824.12	1655.46
273.28	1185.60	699.303	1090.23	1090.26	362.30
179.92	1076.19	586.163	959.15	958.38	278.13
1.00	1.00	1.000	1.00	1.00	1.00
0.00	0.00	0.000	0.00	0.00	0.00

#24	#25	#26	#27	#28	#29
865.640	906.033	256.98	256.98	2878.19	2878.19
809.658	780.742	1069.91	1033.76	1828.96	1821.73
559.963	554.623	221.73	228.01	3509.60	3510.85
660.533	673.120	246.69	252.86	3708.16	3709.64
1.000	1.000	1.00	1.00	1.00	1.00
0.000	0.000	0.00	0.00	0.00	0.00

#30	delta	_type_	_rhs_		
2569.81	1027.92	<=	2055.85		
1763.90	527.72	<=	1055.45		
3352.76	448.10	<=	896.21		
3528.04	-404.99	>=	0.00		
1.00	0.00	=	1.00		
0.00	1.00	max	.		

Exhibit: 4.2. *SAS output of the graph efficiency problem for Firm #6*

				Solution Summary			

Objective Value					1.1149622		

				Variable Summary			

#	Variable Name	Status	Type	Price	Activity	Reduced Cost
1	#1		NON-NEG	0	0	−0.126945
2	#2		NON-NEG	0	0	−0.164165
3	#3		NON-NEG	0	0	−0.338569
4	#4		NON-NEG	0	0	−0.205138
5	#5		NON-NEG	0	0	−0.200211
6	#6		NON-NEG	0	0	−0.114962
7	#7	BASIC	NON-NEG	0	0.0380436	0
8	#8		NON-NEG	0	0	−0.004223
9	#9		NON-NEG	0	0	−0.116898
10	#10		NON-NEG	0	0	−0.020437
11	#11		NON-NEG	0	0	−0.00181
12	#12	BASIC	NON-NEG	0	0.4715774	0
13	#13		NON-NEG	0	0	−0.001988
14	#14		NON-NEG	0	0	−0.324491
15	#15		NON-NEG	0	0	−0.245413
16	#16		NON-NEG	0	0	−0.24584
17	#17		NON-NEG	0	0	−0.31516
18	#18		NON-NEG	0	0	−0.318587
19	#19		NON-NEG	0	0	−0.354734
20	#20		NON-NEG	0	0	−0.232508
21	#21		NON-NEG	0	0	−0.261651
22	#22		NON-NEG	0	0	−0.259256
23	#23		NON-NEG	0	0	−0.411942
24	#24		NON-NEG	0	0	−0.025093
25	#25	BASIC	NON-NEG	0	0.490379	0
26	#26		NON-NEG	0	0	−0.17015
27	#27		NON-NEG	0	0	−0.162037
28	#28		NON-NEG	0	0	−0.08243
29	#29		NON-NEG	0	0	−0.080541
30	#30		NON-NEG	0	0	−0.095851
31	delta	BASIC	NON-NEG	1	1.1149622	0
32	_OBS1_	BASIC	SLACK	0	363.00291	0
33	_OBS2_		SLACK	0	0	−0.000224
34	_OBS3_		SLACK	0	0	−0.001023
35	_OBS4_		SURPLUS	0	0	−0.001046

			Constraint Summary			

Row	Constraint Name	Type	S/S #	Rhs	Activity	Dual Activity
1	_OBS1_	LE	32	2055.8474	1692.8445	0
2	_OBS2_	LE	33	1055.4471	1055.4471	0.0002235
3	_OBS3_	LE	34	896.20752	896.20752	0.001023
4	_OBS4_	GE	35	0	0	−0.001046
5	_OBS5_	EQ	.	1	1	−0.037765
6	_OBS6_	OBJECTVE	.	0	1.1149622	.

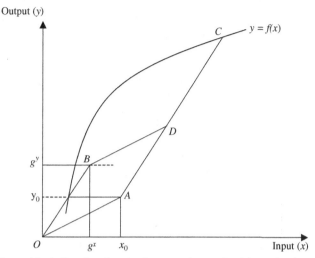

Figure 4.2 A directional projection onto the graph of the technology.

Clearly, the directional distance function evaluated at any specific input–output bundle will depend on (g^x, g^y) as well as on the reference technology. The arbitrarily chosen bundle (g^x, g^y) defines the direction along which the observed bundle, if it is an interior point, is projected onto the efficient frontier of the production possibility set. This is illustrated in Figure 4.2. Point A represents the observed input–output bundle (x_0, y_0) of firm 0 and point B represents the bundle (g^x, g^y). The point C on the frontier is the efficient projection of A in the direction defined by the point B. Thus,

$$AC = (1 + \beta)OB \quad \text{and} \quad \beta = \frac{CD}{AC}.$$

Choice of the bundle (g^x, g^y) is arbitrary. As suggested by Chambers, Chung, and Färe (1996), we may select $(-x^0, y^0)$ for (g^x, g^y) and, in that case, the directional distance function becomes

$$\vec{D}(x^0, y^0) = \max \beta : \{(1 - \beta)x^0, (1 + \beta)y^0\} \in T. \tag{4.15}$$

In other words, we seek to increase the output and reduce the input by the proportion β. For example, if β equals 10%, we expand all outputs by 10%, while at the same time reducing all inputs by 10%. This is illustrated diagrammatically in Figure 4.3. As before, the point A shows the actual input–output bundle (x_0, y_0) while the point B represents $(-x_0, y_0)$. Point D on the production frontier is the projection of the point A in the direction OB. It represents

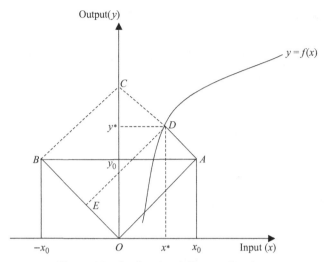

Figure 4.3 The directional distance function.

the bundle (x^*, y^*) where $x^* = (1 - \beta)x_0$, $y^* = (1 + \beta)y_0$ and

$$\beta = \frac{AD}{AC} = \frac{OE}{OB}.$$

The VRS DEA formulation for this problem is

$$\max \beta$$

$$\text{s.t.} \quad \sum_{j=1}^{N} \lambda_j y^j - \beta y^0 \geq y^0;$$ (4.16)

$$\sum_{j=1}^{N} \lambda_j x^j + \beta x^0 \leq x^0;$$

$$\sum_{j=1}^{N} \lambda_j = 1;$$

$$\lambda_j \geq 0 \, (j = 1, 2, \ldots, N); \quad \beta \text{ unrestricted.}$$

This is a straightforward LP problem and can be solved quite easily. The factor β measures the level of technical *inefficiency* of the firm.

Exhibits 4.3 and 4.4 show, respectively, the DEA LP problem for measuring the directional distance function and the output from the relevant SAS program.

Exhibit: 4.3. *DEA LP problem for measuring the directional distance function for firm #6 from the Korean electrical utilities data*

FIRM	#1	#2	#3	#4	#5
Capital	706.698	1284.90	1027.92	1027.92	1027.92
Labor	643.389	1142.20	1749.44	1019.30	1033.76
Fuel	648.946	1101.65	531.19	640.32	640.41
Output	614.661	1128.39	533.52	611.80	619.68
Lambda	1.000	1.00	1.00	1.00	1.00
Objective	0.000	0.00	0.00	0.00	0.00

#6	#7	#8	#9	#10	#11
1027.92	2055.85	2055.85	2055.85	51.396	51.396
527.72	1048.22	1055.45	1062.68	86.749	101.207
448.10	2136.09	2140.03	2140.18	111.276	91.632
404.99	2276.89	2278.26	2172.23	71.720	73.405
1.00	1.00	1.00	1.00	1.000	1.000
0.00	0.00	0.00	0.00	0.000	0.000

#12	#13	#14	#15	#16	#17
51.3962	51.396	1669.35	308.377	308.377	256.98
93.9782	101.207	1612.09	910.865	903.636	1178.34
91.9232	92.244	1585.23	344.508	344.483	273.29
73.8759	73.834	1548.44	260.830	258.853	181.65
1.0000	1.000	1.00	1.000	1.000	1.00
0.0000	0.000	0.00	0.000	0.000	0.00

#18	#19	#20	#21	#22	#23
256.98	1027.92	642.452	1027.92	1027.92	385.47
1185.57	1366.30	751.825	838.57	824.12	1655.46
273.28	1185.60	699.303	1090.23	1090.26	362.30
179.92	1076.19	586.163	959.15	958.38	278.13
1.00	1.00	1.000	1.00	1.00	1.00
0.00	0.00	0.000	0.00	0.00	0.00

#24	#25	#26	#27	#28	#29
865.640	906.033	256.98	256.98	2878.19	2878.19
809.658	780.742	1069.91	1033.76	1828.96	1821.73
559.963	554.623	221.73	228.01	3509.60	3510.85
660.533	673.120	246.69	252.86	3708.16	3709.64
1.000	1.000	1.00	1.00	1.00	1.00
0.000	0.000	0.00	0.00	0.00	0.00

#30	beta	_type_	_rhs_		
2569.81	1027.92	<=	1027.92		
1763.90	527.72	<=	527.72		
3352.76	448.10	<=	448.10		
3528.04	−404.99	>=	404.99		
1.00	0.00	=	1.00		
0.00	1.00	max	.		

Exhibit: 4.4. *SAS output of the directional distance function problem for firm #6*

		Solution Summary			

Objective Value		0.1149622

		Variable Summary			

#	Variable Name	Status	Type	Price	Activity	Reduced Cost
1	#1		NON-NEG	0	0	−0.126945
2	#2		NON-NEG	0	0	−0.164165
3	#3		NON-NEG	0	0	−0.338569
4	#4		NON-NEG	0	0	−0.205138
5	#5		NON-NEG	0	0	−0.200211
6	#6		NON-NEG	0	0	−0.114962
7	#7	BASIC	NON-NEG	0	0.0380436	0
8	#8		NON-NEG	0	0	−0.004223
9	#9		NON-NEG	0	0	−0.116898
10	#10		NON-NEG	0	0	−0.020437
11	#11		NON-NEG	0	0	−0.00181
12	#12	BASIC	NON-NEG	0	0.4715774	0
13	#13		NON-NEG	0	0	−0.001988
14	#14		NON-NEG	0	0	−0.324491
15	#15		NON-NEG	0	0	−0.245413
16	#16		NON-NEG	0	0	−0.24584
17	#17		NON-NEG	0	0	−0.31516
18	#18		NON-NEG	0	0	−0.318587
19	#19		NON-NEG	0	0	−0.354734
20	#20		NON-NEG	0	0	−0.232508
21	#21		NON-NEG	0	0	−0.261651
22	#22		NON-NEG	0	0	−0.259256
23	#23		NON-NEG	0	0	−0.411942
24	#24		NON-NEG	0	0	−0.025093
25	#25	BASIC	NON-NEG	0	0.490379	0
26	#26		NON-NEG	0	0	−0.17015
27	#27		NON-NEG	0	0	−0.162037
28	#28		NON-NEG	0	0	−0.08243
29	#29		NON-NEG	0	0	−0.080541
30	#30		NON-NEG	0	0	−0.095851
31	phi	BASIC	NON-NEG	1	0.1149622	0
32	_OBS1_	BASIC	SLACK	0	363.00291	0
33	_OBS2_		SLACK	0	0	−0.000224
34	_OBS3_		SLACK	0	0	−0.001023
35	_OBS4_		SURPLUS	0	0	−0.001046

		Constraint Summary				

Row	Constraint Name	Type	S/S #	Rhs	Activity	Dual Activity
1	_OBS1_	LE	32	1027.9237	664.92079	0
2	_OBS2_	LE	33	527.72356	527.72356	0.0002235
3	_OBS3_	LE	34	448.10376	448.10376	0.001023
4	_OBS4_	GE	35	404.98544	404.98544	−0.001046
5	_OBS5_	EQ	.	1	1	−0.037765
6	_OBS6_	OBJECTVE	.	0	0.1149622	

This time, the actual input quantities and the negative of the actual output quantity of the firm appear in the column called "beta" in the left-hand side and the actual input and output quantities also appear on the right-hand side. The optimal value of "beta" is 0.11496. This again shows that the output can be expanded by 11.496% while all inputs can simultaneously be contracted by the same percentage. Note that the presence of positive slack in the capital input at the optimal solution implies that the efficient input–output projection is not showing the potential contraction in all inputs and the (in)efficiency measure obtained from the directional distance function (as also the graph efficiency measure) is less than accurate. We consider the question of slacks at an optimal solution in detail in Chapter 7.

4.4 Ranking Efficient Units and Influential Observations

The standard DEA models – both the CCR model for CRS and the BCC model for VRS – provide measures of technical efficiency of a firm relative to the others within the same sample. Firms that are found to be technically inefficient can be ranked in order of their measured levels of efficiency. Firms that are found to be efficient are, however, all ranked equally by this criterion. Andersen and Petersen (1993) suggest a criterion that permits one to rank-order firms that have all been found to be at 100% technical efficiency by DEA. The underlying idea behind this criterion is quite simple. Consider the single-input, single-output case. Suppose that a firm with input–output (x_0, y_0) has been found to be technically efficient in an output-oriented DEA problem. Obviously, if its output had been any larger than y_0, it would have remained efficient. But a small reduction in its output may not necessarily lower its technical efficiency rating from 100%. In that sense, this firm may permit some deterioration in its performance without becoming inefficient. In other words, its observed output exceeds what is necessary for this firm to be considered efficient relative to other firms in the sample. In that case, the firm may be regarded as *superefficient*. Naturally, between two firms, both of which are technically efficient, the one with greater room for reducing its output without becoming inefficient is, in a sense, more *superefficient* than the other.

Consider a simple numerical example. Suppose that the input–output quantities of seven firms are as shown in Table 4.1. In Figure 4.4, the broken line *HACDE-extension* is the frontier of the VRS production possibility set constructed from the observed points – A, B, C, D, E, F, and G. Points A, C, D, and E are efficient, whereas points B, F, and G are inefficient. The

Table 4.1. *Input–output data of hypothetical firms*

Firm	A	B	C	D	E	F	G
Input (x)	4	5	8	12	16	8	14
Output (y)	6	7	14	20	22	9	19

output-oriented technical efficiency levels of B, F, and G are 0.875, 0.643, and 0.905, respectively. Thus, B ranks above F and G ranks above B. But all the efficient points are ranked equally at 1.0. Focus, now, on the two points C and D. The firm at point C uses 8 units of the input x to produce 14 units of the output y. Even if this firm allowed its output to fall to 13 units, it would still remain efficient at the point C^* on the new frontier *HADE-extension*. It will be considered inefficient only when its output falls below this level. In this sense, the firm at point C is *superefficient*. This critical output level corresponds to the maximum output producible from the observed input of this firm within the VRS production possibility set constructed using the input–output data from

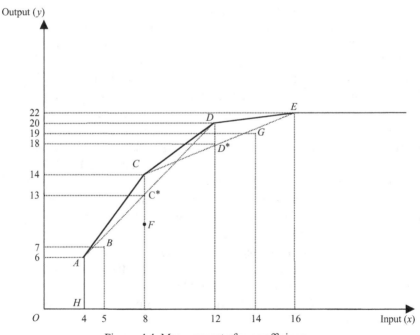

Figure 4.4 Measurement of superefficiency.

all other firms. Point C^* on the frontier *HADE-extension* shows this critical input–output combination. Similarly, for the firm at point D, the critical point is D^* on the frontier *HACE-extension*, where the output from its observed input quantity of 12 units of x needs to be only 18 units of y. Firm D can allow its output to fall by 10% without becoming technically inefficient. By contrast, firm C can only lose 7.14% of its output and still remain efficient. Hence, firm D is more *superefficient* than firm C even though *at their observed input–output bundles, both are equally ranked at 100% technical efficiency.*

In the general case of N firms with the observed input–output bundle (x^j, y^j) for firm j $(= 1, 2, \ldots, N)$, for each technically efficient firm k, we solve the following DEA problem:

$$\phi_k^- = \max \phi$$

$$\text{s.t.} \quad \sum_{j \neq k} \lambda_j y^j \geq \phi y^k;$$

$$\sum_{j \neq k} \lambda_j x^j \leq x^k; \tag{4.17}$$

$$\sum_{j \neq k} \lambda_j = 1; \quad \lambda_j \geq 0 \, (j = 1, 2, \ldots, N; \, j \neq k).$$

The output bundle $y_k^- = \phi_k^- y^k$ is what the firm k needs to produce from the input bundle x^k in order to remain (output-oriented) technically efficient relative to the other firms in the sample. Thus, $(1 - \phi_k^-)$ is a measure of its *supereffi-ciency.* Hence, between two technically efficient firms i and j, both technically efficient, j is ranked above i, if $\phi_j^- < \phi_i^-$.

A potential problem of feasibility with these *superefficiency* models has been noted by Dulá and Hickman (1997), Seiford and Zhu (1999), Harker and Xue (2002), and Lovell and Rouse (2003).[1] For some efficient observations, there may not exist any input- or output-oriented projection onto a frontier that is constructed from the remaining observations in the data set. For example, if the firm k under evaluation has the smallest quantity of any individual input in the sample, there cannot be *any* convex combination of the input bundles of the other firms that would satisfy the relevant input constraint in the problem (4.17). Thus, one cannot measure the level of *superefficiency* of such a firm.

---

[1] The problem of feasibility was noted in a general context by Chavas and Cox (1999), who proposed a generalized distance function.

In a more general context, the frontier of the production possibility set in any DEA application is defined by a subset of the observed input–output bundles. Deletion of any one of these observations from the data set results in a revision of the frontier causing the measured efficiency level of some of the other observations in the data set to change. Wilson (1993) suggests two different criteria for measuring the influence of any such observation. The first is based on the number of observations that experience a change in measured technical efficiency due to the deletion of this observation. The other is based on the magnitude of changes in such efficiency measures of the affected firms. In Figure 4.4, if the observation C is deleted, the new frontier becomes *HADE-extension*. This affects the technical efficiency of two firms, B and F. But the firm G is not affected. On the other hand, if D is excluded from the data set,[2] the new frontier is *HACE-extension*. In this case, technical efficiency of only one firm, G, is affected. By this criterion, firm C is more influential than firm D.

To consider the other criterion, we need to compute the revised technical-efficiency measures of the affected firms. Consider the maximization problem

$$\phi_s^k = \max \phi$$

$$\text{s.t.} \quad \sum_{j \neq k} \lambda_j y^j \geq \phi y^s;$$

$$\sum_{j \neq k} \lambda_j x^j \leq x^s; \tag{4.18}$$

$$\sum_{j \neq k} \lambda_j = 1; \quad \lambda_j \geq 0 \, (j = 1, 2, \ldots, N; \, j \neq k).$$

Then

$$\text{TE}_s^k = \frac{1}{\phi_s^k}$$

is the measured technical efficiency of firm s when all observed input–output bundles *except the bundle k* are included. For any observation s that is influenced by the observation k, this will be different from its technical efficiency, TE_s. Hence,

$$\delta_s^k = \text{TE}_s^k - \text{TE}_s \tag{4.19}$$

---

[2] Once any observation has been deleted from the sample, the remaining observations constitute its deleted data domain.

is a measure of the degree of influence of observation k on the observation s. The overall influence of observation k on the entire sample can be measured as

$$\Delta^k = \sum_{s \neq k} \left(\delta_s^k \right)^2. \tag{4.20}$$

For the firms shown in Figure 4.4,

$$\delta_B^C = \frac{3}{3.8} - \frac{1}{2} = 0.0289; \quad \delta_F^C = \frac{5.6}{9} - \frac{5}{9} = 0.0667, \quad \text{and}$$

$$\delta_G^D = \frac{63}{74} - \frac{63}{76} = 0.0224.$$

All other $\delta_s^k = 0$. Thus,

$$\Delta^C = (0.0289)^2 + (0.0667)^2 = 0.0053 \quad \text{and} \quad \Delta^D = (0.0224)^2 = 0.0005.$$

Hence, by this criterion also, the observation C is more influential than observation D in this data set. In this discussion of influential observations, we have focused only on the technically efficient firms. A natural question to ask in this context is *How would the distribution of technical efficiency of firms in a sample data set be affected if a technically inefficient observation is deleted?*

We have seen before that in DEA, technical efficiency of a firm is measured by comparing it with a hypothetical observation that is generated either as a convex combination of the actually observed input–output bundles if VRS is assumed, or simply a positive linear combination if CRS is specified for the reference technology. Thus, for any observed input–output pair (x^k, y^k), the benchmark for comparison is a bundle (x^*, y^*), where $x^* = \sum_j \lambda_j x^j$ and $y^* = \sum_j \lambda_j y^j$. The values of the λ_j's are determined by the optimal solution of a LP problem. At any such optimal solution, only some of the λ_j's will be strictly positive and the others will be zero. For any specific firm, say firm k, its reference group consists of all such observations j such that λ_j is strictly positive. Because (x^*, y^*) is defined only by the input–output bundles of the firms in its reference group, the technical efficiency of firm k is unaffected by the deletion of any firm that is not in its reference group. We now prove an extremely important theorem showing that *any observed firm helps to define* *the frontier of the production possibility set only if the firm itself is technically efficient.*

Theorem: An individual firm s with input–output bundle (x^s, y^s) cannot be in the reference group of any firm k $(k = 1, 2, \ldots, s, \ldots, N)$ unless it has technical efficiency equal to unity.

Proof. Consider the primal problem output-oriented CCR model for firm k:

$$\max \phi$$

$$\text{s.t.} \quad \sum_{j=1}^{N} \lambda_j y^j \geq \phi y^k; \tag{4.21}$$

$$\sum_{j=1}^{N} \lambda_j x^j \leq x^k;$$

$$\lambda_j \geq 0 \, (j = 1, 2, \ldots, N); \quad \phi \text{ unrestricted.}$$

The corresponding dual problem is

$$\min v' x^k$$

$$\text{s.t.} \quad v' x^j \geq u' y^j \, (j = 1, 2, \ldots, k, \ldots, N); \tag{4.22}$$

$$u' y^k = 1;$$

$$u \geq 0; \quad v \geq 0.$$

Here, u and v are multiplier or shadow price vectors commensurate with the output and input vectors, respectively. Suppose that λ_s^* is positive at any optimal solution. Then, by virtue of the Kuhn–Tucker theorem, at the optimal solution of the dual problem the constraint for firm s holds as an equation. That is, an optimal solution (u^*, v^*) of the dual problem (4.22) will satisfy

$$v^{*\prime} x^j \geq u^{*\prime} y^j (j = 1, 2, \ldots, N); \quad v^* x^s = u^{*\prime} y^s; \quad u^* y^k = 1;$$

$$u^* \geq 0; \quad v^* \geq 0. \tag{4.23}$$

Now, define

$$t = \frac{1}{u^{*\prime} y^s}; \quad u^{**} = t u^*; \quad v^{**} = t v^*. \tag{4.24}$$

Then, the relations in (4.23) can be expressed as

$$v^{**\prime}x^j \geq u^{**}y^j\,(j = 1, 2, \ldots, N); \quad v^{**\prime}x^s = u^{**}y^s; \quad u^{**}y^k = 1;$$
$$u^{**} \geq 0; \quad v^{**} \geq 0. \qquad (4.25)$$

Now, suppose that we were evaluating the technical efficiency of firm s rather than firm k. In that case, in the primal–dual problems (4.21–4.22), (x^k, y^k) would be replaced by (x^s, y^s). The relations in (4.23) imply that (u^{**}, v^{**}) is a feasible solution for the dual form of the DEA problem evaluating the technical efficiency of firm s. The value of the objective function for this solution is unity. Again, by the duality theorem, the optimal value of the primal-maximization problem cannot be greater than the objective function value at any feasible solution of the dual-minimization problem. In other words, $\phi^* \leq 1$ for firm s. Of course, a feasible solution for the primal problem is $\lambda_j^* = 1\,(j = s), \lambda_j^* = 0\,(j \neq s), \phi^* = 1$. Hence, $\phi^* = 1$ at the optimal solution and firm s is technically efficient. This completes the proof of this theorem. A logical corollary of this theorem is that a technically inefficient firm cannot be an influential observation.

It may be noted here in passing that although this theorem was formally proven by Ray (1988), it apparently was a part of the "oral literature" on DEA at that time. An implication of this theorem is that if a firm is not technically efficient, it can never play a role in defining the benchmark input–output bundle for evaluating the efficiency of any other firm. Thus, a technically inefficient firm is never an influential observation.

4.5 Nondiscretionary Factors and Technical Efficiency

In an output-oriented DEA model, in the single-output case, one measures the efficiency of a firm by comparing its actual output with what is considered to be maximally feasible from its observed bundle of inputs. In practice, however, the maximum producible quantity of output from any specific input bundle depends on a number of environmental or contextual variables. In agriculture, for example, the same input can produce a greater volume of output in a year with good rainfall than in a drought year. Similarly, in education, the performance of the student in standardized tests depends not only on the resources utilized by the school but also on the pupil's socioeconomic status. These variables are essentially exogenous to the decision-making process of the firm. Nevertheless, they shift the production possibility frontier in the input–output space, thereby affecting the measured technical efficiency of a firm. Some of these factors are favorable to the production process and enhance the maximum output producible from a bundle of inputs within the firm's control. Others are detrimental to production and lower efficiency measured from the controlled inputs and outputs alone. In the DEA literature, these factors are treated as *nondiscretionary variables*. We may extend the free disposability assumption to these nondiscretionary variables in the following manner. It may be assumed that increase in a favorable factor does not reduce output. Decline in an unfavorable factor has a similar effect.

It is, of course, possible to incorporate these nondiscretionary variables directly into an appropriately modified DEA model. Suppose the firm 0 under review produces an output vector y^0 using the input vector x^0. Further, suppose that it has the vector w^0 of favorable and the vector z^0 of unfavorable nondiscretionary variables. Thus, because $(x^0, y^0; w^0, z^0)$ is feasible, $(x^0, y^0; w, z^0)$ is feasible so long as $w \geq w^0$. Similarly, $(x^0, y^0; w^0, z)$ is feasible for any $z \leq z^0$. Based on the observed data $(x^j, y^j; w^j, z^j)$ for $(j = 1, 2, \ldots, N)$, we may set up the following output-oriented DEA model:

$$\max \phi$$

$$\text{s.t.} \quad \sum_{j=1}^{N} \lambda_j y^j \geq \phi y^0;$$

$$\sum_{j=1}^{N} \lambda_j x^j \leq x^0;$$

$$\sum_{j=1}^{N} \lambda_j w^j \leq w^0; \tag{4.26}$$

$$\sum_{j=1}^{N} \lambda_j z^j \geq z^0;$$

$$\sum_{j=1}^{N} \lambda_j = 1;$$

$$\lambda_j \geq 0 \ (j = 1, 2, \ldots, N); \quad \phi \text{ unrestricted.}$$

On the other hand, if we were to take the input-oriented approach, the focus would be on the extent of radial contraction of the discretionary input vector x^0, with (y^0, w^0, z^0) only defining the constraints but not appearing directly in the objective function. Thus, the input-oriented BCC model would be

$$\min \theta$$

$$\text{s.t.} \quad \sum_{j=1}^{N} \lambda_j y^j \geq y^0;$$

$$\sum_{j=1}^{N} \lambda_j x^j \leq \theta x^0;$$

$$\sum_{j=1}^{N} \lambda_j w^j \leq w^0; \qquad (4.27)$$

$$\sum_{j=1}^{N} \lambda_j z^j \geq z^0;$$

$$\sum_{j=1}^{N} \lambda_j = 1;$$

$$\lambda_j \geq 0 \ (j = 1, 2, \ldots, N); \quad \theta \text{ unrestricted.}$$

There are several difficulties with this approach of including the nondiscretionary factors in the DEA model itself. To appropriately specify the direction of the inequality restriction involving these variables, one needs to decide *a priori* whether a specific variable is favorable or detrimental to production. This may not always be possible in practice. At the conceptual level, the disposability assumption may be inappropriate for a nondiscretionary variable in some cases. For example, the amount of rainfall does influence production and is nondiscretionary. Moreover, the farmer has to cope with the actual amount of rainfall and cannot keep some part of it idle, as in the case of a controllable input like labor. Finally, the convexity assumption also may be questionable for such variables. This is particularly the case for categorical variables. Often a categorical variable[3] like "good" or "bad" rainfall is coded as a binary 0–1 variable. In this case, convexity will artificially create an intermediate state with a fractional value. It is much better to maintain the convexity assumption for the controlled inputs and outputs and to allow the production possibility frontier to shift due to differences in the nondiscretionary factors.

---

[3] For two of the earlier applications incorporating exogenously fixed and categorical variables, see Banker and Morey (1986a, 1986b).

The effects of these factors on the measured technical efficiency of a firm may be then analyzed via a second-stage regression of the DEA efficiency scores on these variables.

Ray (1988) provides a conceptual link between the DEA efficiency measure and the nondiscretionary environmental variables faced by a firm. Consider a single-output, multiple-input production technology, where the maximum output (y^*) producible from any given input bundle (x) depends on the nondiscretionary environmental variables (a) faced by the firm. Let the production function be

$$y = f(x; a). \tag{4.28}$$

Assume further that the production function is multiplicatively separable as

$$f(x; a) = g(x) \cdot h(a). \tag{4.29}$$

Further, the function $g(x)$ is nondecreasing and homogeneous of degree 1 in x. Also, $h(a)$ lies between 0 and 1. Then, the maximum output is produced from a given input bundle x only when $h(a)$ equals unity. Thus,

$$y^* = g(x) \tag{4.30}$$

and a measure of the technical efficiency of a firm is

$$\text{TE}(x, y; a) = \frac{y}{y^*} = h(a). \tag{4.31}$$

We now show that the output-oriented CCR technical efficiency of any firm provides a measure of $h(a)$ for that firm. Let (x^j, a^j) be the input bundle used and the vector of environmental variables faced by firm j and y_j its observed output. In the CCR model, the technical efficiency of firm 0 producing output y_0 from input x^0 is measured by comparing it with the pair (x^*, y^*), where $y^* = \sum_{j=1}^{N} \lambda_j y_j = \phi^* y_0$ and $x^* = \sum_{j=1}^{N} \lambda_j x^j \leq x^0$. Thus,

$$y^* = \sum_{j=1}^{N} \lambda_j y_j = \sum_{j=1}^{N} \lambda_j g(x^j) h(a^j). \tag{4.32}$$

Now, suppose that we select the λ's such that $\lambda_j = 0$ unless $h(a^j) = 1$. In that case,

$$y^* = \phi^* y_0 = \sum_{j=1}^{N} \lambda_j y_j = \sum_{j=1}^{N} \lambda_j g(x^j) = g\left(\sum_{j=1}^{N} \lambda_j x^j\right) = g(x^*). \tag{4.33}$$

If there is no slack in any of the inputs, $x^* = x^0$ and $g(x^*) = g(x^0)$. Even when there are slacks in some inputs, there will be no slack in at least one input. If we specify a Leontief-type production function for $g(x)$, $g(x^*)$ equals $g(x^0)$.
Hence,

$$\frac{1}{\phi^*} = \frac{y_0}{y^*} = h(a^0). \tag{4.34}$$

Of course, when any firm j is technically efficient, $\phi^* = 1$, implying $h(a^j)$ equal to unity as well. Now recall that as shown in the previous theorem, at the optimal solution of the DEA LP problem for any firm, $\lambda_j^* = 0$ unless firm j is efficient. Therefore, the DEA technical efficiency score for (x^0, y^0) does, indeed, measure $h(a^0)$. Hence, one can specify an appropriate functional relation between the DEA efficiency score of a firm and the relevant nondiscretionary variables and econometrically estimate the coefficients of the model. This two-step analysis – DEA followed by regression – has two distinct advantages. First, one need not prespecify the algebraic sign of any regression coefficient. This avoids deciding *a priori* whether any particular variable has a favorable or unfavorable effect on production. Second, one can change the list of nondiscretionary variables included in the model without having to recompute the DEA efficiency scores every time any such change is made. Only the second-stage regression model needs to be re-estimated.

The second-stage regression has its own problems, however. First, the technical efficiency of a firm can vary only between 0 and 1. This raises the problem of a limited dependent variable problem. If we take the natural log of technical efficiency, the lower bound goes to negative infinity but the upper bound is at 0. One can define $\tau_j = \frac{1}{\phi_j^*}$ and specify the model

$$\ln \tau_j = \gamma_0 + \sum_i \gamma_i a_{ij} + u_j. \tag{4.35}$$

In that case, $\ln \tau_j = 0$ whenever $u_j \geq -(\gamma_0 + \sum_i \gamma_i a_{ij})$. One must, therefore, apply the Tobit model instead of the usual ordinary least squares regression.

Another problem is that although the coefficients of the fitted model show how the different nondiscretionary variables influence the technical efficiency measure obtained from DEA, we cannot get a measure of managerial inefficiency or pure waste from the residuals. This is because these residuals (e_j) may be either positive or negative. Hence, the antilog of these residuals may exceed unity in some cases and cannot be properly used as a measure of efficiency. One may apply the so-called Greene correction and subtract the largest positive residual from each of the residuals. These modified residuals are, by construction, all nonpositive. The antilogs of the modified residuals can then be used as measures of pure inefficiency not systematically related to any of the nondiscretionary variables.

4.6 Data Transformation and Invariance of DEA Measures of Efficiency

The input–output quantities of a firm can be measured in many different ways. For example, the quantity of power generated by an electric utility plant may be measured in kilowatt- or in megawatt-hours. Oil used as fuel may be measured in liters or gallons. These represent differences in the scale or unit of measurement. Similarly, in some cases, one may add a constant to the measured quantity of any output of all of the firms. This is often the practice when some of the measured output quantities are negative. This is equivalent to a translation of the axes (in the input or output space) so that the origin is shifted to a point in the positive orthant. Such transformations of the data are quite arbitrary and are often carried out for computational convenience. It is important to recognize that some of the DEA measures of efficiency will be affected by certain kinds of data transformation. When a change in the unit of measurement of any input or output quantity does not alter the DEA efficiency measure obtained from a specific model, we call that model *scale invariant*. Similarly, if the change of origin leaves the optimal solution unchanged, the model is called *translation invariant*.

Consider first the question of scale invariance. Suppose that the observed input vector of an individual firm j ($j = 1, 2, \ldots, N$) is $x^j = (x_{1j}, x_{2j}, \ldots, x_{nj})$ and the output vector is $y^j = (y_{1j}, y_{2j}, \ldots, y_{mj})$. Now, redefine the input bundles of all firms as $\tilde{x}^j = (\tilde{x}_{1j}, \tilde{x}_{2j}, \ldots, \tilde{x}_{nj})$, where $\tilde{x}_{ij} = \alpha_i x_{ij} (\alpha_i > 0)$ for all j. Similarly, define the transformed output bundles as $\tilde{y}^j = (\tilde{y}_{1j}, \tilde{y}_{2j}, \ldots, \tilde{y}_{mj})$, where $\tilde{y}_{rj} = \beta_r y_{rj} (\beta_r > 0)$ for all j. Now, consider the output-oriented CCR DEA model for firm k using the transformed data:

$$\max \phi$$

$$\text{s.t.} \quad \sum_{j=1}^{N} \lambda_j \tilde{x}_{ij} \le \tilde{x}_{ik} \quad (i = 1, 2, \ldots, n);$$

$$\sum_{j=1}^{N} \lambda_j \tilde{y}_{rj} \ge \phi \tilde{y}_{rk} \quad (r = 1, 2, \ldots, m); \tag{4.36}$$

$$\lambda_j \ge 0 \ (j = 1, 2, \ldots, N); \quad \phi \text{ free.}$$

If we substitute $\alpha_i x_{ij}$ for $\tilde{x}_{ij}$ in the input constraints and $\beta_r y_{rj}$ for $\tilde{y}_{rj}$ in the output constraints, problem (4.36) becomes

$$\max \phi$$

$$\text{s.t.} \quad \sum_{j=1}^{N} \lambda_j \alpha_i x_{ij} \le \alpha_i x_{ik} \quad (i = 1, 2, \dots, n); \qquad (4.36a)$$

$$\sum_{j=1}^{N} \lambda_j \beta_r y_{rj} \ge \phi \beta_r y_{rk} \quad (r = 1, 2, \dots, m);$$

$$\lambda_j \ge 0 \ (j = 1, 2, \dots, N); \quad \phi \text{ free}.$$

Cancellation of the common factors from both sides of the inequalities reduces this problem to the output-oriented CCR model in terms of the untransformed data. It is easy to see that the similar reasoning would apply in the case of the input-oriented CCR model as well. Also, an additional restriction that the λ's have to add up to unity does not involve the input–output quantities and, therefore, would not be affected by any data transformation. This implies that the input- and output-oriented BCC DEA models are also scale invariant.

Next, consider translation invariance. For this, we define the transformed input quantities

$$\breve{x}_{ij} = \gamma_i + x_{ij} \quad (i = 1, 2, \dots, n; j = 1, 2, \dots, N)$$

and output quantities

$$\breve{y}_{rj} = \delta_r + y_{rj} \quad (r = 1, 2, \dots, m; j = 1, 2, \dots, N).$$

Now, consider the output-oriented CCR DEA model in terms of the transformed data:

$$\max \phi$$

$$\text{s.t.} \quad \sum_{j=1}^{N} \lambda_j \breve{x}_{ij} \le \breve{x}_{ik} \quad (i = 1, 2, \dots, n);$$

$$\sum_{j=1}^{N} \lambda_j \breve{y}_{rj} \ge \phi \breve{y}_{rk} \quad (r = 1, 2, \dots, m); \qquad (4.37)$$

$$\lambda_j \ge 0 \ (j = 1, 2, \dots, N); \quad \phi \text{ free}.$$

Problem (4.37) is equivalent to the following problem:

$$\max \phi$$

$$\text{s.t.} \quad \sum_{j=1}^{N} \lambda_j x_{ij} + \gamma_i \left(\sum_{j=1}^{N} \lambda_j \right) \leq x_{ik} + \gamma_i \quad (i = 1, 2, \ldots, n);$$

$$\sum_{j=1}^{N} \lambda_j y_{rj} + \delta_r \left(\sum_{j=1}^{N} \lambda_j \right) \geq \phi (y_{rk} + \delta_r) \quad (r = 1, 2, \ldots, m);$$

$$(4.37a)$$

$$\lambda_j \geq 0 \, (j = 1, 2, \ldots, N); \quad \phi \text{ free.}$$

This does not reduce to the corresponding problem in the untransformed data.
The input-oriented CCR DEA problem would be

$$\min \theta$$

$$\text{s.t.} \quad \sum_{j=1}^{N} \lambda_j \breve{x}_{ij} \leq \theta \breve{x}_{ik} \quad (i = 1, 2, \ldots, n);$$

$$\sum_{j=1}^{N} \lambda_j \breve{y}_{rj} \geq \breve{y}_{rk} \quad (r = 1, 2, \ldots, m); \quad (4.38)$$

$$\lambda_j \geq 0 \, (j = 1, 2, \ldots, N); \quad \phi \text{ free.}$$

This is equivalent to the problem

$$\min \theta$$

$$\text{s.t.} \quad \sum_{j=1}^{N} \lambda_j x_{ij} + \gamma_i \left(\sum_{j=1}^{N} \lambda_j \right) \leq \theta(x_{ik} + \gamma_i) \quad (i = 1, 2, \ldots, n);$$

$$\sum_{j=1}^{N} \lambda_j y_{rj} + \delta_r \left(\sum_{j=1}^{N} \lambda_j \right) \geq (y_{rk} + \delta_r) \quad (r = 1, 2, \ldots, m);$$

$$(4.38a)$$

$$\lambda_j \geq 0 \, (j = 1, 2, \ldots, N); \quad \phi \text{ free.}$$

Again, this does not reduce to an input-oriented CCR DEA problem in terms of the untransformed data. Thus, neither the output-oriented nor the input-oriented CCR DEA problem is translation invariant.

For the BCC DEA problems, however, the additional restriction on the sum of the λ's ensures that the γ_i's disappear from the input restrictions in the output-oriented model. Similarly, the δ_r's disappear from the output restrictions in the input-oriented model. Hence, if each δ_r equals zero (i.e., if there is no translation of outputs), the input-oriented BCC model is invariant to input translation. Similarly, the input-oriented BCC model is invariant to output translation.

4.7 Summary

The standard DEA models are either output- or input-oriented. The main focus in these models is on either output augmentation or input contraction. By contrast, the DEA models based on the graph hyperbolic distance function and the directional distance function seek an efficient projection of an observed input–output bundle so as to expand outputs and contract inputs simultaneously.

Although all firms with measured technical efficiency of 100% are conceptually ranked equally in terms of performance, it is possible to obtain a ranking of firms even within the subset of efficient firms. This can be achieved by evaluating the extent that the actual output of a firm exceeds what is minimally necessary for it to produce in order to remain efficient relative to a production frontier constructed on the basis of the observed input–output bundles of the *other firms* in the sample. One can also measure the degree of influence an efficient observation has in any specific DEA application by measuring how the distribution of technical efficiency of the other firms in the sample would change if this observation were to be deleted.

Usually, the technical efficiency of a firm depends on a variety of factors outside the control of the decision maker within the firm. One may capture the effects of differences in such external factors by a second-stage statistical analysis, where the measured DEA efficiency scores are regressed on these factors. This permits the analyst to isolate inefficiency from the effects of environmental heterogeneity.

In empirical applications, the input–output data of firms to be used for DEA can be transformed by changes of scale and origin. The CCR and BCC DEA models – both input- and output-oriented – are scale invariant with respect to inputs as well as outputs. The CCR model is not translation invariant. The output-oriented BCC model is translation invariant with respect to inputs. The input-oriented BCC model, on the other hand, is translation invariant with respect to outputs.

Guide to the Literature

Färe, Grosskopf, and Lovell (FGL) (1985, 1994) developed the graph hyperbolic distance function. Chambers, Chung, and Färe (1996) introduced the directional distance function as an extension of the Luenberger *benefit function*

(1992). An application of the graph efficiency approach in the context of un-desirable outputs can be found in Färe, Grosskopf, Lovell, and Pasurka (1989). The method of ranking of technically efficient firms was proposed by Ander-sen and Petersen (1993). Torgersen, Førsund, and Kittelsen (1996) propose a method of ranking efficient firms using a slack-adjusted measure of efficiency. Wilson (1993) developed the method of identifying influential firms and mea-suring the degree of influence discussed in this chapter. The rationale for the second-stage regression of DEA efficiency scores is from Ray (1988). For an early application of the second-stage regression analysis, see Lovell, Walters, and Wood (1994). The question of invariance of DEA efficiency scores was first addressed by Ali and Seiford (1990). See also Lovell and Pastor (1995).

5

Nonradial Models and Pareto–Koopmans Measures of Technical Efficiency

5.1 Introduction

One major problem with a radial measure of technical efficiency is that it does not reflect all identifiable potential for increasing outputs and reducing inputs. In economics, the concept of efficiency is intimately related to the idea of Pareto optimality. An input–output bundle is not Pareto optimal if there remains the possibility of any net increase in outputs or net reduction in inputs. When positive output and input slacks are present at the optimal solution of a CCR or BCC DEA LP problem, the corresponding radial projection of an observed input–output combination does not meet the criterion of Pareto optimality and should not qualify as an efficient point. Note that this problem arises not only for input- or output-oriented models but also for graph efficiency or directional distance function models.

In this chapter, we consider a number of nonradial models that allow reduction of individual inputs and/or increase in individual outputs at different rates. The output- and input-oriented nonradial models developed independently of the DEA models by Färe and Lovell (FL) (1978) provide appropriately oriented summary measures of technical efficiency. Although the output-oriented nonradial projection allows no slacks in outputs, it does not exclude input slacks, however. Similarly, the input-oriented projection permits output slacks. The more general Pareto–Koopmans measure proposed by Pastor, Ruiz, and Sirvent (1999), on the other hand, does not permit any slack in either any input or any output at the efficient projection. This chapter is organized as follows: Section 5.2 introduces two alternative, but equivalent, representations of the set of all feasible input–output bundles, in terms of input sets and output sets. The input- and output-oriented nonradial measures of technical efficiency are discussed in Section 5.3. The Pareto–Koopmans measure is presented in Section 5.4. Section 5.5 provides an example of the alternative nonradial

111

measures of efficiency using an airlines data set constructed by Coelli, Griffel-Tatje, and Perelman (2002). The main points of the chapter are summarized in Section 5.6.

5.2 Input and Output Sets

Consider the production possibility set T, an m-element output vector y^0, and an n-element input vector x^0. If (x^0, y^0) is a feasible production plan, then $(x^0, y^0) \in T$, implying that y^0 can be produced from x^0. There will, in general, be many input bundles other than x^0, all of which can also produce y^0. For the specific output bundle y^0, we can define the *input (requirement) set*

$$V(y^0) = \{x : y^0 \text{ can be produced from } x\}. \tag{5.1}$$

Several points may be noted. First, while T is a set in the $(m + n)$ dimensional input–output space, $V(y^0)$ is a set in the n-dimensional input space. Second, for each specific output bundle, y, there is a specific input set $V(y)$. Thus, the same production possibility set T generates a family of input sets.

Consider the following example for the one-output, two-input case. Let the production possibility set be

$$T = \{(x_1, x_2; y) : y \leq 2\sqrt{x_1 x_2}; (x_1, x_2, y \geq 0)\}. \tag{5.2}$$

Then, for any given output level, y_0,

$$V(y_0) = \{(x_1, x_2) : 2\sqrt{x_1 x_2} \geq y_0; (x_1, x_2 \geq 0)\}. \tag{5.3}$$

Figure 5.1 shows the input set for the output level $y_0 = 10$ in the $x_1 - x_2$ plane. All points on or to the right of the curve AB represent input bundles that are in the input set of y_0.

The following properties of input sets follow from the assumptions made about the production possibility set:

(V1) If (x^j, y^j) is an actually observed input–output combination, then $x^j \in V(y^j)$. Clearly, every observed $(x^j, y^j) \in T$. Hence, by definition of an input set, $x^j \in V(y^j)$.

(V2) If $x^0 \in V(y^0)$ and $x^1 \geq x^0$, then $x^0 \in V(y^0)$. This follows from the assumption of free disposability of inputs. Because $(x^1, y^0) \in T$, whenever $x^1 \geq x^0$ and $(x^0, y^0) \in T$, (V2) follows. Varian (1984) calls this the *monotonicity property of input sets*.

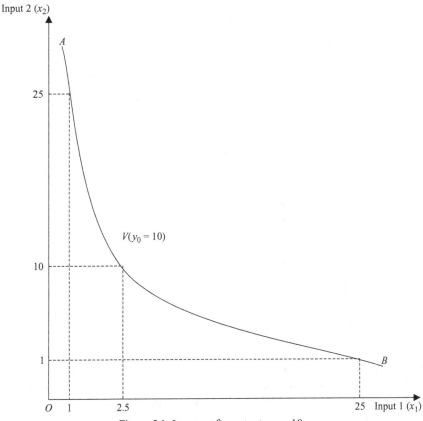

Figure 5.1 Input set for output $y_0 = 10$.

(V3) If $x^0 \in V(y^0)$ and $y^1 \leq y^0$, then $x^0 \in V(y^1)$. This follows from the assumption of free disposability of outputs. Because $(x^0, y^1) \in T$, whenever $y^1 \leq y^0$ and $(x^0, y^0) \in T$, (V3) follows. Varian (1984) calls this the "nestedness" property of input sets. This implies that the input set of a larger output bundle is a subset of the input set of a smaller output bundle.

(V4) Each input set $V(y)$ is convex.

Convexity of the production possibility set is sufficient, but not necessary, for the convexity of input sets. Consider two different input bundles x^0 and x^1 such that $(x^0, y^0) \in T$ and that $(x^1, y^0) \in T$. Let $\bar{x} = \lambda x^0 + (1 - \lambda)x^1$, where $0 < \lambda < 1$. Then, by convexity of T, $(\bar{x}, y^0) \in T$. That, of course, implies that $\bar{x} \in V(y^0)$. It should be noted, however, that the input set will be convex

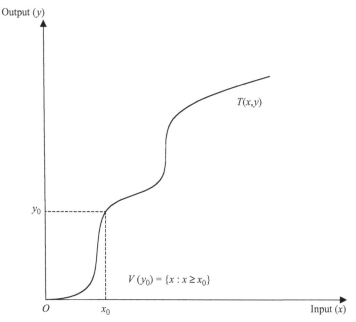

Figure 5.2 Quasi-concave production function and convex input sets.

whenever the production function is quasi-concave. But a quasi-concave production function may quite easily correspond to a nonconvex production possibility set. This is shown in Figure 5.2 for the one-input, one-output case. Here, the area under the production function is a nonconvex production possibility set. But, for the output level y_0, the input set

$$V(y_0) = \{x : x \geq x_0\}$$

is a convex set.

As is apparent from (V2), many input bundles in the input set of a specific output bundle are inefficient because it may be possible to produce the target output from a smaller input bundle. These are strictly interior points of the input set. By contrast, the *isoquant* of an output bundle y^0 consists only of boundary points of $V(y^0)$. The isoquant of y^0 is

$$\bar{V}(y^0) = \{x : x \in V(y^0) \text{ and } \lambda x \notin V(y^0) \text{ if } \lambda < 1\}. \tag{5.4}$$

Thus, if $x^0 \in \bar{V}(y^0)$, then it is not possible to reduce all inputs simultaneously even by the smallest amount and still produce the output level y^0. The quantity of at least one input in the x^0 bundle must be strictly binding. In Figure 5.1, the isoquant of y^0 is the set of points on the curve AB. It is obvious from the definition of the isoquant that if $x^0 \in \bar{V}(y^0)$, then the input-oriented technical efficiency of (x^0, y^0) equals unity. Indeed, every input-oriented radial projection of an inefficient input–output bundle (x, y) lies in the isoquant of the output bundle y.

The *efficient subset of the isoquant* of any output bundle y^0 can be defined as

$$V^*(y^0) = \{x : x \in V(y^0) \text{ and } x' \notin V(y^0) \text{ if } x' \leq x\}. \tag{5.5}$$

Note that if $x^0 \in V^*(y^0)$, then reducing *any* input in the x^0 bundle will render the output bundle y^0 infeasible. Thus, every input bundle in the efficient subset of the isoquant of an output bundle is technically efficient and there is no slack in any individual input.

Consider the production possibility set implied by the piecewise linear production function

$$y = \min(3x_1, 1.5x_2); \quad x_1 \leq \tfrac{1}{2}x_2;$$

$$y = x_1 + x_2; \quad \tfrac{1}{2}x_2 \leq x_1 \leq 2x_2; \tag{5.6}$$

$$y = \min(1.5x_1, 3x_2); \quad x_1 \geq 2x_2.$$

The input set for the output level $y = 12$ consists of all points on and to the right of the broken line $ABCD$ shown in Figure 5.3. The isoquant consists of the points on the line $ABCD$. But the efficient subset of the isoquant includes only points on the segment BC. Now, consider the point E in $V(y)$ showing the input bundle $(x_1 = 15, x_2 = 5)$. The input-oriented radial projection of this point onto the isoquant would be the point $F(x_1 = 12, x_2 = 4)$. Thus, the radial technical efficiency measure would be

$$\theta^* = \frac{OF}{OE} = 0.8.$$

This implies that one could reduce both inputs of the firm using the input bundle E and still produce the output level $y = 20$. But the move from E to F does not exhaust the potential for reduction in all inputs. It is possible to move to the point C within $V(y)$. As a result, we can achieve a reduction in input x_1 by another 3 units, although no additional reduction in x_2 is feasible without reducing the output. Clearly, a movement from E to F leads to improvement in technical efficiency. But so does a move from F to C because the same output is

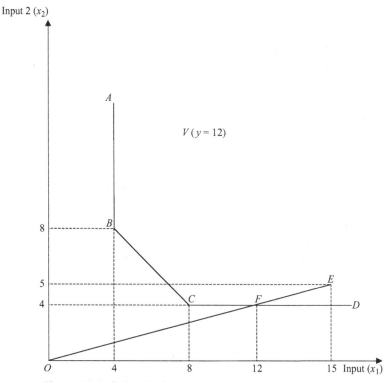

Figure 5.3 Radial projection onto the isoquant and input slacks.

being produced from a smaller input bundle. The input-oriented radial measure of technical efficiency fails to capture the effect of the input slack that exists at the radial projection onto the isoquant. One may, of course, further adjust the projected input bundle for positive slacks in individual inputs that may exist at the optimal solution. The resulting input bundle will be a point in the efficient subset of the isoquant. But, as a summary measure of technical efficiency, θ^* does not reflect the presence of such slacks. The nonradial measure proposed by FL (1978) described herein measures the technical efficiency of a firm relative to a point in the efficient subset of the isoquant.

In an output-oriented analysis of technical efficiency, the objective is to produce the maximum output from a given quantity of inputs. For this we first define the *(producible) output set* of any given input bundle. For the input bundle x^0, the output set

$$P(x^0) = \{\, y : (x^0, y) \in T \,\} \tag{5.7}$$

consists of all output bundles that can be produced from x^0. Indeed, the familiar production possibility frontier of a country shown in textbooks on principles of economics shows the output set of an input bundle consisting of the total factor endowments of a nation.

Because there are different output sets for different input bundles, the production possibility set is equivalently characterized by a family of output sets. Each output set is a subset of the m-dimensional output space.[1] The following properties of output sets follow from the relevant assumptions made about the production possibility set:

(P1) If (x^j, y^j) is an actually observed input–output combination, then $y^j \in P(x^j)$.

(P2) If $y^0 \in P(x^0)$ and if $x^1 \geq x^0$, then $y^0 \in P(x^1)$. This property follows from free disposability of inputs and can be called "reverse nestedness" of output sets. Thus, the output set of a smaller input bundle is contained in the output set of a bigger input bundle.

(P3) If $y^0 \in P(x^0)$ and if $y^1 \leq y^0$, then $y^1 \in P(x^0)$. This property follows from the assumption of free disposability of outputs.

(P4) Each output set $P(x)$ is convex. Again, this follows from convexity of the production possibility set.

The *output isoquant* of any input bundle x^0 can be defined as

$$\bar{P}(x^0) = \{y : y \in P(x^0) \text{ and } \lambda y \notin P(x^0) \text{ if } \lambda > 1\}. \tag{5.8}$$

Thus, if $y^0 \in \bar{P}(x^0)$, then the output-oriented radial technical efficiency of the pair of vectors (x^0, y^0) equals unity because it is not possible to increase *all* outputs holding the input bundle unchanged. This does not, of course, rule out the possibility that some individual components of the y^0 output bundle can be increased.

The *efficient subset* of the output isoquant of x^0, on the other hand, is

$$P^*(x^0) = \{y : y \in P(x^0) \text{ and } y' \notin P(x^0) \text{ if } y' \geq y^0\}. \tag{5.9}$$

Thus, an output-oriented radial technically efficient projection of y^0 produced from x^0 onto $\bar{P}(x^0)$ may include slacks in individual outputs. But no such slacks may exist if the projection is onto $P^*(x^0)$.

---

[1] It can easily be seen that $x \in V(y)$ if and only if $y \in P(x)$.

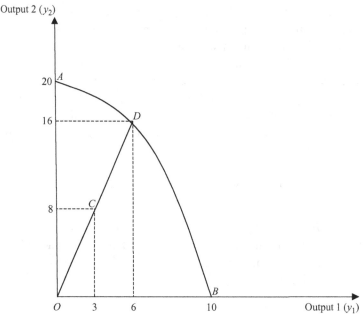

Figure 5.4 Projection onto the efficient output isoquant and absence of output slacks.

Figure 5.4 shows the output set in the one-input, two-output case for input $x_0 = 400$ for the production correspondence

$$x = 4y_1^2 + y_2^2. \tag{5.10}$$

In this diagram, points on the curve AB constitute the output isoquant of x_0 while the output set includes all points on or to the left of the line. In this example, the entire isoquant coincides with its efficient subset. Now, consider the output bundle y^0 shown by the point C with $y_1 = 3$ and $y_2 = 8$. Its radial projection onto the output isoquant of x_0 is the point D, where both outputs are doubled. Thus, the output-oriented technical efficiency of (x_0, y^0) is $\frac{1}{2}$. Note that in this case, no further increase in any output is feasible.

Figure 5.5 shows a different two-output case where $ABCD$ is a piecewise linear isoquant for some input bundle x_0. In this diagram, the *efficient subset* of the isoquant is only the downward sloping segment. Along the output isoquant

$$y_2 = 12 \quad \text{for } 0 \le y_1 \le 6 \quad \text{over the } AB \text{ segment,}$$

$$y_2 = 24 - 2y_1 \quad \text{for } 6 \le y_1 \le 9 \quad \text{over the } BC \text{ segment, and} \tag{5.11}$$

$$0 \le y_2 \le 6 \quad \text{for } y_1 = 9 \quad \text{over the } CD \text{ segment.}$$

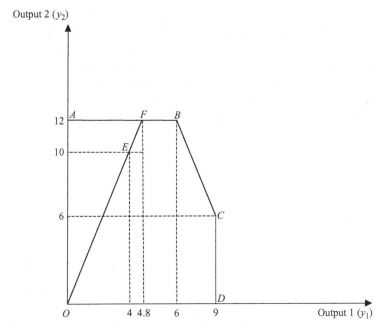

Figure 5.5 Presence of slacks at the radial projection onto the output isoquant.

At the output bundle E, which is an interior point of $P(x^0)$, $y_1 = 4$ and $y_2 = 10$. The radial output-oriented projection of E onto $\bar{P}(x^0)$ is the point F, where the output bundle has been scaled up by 20%. Thus, the radial output-oriented technical efficiency of a firm operating at point E is $\frac{5}{6}$. But this radial projection F with $y_1 = 4.8$ and $y_2 = 12$ is not in the efficient subset of the output isoquant of x^0. One can further increase y_1 to 6 while keeping y_2 at 12 by moving to the point B, which lies in the efficient subset of the output isoquant. The radial measure of output-oriented technical efficiency does not reflect this unutilized potential for increasing y_1. Again, as is shown herein, a nonradial output-oriented measure does take account of all potential increase in any component of the output bundle.

5.3 Nonradial Measures of Technical Efficiency

The problem of slacks in any optimal solution of a radial DEA model arises because we seek to expand all outputs or contract all inputs by the same proportion. In nonradial models, one allows the individual outputs to increase or the inputs to decrease at different rates. By far the simplest, though not particularly useful, nonradial approach is the so-called *additive* variant of the DEA model. In an output-oriented additive DEA model, one seeks to maximize the total slacks in all outputs that exist in the observed input–output bundles. Similarly, in an input-oriented model, one would maximize the total slacks in inputs. The additive model does yield a projection onto the efficient subset of the output isoquant of the observed input bundle.

The output-oriented additive DEA model for the VRS technology is

$$\max \ S = \sum_r s_r^+$$

$$\text{s.t.} \sum_j \lambda_j y_{rj} + s_r^+ = y_{r0}; (r = 1, 2, \ldots, m);$$

$$\sum_j \lambda_j x_{ij} \leq x_{i0}; (i = 1, 2, \ldots, n); \qquad (5.12)$$

$$\lambda_j \geq 0; \quad (j = 1, 2, \ldots, N); \quad s_r^+ \geq 0; \quad (r = 1, 2, \ldots, m).$$

Clearly, there cannot be any remaining output slack at the projected bundle

$$y^* = y^0 + s_*^+$$

where $s_*^+ = (s_{1*}^+, s_{2*}^+, \ldots, s_{m*}^+)$ is obtained from the optimal solution of the previous DEA model. Indeed, y^* is the point in the efficient subset of the output isoquant of x^0 that is the farthest from y^0. But the only usefulness of the additive model is that it helps to determine whether or not $y^0 \in P^*(x^0)$. We can conclude that $y^0 \notin P^*(x^0)$ unless the objective function S equals 0 at the optimal solution. But because S is the sum of the slacks in the various output quantities measured in different units, it has no clear interpretation. Moreover, the magnitude of S depends on the scale of measurement of the outputs.

FL (1978) introduced the following output-oriented nonradial measure of technical efficiency, which they called the Russell measure:

$$\text{RM}_y = \frac{1}{\rho_y}, \text{ where}$$

$$\rho_y = \max \frac{1}{m} \sum_r \phi_r$$

$$\text{s.t.} \sum_j \lambda_j y_{rj} = \phi_r y_{r0}; (r = 1, 2, \ldots, m);$$

$$\sum_j \lambda_j x_{ij} \leq x_{i0}; (i = 1, 2, \ldots, n); \qquad (5.13)$$

$$\sum_j \lambda_j = 1; \quad \phi_r \geq 1; \quad (r = 1, 2, \ldots, m);$$

$$\lambda_j \geq 0; \quad (j = 1, 2, \ldots, N).$$

The output-oriented Russell measure is, in effect, a scale invariant version of the simple additive model. To see this, define

$$y_{r0} + s_r^+ = y_{r0}\left(1 + \frac{s_r^+}{y_{r0}}\right) \equiv \phi_r y_{r0}; \quad (r = 1, 2, \ldots, m). \tag{5.14}$$

Then, clearly,

$$\rho_y = 1 + \frac{1}{m}\sum_r \frac{s_r^+}{y_{r0}}. \tag{5.15}$$

Of course, the constraints of the FL model are exactly the same as those of the additive model. Because the slacks in the individual outputs are scaled by the respective observed quantities of those outputs, ρ_y (and, hence, RM_y) is scale invariant. But when output slacks do exist at the optimal solution of a radial DEA model, the nonradial Russell measure is lower than the conventional measure obtained from an output-oriented BCC model. In the example shown in Figure 5.5, the optimal nonradial projection of the point E is the point B, where y_1 increases from 4 to 6 while y_2 increases from 10 to 12. Thus,

$$\phi_1^* = 1.5 \quad \text{and} \quad \phi_2^* = 1.2; \quad \text{thus,} \quad \rho_y = 1.35 \quad \text{and} \quad RM_y = 0.7407.$$

By contrast, the radial measure is 0.833. Thus, the presence of 3 units of output slack in y_1 at the efficient radial projection results in a lower nonradial measure of output-oriented technical efficiency. One may be inclined to believe that if the radial projection of y^0 lies in $P^*(x^0)$, ρ_y coincides with ϕ^* so that the non-radial measure equals the radial measure. This is not necessarily true, however. Figure 5.6 provides an example. The radial projection of the point E onto the output isoqant is the point F in the efficient subset and there is no output slack at this point. But this is not where ρ_y is maximized for the Russell measure. The objective is to maximize

$$S = \left(\frac{1}{y_{10}}\right)s_1^+ + \left(\frac{1}{y_{20}}\right)s_2^+. \tag{5.16}$$

If we shift the origin to (y_{10}, y_{20}) at E, nonnegativity of the output slacks ensures that we seek a projection onto the segment of $P^*(x^0)$ in the positive quadrant with reference to this new origin. The objective function can be alternatively

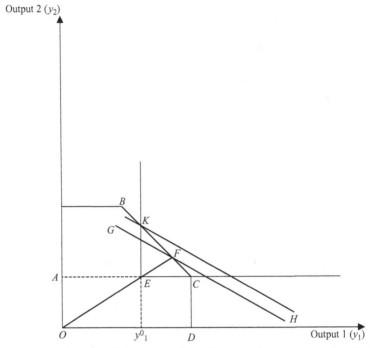

Figure 5.6 Efficient radial and nonradial projections of a given output bundle.

expressed as

$$s_2^+ = (y_{20}S) - \left(\frac{y_{20}}{y_{10}}\right) s_1^+. \tag{5.17}$$

This is shown for an arbitrary value of S by the line GH that has a slope equal to the negative of the slope of the line EF. Maximization of S occurs at the point of tangency of a line parallel to GH with the output isoquant of x^0 in the northeast quadrant of E. In the example shown in Figure 5.6, this occurs at the point K, which is different from the radial projection F. It is easy to see that because the radial projection is always a feasible point for this problem, $\rho_y \geq \phi^*$. Hence, the nonradial Russell measure of technical efficiency is never greater than the corresponding radial measure.

The analogous input-oriented nonradial model is

$$\text{RM}_x = \rho_x, \text{ where}$$

$$\rho_x = \min \frac{1}{n} \sum_i \theta_i$$

$$\text{s.t. } \sum_j \lambda_j y_{rj} \geq y_{r0}; \quad (r = 1, 2, \ldots, m);$$

$$\sum_j \lambda_j x_{ij} - s_i^- = \theta_i x_{i0}; \quad (i = 1, 2, \ldots, n); \quad (5.18)$$

$$\sum_j \lambda_j = 1; \theta_i \leq 1; \quad (i = 1, 2, \ldots, n);$$

$$\lambda_j \geq 0; \quad (j = 1, 2, \ldots, N).$$

The optimal solution projects the observed input bundle x^0 onto the bundle $x^* = (\theta_1^* x_{10}, \theta_2^* x_{20}, \ldots, \theta_n^* x_{n0})$ in the efficient subset of the isoquant of the output y^0.

5.4 Pareto–Koopmans Model of Nonradial Technical Efficiency

An input–output combination (x^0, y^0) is not Pareto–Koopmans efficient if it violates either of the following inefficiency postulates:

(A) It is possible to increase at least one output in the bundle y^0 without reducing any other output and/or without increasing any input in the bundle x^0.

(B) It is possible to reduce at least one input in the bundle x^0 without increasing any other input and/or without reducing any output in the bundle y^0.

Clearly, unless

$$RM_x(x^0, y^0) = RM_y(x^0, y^0) = 1,$$

at least one of the two inefficiency postulates is violated and (x^0, y^0) is not Pareto–Koopmans efficient. For (x^0, y^0) to be Pareto–Koopmans efficient, both of the following must be true:

(i) $x^0 \in V^*(y^0)$; and

(ii) $y^0 \in P^*(x^0)$.

Consider the vectors

$$\theta = (\theta_1, \theta_2, \ldots, \theta_n) \text{ and}$$

$$\phi = (\phi_1, \phi_2, \ldots, \phi_m).$$

A nonradial Pareto–Koopmans measure of technical efficiency of the input–output pair (x^0, y^0) can be computed as

$$\Gamma = \min \frac{\frac{1}{n} \sum_i \theta_i}{\frac{1}{m} \sum_r \phi_r}$$

s.t. $\displaystyle\sum_{j=1}^{N} \lambda_j y_{rj} \geq \phi_r y_{r0}; \quad (r = 1, 2, \ldots, m);$

$$\sum_{j=1}^{N} \lambda_j x_{ij} \leq \theta_i x_{i0}; \quad (i = 1, 2, \ldots, n); \qquad (5.19)$$

$$\phi_r \geq 1; \quad (r = 1, 2, \ldots, m);$$

$$\theta_i \leq 1; \quad (i = 1, 2, \ldots, n);$$

$$\sum_{j=1}^{N} \lambda_j = 1; \lambda_j \geq 0; \quad (j = 1, 2, \ldots, N).$$

Note that the efficient input–output projection (x^*, y^*) satisfies

$$x^* = \sum_{j=1}^{N} \lambda_j^* x^j \leq x^0 \text{ and}$$

$$y^* = \sum_{j=1}^{N} \lambda_j^* y^j \geq y^0.$$

Thus, (x^0, y^0) is Pareto–Koopmans efficient if and only if $\phi_r^* = 1$ for each output r and $\theta_i^* = 1$ for each input i implying $\Gamma = 1$.

The objective function in this mathematical programming problem is nonlinear. But it is possible to linearize it as

$$\Gamma = f(\theta, \phi) \approx f(\theta^0, \phi^0) + \sum_i (\theta_i - \theta_i^0) \left(\frac{\partial f}{\partial \theta_i} \right)_0$$

$$+ \sum_r (\phi_r - \phi_r^0) \left(\frac{\partial f}{\partial \phi_r} \right)_0. \qquad (5.20)$$

Note that

$$\frac{\partial f}{\partial \theta_i} = \frac{\frac{1}{n}}{\frac{1}{m} \sum_r \phi_r} \qquad (5.21a)$$

and

$$\frac{\partial f}{\partial \phi_r} = -\frac{\frac{1}{n} \sum_i \theta_i}{\frac{1}{m} \left(\sum_r \phi_r \right)^2}. \tag{5.21b}$$

Thus, using $\theta_i^0 = 1$ for all i and $\phi_r^0 = 1$ for all r,

$$\Gamma \approx 1 + \frac{1}{n} \sum_i \theta_i - \frac{1}{m} \sum_r \phi_r. \tag{5.22}$$

We may, therefore, solve the LP problem

$$\min \widetilde{\Gamma} = \frac{1}{n} \sum_i \theta_i - \frac{1}{m} \sum_r \phi_r$$

$$\text{s.t.} \sum_{j=1}^{N} \lambda_j y_{rj} \geq \phi_r y_{r0}; \quad (r = 1, 2, \ldots, m);$$

$$\sum_{j=1}^{N} \lambda_j x_{ij} \leq \theta_i x_{i0}; \quad (i = 1, 2, \ldots, n); \tag{5.23}$$

$$\phi_r \geq 1; \quad (r = 1, 2, \ldots, m);$$

$$\theta_i \leq 1; \quad (i = 1, 2, \ldots, n);$$

$$\sum_{j=1}^{N} \lambda_j = 1; \quad \lambda_j \geq 0; \quad (j = 1, 2, \ldots, N).$$

Once we obtain the optimal (θ^*, ϕ^*) from this problem,[2] we use

$$\Gamma^* = \frac{\frac{1}{n} \sum_i \theta_i^*}{\frac{1}{m} \sum_r \phi_{rr}^*} \tag{5.24}$$

as a measure of the Pareto–Koopmans efficiency of (x^0, y^0).

It is interesting to note that this LP problem is a special case of the more general optimization problem with the same constraints but the objective function

---

[2] Indeed, one may iterate this procedure using the (θ^*, ϕ^*) obtained at the optimal solution of (5.23) as the new point of approximation.

$$\min \Omega = \sum_i \alpha_i \theta_i - \sum_r \beta_r \phi_r$$

$$\text{s.t.} \sum_{j=1}^{N} \lambda_j y_{rj} \geq \phi_r y_{r0}; \quad (r = 1, 2, \ldots, m);$$

$$\sum_{j=1}^{N} \lambda_j x_{ij} \leq \theta_i x_{i0}; \quad (i = 1, 2, \ldots, n); \qquad (5.25)$$

$$\phi_r \geq 1; \quad (r = 1, 2, \ldots, m);$$

$$\theta_i \leq 1; \quad (i = 1, 2, \ldots, n);$$

$$\sum_{j=1}^{N} \lambda_j = 1; \quad \lambda_j \geq 0; \quad (j = 1, 2, \ldots, N).$$

Setting $\alpha_i = \frac{1}{n}$ for all i and $\beta_r = \frac{1}{m}$ for all r, we get the Pareto–Koopmans problem. If, on the other hand, we set $\beta_r = 0$ for all r, we get the input-oriented Russell measure. When we further restrict each $\alpha_i = \alpha$, we get the usual input-oriented radial DEA problem. Similarly, the restrictions $\alpha_i = 0$ for all i lead to the output-oriented Russell problem and further restricting $\beta_r = \beta$, for all r we get the usual output-oriented radial DEA problem.

5.5 An Empirical Example: Nonradial Measures of Efficiency in the Airline Industry

This example considers the performance of 28 international airlines from North America, Europe, and Asia–Australia during the year 1990. The data set is taken from Coelli, Grifell-Tatje, and Perelman (2002, Table 1). Each firm produces two outputs: (a) passenger-kilometers flown (y_1), and (b) freight tonne-kilometers flown (y_2). Inputs used are (i) labor (number of employees) (x_1), (ii) fuel (millions of gallons) (x_2), (iii) other inputs (millions of U.S. dollar equivalent) consisting of operating and maintenance expenses excluding labor and fuel expenses (x_3), and (iv) capital (sum of the maximum takeoff weights of all aircraft flown multiplied by the number of days flown) (x_4). The input–output data set is shown in Table 5.1.

Exhibit 5.1 shows the appropriate SAS program for obtaining the Pareto–Koopmans efficiency measure of British Airways (airline #10). The variables PHI1 and PHI2 are the factors by which the two outputs, y_1 and y_2, respectively, can be expanded. The other variables THETA1 through THETA4 are the factors

Table 5.1. *Input–output data for selected international airlines for the year 1990*

Obs	Name	Pass	Cargo	Lab	Fuel	Matl	Cap
1	NIPPON	35261	614	12222	860	2008	6074
2	CATHAY	23388	1580	12214	456	1492	4174
3	GARUDA	14074	539	10428	304	3171	3305
4	JAL	57290	3781	21430	1351	2536	17932
5	MALAYSIA	12891	599	15156	279	1246	2258
6	QUANTAS	28991	1330	17997	393	1474	4784
7	SAUDIA	18969	760	24708	235	806	6819
8	SINGAPORE	32404	1902	10864	523	1512	4479
9	AUSTRIA	2943	65	4067	62	241	587
10	BRITISH	67364	2618	51802	1294	4276	12161
11	FINNAIR	9925	157	8630	185	303	1482
12	IBERIA	23312	845	30140	499	1238	3771
13	LUFTHANSA	50989	5346	45514	1078	3314	9004
14	SAS	20799	619	22180	377	1234	3119
15	SWISSAIR	20092	1375	19985	392	964	2929
16	PORTUGAL	8961	234	10520	121	831	1117
17	AIR CANADA	27676	998	22766	626	1197	4829
18	AM. WEST	18378	169	11914	309	611	2124
19	AMERICAN	133796	1838	80627	2381	5149	18624
20	CANADIAN	24372	625	16613	513	1051	3358
21	CONTINENTAL	69050	1090	35661	1285	2835	9960
22	DELTA	96540	1300	61675	1997	3972	14063
23	EASTERN	29050	245	21350	580	1498	4459
24	NORTHWEST	85744	2513	42989	1762	3678	13698
25	PANAM	54054	1382	28638	991	2193	7131
26	TWA	62345	1119	35783	1118	2389	8704
27	UNITED	131905	2326	73902	2246	5678	18204
28	USAIR	59001	392	53557	1252	3030	8952

Source: Coelli, Griffel-Tatje, and Perelman (2002), Table 1.

by which the four respective inputs can be scaled down. Each output expansion factor is restricted to be greater than or equal to unity. Similarly, the input contraction factors are all restricted to be less than or equal to unity.

Exhibit 5.2 shows the DEA problem for airline #10 in the standard LP format and Exhibit 5.3 shows the relevant SAS output. At the optimal solution, the λ^*s are strictly positive for airline #8 (Singapore Airlines), airline #13 (Lufthansa), and airline #27 (United Airlines). The hypothetical airline constructed by the appropriate convex combination of these three airlines would produce the same quantity of y_1 but 69.63% more of output y_2. At the same time, x_1 could be reduced by 4.91%, x_2 would be unchanged, x_3 reduced by 13.4%,

Exhibit: 5.1. *The SAS program for measuring the Pareto–Koopmans efficiency of airline #10*

```
OPTIONS NOCENTER;
DATA CORE;
INPUT NAME $ PASS CARGO LAB FUEL MATL CAP;
A1=0;A2=0;B1=0;B2=0;B3=0;B4=0;
C=1;D=0;
CARDS;
NIPPON      35261     614   12222     860    2008    6074
CATHAY      23388    1580   12214     456    1492    4174
GARUDA      14074     539   10428     304    3171    3305
JAL         57290    3781   21430    1351    2536   17932
..            ...     ...     ...     ...     ...     ...
..            ...     ...     ...     ...     ...     ...
SINGAPR     32404    1902   10864     523    1512    4479
AUSTRIA      2943      65    4067      62     241     587
BRITISH     67364    2618   51802    1294    4276   12161
FINNAIR      9925     157    8630     185     303    1482
IBERIA      23312     845   30140     499    1238    3771
LUFTHNSA    50989    5346   45514    1078    3314    9004
..            ...     ...     ...     ...     ...     ...
..            ...     ...     ...     ...     ...     ...
UNITED     131905    2326   73902    2246    5678   18204
USAIR       59001     392   53557    1252    3030    8952
;
proc print; var name pass cargo lab fuel matl cap;
PROC TRANSPOSE OUT=NEXT;
DATA MORE;
INPUT PHI1 PHI2 THETA1-THETA4 _TYPE_ $ _RHS_;
CARDS;
-1      0      0      0      0      0     >=    0
 0     -1      0      0      0      0     >=    0
 0      0     -1      0      0      0     <=    0
 0      0      0     -1      0      0     <=    0
 0      0      0      0     -1      0     <=    0
 0      0      0      0      0     -1     <=    0
 1      0      0      0      0      0     >=    1
 0      1      0      0      0      0     >=    1
 0      0      1      0      0      0     <=    1
 0      0      0      1      0      0     <=    1
 0      0      0      0      1      0     <=    1
 0      0      0      0      0      1     <=    1
 0      0      0      0      0      0      =    1
-.5    -.5    .25    .25    .25    .25    MIN   .
```

(continued)

Exhibit: 5.1 *(continued)*

```
;
.DATA LAST; MERGE NEXT MORE;
IF _N_=1 THEN PHI1=-COL10;
IF _N_=2 THEN PHI2=-COL10;
IF _N_=3 THEN THETA1=-COL10;
IF _N_=4 THEN THETA2=-COL10;
IF _N_=5 THEN THETA3=-COL10;
IF _N_=6 THEN THETA4=-COL10;
PROC PRINT;
PROC LP;
```

and x_4 reduced by 12.06%. Using these optimal values of the ϕ's and θ's, we get a nonradial Pareto–Koopmans measure of efficiency

$$\Gamma = \frac{0.9241}{1.3482} = 0.6854.$$

This may be contrasted with what one obtains from the DEA problems for input- and output-oriented nonradial technical efficiency measurement. For the input-oriented Russell efficiency measure, we get $\theta_1^* = 0.7117$, $\theta_2^* = 0.9024$, $\theta_3^* = 0.736$, and $\theta_4^* = 0.7920$, leading to

$$\text{RM}_x = \rho_x = 0.7856.$$

On the other hand, for the output-oriented problem, we get $\varphi_1^* = 1$ and $\varphi_2^* = 1.0762$ and the Russell efficiency measure

$$\text{RM}_y = \frac{1}{\rho_y} = \frac{1}{1.3531} = 0.7390.$$

Finally, the input-oriented BCC model yields the radial efficiency measure $\theta^* = 0.8915$ whereas the optimal ϕ^* from the output-oriented BCC model is 1.1031, implying an efficiency level of 0.9065.

This example shows how the radial measures overestimate the efficiency of a firm because they ignore the presence of input and/or output slacks at the optimal solution of the relevant DEA LP problem. The input (output)-oriented nonradial measures ignore output (input) slacks present at the optimal solution. Only the Pareto–Koopmans measure ensures that neither input nor

Exhibit: 5.2. *The DEA-LP problem for airline #10*

NAME	COL1	COL2	COL3	COL4	COL5	COL6	COL7	COL8
PASS	35261	23388	14074	57290	12891	28991	18969	32404
CARGO	614	1580	539	3781	599	1330	760	1902
LAB	12222	12214	10428	21430	15156	17997	24708	10864
FUEL	860	456	304	1351	279	393	235	523
MATL	2008	1492	3171	2536	1246	1474	806	1512
CAP	6074	4174	3305	17932	2258	4784	6819	4479
A1	0	0	0	0	0	0	0	0
A2	0	0	0	0	0	0	0	0
B1	0	0	0	0	0	0	0	0
B2	0	0	0	0	0	0	0	0
B3	0	0	0	0	0	0	0	0
B4	0	0	0	0	0	0	0	0
C	1	1	1	1	1	1	1	1
D	0	0	0	0	0	0	0	0

COL9	COL10	COL11	COL12	COL13	COL14	COL15	COL16	COL17
2943	67364	9925	23312	50989	20799	20092	8961	27676
65	2618	157	845	5346	619	1375	234	998
4067	51802	8630	30140	45514	22180	19985	10520	22766
62	1294	185	499	1078	377	392	121	626
241	4276	303	1238	3314	1234	964	831	1197
587	12161	1482	3771	9004	3119	2929	1117	4829
0	0	0	0	0	0	0	0	0
0	0	0	0	0	0	0	0	0
0	0	0	0	0	0	0	0	0
0	0	0	0	0	0	0	0	0
0	0	0	0	0	0	0	0	0
0	0	0	0	0	0	0	0	0
1	1	1	1	1	1	1	1	1
0	0	0	0	0	0	0	0	0

COL18	COL19	COL20	COL21	COL22	COL23	COL24	COL25	COL26
18378	133796	24372	69050	96540	29050	85744	54054	62345
169	1838	625	1090	1300	245	2513	1382	1119
11914	80627	16613	35661	61675	21350	42989	28638	35783
309	2381	513	1285	1997	580	1762	991	1118
611	5149	1051	2835	3972	1498	3678	2193	2389
2124	18624	3358	9960	14063	4459	13698	7131	8704
0	0	0	0	0	0	0	0	0
0	0	0	0	0	0	0	0	0
0	0	0	0	0	0	0	0	0
0	0	0	0	0	0	0	0	0
0	0	0	0	0	0	0	0	0
0	0	0	0	0	0	0	0	0
1	1	1	1	1	1	1	1	1
0	0	0	0	0	0	0	0	0

COL27	COL28	PHI1	PHI2	THETA1	THETA2	THETA3	THETA4	_TYPE_	_RHS_
131905	59001	-67364.0	0.0	0.00	0.00	0.00	0.00	>=	0
2326	392	0.0	-2618.0	0.00	0.00	0.00	0.00	>=	0
73902	53557	0.0	0.0	-51802.00	0.00	0.00	0.00	<=	0
2246	1252	0.0	0.0	0.00	-1294.00	0.00	0.00	<=	0
5678	3030	0.0	0.0	0.00	0.00	-4276.00	0.00	<=	0
18204	8952	0.0	0.0	0.00	0.00	0.00	-12161.00	<=	0
0	0	1.0	0.0	0.00	0.00	0.00	0.00	>=	1
0	0	0.0	1.0	0.00	0.00	0.00	0.00	>=	1
0	0	0.0	0.0	1.00	0.00	0.00	0.00	<=	1
0	0	0.0	0.0	0.00	1.00	0.00	0.00	<=	1
0	0	0.0	0.0	0.00	0.00	1.00	0.00	<=	1
0	0	0.0	0.0	0.00	0.00	0.00	1.00	<=	1
1	1	0.0	0.0	0.00	0.00	0.00	0.00	=	1
0	0	-0.5	-0.5	0.25	0.25	0.25	0.25	MIN	.

Solution Summary

Objective Value	-0.424066

Variable Summary

Col	Variable Name	Status	Type	Price	Activity	Reduced Cost
1	COL1		NON-NEG	0	0	0.8255815
2	COL2		NON-NEG	0	0	0.293577
3	COL3		NON-NEG	0	0	0.6513861
4	COL4		NON-NEG	0	0	0.5769517
5	COL5		NON-NEG	0	0	0.5292137
6	COL6		NON-NEG	0	0	0.0420388
7	COL7		NON-NEG	0	0	0.2903089
8	COL8	BASIC	NON-NEG	0	0.0710373	0
9	COL9		NON-NEG	0	0	0.4765634
10	COL10		NON-NEG	0	0	0.4240662
11	COL11		NON-NEG	0	0	0.4543679
12	COL12		NON-NEG	0	0	0.5800132
13	COL13	BASIC	NON-NEG	0	0.7102763	0
14	COL14		NON-NEG	0	0	0.4446172
15	COL15		NON-NEG	0	0	0.3257467
16	COL16		NON-NEG	0	0	0.3917515
17	COL17		NON-NEG	0	0	0.5970051
18	COL18		NON-NEG	0	0	0.394043
19	COL19		NON-NEG	0	0	0.2785944
20	COL20		NON-NEG	0	0	0.5212755
21	COL21		NON-NEG	0	0	0.4250352
22	COL22		NON-NEG	0	0	0.8916024
23	COL23		NON-NEG	0	0	0.6043148
24	COL24		NON-NEG	0	0	0.5372937
25	COL25		NON-NEG	0	0	0.2889633
26	COL26		NON-NEG	0	0	0.3243596
27	COL27	BASIC	NON-NEG	0	0.2186864	0
28	COL28		NON-NEG	0	0	0.9723111
29	PHI1	BASIC	NON-NEG	-0.5	1	0
30	PHI2	BASIC	NON-NEG	-0.5	1.6963004	0
31	THETA1	BASIC	NON-NEG	0.25	0.9509406	0
32	THETA2	BASIC	NON-NEG	0.25	1	0
33	THETA3	BASIC	NON-NEG	0.25	0.8659882	0
34	THETA4	BASIC	NON-NEG	0.25	0.8794072	0
35	_OBS1_		SURPLUS	0	0	0.0000396
36	_OBS2_		SURPLUS	0	0	0.000191

(continued)

131

Exhibit: 5.3. *(continued)*

Solution Summary

Objective Value	−0.424066

Variable Summary

Col	Variable Name	Status	Type	Price	Activity	Reduced Cost
37	_OBS3_		SLACK	0	0	4.8261E-6
38	_OBS4_		SLACK	0	0	0.0018529
39	_OBS5_		SLACK	0	0	0.0000585
40	_OBS6_		SLACK	0	0	0.0000206
41	_OBS7_		SURPLUS	0	0	2.1684644
42	_OBS8_	BASIC	SURPLUS	0	0.6963004	0
43	_OBS9_	BASIC	SLACK	0	0.0490594	0
44	_OBS10_		SLACK	0	0	2.1476374
45	_OBS11_	BASIC	SLACK	0	0.1340118	0
46	_OBS12_	BASIC	SLACK	0	0.1205928	0

Constraint Summary

Constraint Row	Name	Type	S/S Col	Rhs	Activity	Dual Activity
1	_OBS1_	GE	35	0	0	0.0000396
2	_OBS2_	GE	36	0	0	0.000191
3	_OBS3_	LE	37	0	0	−4.826E-6
4	_OBS4_	LE	38	0	0	−0.001853
5	_OBS5_	LE	39	0	0	−0.000058
6	_OBS6_	LE	40	0	0	−0.000021
7	_OBS7_	GE	41	1	1	2.1684644
8	_OBS8_	GE	42	1	1.6963004	0
9	_OBS9_	LE	43	1	0.9509406	0
10	_OBS10_	LE	44	1	1	−2.147637
11	_OBS11_	LE	45	1	0.8659882	0
12	_OBS12_	LE	46	1	0.8794072	0
13	_OBS13_	EQ	.	1	1	−0.444893
14	_OBS14_	OBJECTVE	.	0	−0.424066	.

output slacks will be present at the optimal solution of the relevant DEA problem.

5.6 Summary

Presence of input and/or output slacks at the optimal solution of a CCR or BCC DEA model can undermine the usefulness of the relevant radial efficiency measure. The additive model does ensure that a firm is not rated efficient if any positive slack exists in any input or output. But the usefulness of the additive model for measuring efficiency is limited because the objective function is the sum of input and output slacks that are expressed in heterogeneous units. A different way to avoid input or output slacks is to allow different inputs to be contracted at different rates in an input-oriented nonradial model or to allow outputs to expand at unequal rates in an output-oriented nonradial model. The resulting Russell efficiency measures may still leave positive output or input slacks at the optimal solution. But the Pareto–Koopmans measure of technical efficiency reflects all potential increase in outputs and reduction in inputs. A firm cannot be found to be technically efficient by this criterion as long as there is any slack in any input or output.

Guide to the Literature

The additive model was developed by Charnes, Cooper, Golany, Seiford, and Stutz (1985). The nonradial Russell measure was proposed by Färe and Lovell (1978). Russell (1984) pointed out that this measure fails to satisfy a number of desirable properties of an efficiency measure. Zieschang (1985) proposed an extended Russell measure that is obtained in a two-step procedure by first obtaining the radial component and subsequently maximizing the sum of input and output slacks in the second stage. Coelli (1998) proposed a multistage procedure for maximizing slacks. A different nonradial measure called the Range-Adjusted Measure (RAM) of efficiency was proposed by Cooper, Park, and Pastor (1999). The Pareto–Koopmans efficiency measure was introduced by Pastor, Ruiz, and Sirvent (1999) as an extension of an earlier Generalized Efficiency Measure (GEM) due to Cooper and Pastor (1995). Ray (2000) proposed the linear approximation of the objective function in the problem for obtaining the Pareto–Koopmans measure.

6

Efficiency Measurement without Convexity Assumption:
Free Disposal Hull Analysis

6.1 Introduction

Of the different assumptions made about the technology in defining the production possibility set faced by a firm, by far the strongest is the assumption of convexity. Clearly, the feasibility of any observed input–output bundle (x^j, y^j) is demonstrated by the fact that some firm has been actually observed producing outputs y^j from inputs x^j. Similarly, free disposability of either inputs or outputs can be easily justified intuitively. Both rest on the possibility of less than full utilization of resources by a firm. After all, if a firm has been found to have actually produced output y^0 from input x^0, it could produce the same output from a larger input bundle x^1 by leaving some of the input unused. Similarly, it could produce less output than y^0 from the input x^0 by keeping some of its input idle. By contrast, the assumption of convexity is much more contentious.

Consider an example for the one-output, one-input case. Suppose two observed input–output combinations are $(x_0 = 5, y_0 = 8)$ and $(x_1 = 9, y_1 = 12)$. Then, convexity would imply that the simple average of these two bundles $(\bar{x} = 7, \bar{y} = 10)$ is feasible. Note that it is not intuitively obvious, however, from the two observed bundles. Compared to the smaller input–output bundle, this average bundle does use more input. But the corresponding output is also larger and is not necessarily producible from this input level. Similarly, compared to the larger bundle, the average does target a smaller quantity of output. But the input level is also smaller and may not be adequate for producing this target output. Thus, feasibility of the average bundle does not follow from any "proof by way of examples."

At a more abstract level, convexity of the production possibility set rules out increasing marginal productivity of any input. In this chapter we consider a modification of the standard DEA model called Free Disposal Hull (FDH) analysis introduced by Deprins, Simar, and Tulkens (1984) and further developed by Tulkens (1993). This alternative approach retains the disposability assumptions about inputs and outputs but dispenses with the convexity assumption. Section 6.2 defines the *disposal hull* of any input–output bundle and explains how the concept of dominance can be utilized without additional assumptions to measure technical efficiency. Section 6.3 describes how the input- or the output-oriented measure of technical efficiency of any firm can be computed by means of FDH analysis in a n-input, m-output framework. Section 6.4 addresses the question of CRS in FDH models. Section 6.5 includes an empirical example of FDH analysis. Section 6.6 summarizes the main points of the chapter.

6.2 Free Disposal Hull and Dominant Input–Output Bundles

We start with a single-output, single-input technology. Consider an input–output combination (x_0, y_0). Note that it may or may not be a feasible production plan. The set of input–output bundles *dominated* by (x_0, y_0) is

$$FDH(x_0, y_0) = \{(x, y) : x \geq x_0; y \leq y_0\}. \tag{6.1}$$

Compared to (x_0, y_0), every input–output combination $(x, y) \in FDH(x_0, y_0)$ involves no less input and no more output. The set $FDH(x_0, y_0)$ is the *Free Disposal Hull* (FDH) of the bundle (x_0, y_0). Now, suppose that (x_0, y_0) is indeed a feasible input–output combination. Then, by free disposability of inputs and outputs, all bundles in the FDH of this bundle are also feasible.

Note that for any $(x, y) \in FDH(x_0, y_0)$, at least one of the following would be true:

$$\begin{align} \text{(a)} \quad & x > x_0, \quad y = y_0; \\ \text{(b)} \quad & x = x_0; \quad y < y_0; \tag{6.2} \\ \text{(c)} \quad & x > x_0; \quad y < y_0. \end{align}$$

If (a), free disposability of inputs ensures feasibility of (x, y). If (b), feasibility follows from free disposability of outputs. If (c), (x, y) is feasible on both counts. Note that compared to a point in its FDH, the bundle (x_0, y_0) is more efficient in the sense that it either produces the same output with less input or produces more output from the same input, or uses less input to produce more output. In this sense, (x_0, y_0) dominates (x, y). Also, because inputs get depleted in stock in the production process, they may be treated as negative outputs and the input–output bundle (x, y) can be expressed as the *netput*

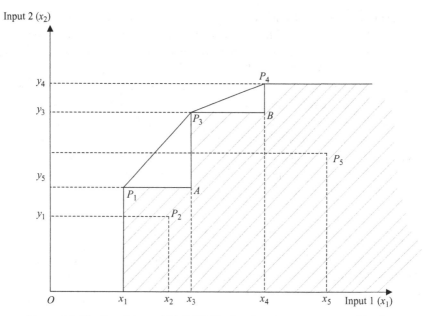

Figure 6.1 The Free Disposal Hull (FDH) of a given input–output combination.

bundle $(-x, y)$. Hence, if (x, y) lies in the FDH of (x_0, y_0), then $(-x_0, y_0) \geq (-x, y)$.

Figure 6.1 illustrates this for the single-output, single-input case. Points P_1 through P_5 show the observed input–output combinations (x_j, y_j) for $j = 1, 2, \ldots, 5$. Because any observed input–output combination (x_j, y_j) is feasible by assumption, any (x, y) that lies in the FDH of any observed input–output combination is also feasible. All points in the southeast quadrant of any point P_j are feasible input–output combinations. Thus, the shaded area to the right of the broken line $x_1 P_1 A P_3 B P_4$-*extension* represents the production possibility set derived from the FDH of the observed data. The frontier of this production possibility set is a step function. Note that if we had assumed convexity, the production possibility set would have been the free disposal *convex* hull of the observed data points and the frontier would have been the broken line $x_1 P_1 P_3 P_4$-*extension*.

Now consider the n-input m-output technology. The FDH of any observed input–output combination (x^j, y^j) is

$$\text{FDH}(x^j, y^j) = \{(x, y) : x \geq x^j; y \leq y^j\}. \tag{6.3}$$

The production possibility set is the union of the FDH of all the individual input–output bundles in the data and can be specified as

$$T_{\text{FDH}} = \{(x, y) : x \ge x^j; \, y \le y^j; \, \text{for some } j = 1, 2, \dots, N\}. \tag{6.4}$$

Alternatively,

$$T_{\text{FDH}} = \left[(x, y) : x \ge \sum_{j=1}^{N} \lambda_j x^j; \, y \le \sum_{j=1}^{N} \lambda_j y^j; \, \sum_{j=1}^{N} \lambda_j = 1; \right.$$

$$\left. \lambda_j \in \{0, 1\}; j = 1, 2, \dots, N \right]. \tag{6.5}$$

Note that each λ_j must be either 0 or 1. Moreover, the λ_j's add up to 1. Hence, one and only one λ will be unity and the others have to be equal to 0. Thus, T_{FDH} differs from the production possibility set for DEA (T_{DEA}) in respect of how the λ_j's are restricted.

The FDH production possibility set T_{FDH} yields the families of input sets

$$V_{\text{FDH}}(y) = \{x : x \ge x^j; \, y \le y^j; \, \text{for some } j = 1, 2, \dots, N\} \tag{6.6a}$$

and output sets

$$P_{\text{FDH}}(x) = \{y : y \le y^j; \, x \ge x^j; \, \text{for some } j = 1, 2, \dots, N\} \tag{6.6b}$$

The radial input-oriented FDH technical efficiency of the input–output pair (x^0, y^0) is

$$\theta_{\text{FDH}}^* = \min \theta : (\theta x^0) \in V_{\text{FDH}}(y^0). \tag{6.7}$$

The corresponding radial output-oriented FDH technical efficiency can be defined in an analogous manner.

In the multiple-input case, it is often more convenient to define the free disposal input hull (FDH^{I}) of an input bundle x^0 as

$$\text{FDH}^{\text{I}}(x^0) = \{x : x \ge x^0\}. \tag{6.8}$$

Clearly, all bundles inside FDH$^{\text{I}}(x^0)$ are larger than the bundle x^0 in some components but smaller in none. Hence, for any output bundle y, if (x^0, y) is feasible, then (x, y) is also feasible for any $x \in \text{FDH}^{\text{I}}(x^0)$. Consider the following example for the one-output, two-input case. Suppose that we observe the input–output bundles for five firms shown in Table 6.1.

Table 6.1. *Data for a two-input, one-output example*

Firm	Input 1 (x_1)	Input 2 (x_2)	Output (y)
#1	4	10	8
#2	7	12	10
#3	6	9	7
#4	10	8	6
#5	8	10	7

Figure 6.2 shows the free disposal input hulls for each of the input bundles from Table 6.1. All points to the northeast of P_1 show input bundles that include more than 4 units of input 1 and or more than 10 units of input 2. Thus, they are in the free disposal input hull of P_1. Similar reasoning applies to the points towards the northeast of the other input bundles from Table 6.1. Now, consider the output level 7 produced by firm #5. All firms in this data set except firm #4 produce 7 or more units of the output. Therefore, all of these input bundles

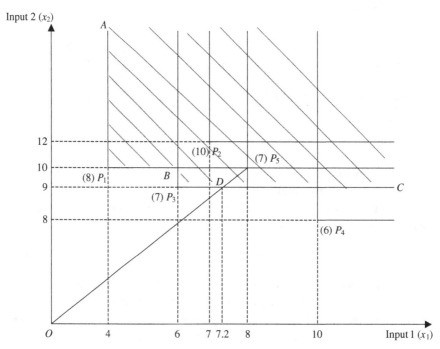

Figure 6.2 The free disposal input hull.

except P_4 can produce $y = 7$. Thus, all input bundles in the free disposal input hulls of P_1, P_2, P_3, and P_5 are in the input set of $y = 7$. This yields the shaded area to the right of AP_1BP_3C as the relevant input set. Now, suppose that we seek the input-oriented radial efficiency of firm #5. With reference to this input set, the efficient projection is the point D on the P_3C segment of the isoquant with 7.2 units of input 1 and 9 units of input 2. It needs to be emphasized that the principal merit of FDH analysis is that it always uses a single actually observed input–output bundle as the basis for comparison and efficiency evaluation of any firm. In this example, the comparison of firm #5 is with firm #3. The input bundle P_3 requires only 75% of input 1 and 90% of input 2 compared to the bundle P_5. One could demonstrably switch over to P_3 and still produce $y = 7$. This would lower both inputs by at least 10%. In fact, input 1 could be lowered even further. But a radial measure ignores slacks in individual inputs. Thus, even a generous evaluation of the technical efficiency of the bundle P_5 is 0.90.

For any output bundle y^0, we may define its free disposal output hull as

$$\text{FDH}^O(y^0) = \{y : y \leq y^0\} \tag{6.9}$$

Clearly, all bundles inside $\text{FDH}^O(y^0)$ are smaller than the bundle y^0 in some components but larger in none. Hence, for any input bundle x, if (x, y^0) is feasible, then (x, y) is also feasible for any $y \in \text{FDH}^O(y^0)$. Consider the following example for the two-output, one-input case. Suppose that we observe the input–output bundles for five firms shown in Table 6.2.

In Figure 6.3, points Q_1 through Q_5 show the output bundles of firm #1 through #5. Any point towards the southwest of point Q_1 represents an output bundle that is in the free disposal output hull of Q_1. Similar reasoning applies to the points towards the southwest of the other output bundles from Table 6.2. Now, consider the input level 12 used by firm #4. All firms in this data set except firm #5 use fewer units of the input. Therefore, all of these output

Table 6.2. *Data for a two-output, one-input example*

Firm	Output 1 (y_1)	Output 2 (y_2)	Input (x)
#1	4	15	9
#2	6	10	8
#3	10	8	10
#4	7	6	12
#5	9	12	15

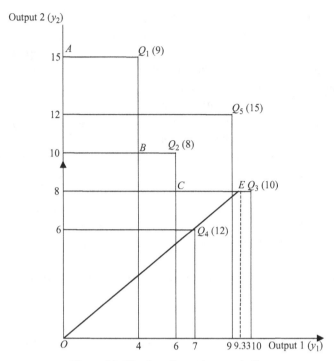

Figure 6.3 The free disposal output hull.

bundles except Q_5 can be produced from $x = 12$. Thus, all output bundles in the free disposal output hulls of Q_1, Q_2, Q_3, and Q_4 are in the output set of $x = 12$. This yields the area to the left of $AQ_1BQ_2CQ_3D$ as the relevant output set. Now, suppose that we measure the output-oriented radial efficiency of firm #4 with reference to this output set. The efficient projection of Q_4 is the point E on the CQ_3 segment of the output isoquant with 9.33 units of output 1 and 8 units of output 2. As in the previous input-oriented example, here again we use a single actually observed input–output bundle as the basis for comparison and efficiency evaluation of any firm. In this output-oriented example, the comparison of firm #4 is with firm #3. The output bundle Q_3 produces $1\frac{1}{3}$ times the quantity of output 1 and $1\frac{3}{7}$ times the quantity of output 2 compared to the bundle Q_4. One could switch over to Q_3 and use 2 units less of the input compared to firm #4. This would increase both outputs by at least 33%. Output 2 could be expanded even further. But even when we take the lower rate at which both outputs can be expanded, the radial output-oriented FDH measure of technical efficiency of firm #4 is $\frac{3}{4}$.

6.3 The FDH Methodology

We first consider the input-oriented FDH problem

$$\theta^* = \min \theta$$

$$\text{s.t.} \sum_{j=1}^{N} \lambda_j x_{ij} \leq \theta x_{i0} \quad (i = 1, 2, \ldots, n);$$

$$\sum_{j=1}^{N} \lambda_j y_{rj} \geq y_{r0} \quad (r = 1, 2, \ldots, m);$$ (6.10)

$$\sum_{j=1}^{N} \lambda_j = 1;$$

$$\lambda_j \in \{0, 1\}; \quad (j = 1, 2, \ldots, N); \quad \theta \text{ unrestricted.}$$

Note that if at the optimal solution of the FDH analysis problem λ_k^* equals 1, then x^0 lies in the free disposal input hull of x^k and, at the same time, y^0 lies in the free disposal output hull of y^k. In other words,

$$(x^0, y^0) \in \text{FDH}(x^k, y^k).$$

This is a mixed-integer programming problem because the choice variables λ_j can take only 0 or 1 as admissible values. But the restriction that the λ_j's add up to unity makes this problem much easier to solve.

Note that these restrictions imply that at any solution (including an optimal solution), only one of the λ_j's will equal unity and the others will be equal to 0. Thus, we can have at most N solutions. However, of these N possible solutions, not all will be feasible. To see this, suppose that we selected a solution where λ_k^* equals unity and the other λ's are all 0. For this to be a feasible solution, y_{rk} must be greater than or equal to y_{r0} for each output r. In other words, the output bundle y^0 must lie in the free disposal output hull of the bundle y^k. Hence, if, for any firm j, y_{rj} is less than y_{r0} for *any* individual output r, then the firm j need not be considered as a possible benchmark for comparison. To evaluate any observed input–output bundle for input-oriented technical efficiency using FDH analysis, we first eliminate all observations that produce any output in a smaller quantity than the firm under evaluation. Call the remaining set of observations J^0. Thus,

$$j \in J^0 \Rightarrow y^j \geq y^0.$$ (6.11)

Next we make a pairwise comparison of the input bundle of the firm under evaluation with the input bundle of each of these remaining firms. Suppose that x^s observed for firm s is one such bundle. Then, for each input i we compute the ratio

$$\theta_{is} = \frac{x_{is}}{x_{i0}} \quad (i = 1, 2, \ldots, n). \tag{6.12}$$

If $\theta_{is} < 1$ for every input i then compared to x^0 one can reduce every input by switching over to the bundle x^s. Of course, the fact that $s \in J^0$ ensures that one need not reduce any output while reducing inputs in this manner. In this pairwise comparison with the firm s, let

$$\theta_s^* = \max \{\theta_{1s}, \theta_{2s}, \ldots, \theta_{ns}\}. \tag{6.13}$$

Then, θ_s^* denotes the factor by which *all* inputs could be scaled down if the firm switched from the input bundle x^0 to the bundle x^s. Of course, it may be possible to reduce some inputs even further. In this sense, it is a conservative estimate of the efficiency of the firm producing y^0 from x^0. This, however, is a measure of input-oriented technical efficiency of the firm under evaluation if firm s is used as the benchmark. Note that we are free to use any firm from the set J^0 as the benchmark for comparison. Naturally, we select that particular firm j for which θ_j^* is the lowest across all firms in J^0. It is possible that even this lowest measure exceeds 1. In that case, the input-oriented FDH technical efficiency firm under evaluation is 1.

The actual implementation of this procedure to measure input-oriented technical efficiency of a firm using FDH analysis consists of the following steps:

Step 1: Eliminate any observation j if y_{rj} is less than y_{r0} for any output r. Call the remaining set of observations J^0.

Step 2: Eliminate any observation $j \in J^0$ if x_{i0} is less than x_{ij} for any input i. Call the remaining set of observations J^1.

Step 3: For each observation $j \in J^1$, compute

$$\theta_{ij} = \frac{x_{ij}}{x_{i0}} \quad \text{for each input } i.$$

Note that by virtue of step 2, $\theta_{ij} \leq 1$ for all i and j.

Step 4: For each $j \in J^1$, define

$$\theta_j^* = \max \{\theta_{1j}, \theta_{2j}, \ldots, \theta_{nj}\}.$$

Again, $\theta_j^* \leq 1$ for all j.

Step 5: Define

$$\theta^* = \min \{\theta_j^* : j \in J^1\}.$$

$$\theta_{\text{FDH}}^* = \min \{\theta^*, 1\}.$$

Next, consider the output-oriented measure of technical efficiency. For that, we need to solve the following mixed integer programming problem:

$$\max \phi$$

$$\text{s.t.} \quad \sum_{j=1}^{N} \lambda_j y_{rj} \geq \phi y_{r0} \quad (r = 1, 2, \ldots, m);$$

$$\sum_{j=1}^{N} \lambda_j x_{ij} \leq x_{i0} \quad (i = 1, 2, \ldots, n); \tag{6.14}$$

$$\sum_{j=1}^{N} \lambda_j = 1; \quad \lambda_j \in \{0, 1\}; \quad (j = 1, 2, \ldots, N); \quad \phi \text{ unrestricted.}$$

The solution procedure for the output-oriented model closely parallels the procedure outlined herein for the input-oriented model and consists of the following steps:

Step 1: Eliminate any observation j if y_{rj} is less than y_{r0} for any output r. Call the remaining set of observations J^0.

Step 2: Eliminate any observation $j \in J^0$ if x_{i0} is less than x_{ij} for any input i. Call the remaining set of observations J^1.

Step 3: For each observation $j \in J^1$, compute

$$\phi_{rj} = \frac{y_{rj}}{y_{r0}} \quad \text{for each output } r. \tag{6.15}$$

Step 2 ensures that $\phi_{rj} \geq 1$ for all r and j.

Step 4: For each $j \in J^1$, define

$$\phi_j^* = \min \{\phi_{1j}, \phi_{2j}, \ldots, \phi_{mj}\}. \tag{6.16}$$

Note that $\phi_j^* \geq 1$ for all $j \in J^1$.

Step 5: Define

$$\phi^* = \max\{\phi_j^* : j \in J^1\}. \tag{6.17}$$

$$\phi_{\text{FDH}}^* = \max\{\phi^*, 1\}. \tag{6.18}$$

The output-oriented FDH measure of technical efficiency is $\frac{1}{\phi_{\text{FDH}}^*}$.

6.4 Additivity and Replication in FDH Analysis

If the technology is assumed to be additive, the sum of two or more feasible input–output bundles is also feasible. Thus, if (x^0, y^0) and (x^1, y^1) are feasible bundles, $(x^0 + x^1, y^0 + y^1)$ is also a feasible input–output bundle. Further, a basic assumption in DEA is that if a firm can produce output y^0 from input x^0, so could any other firm in the same industry. That is, an observed input–output bundle can be *replicated* any number of times. Thus, additivity and replication together imply that if (x, y) is a feasible bundle, then, for any positive integer K, the bundle (Kx, Ky) is also feasible. The free replication hull (FRH) of any input–output bundle (x^0, y^0) is

$$\text{FRH}\,(x^0, y^0) = \{(x, y) : x \geq Kx^0; y \leq Ky^0; K \in \{1, 2, 3, \ldots\}\}. \tag{6.19}$$

The FRH is shown in Figure 6.4 for the single-input, single-output case. Consider the bundle $x^0 = (x_1^0, x_2^0) = (4, 5)$ shown by the point A_0 in the diagram. The point $B_0 = (8, 10)$ is a two-fold replication of A_0. Similarly, $C_0 = (12, 15)$ is a three-fold replication and so on. The shaded area to the southwest of each of these points is the corresponding FDH of the relevant point. The union of all of these is the FRH of A_0.

For a sample data set of input–output bundles $(x^j, y^j)\,(j = 1, 2, \ldots, N)$, the FRH production possibility set is

$$T_{\text{FRH}} = \left\{ (x, y) : x \geq \sum_1^N \lambda_j x^j; y \leq \sum_1^N \lambda_j y^j; \lambda_j \in \{1, 2, 3, \ldots\}; \right.$$

$$\left. (j = 1, 2, \ldots, N) \right\}. \tag{6.20}$$

Clearly, $T_{\text{FDH}} \subset T_{\text{FRH}}$ just as the VRS production possibility set lies inside the corresponding CRS production possibility set in DEA.

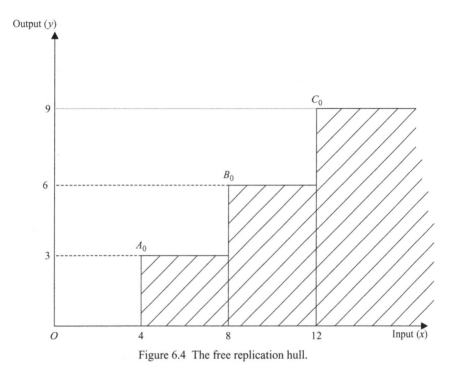

Figure 6.4 The free replication hull.

Figure 6.5 shows the FRH production possibility set along with the FDH production possibility set constructed from four observed input–output bundles:

$$A = (x_A = 4, y_A = 3); \quad B = (x_B = 6, y_B = 4); \quad C = (x_C = 11, y_C = 5);$$

$$\text{and} \quad D = (x_D = 21, y_D = 9).$$

The FDH frontier is the broken line *EAFBGCHD-extension*. By contrast, the FRH frontier is *EAFBJA₂KLMA₃NPQA₄RSTU-extension*. Here, the point A_2 is a twofold replication of A, L is the sum of the bundles A and B, A_3 is a threefold replication of A, and U is a twofold replication of L. The point D lies on the FDH frontier and is efficient relative to T_{FDH}. But its efficient output-oriented projection onto the FRH frontier is the point D^*, where 14 units of the output is produced from 21 units of the input. Thus,

$$\phi^{\text{FRH}} = \frac{14}{9}$$

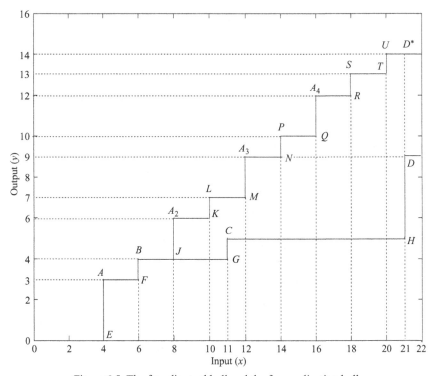

Figure 6.5 The free disposal hull and the free replication hull.

and the corresponding output-oriented efficiency is

$$\text{TE}_{\text{FRH}} = \frac{9}{14}.$$

For the multiple-input, multiple-output case, the FRH technical efficiency of the bundle (x^0, y^0) is the inverse of the optimal solution of the following mixed integer programming problem:

$$\max \phi$$

$$\text{s.t.} \ \sum_{j=1}^{N} \lambda_j y_{rj} \geq \phi y_{r0} \quad (r = 1, 2, \ldots, m);$$

$$\sum_{j=1}^{N} \lambda_j x_{ij} \leq x_{i0} \quad (i = 1, 2, \ldots, n); \tag{6.21}$$

$$\lambda_j \in \{0, 1, 2, 3, \ldots\}; \quad (j = 1, 2, \ldots, N); \quad \phi \text{ unrestricted.}$$

6.5 Empirical Applications of FDH Analysis

Christensen and Greene (1976) analyzed the data from a number of electrical utility companies in the United States for the year 1970 to estimate a dual cost function. They conceptualized a single-output, three-input production technology for the electric power industry. Output was measured by millions of kilowatt hours of electric power generated. Quantity indexes of labor, fuel, and capital were constructed from the available expenditure and price information for individual inputs at the firm level. We use their input–output quantity data for a sample of 99 firms (shown in Table 6.3) from their 1970 data set to illustrate the application of FDH and FRH analysis.

The SAS program measuring technical efficiency of firm #48 using input-oriented FDH analysis is shown in Exhibit 6.1. Exhibit 6.2 shows the relevant portion of the output of this program. Of the 51 firms producing greater output than firm #48, only 4 used lower quantities of all inputs than this firm. These were firms #49, #50, #51, and #54. Firm #48 is in the FDH of these firms. The columns RL0, RK0, and RF0 show the quantities of labor, capital, and fuel inputs of these firms as proportions of the corresponding input quantities used by firm #48. For any firm, the entry in the column labeled THETA shows the radial contraction possible in *all of the inputs* of firm #48 without reducing output. For example, the row for firm #49 shows that if firm #48 switched to the input–output bundle of #49, it would be using only 40.03% of labor, 54.173% of capital, and 90.72% of fuel compared to what it is currently using. Thus, every input could be scaled down by a factor of 0.9072 or less. The optimal reference bundle for firm #48 is that of #50, where all inputs can be scaled down to about 86% of its current level or lower. This factor (0.8599) measures the input-oriented FDH efficiency of firm #48.

Exhibits 6.3 and 6.4 show the SAS program and the relevant output for the output-oriented FDH analysis of the same firm. As in the input-oriented case, the same four firms appear in Exhibit 6.4 as dominating firm #48. But this time we measure the ratio of the output quantity of each of these firms to that of firm #48. Firm #54 produces 20.13% more output without requiring any increase in any input compared to firm #48. Thus, the output-oriented FDH efficiency of firm #48 is 0.8324.

The SAS program file for the mixed integer programming problem to measure the FRH output-oriented technical efficiency of firm #89 is shown in Exhibit 6.5. The commands are quite similar to those in an output-oriented CCR model except for the integer constraints on λ_j's incorporated by including two additional rows. The first has the name "INTEGER" for the type of

Table 6.3. *Christensen–Greene data on U.S. electrical utilities*

FIRM	KWH	LABOR	CAPITAL	FUEL
1	8	1.0204	1.376	2.973
2	14	2.6902	2.594	3.485
3	50	1.9827	0.668	11.630
4	65	2.3754	2.364	15.767
5	67	2.3251	4.013	9.717
6	90	4.5563	3.007	27.064
7	183	2.5447	4.741	24.232
8	295	4.8701	5.096	38.064
9	374	5.3485	3.008	52.592
10	378	3.9104	10.432	52.106
11	467	13.2520	11.319	94.127
12	643	13.5461	14.023	86.351
13	856	12.0581	20.379	109.640
14	869	3.7430	12.991	87.481
15	938	11.4583	16.980	133.978
16	1025	17.8433	21.046	141.289
17	1090	24.3545	39.050	147.902
18	1293	22.1513	31.356	162.186
19	1328	9.7280	30.266	150.139
20	1412	10.5273	36.221	170.815
21	1500	10.6548	25.468	173.143
22	1627	12.1292	22.705	187.082
23	1627	17.4942	30.327	191.893
24	1886	12.4658	62.022	205.627
25	1901	31.1495	32.814	248.157
26	2001	11.6434	30.695	351.391
27	2020	31.4233	37.854	266.281
28	2258	16.2611	32.008	258.602
29	2325	25.5840	35.211	279.146
30	2437	21.0152	53.581	275.995
31	2445	19.9365	42.013	293.332
32	2487	27.4192	47.906	330.088
33	2506	17.2205	41.228	267.304
34	2632	12.0355	47.353	272.244
35	2682	22.5875	47.206	271.701
36	2689	12.5604	25.877	290.122
37	2764	26.6733	35.572	289.789
38	2969	22.1125	37.176	304.568
39	3571	35.3054	52.846	381.036
40	3886	28.2969	68.947	468.661
41	3965	28.8538	60.265	420.306
42	3981	27.6883	65.972	406.980
43	4148	27.2748	48.054	482.731
44	4187	39.2059	73.337	447.717
45	4560	34.7745	65.514	481.773
46	5286	37.6939	81.114	563.110
47	5316	47.1379	57.096	555.471
48	5643	52.2177	111.490	673.429
49	5648	20.9029	60.397	610.932
50	5708	33.4168	79.428	579.140

(continued)

Table 6.3. *(continued)*

FIRM	KWH	LABOR	CAPITAL	FUEL
51	5785	27.2934	60.331	601.816
52	6754	75.3867	113.461	805.255
53	6770	50.4825	147.968	724.068
54	6779	45.8872	90.295	485.152
55	6793	48.6601	112.713	718.082
56	6837	53.6128	118.976	731.155
57	6891	53.582	130.847	756.24
58	7320	62.089	94.725	762.05
59	7382	62.823	116.400	803.21
60	7484	66.475	117.207	765.06
61	7896	45.494	90.286	851.15
62	7930	55.336	184.344	858.62
63	9145	103.101	128.891	880.56
64	9275	49.801	177.613	949.23
65	9530	78.681	118.974	994.47
66	9602	39.687	108.847	1031.63
67	9660	30.006	86.530	982.08
68	10004	161.064	178.703	1198.26
69	10057	54.320	103.716	1049.70
70	10149	58.085	103.523	1115.62
71	10361	103.336	183.107	1044.31
72	10855	81.581	182.301	1119.68
73	11114	74.394	204.139	1222.35
74	11667	81.833	161.468	1187.07
75	11837	123.487	184.421	1328.30
76	12542	112.355	143.801	1334.84
77	12706	94.382	224.423	1460.51
78	12936	55.772	136.867	1431.58
79	12954	56.101	147.493	1336.88
80	13702	132.695	233.160	1485.23
81	13846	125.447	227.241	1528.59
82	16311	58.151	131.748	1595.84
83	16508	127.072	158.744	1309.70
84	17280	90.604	223.165	1792.37
85	17875	60.810	220.204	1849.23
86	18455	244.193	297.329	2091.73
87	19445	239.797	364.271	2217.38
88	21956	132.812	323.585	2306.28
89	22522	233.765	384.349	2459.34
90	23217	138.172	267.667	2393.17
91	24001	155.437	414.068	2478.45
92	27118	236.563	528.823	2832.44
93	27708	144.754	309.101	2867.48
94	29613	403.141	593.415	3687.48
95	30958	319.464	419.813	3608.86
96	34212	192.852	285.081	3318.65
97	38343	123.068	562.133	3827.24
98	46870	440.530	851.127	5047.70
99	53918	382.789	566.391	5541.24

Exhibit: 6.1. *Input-oriented FDH analysis for firm #48*

```
OPTIONS NOCENTER;
DATA GREENE;
INPUT   FIRM      KWH        L          K        F;
SELECT OUTPUT LEVEL OF THE FIRM EVALUATED (#48 HERE);
KWH0= 5643;
DELETE FIRMS WITH LOWER OUTPUT;
IF KWH < KWH0 THEN DELETE;
SELECT INPUT LEVELS OF THE FIRM EVALUATED;
L0=52.2177;K0=111.490;F0=673.429;
COMPUTE RATIOS OF INDIVIDUAL INPUTS;
RL0=L/L0;RK0=K/K0;RF0=F/F0;
COMPUTE THE RADIAL SCALEDOWN FACTOR IN PAIRWISE COMPARISON;
THETA=MAX(RL0,RK0);THETA=MAX(THETA,RF0);
DELETE FIRMS USING LARGER QUANTITY OF ANY INPUT;
IF THETA >1 THEN DELETE;
CARDS;
      1         8      1.0204      1.376       2.973
      2        14      2.6902      2.594       3.485
      3        50      1.9827      0.668      11.630
      4        65      2.3754      2.364      15.767
      5        67      2.3251      4.013       9.717
      .        ..        ..         ..          ..
      .        ..        ..         ..          ..
     46      5286     37.6939     81.114     563.110
     47      5316     47.1379     57.096     555.471
     48      5643     52.2177    111.490     673.429
     49      5648     20.9029     60.397     610.932
     50      5708     33.4168     79.428     579.140
      .        ..        ..         ..          ..
      .        ..        ..         ..          ..
     89     22522    233.765     384.349    2459.34
     90     23217    138.172     267.667    2393.17
     91     24001    155.437     414.068    2478.45
     92     27118    236.563     528.823    2832.44
     93     27708    144.754     309.101    2867.48
     94     29613    403.141     593.415    3687.48
     95     30958    319.464     419.813    3608.86
     96     34212    192.852     285.081    3318.65
     97     38343    123.068     562.133    3827.24
     98     46870    440.530     851.127    5047.70
     99     53918    382.789     566.391    5541.24
;
PROC PRINT; VAR FIRM KWH RL0 RK0 RF0 THETA;
PROC MEANS MIN;VAR THETA;
```

Exhibit: 6.2. *Findings from input-oriented FDH analysis of firm #48*

Obs	FIRM	KWH	RL0	RK0	RF0	THETA
1	48	5643	1.00000	1.00000	1.00000	1.00000
2	49	5648	0.40030	0.54173	0.90720	0.90720
3	50	5708	0.63995	0.71242	0.85999	0.85999
4	51	5785	0.52268	0.54113	0.89366	0.89366
5	54	6779	0.87877	0.80989	0.72042	0.87877

Analysis Variable : THETA

Minimum 0.8599867

Exhibit: 6.3. *SAS program for output-oriented FDH analysis of firm #48*

```
Data Greene;
input FIRM        KWH   l k f;
kwh0=5643; l0=52.2177; k0=111.490; f0=673.429;
if l>l0 then delete;
if k>k0 then delete;
if f>f0 then delete;
if kwh < kwh0 then delete;
phi=kwh/kwh0;
cards;
    1         8       1.0204       1.376        2.973
    2        14       2.6902       2.594        3.485
    3        50       1.9827       0.668       11.630
    4        65       2.3754       2.364       15.767
    5        67       2.3251       4.013        9.717
    .         .          .           .            .
    .         .          .           .            .
   44      4187      39.2059      73.337      447.717
   45      4560      34.7745      65.514      481.773
   46      5286      37.6939      81.114      563.110
   47      5316      47.1379      57.096      555.471
   48      5643      52.2177     111.490      673.429
   49      5648      20.9029      60.397      610.932
   50      5708      33.4168      79.428      579.140
    .         .          .           .            .
    .         .          .           .            .
   97     38343     123.068      562.133     3827.24
   98     46870     440.530      851.127     5047.70
   99     53918     382.789      566.391     5541.24
;
proc print; var firm kwh kwh0 phi;
proc means max; var phi;
```

Exhibit: 6.4. *Findings from an output-oriented FDH analysis of firm #48*

Obs	FIRM	KWH	kwh0	phi
1	48	5643	5643	1.00000
2	49	5648	5643	1.00089
3	50	5708	5643	1.01152
4	51	5785	5643	1.02516
5	54	6779	5643	1.20131

The MEANS Procedure

Analysis Variable : phi

Maximum 1.2013114

the constraint. Each entry in the left-hand side of the constraint is 1 except for a 0 in the column for PHI. The other row, with "UPPERBD" for type, specifies an upper bound (set equal to 100 in this example) for each integer variable (and a missing value for the other variable PHI). As in the case of radial DEA, the input quantities of firm #89 appear in the right-hand side of appropriate constraints and the negative of its output quantity appears in the column for PHI at the output row.

The objective value (1.41275) in the solution summary section in Exhibit 6.6 shows that it is possible to increase the output of firm #89 by 41.275% from its current level of 22522. The benchmark bundle would be constructed by adding the input–output bundles of firms #2 and #83 with two-fold replications of the bundles of firms #14 and #54. This can be found from the entries in the "Activity" column in the "Variable Summary" section in Exhibit 6.6 (1 for COL2, 2 for COL14, 2 for COL54, and 1 for COL83). The "Activity" column in the "Constraint Summary" section shows the quantities of the inputs (229.0226 of labor, 367.91 of capital, and 2458.451 of fuel) used in this benchmark bundle. Comparison of these quantities with the entries in the corresponding rows of the column "RHS" in the same section of the output reveals the quantities of input slacks (shown in the bottom rows in the "Variable Summary" section).

6.6 Summary

FDH analysis provides a method of efficiency measurement without the assumption of convexity. It is shown to be a special case of the BCC DEA problem with additional $(0, 1)$ constraints on the λ_j's. The resulting

Exhibit: 6.5. *SAS program for the output-oriented free replication hull analysis of firm #48*

```
OPTIONS NOCENTER;
DATA CG;
INPUT OBS KWH L K F ;
C=1;D=100;E=0;
DROP OBS;
CARDS;
    1         8         1.0204        1.376          2.973
    2        14         2.6902        2.594          3.485
    3        50         1.9827        0.668         11.630
    4        65         2.3754        2.364         15.767
    5        67         2.3251        4.013          9.717
   85     17875        60.810       220.204       1849.23
   86     18455       244.193       297.329       2091.73
   87     19445       239.797       364.271       2217.38
   88     21956       132.812       323.585       2306.28
   89     22522       233.765       384.349       2459.34
   90     23217       138.172       267.667       2393.17
   91     24001       155.437       414.068       2478.45
   92     27118       236.563       528.823       2832.44
   93     27708       144.754       309.101       2867.48
   94     29613       403.141       593.415       3687.48
   95     30958       319.464       419.813       3608.86
   96     34212       192.852       285.081       3318.65
   97     38343       123.068       562.133       3827.24
   98     46870       440.530       851.127       5047.70
   99     53918       382.789       566.391       5541.24
;
PROC TRANSPOSE OUT=NEW;
DATA MORE;
INPUT PHI _TYPE_ $ _RHS_;
CARDS;
0 >= 0
0 <= 0
0 <= 0
0 <= 0
. INTEGER .
. UPPERBD .
1 MAX .
;
DATA LAST; MERGE NEW MORE;
IF _N_ <=4 THEN _RHS_=COL89;
IF _N_=1 THEN _RHS_=0;
IF _N_=1 THEN PHI=-COL89;
PROC PRINT;
PROC LP IMAXIT=1500;
```

Exhibit: 6.6. *SAS output of the output-oriented free replication hull analysis of firm #48: the LP procedure*

Solution Summary

Integer Optimal Solution

Objective Value   1.4127519758

Variable Summary

Col	Variable Name	Status	Type	Price	Activity	Reduced Cost
1	COL1		INTEGER	0	0	0.0003552
2	COL2		INTEGER	0	1	0.0006216
3	COL3		INTEGER	0	0	0.0022201
4	COL4		INTEGER	0	0	0.0028861
5	COL5		INTEGER	0	0	0.0029749
6	COL6		INTEGER	0	0	0.0039961
7	COL7		INTEGER	0	0	0.0081254
8	COL8		INTEGER	0	0	0.0130983
9	COL9		INTEGER	0	0	0.016606
10	COL10		INTEGER	0	0	0.0167836
11	COL11		INTEGER	0	0	0.0207353
12	COL12		INTEGER	0	0	0.0285499
13	COL13		INTEGER	0	0	0.0380073
14	COL14		INTEGER	0	2	0.0385845
15	COL15		INTEGER	0	0	0.0416482
16	COL16		INTEGER	0	0	0.0455111
17	COL17		INTEGER	0	0	0.0483971
18	COL18		INTEGER	0	0	0.0574105
19	COL19		INTEGER	0	0	0.0589646
20	COL20		INTEGER	0	0	0.0626943
21	COL21		INTEGER	0	0	0.0666015
22	COL22		INTEGER	0	0	0.0722405
23	COL23		INTEGER	0	0	0.0722405
24	COL24		INTEGER	0	0	0.0837403
25	COL25		INTEGER	0	0	0.0844064
26	COL26		INTEGER	0	0	0.0888465
27	COL27		INTEGER	0	0	0.0896901
28	COL28		INTEGER	0	0	0.1002575
29	COL29		INTEGER	0	0	0.1032324
30	COL30		INTEGER	0	0	0.1082053

(continued)

Exhibit: 6.6. *(continued)*

Solution Summary

Integer Optimal Solution

Objective Value	1.4127519758

Variable Summary

Col	Variable Name	Status	Type	Price	Activity	Reduced Cost
31	COL31		INTEGER	0	0	0.1085605
32	COL32		INTEGER	0	0	0.1104254
33	COL33		INTEGER	0	0	0.111269
34	COL34		INTEGER	0	0	0.1168635
35	COL35		INTEGER	0	0	0.1190836
36	COL36		INTEGER	0	0	0.1193944
37	COL37		INTEGER	0	0	0.1227244
38	COL38		INTEGER	0	0	0.1318267
39	COL39		INTEGER	0	0	0.1585561
40	COL40		INTEGER	0	0	0.1725424
41	COL41		INTEGER	0	0	0.1760501
42	COL42		INTEGER	0	0	0.1767605
43	COL43		INTEGER	0	0	0.1841755
44	COL44		INTEGER	0	0	0.1859071
45	COL45		INTEGER	0	0	0.2024687
46	COL46		INTEGER	0	0	0.2347038
47	COL47		INTEGER	0	0	0.2360359
48	COL48		INTEGER	0	0	0.250555
49	COL49		INTEGER	0	0	0.250777
50	COL50		INTEGER	0	0	0.2534411
51	COL51		INTEGER	0	0	0.25686
52	COL52		INTEGER	0	0	0.2998846
53	COL53		INTEGER	0	0	0.300595
54	COL54		INTEGER	0	2	0.3009946
55	COL55		INTEGER	0	0	0.3016162
56	COL56		INTEGER	0	0	0.3035698
57	COL57		INTEGER	0	0	0.3059675
58	COL58		INTEGER	0	0	0.3250155
59	COL59		INTEGER	0	0	0.3277684
60	COL60		INTEGER	0	0	0.3322973
61	COL61		INTEGER	0	0	0.3505905
62	COL62		INTEGER	0	0	0.3521002

(continued)

Exhibit: 6.6. *(continued)*

Solution Summary

Integer Optimal Solution

Objective Value   1.4127519758

Variable Summary

Col	Variable Name	Status	Type	Price	Activity	Reduced Cost
63	COL63		INTEGER	0	0	0.4060474
64	COL64		INTEGER	0	0	0.4118196
65	COL65		INTEGER	0	0	0.4231418
66	COL66		INTEGER	0	0	0.4263387
67	COL67		INTEGER	0	0	0.428914
68	COL68		INTEGER	0	0	0.4441879
69	COL69		INTEGER	0	0	0.4465412
70	COL70		INTEGER	0	0	0.4506261
71	COL71		INTEGER	0	0	0.4600391
72	COL72		INTEGER	0	0	0.4819732
73	COL73		INTEGER	0	0	0.493473
74	COL74		INTEGER	0	0	0.5180268
75	COL75		INTEGER	0	0	0.525575
76	COL76		INTEGER	0	0	0.5568777
77	COL77		INTEGER	0	0	0.5641595
78	COL78		INTEGER	0	0	0.5743717
79	COL79		INTEGER	0	0	0.5751709
80	COL80		INTEGER	0	0	0.6083829
81	COL81		INTEGER	0	0	0.6147767
82	COL82		INTEGER	0	0	0.7242252
83	COL83		INTEGER	0	1	0.7329722
84	COL84		INTEGER	0	0	0.7672498
85	COL85		INTEGER	0	0	0.7936684
86	COL86		INTEGER	0	0	0.819421
87	COL87		INTEGER	0	0	0.863378
88	COL88		INTEGER	0	0	0.974869
89	COL89		INTEGER	0	0	1
90	COL90		INTEGER	0	0	1.0308587
91	COL91		INTEGER	0	0	1.0656691
92	COL92		INTEGER	0	0	1.2040671
93	COL93		INTEGER	0	0	1.2302637
94	COL94		INTEGER	0	0	1.3148477

(continued)

Exhibit: 6.6. *(continued)*

Solution Summary

Integer Optimal Solution

Objective Value	1.4127519758

Variable Summary

Col	Variable Name	Status	Type	Price	Activity	Reduced Cost
95	COL95		INTEGER	0	0	1.3745671
96	COL96		INTEGER	0	0	1.519048
97	COL97		INTEGER	0	0	1.7024687
98	COL98		INTEGER	0	0	2.0810763
99	COL99		INTEGER	0	0	2.3940147
100	PHI	BASIC	NON-NEG	1	1.412752	0
101	_OBS1_		SURPLUS	0	0	−0.000044
102	_OBS2_	BASIC	SLACK	0	4.7424	0
103	_OBS3_	BASIC	SLACK	0	16.439	0
104	_OBS4_	BASIC	SLACK	0	0.889	0

Constraint Summary

Row	Constraint Name	Type	S/S Col	Rhs	Activity	Dual Activity
1	_OBS1_	GE	101	0	0	−0.000044
2	_OBS2_	LE	102	233.765	229.0226	0
3	_OBS3_	LE	103	384.349	367.91	0
4	_OBS4_	LE	104	2459.34	2458.451	0
5	_OBS7_	OBJECTVE	.	0	1.412752	.

production possibility set is a proper subset of the familiar free disposal convex hull of the data points. As a result, the efficiency measure under FDH analysis is, in general, higher than what is obtained from the BCC model under the convexity assumption. The nonconvex counterpart of CRS is free replication under which every integer multiple of any observed input–output bundle is feasible. One can exploit this added assumption to define a FRH of the data points and obtain corresponding efficiency measures.

Guide to the Literature

The concept of a FDH and the associated method of FDH analysis were introduced by Deprins, Simar, and Tulkens (1984). Subsequently, in a number of papers, Tulkens and his associates (especially Tulkens [1993]) have further refined the methodology of FDH analysis within the broad framework of dominance analysis. Thrall (1999) contested the economic meaningfulness of FDH analysis on the ground that the shadow prices of all inputs and/or outputs need not be positive at the optimal solution. For a response to Thrall, see Cherchiye, Kuosomanen, and Post (2000).

7

Dealing with Slacks: Assurance Region/Cone Ratio Analysis, Weak Disposability, and Congestion

7.1 Introduction

The presence of any positive input or output slacks at the optimal solution of a CCR or BCC DEA model has already been recognized as a potential problem with the technical efficiency measure in such cases. The nonradial models considered in Chapter 5 ensure that no slacks are present at the projection of an observed input or output bundle onto the isoquant. In this chapter, we consider several other approaches that address the problem of slacks. It may be noted that when a slack is present at the optimal solution, the relevant input or output constraint is nonbinding and the shadow price of the resource (i.e., the dual variable associated with the constraint) equals 0. An alternative approach known as assurance region (AR) analysis avoids the problem of slacks by imposing restrictions on the shadow prices of inputs and/or outputs. This leads to a reconstruction of the input or output isoquant in such a way that no slacks can exist at the radial projection of any input or output bundle onto the modified isoquant. Use of prior weight restrictions also allows incorporation of expert opinion regarding the relative significance of individual inputs and outputs in the production process.

The approach of AR analysis was introduced by Thompson, Singleton, Thrall, and Smith (1986) and was applied for choosing a "best site" for the location of a high-energy physical laboratory. Subsequently, Charnes, Cooper, Huang, and Sun (1990) developed a different approach called Cone Ratio (CR) analysis incorporating bounds on shadow prices or multipliers. An altogether different approach is to modify the free disposability assumption about inputs and outputs. If one assumes weak rather than strong disposability, no slacks can exist in any region of the frontier. In fact, as shown by Färe, Grosskopf, and Lovell (1994), when the radial technical efficiency measure under the weak disposability assumption exceeds the usual radial measure under strong or free disposability, one may conclude that congestion is being caused by one or more inputs or outputs.

AR analysis is explained for the one-output, two-input case in Section 7.2 followed by the multiple-output, multiple-input case in Section 7.3. CR analysis is described in Section 7.4. Section 7.5 includes empirical examples of the two approaches using the Christensen and Greene data set shown in Table 6.3. The difference between weak and strong disposability is explained and congestion efficiency is defined in Section 7.6. The main points of this chapter are summarized in Section 7.7.

7.2 Assurance Region Analysis: The One-Output, Two-Input Case

Consider an industry producing a single output (y) from two inputs (x_1 and x_2) and a sample of N firms. Let $x^j = (x_{1j}, x_{2j})$ be the input bundle and y_j the output level of firm j ($j = 1, 2, \ldots, N$). Further assume that the technology exhibits globally CRS. The dual or multiplier form of the input-oriented CCR DEA model for firm k is

$$\max u y_k$$

$$\text{s.t. } u y_j - v_1 x_{1j} - v_2 x_{2j} \leq 0; \quad (j = 1, 2, \ldots, N); \tag{7.1}$$

$$v_1 x_{1k} + v_2 x_{2k} = 1;$$

$$u, v_1, v_2 \geq 0.$$

Note that in the single-output CCR model, the output constraint is always binding. Thus, the shadow price of the output is strictly positive at the optimal solution. On the other hand, although the shadow prices of the inputs are constrained to be merely nonnegative, any one shadow price can take the value 0 at the optimal solution. At the same time, however, the normalization condition (i.e., the shadow value of the input bundle x^k is unity) ensures that v_1 and v_2 cannot be zero simultaneously.

Consider now the restrictions

$$c_1 \leq \frac{v_2}{v_1} \leq c_2, \quad \text{where} \quad 0 < c_1 < c_2. \tag{7.2}$$

Alternatively,

$$c_1 v_1 \leq v_2 \tag{7.2a}$$

and

$$v_2 \leq c_2 v_1. \tag{7.2b}$$

Now, if $v_1 = 0$, v_2 cannot be positive. At the same time, if $v_2 = 0$, v_1 cannot be positive. Thus, the normalization condition cannot be satisfied unless both shadow prices are strictly positive.

We now incorporate the restrictions (7.2a–2b) into (7.1) to get the revised LP problem:

$$\max u y_k$$

$$\text{s.t. } u y_j - v_1 x_{1j} - v_2 x_{2j} \leq 0; \quad (j = 1, 2, \ldots, N);$$

$$v_1 x_{1k} + v_2 x_{2k} = 1;$$

$$c_1 v_1 - v_2 \leq 0; \tag{7.3}$$

$$-c_2 v_1 + v_2 \leq 0;$$

$$u, v_1, v_2 \geq 0.$$

The dual LP problem for (7.3) is

$$\min \theta$$

$$\text{s.t. } \sum_{1}^{N} \lambda_j y_j \geq y_k;$$

$$\sum_{1}^{N} \lambda_j x_{1j} \leq \theta x_{1k} + c_1 \delta_1 - c_2 \delta_2; \tag{7.4}$$

$$\sum_{1}^{N} \lambda_j x_{2j} \leq \theta x_{2k} - \delta_1 + \delta_2;$$

$$\lambda_j \geq 0; \quad (j = 1, 2, \ldots, N); \quad \delta_1, \delta_2 \geq 0; \quad \theta \text{ unrestricted.}$$

Suppose that at the optimal solution of (7.2), the ratio of the shadow prices ($\frac{v_2}{v_1}$) lies strictly between c_1 and c_2. In that case, neither (7.2a) nor (7.2b) is a binding constraint and both δ_1 and δ_2 will be 0 at the optimal solution of (7.4). Otherwise, at most, one of the constraints (7.2a–b) can be binding and either δ_1 or δ_2 (but not both) will be strictly positive. Assume arbitrarily that v_2 is 0 at the optimal solution of (7.1). This, in its turn, implies that (7.2a) is binding in (7.3) and that δ_1 is positive at the optimal solution of (7.4). Thus, the radial projection $(\theta^* x^k)$ does not lie inside the free disposal conical hull of the observed input–output bundles. In particular, $\theta^* x_{1k}$ includes a negative slack of $c_1 \delta_1^*$.

The optimization problem in (7.4) is best understood from the following numerical example shown in Table 7.1 and the accompanying Figure 7.1.

Table 7.1. *Data for the two-input CRS example*

Firm	1	2	3	4	5
Input 1	4	5	6	7	10
Input 2	7	10	6	3	2

Suppose that we have the input–output data for five firms. Because CRS is assumed, we can scale the output bundle of each firm by its output quantity. Table 7.1 shows the quantities of the two inputs used by each firm per unit of the output. Points P_1 through P_5 show the input bundles per unit of the output. The input isoquant for output level 1 is shown by the broken line $AP_1 P_4 P_5 B$. The efficient radial projection of the bundle x^2 shown by the point P_2 is the point $C(x_1 = 4, x_2 = 8)$ on the vertical segment of the isoquant. The CCR

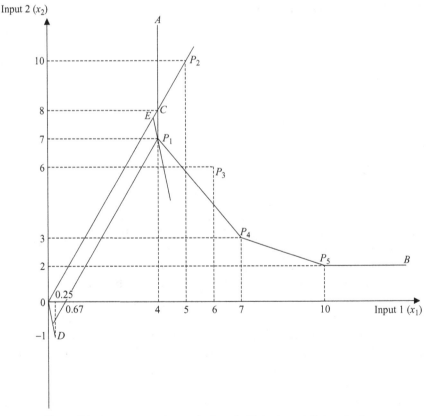

Figure 7.1 Assurance region analysis and efficient nonradial projection.

measure of efficiency of firm 2 is ($\theta_C = 0.8$). But there is a 1-unit slack in input x_2 at the point C and the shadow price v_2 equals 0.

Suppose, however, that the lower bound on the ratio of the shadow prices ($\frac{v_2}{v_1}$) is 0.25. Now, define the direction vector $\beta = (0.25, -1)$ shown by the point D in the quadrant to the southeast of the origin. Next, consider the positive linear combination $\mu = \theta x^2 + \delta\beta$. We may freely choose nonnegative values of θ and δ subject to the constraint that the resulting bundle μ lies in the input requirement set of the unit output level. This can be regarded as the feasibility constraint. Clearly, the point P_2 with θ equal to 1 and δ equal to 0 is a trivial solution. The objective is to select the minimum value of θ that satisfies the feasibility constraint when supplemented by the appropriate value of δ. Clearly, ($\theta = 0.8, \delta = 0$) corresponding to the point C is a superior but not the optimal solution. We move towards the origin along the ray OP_2 and at the same time move the minimum distance necessary in the direction defined by β to reach a point in the feasible region. For ($\theta = 0.767, \delta = 0.67$), one obtains the point P_1 in the feasible set. If θ is reduced any further, there is no value of δ for which $\theta x^2 + \delta\beta$ would be a feasible point. Effectively, one needs to draw a tangent with slope defined by the direction vector β to the isoquant. The point of intersection of the ray OP_2 with this tangent (point E in this diagram) defines the optimal value of θ in AR analysis. The tangency point is the optimal nonradial projection of the inefficient point P_2.[1]

7.3 AR Analysis with Multiple Outputs and Inputs

In the preceding model for measuring input-oriented technical efficiency, restrictions on shadow prices in order to eliminate slacks were imposed only for the inputs. It was assumed that the constraint for the single output will always be binding and the shadow price will be strictly positive. Although this assumption holds for the single-output case under CRS, output slacks can exist even in the single-output case under VRS and in the multiple-output case under CRS. For such models, one needs to impose restrictions on the shadow prices of outputs as well. In this section, we consider an input-oriented model with two outputs and two inputs under VRS.

Consider again a sample of N firms each producing two outputs (y_1, y_2) using two inputs (x_1, x_2). Let $x^j = (x_{1j}, x_{2j})$ be the input bundle and $y^j = (y_{1j}, y_{2j})$ the corresponding output bundle of firm j. Then, the dual LP form

---

[1] The input-oriented AR efficiency of a firm can be interpreted as its "shadow" cost efficiency.

of the input-oriented CCR DEA model for firm k is

$$\max u_1 y_{1k} + u_2 y_{2k}$$

$$\text{s.t. } u_1 y_{1j} - u_2 y_{2j} - v_1 x_{1j} - v_2 x_{2j} \leq 0; \quad (j = 1, 2, \ldots, N); \quad (7.5)$$

$$v_1 x_{1k} + v_2 x_{2k} = 1;$$

$$u_1, u_2, v_1, v_2 \geq 0.$$

For AR analysis, we incorporate the restrictions

$$d_1 \leq \frac{u_2}{u_1} \leq d_2 \tag{7.6}$$

along with

$$c_1 \leq \frac{v_2}{v_1} \leq c_2. \tag{7.7}$$

Equivalently,

$$d_1 u_1 - u_2 \leq 0. \tag{7.8a}$$

$$-d_2 u_1 + u_2 \leq 0. \tag{7.8b}$$

$$c_1 v_1 - v_2 \leq 0. \tag{7.9a}$$

$$-c_2 v_1 + v_2 \leq 0. \tag{7.9b}$$

The dual of the LP problem (7.5) with the additional restrictions (7.8a–b) and (7.9a–b) is the input-oriented AR problem:

$$\min \theta$$

$$\text{s.t. } \sum_{j=1}^{N} \lambda_j y_{1j} + d_1 \sigma_1 - d_2 \sigma_2 \geq y_{1k};$$

$$\sum_{j=1}^{N} \lambda_j y_{2j} - \sigma_1 + \sigma_2 \geq y_{2k};$$

$$\sum_{j=1}^{N} \lambda_j x_{ij} - c_1 \delta_1 + c_2 \delta_2 \leq \theta x_{ik}; \tag{7.10}$$

$$\sum_{j=1}^{N} \lambda_j x_{2ij} - \delta_1 + \delta_2 \leq \theta x_{2k};$$

$$\lambda_j \geq 0; \quad (j = 1, 2, \ldots, N); \quad \delta_1, \delta_2, \sigma_1, \sigma_2 \geq 0; \quad \theta \text{ unrestricted.}$$

Table 7.2. *Data for the two-output two-input*
example of AR analysis

Firm	1	2	3	4	5
Output 1	9	10	12	14	18
Output 2	12	20	15	16	4
Input 1	6	4	3	6	2
Input 2	5	2	7	8	10

For a numerical example, consider the input–output data shown in Table 7.2. Assume further that

$$0.33 \le \frac{u_2}{u_1} \le 2 \quad \text{and} \quad 0.25 \le \frac{v_2}{v_1} \le 4.$$

Then, the input-oriented AR efficiency of firm 1 is 0.4739 with ($\lambda_2^* = 0.6582$, $\lambda_5^* = 0.1053$) at the optimal solution. Further, σ_1^* equals 1.5845. This positive value implies that the lower bound on the ratio of shadow prices of outputs is binding. As argued before, this happens when the unrestricted shadow price of output 2 (u_2) equals 0. The input-oriented CCR technical efficiency of firm 1, by contrast, is 0.5031. A positive slack of 2.4224 units in output 2 exists at the optimal solution and the optimal shadow price of this output is 0. Imposition of restrictions on the shadow prices rules out the presence of slacks in any input or output at the optimal solution and yields a lower measure of technical efficiency.

In the examples considered previously, shadow prices of inputs or outputs are restricted separately. In a linked AR model, bounds are imposed on the ratios of shadow prices of inputs and outputs. For example, in the two-input, two-output case, we may specify the bounds

$$a_1 \le \frac{u_2}{u_1} \le a_2; \tag{7.11}$$

$$b_1 \le \frac{v_1}{u_1} \le b_2; \tag{7.12}$$

$$c_1 \le \frac{v_2}{u_1} \le c_2. \tag{7.13}$$

Equivalently,

$$a_1 u_1 - u_2 \le 0; \tag{7.14a}$$

$$-a_2 u_1 + u_2 \le 0; \tag{7.14b}$$

$$b_1 u_1 - v_1 \leq 0; \qquad (7.15\text{a})$$

$$- b_2 u_1 + v_1 \leq 0; \qquad (7.15\text{b})$$

$$c_1 u_1 - v_2 \leq 0; \qquad (7.16\text{a})$$

$$- c_2 u_1 + v_2 \leq 0. \qquad (7.16\text{b})$$

The linked AR model in the multiplier form consists of problem (7.10) with the added restrictions (7.14a–b), (7.15a–b), and (7.16a–b). The dual of the multiplier problem is the input-oriented linked AR problem:

$$\min \theta$$

$$\text{s.t.} \quad \sum_{j=1}^{N} \lambda_j y_{1j} + a_1 \alpha_1 - a_2 \alpha_2 + b_1 \beta_1 - b_2 \beta_2 + c_1 \gamma_1 - c_2 \gamma_2 \geq y_{1k};$$

$$\sum_{j=1}^{N} \lambda_j y_{2j} - \alpha_1 + \alpha_2 \geq y_{2k};$$

$$\sum_{j=1}^{N} \lambda_j x_{ij} - \beta_1 + \beta_2 \leq \theta x_{ik}; \qquad (7.17)$$

$$\sum_{j=1}^{N} \lambda_j x_{2ij} - \gamma_1 + \gamma_2 \leq \theta x_{2k};$$

$$\lambda_j \geq 0; \quad (j = 1, 2, \ldots, N); \quad \alpha_1, \alpha_2, \beta_1, \beta_2, \gamma_1, \gamma_2 \geq 0; \quad \theta \text{ unrestricted.}$$

7.4 Cone Ratio Analysis

Charnes, Cooper, and Sun, Huang (1990) incorporate the upper and lower bounds on the ratio of shadow prices in a different way. They recognize that the restrictions define a convex cone in the positive quadrant in the multiplier of shadow price space. This is shown in Figure 7.2 for the two-input case. Consider the points A $(v_1 = 1, v_2 = c_1)$ and B $(v_1 = 1, v_2 = c_2)$. All points in the cone formed by the rays OB and OA through the origin satisfy the restrictions on the ratio of the shadow prices. Thus, the feasible set of the shadow prices can be represented by the cone formed by all positive linear combinations of the two points A and B:

$$W = \{v_1 = \rho_1 + \rho_2; v_2 = c_1 \rho_1 + c_2 \rho_2; \rho_1, \rho_2 \geq 0\} \qquad (7.18)$$

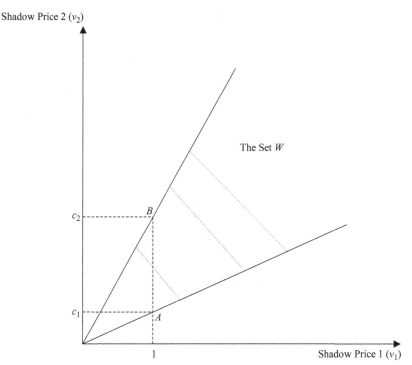

Figure 7.2 Bounds on the ratio of multipliers and the cone of feasible shadow prices.

If we restrict the multipliers in (7.2) to lie in W above, we get the transformed model:

$$\max \ uy_k$$

$$\text{s.t. } uy_j - (\rho_1 + \rho_2)x_{1j} - (c_1\rho_1 + c_2\rho_2)x_{2j} \leq 0; (j = 1, 2, \ldots, N); \quad (7.19)$$

$$(\rho_1 + \rho_2)x_{1k} + (c_1\rho_1 + c_2\rho_2)x_{2k} = 1;$$

$$u, \rho_1, \rho_2 \geq 0.$$

Define the transformed variables

$$\bar{x}_{1j} = x_{1j} + c_1 x_{2j} \qquad (7.20a)$$

and

$$\bar{x}_{2j} = x_{1j} + c_2 x_{2j} \qquad (7.20b)$$

Then, (7.19) can be revised as

$$\max \ uy_k$$

$$\text{s.t. } uy_j - \rho_1 \bar{x}_{1j} - \rho_2 \bar{x}_{2j} \leq 0; \quad (j = 1, 2, \ldots, N); \qquad (7.21)$$

Table 7.3. *Transformed data for the two-input CRS example*

Firm	1	2	3	4	5
(Transformed) Input 1	5.75	7.5	7.5	7.75	10.5
(Transformed) Input 2	32	45	30	19	18

$$\rho_1 \bar{x}_{1k} + \rho_2 \bar{x}_{2k} = 1;$$

$$u, \rho_1, \rho_2 \geq 0.$$

The dual of the problem (7.21) is

$$\min \theta$$

$$\text{s.t.} \sum_{j=1}^{N} \lambda_j y_j \geq y_k;$$

$$\sum_{j=1}^{N} \lambda_j \bar{x}_{1j} \leq \theta \bar{x}_{1k}; \qquad (7.22)$$

$$\sum_{j=1}^{N} \lambda_j \bar{x}_{2j} \leq \theta \bar{x}_{2k};$$

$$\lambda_j \geq 0; \quad (j = 1, 2, \ldots, N); \quad \theta \text{ unrestricted.}$$

This is, clearly, an input-oriented CCR model. Consider again the input bundles shown in Table 7.1. The transformed input quantities of the firms considered in the numerical example are shown in Table 7.3 for $c_1 = 0.25$ and $c_2 = 4$. In Figure 7.3, points P_1 through P_5 show the actual input bundles and Q_1 through Q_5 denote the transformed input bundles. The input isoquant defined by these transformed input quantities is the broken line $RQ_1Q_4Q_5S$. The radial efficient projection of the bundle Q_2 is the point T on the vertical segment RQ_1. The CCR input-oriented efficiency measure of firm 2 relative to the transformed isoquant shown in Figure 7.3 is its CR efficiency for the upper and lower bounds specified for the shadow price ratio of inputs.

7.5 An Empirical Application of AR Analysis

In this section, we evaluate the input-oriented AR technical efficiency of firm #89 from the Christensen–Greene data set of U.S. electrical utilities described earlier and shown in Chapter 6. We assume that the technology exhibits VRS

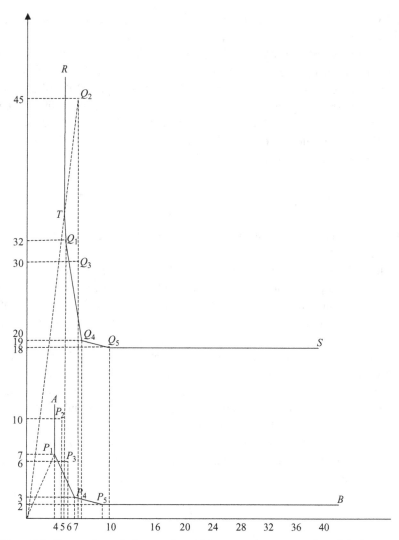

Figure 7.3 Cone-ratio analysis, transformed inputs, and reconstruction of the isoquant.

so that the appropriate model is the restricted version of the input-oriented BCC DEA problem.

In AR analysis, the upper and lower bounds on the shadow price ratios need to be specified with great care. In situations where no guidance can be found from the market, one needs to rely on the opinions of experts or the practitioners. After all, the shadow price of any input represents the imputed value of its marginal product. It is sensible to assume that the manager at the production facility would have a reasonable estimate of the marginal rate of substitution between a pair of inputs. Alternatively, one may look at the shadow prices of inputs from the optimal solution of the CCR or BCC model for the firms that have no input slacks. The bounds on the relative shadow prices can be specified as the 5th-percentile and the 95th-percentile of the empirical distribution of the ratios of shadow prices of pairs of inputs for these firms. In the present application, actual prices of inputs are available from the Christensen–Greene data. The appropriate percentiles of the distribution of the actual price ratios were used to define the following bounds:

$$168.610 \leq \frac{v_L}{v_F} \leq 381.637 \quad \text{and} \quad 1.4451 \leq \frac{v_K}{v_F} \leq 3.7812.$$

Here v_K, v_L, and v_F are the shadow prices of the capital, labor, and fuel input, respectively.

Exhibit 7.1 shows the SAS program for the input-oriented AR analysis of firm #89. Its output quantity appears in the right-hand side of the output constraint and its input quantities appear (with a negative sign) in the appropriate rows of the column for THETA. The bounds defined previously appear with the appropriate signs in the inequality constraint for the labor input.

Exhibit 7.2 shows the SAS output from the program. The AR efficiency of the firm is 0.7886. At the optimal solution, the variables C_1 and D_1 associated, respectively, with the lower bounds of the labor–fuel price ratio and the capital–fuel price are both positive. This implies that both the lower bounds are binding. Indeed, at the optimal solution of the input-oriented BCC model there exist 20.969 units of slack in the labor input and 233.77 units of slack in the capital input. Thus, shadow prices of both inputs equal 0. The standard BCC efficiency measure of 0.8091 does not reflect the presence of these slacks.

7.6 Weak Disposability and Congestion

We have assumed so far that both inputs and outputs are freely disposable. Thus, if the input bundle x^0 can produce the output bundle y^0, then any input bundle $x \geq x^0$ can also produce y^0. Similarly, any output bundle $y \leq y^0$ can also be produced from x^0 and, therefore, from all $x \geq x^0$. This implies that an increase in any input cannot have a negative impact on the producible output. In other words, negative marginal productivity of any input is ruled out. The simple intuition behind this assumption is that the additional input quantities can be left idle at no cost. Similarly, one can get rid of appropriate quantities

```
 OPTIONS NOCENTER;
DATA UPDATED;
INPUT FIRM KWH LABOR CAPITAL FUEL;
C=1;D=0;DROP FIRM;
CARDS;
  1       8    1.0204      1.376      2.973
  2      14    2.6902      2.594      3.485
  3      50    1.9827      0.668     11.630
  4      65    2.3754      2.364     15.767
  5      67    2.3251      4.013      9.717
  6      90    4.5563      3.007     27.064
  .      ..      ..         ..         ..
  .      ..      ..         ..         ..
  .      ..      ..         ..         ..
  .      ..      ..         ..         ..
 86   18455   244.193    297.329   2091.73
 87   19445   239.797    364.271   2217.38
 88   21956   132.812    323.585   2306.28
 89   22522   233.765    384.349   2459.34
 90   23217   138.172    267.667   2393.17
 91   24001   155.437    414.068   2478.45
 92   27118   236.563    528.823   2832.44
 93   27708   144.754    309.101   2867.48
 94   29613   403.141    593.415   3687.48
 95   30958   319.464    419.813   3608.86
 96   34212   192.852    285.081   3318.65
 97   38343   123.068    562.133   3827.24
 98   46870   440.530    851.127   5047.70
 99   53918   382.789    566.391   5541.24
;
PROC TRANSPOSE OUT=NEXT;
DATA MORE;
INPUT THETA C1 C2 D1 D2 _TYPE_ $ _RHS_;
CARDS;
0          0          0          0          0     ≥   0
0          1         -1          0          0     ≤   0
0   -168.610    381.637    -1.4451     3.7812     ≤   0
0          0          0          1         -1     ≤   0
0          0          0          0          0     =   1
1          0          0          0          0    MIN   .
;
DATA LAST; MERGE NEXT MORE;
IF _N_ =1 THEN _RHS_=COL89;
IF _N_ =2 THEN THETA=-COL89;
IF _N_ =3 THEN THETA=-COL89;
IF _N_ =4 THEN THETA=-COL89;
PROC PRINT;
PROC LP;
```

171

Exhibit: 7.2. *Output the SAS program for measuring the input-oriented AR efficiency of firm #89*

		Solution Summary				
		Objective Value			0.7886086	
		Variable Summary				
Col	Variable Name	Status	Type	Price	Activity	Reduced Cost
1	COL1		NON-NEG	0	0	0.1855234
2	COL2		NON-NEG	0	0	0.1860205
3	COL3		NON-NEG	0	0	0.1870684
4	COL4		NON-NEG	0	0	0.1882051
5	COL5		NON-NEG	0	0	0.1860517
6	COL6		NON-NEG	0	0	0.191907
7	COL7		NON-NEG	0	0	0.1864775
8	COL8		NON-NEG	0	0	0.1873612
9	COL9		NON-NEG	0	0	0.1891904
10	COL10		NON-NEG	0	0	0.189171
11	COL11		NON-NEG	0	0	0.2033097
12	COL12		NON-NEG	0	0	0.1932018
13	COL13		NON-NEG	0	0	0.1927308
14	COL14		NON-NEG	0	0	0.1810987
15	COL15		NON-NEG	0	0	0.1976
16	COL16		NON-NEG	0	0	0.1986366
17	COL17		NON-NEG	0	0	0.2017502
18	COL18		NON-NEG	0	0	0.1968665
19	COL19		NON-NEG	0	0	0.1874794
20	COL20		NON-NEG	0	0	0.1922033
21	COL21		NON-NEG	0	0	0.1882481
22	COL22		NON-NEG	0	0	0.187992
23	COL23		NON-NEG	0	0	0.1919407
24	COL24		NON-NEG	0	0	0.1874827
25	COL25		NON-NEG	0	0	0.2046215
26	COL26		NON-NEG	0	0	0.2325758
27	COL27		NON-NEG	0	0	0.20667
28	COL28		NON-NEG	0	0	0.18891
29	COL29		NON-NEG	0	0	0.196365
30	COL30		NON-NEG	0	0	0.1909114
31	COL31		NON-NEG	0	0	0.1954971
32	COL32		NON-NEG	0	0	0.2097236
33	COL33		NON-NEG	0	0	0.1825299
34	COL34		NON-NEG	0	0	0.1780828
35	COL35		NON-NEG	0	0	0.1785667
36	COL36		NON-NEG	0	0	0.1802246

(continued)

Solution Summary

Objective Value	0.7886086

Variable Summary

Col	Variable Name	Status	Type	Price	Activity	Reduced Cost
37	COL37		NON-NEG	0	0	0.1816211
38	COL38		NON-NEG	0	0	0.1770918
39	COL39		NON-NEG	0	0	0.1841414
40	COL40		NON-NEG	0	0	0.2022426
41	COL41		NON-NEG	0	0	0.1804555
42	COL42		NON-NEG	0	0	0.1751253
43	COL43		NON-NEG	0	0	0.1937723
44	COL44		NON-NEG	0	0	0.1849568
45	COL45		NON-NEG	0	0	0.1793406
46	COL46		NON-NEG	0	0	0.1800274
47	COL47		NON-NEG	0	0	0.1761699
48	COL48		NON-NEG	0	0	0.211826
49	COL49		NON-NEG	0	0	0.1753318
50	COL50		NON-NEG	0	0	0.1663397
51	COL51		NON-NEG	0	0	0.1678038
52	COL52		NON-NEG	0	0	0.2185058
53	COL53		NON-NEG	0	0	0.1847202
54	COL54		NON-NEG	0	0	0.0901179
55	COL55		NON-NEG	0	0	0.1776312
56	COL56		NON-NEG	0	0	0.1824615
57	COL57		NON-NEG	0	0	0.1904422
58	COL58		NON-NEG	0	0	0.1728417
59	COL59		NON-NEG	0	0	0.1875133
60	COL60		NON-NEG	0	0	0.1702195
61	COL61		NON-NEG	0	0	0.175627
62	COL62		NON-NEG	0	0	0.1886531
63	COL63		NON-NEG	0	0	0.1517504
64	COL64		NON-NEG	0	0	0.1615404
65	COL65		NON-NEG	0	0	0.1692143
66	COL66		NON-NEG	0	0	0.1681635
67	COL67		NON-NEG	0	0	0.1427545
68	COL68		NON-NEG	0	0	0.251351
69	COL69		NON-NEG	0	0	0.1585801
70	COL70		NON-NEG	0	0	0.1797167
71	COL71		NON-NEG	0	0	0.1644214
72	COL72		NON-NEG	0	0	0.1646821
73	COL73		NON-NEG	0	0	0.1912144
74	COL74		NON-NEG	0	0	0.1523047

(continued)

Exhibit: 7.2. *(continued)*

Solution Summary

Objective Value	0.7886086

Variable Summary

Col	Variable Name	Status	Type	Price	Activity	Reduced Cost
75	COL75		NON-NEG	0	0	0.2101113
76	COL76		NON-NEG	0	0	0.1751041
77	COL77		NON-NEG	0	0	0.2169207
78	COL78		NON-NEG	0	0	0.1774835
79	COL79		NON-NEG	0	0	0.143184
80	COL80		NON-NEG	0	0	0.1941483
81	COL81		NON-NEG	0	0	0.2012529
82	COL82		NON-NEG	0	0	0.0919086
83	COL83	BASIC	NON-NEG	0	0	0.6603028
84	COL84		NON-NEG	0	0	0.1395573
85	COL85		NON-NEG	0	0	0.1263007
86	COL86		NON-NEG	0	0	0.2470343
87	COL87		NON-NEG	0	0	0.2555104
88	COL88		NON-NEG	0	0	0.1466592
89	COL89		NON-NEG	0	0	0.2113914
90	COL90		NON-NEG	0	0	0.1200046
91	COL91		NON-NEG	0	0	0.1361634
92	COL92		NON-NEG	0	0	0.1640404
93	COL93		NON-NEG	0	0	0.1052647
94	COL94		NON-NEG	0	0	0.4203306
95	COL95		NON-NEG	0	0	0.294027
96	COL96	BASIC	NON-NEG	0	0	0.3396972
97	COL97		NON-NEG	0	0	0.0154791
98	COL98		NON-NEG	0	0	0.2073829
99	COL99		NON-NEG	0	0	0.040247
100	THETA	BASIC	NON-NEG	1	0	0.7886086
101	C1	BASIC	NON-NEG	0	0	0.0003493
102	C2		NON-NEG	0	0	31.092224
103	D1	BASIC	NON-NEG	0	0	0.1014444
104	D2		NON-NEG	0	0	0.1563664
105	_OBS1_		SURPLUS	0	0	0.0000432
106	_OBS2_		SLACK	0	0	27.063275
107	_OBS3_		SLACK	0	0	0.3657694
108	_OBS4_		SLACK	0	0	0.096746

(continued)

Exhibit: 7.2. *(continued)*

Constraint Summary

Row	Constraint Name	Type	S/S Col	Rhs	Activity	Dual Activity
1	_OBS1_	GE	105	22522	22522	0.0000432
2	_OBS2_	LE	106	0	0	-27.06327
3	_OBS3_	LE	107	0	0	-0.365769
4	_OBS4_	LE	108	0	0	-0.096746
5	_OBS5_	EQ	.	1	1	-0.184373
6	_OBS6_	OBJECTVE	.	0	0.7886086	.

of individual outputs from the bundle y^0 in order to obtain a smaller bundle y from the input bundle x^0 at no additional cost. Indeed, this free disposability assumption in conjunction with convexity leads to the free disposal convex hull of the observed input–output bundles as the empirically constructed production possibility set under VRS.

In many practical situations, however, inputs and/or outputs may not be freely disposable. For example, in a power plant, electricity and smoke pollution are joint outputs. One can reduce pollution without reducing power generation only by using additional resources for pollution control. This is a case where free disposability of outputs fails. Similarly, in farming, although irrigation has a positive marginal impact on output, excessive rain or flooding does lead to crop damage. One needs to use additional labor and capital equipment to pump out the unwanted water from the field. One cannot simply let the flood water remain on the ground without lowering output. Here, the negative marginal productivity of water has to be neutralized by additional application of labor and capital inputs.

Following Färe, Grosskopf, and Lovell (1994), one can distinguish between strong and weak disposability of inputs and outputs. Strong disposability of inputs implies that if x^0 can produce y^0, then x can also produce y^0 as long as $x \geq x^0$. Similarly, strong disposability of outputs implies that if x^0 can produce y^0, then it can also produce y as long as $y \leq y^0$. In other words, strong disposability is the same as what we have so far called free disposability.

Weak disposability, on the other hand, implies that only if *all inputs are increased proportionately* from x^0, then y^0 remains a feasible output bundle. Thus, if the negative marginal productivity of some input(s) causes a decline in the output, proportionate increase in the other input(s) compensates for the

Table 7.4. *Data for the example of weak disposability*

Firm	A	B	C	D	E
Input 1	6	7	8	12	18
Input 2	12	20	20	8	9

loss. Therefore, if x^0 can produce y^0, then βx^0 can also produce y^0 as long as $\beta \geq 1$. It may be noted that weak disposability is necessary but not sufficient for strong disposability.

The production possibility set empirically constructed from a set of N observed input–output bundles (x^j, y^j) under the assumption of convexity, weak disposability, and VRS can be expressed as

$$T_W^V = \left\{ (x, y) : x = \beta \sum_1^N \lambda_j x^j; \ y = \alpha \sum_1^N \lambda_j y^j; \ \sum_1^N \lambda_j \right.$$

$$\left. = 1; 0 \leq \alpha \leq 1; \beta \geq 1; \lambda_j \geq 0; (j = 1, 2, \ldots, N) \right\}. \quad (7.23)$$

This may be called the weak disposal convex hull of the observed input–output bundles. In the single-output case, of course, $y = \alpha y_0$ and $\alpha \geq 1$ together imply $y \geq y_0$ so that strong and weak disposability of output are equivalent. In that case, the corresponding input requirement set for the output level y_0 is:

$$V_W(y_0) = \left\{ x : x = \beta \sum_1^N \lambda_j x^j; \ \sum_1^N \lambda_j y^j \geq y_0; \ \sum_1^N \lambda_j \right.$$

$$\left. = 1; 0 \leq \beta \leq 1; \lambda_j \geq 0; (j = 1, 2, \ldots, N) \right\}. \quad (7.23a)$$

Consider, for a simple example, a two-input, one-output case. Suppose that output is freely disposable and inputs are only weakly disposable. Table 7.4 shows the input quantities of 6 hypothetical firms each producing 12 units of the output.

Points A through E in Figure 7.4 show the input bundles of the individual firms. Because all input bundles produce 12 units of the output, they all lie in the input requirement set for $y = 12$. By convexity, all points in the closed area $ABCED$ also lie inside $V(y = 12)$. By weak disposability of inputs, all radial expansion of points in this area also lie in the input requirement set of

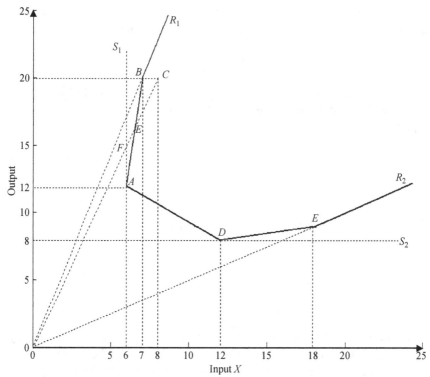

Figure 7.4 Input isoquants under strong and weak disposability assumptions.

the specified output level. Thus, the truncated cone represented by the area $R_1 BADE R_2$ is the weak disposal input requirement set for $y = 12$. If, on the other hand, inputs were assumed to be strongly rather than weakly disposable, the usual free disposal convex hull shown by the area $S_1 ADS_2$ would be the relevant input requirement set.

Now, consider the input-oriented technical efficiency of firm C. If free disposability is assumed, its radial projection onto the free-disposability isoquant is the point F ($x_1 = 6, x_2 = 15$) and the usual BCC measure of efficiency is $\theta = \frac{3}{4}$. On the other hand, if only weak rather than strong (or free) disposability is assumed, the relevant projection is the point G ($x_1 = 6\frac{6}{11}, x_2 = 16\frac{4}{11}$) on the weak-disposability isoquant. In that case, the technical efficiency will be $\theta_W = \frac{9}{11}$. It may be noted that at this point the isoquant is upward sloping and the marginal productivity of x_2 is negative. This corresponds to a negative shadow price for this input.

Färe, Grosskopf, and Lovell attribute the difference between the two iso-quants to input congestion and measure congestion efficiency of a firm as

$$\psi = \frac{\theta}{\theta_W}. \tag{7.24}$$

The DEA LP problem for measuring input-oriented technical efficiency of firm k in the multiple-input, multiple-output case under weak disposability of inputs is

$$\min \theta$$

$$\text{s.t.} \sum_{j=1}^{N} \lambda_j y_{rj} \geq y_{rk}; \quad (r = 1, 2, \ldots, m);$$

$$\sum_{j=1}^{N} \lambda_j x_{ij} = (\alpha) \theta x_{ik}; \quad (i = 1, 2, \ldots, n); \tag{7.25}$$

$$\sum_{j=1}^{N} \lambda_j = 1;$$

$$\lambda_j \geq 0; \quad (j = 1, 2, \ldots, N); \quad \alpha \geq 1; \quad \theta \text{ free.}$$

Note that the input constraints are nonlinear in α and θ. But, as argued by Färe, Grosskopf, and Lovell, α can be set equal to unity without affecting the optimal value of the objective function. That reduces (7.24) to the following LP problem:

$$\min \theta$$

$$\text{s.t.} \sum_{j=1}^{N} \lambda_j y_{rj} \geq y_{rk}; \quad (r = 1, 2, \ldots, m);$$

$$\sum_{j=1}^{N} \lambda_j x_{ij} = \theta x_{ik}; \quad (i = 1, 2, \ldots, n); \tag{7.26}$$

$$\sum_{j=1}^{N} \lambda_j = 1;$$

$$\lambda_j \geq 0; \quad (j = 1, 2, \ldots, N); \quad \theta \text{ free.}$$

Exhibit 7.3 shows the SAS program for measuring the input-oriented weak-disposal technical efficiency of firm 89 from the Christensen–Greene data set considered earlier. Its only difference from a standard input-oriented BCC LP is that the input constraints are equations rather than weak inequalities. The relevant sections of the SAS output from this program appear in Exhibit 7.4.

Exhibit: 7.3. *The SAS program for weak-disposal input-oriented technical efficiency of firm #89*

```
OPTIONS NOCENTER;
DATA UPDATED;
INPUT FIRM KWH LABOR CAPITAL FUEL;
C=1;D=0;DROP FIRM;
CARDS;
1         8    1.0204    1.376    2.973
2        14    2.6902    2.594    3.485
3        50    1.9827    0.668   11.630
4        65    2.3754    2.364   15.767
5        67    2.3251    4.013    9.717
6        90    4.5563    3.007   27.064
.        ..        ..       ..       ..
.        ..        ..       ..       ..
.        ..        ..       ..       ..
.        ..        ..       ..       ..
86    18455   244.193  297.329  2091.73
87    19445   239.797  364.271  2217.38
88    21956   132.812  323.585  2306.28
89    22522   233.765  384.349  2459.34
90    23217   138.172  267.667  2393.17
91    24001   155.437  414.068  2478.45
92    27118   236.563  528.823  2832.44
93    27708   144.754  309.101  2867.48
94    29613   403.141  593.415  3687.48
95    30958   319.464  419.813  3608.86
96    34212   192.852  285.081  3318.65
97    38343   123.068  562.133  3827.24
98    46870   440.530  851.127  5047.70
99    53918   382.789  566.391  5541.24
;
PROC TRANSPOSE OUT=NEXT;
DATA MORE;
INPUT THETA _TYPE_ $ _RHS_;
CARDS;
0 ≥ 0
0 = 0
0 = 0
0 = 0
0 = 1
1 MIN .
;
DATA LAST; MERGE NEXT MORE;
IF _N_=1 THEN _RHS_=COL89;
IF _N_=2 THEN THETA=-COL89;
IF _N_=3 THEN THETA=-COL89;
IF _N_=4 THEN THETA=-COL89;
*PROC PRINT;
PROC LP;
```

Solution Summary

Objective Value		0.9017533

Variable Summary

Col	Variable Name	Status	Type	Price	Activity	Reduced Cost
1	COL1		NON-NEG	0	0	0.2020575
2	COL2		NON-NEG	0	0	0.1932577
3	COL3		NON-NEG	0	0	0.2067098
4	COL4		NON-NEG	0	0	0.2057375
5	COL5		NON-NEG	0	0	0.1962883
6	COL6		NON-NEG	0	0	0.2066248
7	COL7		NON-NEG	0	0	0.2040478
8	COL8		NON-NEG	0	0	0.2033325
9	COL9		NON-NEG	0	0	0.217016
10	COL10		NON-NEG	0	0	0.2086025
11	COL11		NON-NEG	0	0	0.2098209
12	COL12		NON-NEG	0	0	0.1866098
13	COL13		NON-NEG	0	0	0.1957806
14	COL14		NON-NEG	0	0	0.2187085
15	COL15		NON-NEG	0	0	0.2267314
16	COL16		NON-NEG	0	0	0.1968015
17	COL17		NON-NEG	0	0	0.1411973
18	COL18		NON-NEG	0	0	0.1697394
19	COL19		NON-NEG	0	0	0.2078099
20	COL20		NON-NEG	0	0	0.2118756
21	COL21		NON-NEG	0	0	0.2292046
22	COL22		NON-NEG	0	0	0.23705
23	COL23		NON-NEG	0	0	0.2063667
24	COL24		NON-NEG	0	0	0.1710962
25	COL25		NON-NEG	0	0	0.1933132
26	COL26		NON-NEG	0	0	0.38369
27	COL27		NON-NEG	0	0	0.1967211
28	COL28		NON-NEG	0	0	0.2494317
29	COL29		NON-NEG	0	0	0.2243522
30	COL30		NON-NEG	0	0	0.200539
31	COL31		NON-NEG	0	0	0.2444557
32	COL32		NON-NEG	0	0	0.2407444
33	COL33		NON-NEG	0	0	0.2258599
34	COL34		NON-NEG	0	0	0.235017
35	COL35		NON-NEG	0	0	0.1890707
36	COL36		NON-NEG	0	0	0.2886648
37	COL37		NON-NEG	0	0	0.2091523
38	COL38		NON-NEG	0	0	0.2307751

(continued)

Solution Summary

Objective Value	0.9017533

Variable Summary

Col	Variable Name	Status	Type	Price	Activity	Reduced Cost
39	COL39		NON-NEG	0	0	0.2012221
40	COL40		NON-NEG	0	0	0.2797046
41	COL41		NON-NEG	0	0	0.2371327
42	COL42		NON-NEG	0	0	0.2162704
43	COL43		NON-NEG	0	0	0.3244156
44	COL44		NON-NEG	0	0	0.1895991
45	COL45		NON-NEG	0	0	0.2405099
46	COL46		NON-NEG	0	0	0.2522802
47	COL47		NON-NEG	0	0	0.2478255
48	COL48		NON-NEG	0	0	0.2390433
49	COL49		NON-NEG	0	0	0.3927564
50	COL50		NON-NEG	0	0	0.2694382
51	COL51		NON-NEG	0	0	0.3501387
52	COL52		NON-NEG	0	0	0.2285468
53	COL53		NON-NEG	0	0	0.1787674
54	COL54		NON-NEG	0	0	0.0442541
55	COL55		NON-NEG	0	0	0.2430822
56	COL56		NON-NEG	0	0	0.2233397
57	COL57		NON-NEG	0	0	0.2262268
58	COL58		NON-NEG	0	0	0.242655
59	COL59		NON-NEG	0	0	0.2414742
60	COL60		NON-NEG	0	0	0.1787925
61	COL61		NON-NEG	0	0	0.3866716
62	COL62		NON-NEG	0	0	0.1808296
63	COL63		NON-NEG	0	0	0.0507803
64	COL64		NON-NEG	0	0	0.2476015
65	COL65		NON-NEG	0	0	0.2730449
66	COL66		NON-NEG	0	0	0.4877261
67	COL67		NON-NEG	0	0	0.5117101
68	COL68		NON-NEG	0	0	0.0238304
69	COL69		NON-NEG	0	0	0.4344035
70	COL70		NON-NEG	0	0	0.4861037
71	COL71		NON-NEG	0	0	0.0679328
72	COL72		NON-NEG	0	0	0.215604
73	COL73		NON-NEG	0	0	0.3033483
74	COL74		NON-NEG	0	0	0.285594
75	COL75		NON-NEG	0	0	0.2175575
76	COL76		NON-NEG	0	0	0.3097695
77	COL77		NON-NEG	0	0	0.3636957

(continued)

Exhibit: 7.4. *(continued)*

Solution Summary

| | | Objective Value | | | 0.9017533 | |

Variable Summary

Col	Variable Name	Status	Type	Price	Activity	Reduced Cost
78	COL78		NON-NEG	0	0	0.6391532
79	COL79		NON-NEG	0	0	0.5151
80	COL80		NON-NEG	0	0	0.1687223
81	COL81		NON-NEG	0	0	0.248997
82	COL82		NON-NEG	0	0	0.650394
83	COL83	BASIC	NON-NEG	0	0	0.4920294
84	COL84		NON-NEG	0	0	0.5153106
85	COL85		NON-NEG	0	0	0.6748292
86	COL86		NON-NEG	0	0	0.0172507
87	COL87	BASIC	NON-NEG	0	0	0.2626461
88	COL88		NON-NEG	0	0	0.4847004
89	COL89		NON-NEG	0	0	0.0982467
90	COL90		NON-NEG	0	0	0.5969463
91	COL91		NON-NEG	0	0	0.3122729
92	COL92	BASIC	NON-NEG	0	0	0.1116816
93	COL93		NON-NEG	0	0	0.7862203
94	COL94		NON-NEG	0	0	0.0022022
95	COL95		NON-NEG	0	0	0.5107996
96	COL96		NON-NEG	0	0	0.8013073
97	COL97		NON-NEG	0	0	0.9269487
98	COL98	BASIC	NON-NEG	0	0	0.1336429
99	COL99		NON-NEG	0	0	0.943849
100	THETA	BASIC	NON-NEG	1	0	0.9017533
101	_OBS1_		SURPLUS	0	0	0.0000492

Constraint Summary

Row	Constraint Name	Type	S/S Col	Rhs	Activity	Dual Activity
1	_OBS1_	GE	101	22522	22522	0.0000492
2	_OBS2_	EQ	.	0	0	0.0040911
3	_OBS3_	EQ	.	0	0	−0.001081
4	_OBS4_	EQ	.	0	0	0.0018285
5	_OBS5_	EQ	.	1	1	−0.205927
6	_OBS6_	OBJECTVE	.	0	0.9017533	.

The optimal value of the objective function (0.90175) measures the input-oriented weak-disposal technical efficiency of firm #89. This is substantially higher than the efficiency measure (0.80914) that one gets from the standard BCC model based on free disposability. Thus, a measure of its congestion efficiency is

$$\psi = \frac{0.80914}{0.90175} = 0.8890.$$

Obviously, a value of ψ less than unity implies the presence of input congestion. It does not, however, reveal which specific inputs are causing congestion at the projected point on the weak-disposability isoquant. Färe, Grosskopf, and Lovell suggest the following strategy for identifying the congestive inputs. First, the input vector x may be arbitrarily partitioned as (x^S, x^W). Inputs in the subvector x^S are treated as freely (i.e., strongly) disposable whereas those in x^W are treated as weakly disposable. This implies that in the relevant DEA problem, the input restrictions take the form of an equality for each input that is an element of x^W whereas a weak inequality restriction applies to other inputs. If the optimal θ_W from this partitioned model coincides with the θ obtained from a standard BCC model where all inputs are treated as freely disposable, one can infer that inputs currently regarded as weakly disposable are *not causing* congestion. But a value of ψ less than unity confirms that there has to be at least one input that is not freely disposable. One would, then, have to consider a different partition of the input vector x into freely and weakly disposable subvectors.

Clearly, when there is no slack in any individual input at the optimal radial projection under the free-disposability assumption, changing the restriction to an equality from a weak inequality for the relevant input will not make any difference. Hence, only inputs that exhibit positive slacks at the efficient radial projection under free disposability are potential sources of congestion. In the case of firm #89 considered previously, two inputs – labor and capital – had positive slacks at the optimal solution of the BCC model. There was no input slack in the fuel input. Thus, fuel is not a source of congestion. This is verified by the fact that when fuel is treated as weakly disposable when labor and capital are regarded as freely disposable, the measure of technical efficiency does not change from what we get from a BCC model. On the other hand, when either labor or capital is treated, in isolation, as weakly disposable, the technical efficiency measure increases. Hence, both capital and labor are found to be sources of congestion in the case of this firm.

A general note of caution is strongly warranted at this point. Presence of input congestion is quite unlikely in behavioral data. Even though the marginal productivity of an input could *eventually become negative*, it is difficult to imagine a producer *actually using* the input at that level – especially when it has to be procured at a cost. In the example of crop damage due to flooding, excessive irrigation does occur, but only as an act of Nature rather than at the discretion of the farmer. Similarly, the frequently cited case of power generation and air pollution as an example of weak disposability of outputs is somewhat misleading. If one defines a smoke-free environment rather than the degree of pollution as the relevant output, there should be no primary problem in assuming free disposability of outputs. There can, of course, be joint products like beef and cowhide where only weak disposability of outputs holds. In most cases, however, the assumption of weak rather than strong disposability is likely to rationalize simple technical inefficiency.

The diagram shown in Figure 7.5 best explains this. Suppose that we have a sample of 5 firms, each producing output y_0. The points *A, B, C, D,* and

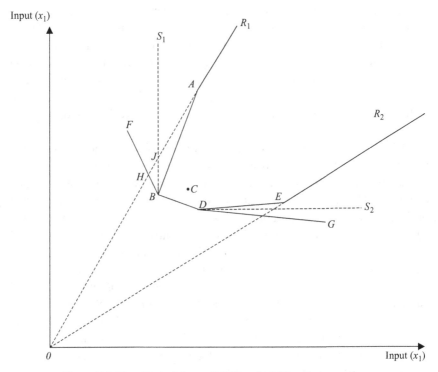

Figure 7.5 The effect of the availability of additional observations
on efficiency measurement.

E show their input bundles. Then, the empirically constructed isoquant for output y_0 is the broken line $S_1 B D S_2$ under free disposability and $R_1 A B D E R_2$ under weak disposability of inputs. Now, suppose that bundles shown by points F and G also can produce y_0. In that case, the isoquant would include the segment $FBDG$. The efficient projection of the point A would be the point H and the technical efficiency of the firm would be $\frac{OH}{OA}$. When points F and G are not observed, the projection of A onto the free-disposal isoquant is the point J and the associated efficiency measure is $\frac{OJ}{OA}$. Note that this is closer to the "true" efficiency than the 100% efficiency measure obtained under weak disposability. The firm at point A is using more of both inputs compared to the one at point B to produce the same level of output. Normally, this would be evidence of inefficiency. But assumption of weak disposability rationalizes the performance of this firm. Therefore, one should consider a possibility of input congestion and implied negative shadow prices only in very special situations and *a priori* rather than on empirical evidence from a sample.

7.7 Summary

At a more fundamental level, availability of inputs acts as a constraint on the producer because there are both private and social opportunity costs of these resources. Similarly, outputs yield private and social benefits. Ideally, shadow prices of both inputs and outputs should be strictly positive. When input or output slacks are present at any point on the frontier, the associated shadow prices become zero. But, in most applications, slacks arise principally out of the limited range of variation of inputs and outputs in any sample of observed points. A parametric characterization of the technology allows out-of-sample extrapolation showing a strictly increasing production function or downward-sloping isoquants. The much weaker assumption underlying DEA can merely project a horizontal production function outside the sample range. Thus, the zero value of the shadow price of any resource does not imply that there is no opportunity cost to it. It merely recognizes that there is not sufficient information in the data to evaluate its marginal contribution.

There have been many attempts in the DEA literature to handle the presence of slacks. The earliest attempt was by Charnes, Cooper, and Rhodes (1979), who modified the original CCR model and incorporated an infinitesimally small penalty for slacks in the objective function. AR analysis and the comparable CR analysis put prior restrictions on the shadow prices. This enlarges the production possibility set beyond the usual free disposal convex hull (or the conical hull, in the case of CRS) of the observed bundles and rules out horizontal or vertical segments of input or output isoquants. Although AR/CR analysis provides a potentially helpful tool for obtaining a more accurate measure of technical efficiency, the multiplier bounds should be specified carefully. The weak disposability and congestion approach works in the opposite direction by actually contracting the production possibility set. Whereas vertical or horizontal segments of isoquants are ruled out, strictly upward rising segments are permitted. By implication, zero shadow prices are ruled out but negative shadow prices are allowed. In the absence of compelling prior reasons, assuming weak disposability may lead to rationalizing inefficiency as congestion.

Guide to the Literature

AR analysis was introduced by Thompson, Singleton, Thrall, and Smith (1986) and was further developed by Thompson, Langemeir, Lee, Lee, and Thrall (1990). CR analysis was developed by Charnes, Cooper, Wei, and Huang (1989) and Charnes, Cooper, Huang, and Sun (1990). Dyson and Thanassoulis (1988); Roll, Cook, and Golany (1991); and Roll and Golany (1993) consider the efficiency implication of various types of restrictions on the multipliers.

Färe and Svensson (1980) introduced the concept of congestion in the context of weak disposability of inputs. Färe and Grosskopf (1983) and Färe, Grosskopf, and Lovell (1983, 1985) developed the measure of congestion efficiency. The concept of weak disposability and congestion has been utilized by Färe, Grosskopf, Lovell, and Pasurka (1989) and Färe, Grosskopf, Lovell, and Yaiswarng (1993) for efficiency measurement and derivation of shadow prices in the context of technologies involving some undesirable outputs. A different approach to measuring input congestion was introduced by Brockett, Cooper, Shin, and Wang (1998).

8

Efficiency of Merger and Breakup of Firms

8.1 Introduction

The primary focus in technical efficiency analysis is on the observed input and output quantities of any individual firm. A pair of input–output bundles is deemed efficient if there is no potential for a radial increase in outputs without any increase in inputs or for an equiproportionate reduction in inputs without a reduction in outputs. In evaluating the technical efficiency of the merger of a number of firms into a single firm, we go beyond the efficiency of the observed input–output bundles of the concerned firms. Instead, we consider the output producible by a single firm from the combined input bundles of these firms and compare it with the total output from the efficient operation of the existing firms operating as separate entities. Merger of firms is quite common in real life. Megamergers between very large banks in the United States or between major airlines like USAir and Piedmont are merely the more notable examples of the ongoing restructuring process in many industries in recent years. There are many reasons why firms decide to merge. But when the output from the combined input bundle is greater than the combined output from the constituent individual input bundles, merger improves technical efficiency.

The flip side of mergers is the breakup of a single firm into a number of smaller firms. The best example from recent years is the breakup of the Bell Telephone companies in the United States into a number of independent Baby Bell firms.[1] Again, whereas breakup of a firm may be justified on a variety of grounds, such breakup would be rational on grounds of technical efficiency when the combined output (at full efficiency) of the constituent smaller units exceeds the technically efficient output of the large firm.

---

[1] For two different perspectives both using a parametric approach on this restructuring of the Bell System, see Evans and Heckman (1983) and Charnes, Cooper, and Sueyoshi (1988).

In this chapter, we consider the technical efficiency gains from mergers or breakup of firms. Potential gains from merger of two or more firms exist when the production technology is superadditive. Similarly, in the presence of subadditivity, breaking up an existing firm into several smaller firms would be technically efficient. The theoretical concepts of and the conditions for super- or subadditivity of the technology are discussed in Section 8.2. In Section 8.3, we describe a decomposition proposed by Bogetoft and Wang (1996) of the gain from merger into a returns to scale effect and a harmony effect. This is followed by an empirical example in Section 8.4. The related concept of *economies of scope* is considered and a relevant DEA model is introduced in Section 8.5. Next, we consider the question of the breakup of a firm and the related concept of "size efficiency" introduced by Maindiratta (1990) in Section 8.6. An empirical example of measuring size efficiency is also included. Section 8.7 summarizes the main points of this chapter.

8.2 Additivity Properties of Technologies

Consider, for simplicity, a single-output, single-input technology. Let the production function be

$$y^* = f(x) \qquad\qquad (8.1a)$$

where y^* is the maximum output producible from the input x. Then, the production possibility set is

$$T = \{(x, y) : y \le f(x)\}. \qquad\qquad (8.1b)$$

As noted earlier, the production function is locally additive, if for n input quantities $x_i(i = 1, 2, \ldots, n)$,

$$f(x_1 + x_2 + \cdots + x_n) = f(x_1) + f(x_2) + \cdots + f(x_n). \qquad (8.2)$$

If, however,

$$f(x_1 + x_2 + \cdots + x_n) > f(x_1) + f(x_2) + \cdots + f(x_n) \qquad (8.3)$$

the production function is locally superadditive. When (8.2) holds for all n-tuples of inputs, the technology is globally additive. Similarly, superadditivity holds globally when (8.3) holds for all n-tuples of inputs. Conversely, the technology is subadditive, if

$$f(x_1 + x_2 + \cdots + x_n) < f(x_1) + f(x_2) + \cdots + f(x_n). \qquad (8.4)$$

As is shown herein, the sub/superadditivity properties of the technology are closely related to but at the same time subtly different from its returns to scale properties.

Consider a simple example. Let the production function be

$$f(x) = 2\sqrt{x} - 4, \quad x \geq 4. \tag{8.5}$$

For the input quantities $x_1 = 6$ and $x_2 = 18$, the corresponding efficient output levels are $f(x_1) = 0.8890$ and $f(x_2) = 4.4853$. Thus, the combined output of two firms using these two input quantities at full technical efficiency is 5.3848. On the other hand, the efficient output of a single firm using the combined input quantity is $f(x_1 + x_2) = 5.7980$. Thus, merger of the two firms would result in a 7.67% increase in the producible output. For this pair of input quantities, the production function exhibits superadditivity.

Now, take a different example. Suppose the two input quantities were $x_1 = 9$ and $x_2 = 25$. This time, the respective output quantities would be $f(x_1) = 2$, $f(x_2) = 6$, and $f(x_1 + x_2) = 7.6619$. Thus, merger would result in a 4.23% decline in the maximum producible output from the separate operation of the individual firms. Hence, the production function exhibits subadditivity for this pair of input quantities.

We now examine why, for the same underlying production function, we get two different verdicts on the technical efficiency of mergers for these two different pairs of input quantities. For this, we consider the expression

$$G(x_1, x_2) = f(x_1 + x_2) - [f(x_1) + f(x_2)]. \tag{8.6}$$

Define $\bar{x} = \frac{1}{2}(x_1 + x_2)$ and $\bar{f}(x_1, x_2) = \frac{1}{2}[f(x_1) + f(x_2)]$.
Then,

$$G(x_1, x_2) = f(2\bar{x}) - 2\bar{f}(x_1, x_2). \tag{8.7}$$

This may also be expressed as

$$G(x_1, x_2) = [f(2\bar{x}) - 2f(\bar{x})] - 2[\bar{f}(x_1, x_2) - f(\bar{x})]. \tag{8.8}$$

The first expression in square brackets on the right-hand side relates to the returns to scale at the mean input level $\bar{x}$ and will be positive (negative) when increasing (diminishing) returns to scale hold over the input range $(\bar{x}, 2\bar{x})$. The other expression in square brackets pertains to the curvature of the production function. If the production function is concave (convex), this expression is negative (positive) so that (with the negative sign attached to it) it contributes positively (negatively) to the gains from merger. This curvature component depends on the second derivative of the production function and also the difference between the two input levels. Assume that $(x_2 - x_1) = \delta > 0$ so that $(x_2 - \bar{x}) = \frac{\delta}{2}$ and $(x_1 - \bar{x}) = -\frac{\delta}{2}$.

Then, a second-order Taylor's series approximation of $f(x)$ at $x = \bar{x}$ is

$$f(x) = f(\bar{x}) + (x - \bar{x})f'(\bar{x}) + \frac{1}{2}f''(\bar{x})(x - \bar{x})^2. \tag{8.9}$$

By this approximation,

$$f(x_1) = f(\bar{x}) + (x_1 - \bar{x})f'(\bar{x}) + \frac{1}{2}f''(\bar{x})(x_1 - \bar{x})^2 \tag{8.10a}$$

and

$$f(x_2) = f(\bar{x}) + (x_2 - \bar{x})f'(\bar{x}) + \frac{1}{2}f''(\bar{x})(x_2 - \bar{x})^2. \tag{8.10b}$$

Therefore,

$$\bar{f}(x_1, x_2) = f(\bar{x}) + \frac{1}{8}f''(\bar{x})\delta^2. \tag{8.11}$$

Hence, the curvature component can be approximated as $-\frac{\delta^2}{8}f''(\bar{x})$. Thus, even when the returns-to-scale component is negative, a sufficiently positive contribution of the curvature component may lead to overall positive gains from a merger. When increasing returns to scale holds at both x_1 and x_2, gains from merger would be positive. This can be shown as follows. Let $\frac{x_1 + x_2}{x_1} = \beta_1$ and $\frac{x_1 + x_2}{x_2} = \beta_2$. Thus, $(x_1 + x_2) = \beta_1 x_1$ and $(x_1 + x_2) = \beta_2 x_2$. Further, both β_1 and β_2 exceed unity. Also, $\frac{1}{\beta_1} + \frac{1}{\beta_2} = 1$. Hence, if increasing returns to scale holds,

$$f(\beta_1 x_1) = f(x_1 + x_2) > \beta_1 f(x_1) \tag{8.12a}$$

and

$$f(\beta_2 x_2) = f(x_1 + x_2) > \beta_2 f(x_2). \tag{8.12b}$$

Thus,

$$\left(\frac{1}{\beta_1} + \frac{1}{\beta_2}\right) f(x_1 + x_2) = f(x_1 + x_2) > f(x_1) + f(x_2). \tag{8.13}$$

Of course, when globally increasing (decreasing) returns holds, gains from merger will necessarily be positive (negative) for any pair of input quantities. Hence, globally increasing returns to scale is a sufficient condition for superadditivity of the technology implying positive gains from merger of smaller firms into a single large firm. That would be an example of natural monopoly. But, as is evident from the numerical example provided previously, positive gains from merger are possible in specific cases even when the production function does not exhibit increasing returns everywhere. Indeed, in the example that we considered, the most productive scale size was $x^* = 16$. For $4 \leq x < 16$, increasing returns to scale held, whereas diminishing returns to scale prevailed for $x > 16$. Thus, in the first numerical example, x_1 was in the region of increasing returns but x_2 was in the region of diminishing returns. Even then, gain from merger was positive. This shows that prevalence of increasing returns at both input levels is not necessary for merger to be technically efficient.

8.3 Measurement and Decomposition of Gains from Merger

In this section, we consider a DEA model for measuring the gain from the merger of a number of firms. Bogetoft and Wang (1996) provide a measure of merger efficiency and its multiplicative decomposition into a harmony effect and a returns-to-scale effect.[2]

Consider the single-output, two-input technology defined by the production function

$$y = g(x_1, x_2). \tag{8.14}$$

The two firms 1 and 2 use the two input bundles $x^1 = (x_{11}, x_{12})$ and $x^2 = (x_{21}, x_{22})$. Assume, initially, that the firms produce the levels of output y_A and y_B, respectively, and both are technically efficient. Thus, both bundles lie on the efficient subset of the isoquants shown in Figure 8.1. The points A and B show the two input bundles. The point C represents the sum of the two input bundles x^1 and x^2. Merger of the two firms will be efficient if the bundle C produces greater output than $y_A + y_D$. First, define the point D representing the input bundle $\bar{x} = \frac{1}{2}(x^1 + x^2)$. Following Bogetoft and Wang, we conceptualize the merger of the two firms as a two-step process. In the first step, we consider a firm that uses the average input bundle $\bar{x}$. In the second step, this average firm is doubled in scale to become the merged firm shown by the point C. Define $\bar{y} = \frac{1}{2}(y_A + y_B)$. Assuming that the isoquants are convex, the bundle $\bar{x}$ shown by the point D will produce output $y_D \geq \bar{y}$. Bogetoft and Wang call this increase in output the *harmony effect* because if the firms shared the combined input equally and used the identical (average)

---

[2] Whereas Bogetoft and Wang consider input-oriented efficiency, the discussion of technical efficiency here is output-oriented.

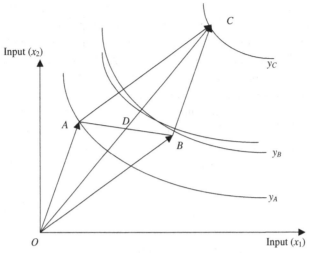

Figure 8.1 Output from the combined input bundles of two firms.

bundle, each would produce this higher level of output. Thus, the *combined output of two identical average firms* would be $2y_D$. Next, consider the output y_T *produced from the combined input bundle by a single firm*. The efficiency of merger can be measured as

$$ME\,(x^1, x^2) = \frac{y_T}{2\bar{y}}. \tag{8.15}$$

When ME exceeds unity, potential gains from merger of the two firms would be positive. We may further decompose the merger efficiency as

$$ME\,(x^1, x^2) = \left(\frac{y_D}{\bar{y}}\right) \cdot \left(\frac{y_T}{2y_D}\right). \tag{8.16}$$

The harmony effect is

$$H = \frac{y_D}{\bar{y}} \tag{8.17a}$$

and the scale effect is

$$S = \frac{y_T}{2y_D}. \tag{8.17b}$$

As noted previously, the harmony effect is generally greater than unity. But the scale effect may be greater than, equal to, or less than unity depending on whether increasing, constant, or diminishing returns holds at the average input bundle.

We now consider the DEA model for measuring the output-oriented merger efficiency and its components in the single-output, multiple-input case. As before, let the vector $x^j = (x_{1j}, x_{2j}, \ldots, x_{nj})$ be the input bundle and the scalar y_j the output of firm $j (j = 1, 2, \ldots, N)$. Suppose that we are considering the potential gains from the merger of K firms – firm 1, firm 2, ..., firm K. For this, we proceed through the following steps:

Step 1: First solve the following output-oriented BCC DEA problem for each firm k $(k = 1, 2, \ldots, K)$:

$$\max \varphi_k$$

$$\text{s. t.} \sum_{j=1}^{N} \lambda_j y^j \geq \varphi_k y_k;$$

$$\sum_{j=1}^{N} \lambda_j x^j \leq x^k; \tag{8.18}$$

$$\sum_{j=1}^{N} \lambda_j x^j = 1;$$

$$\lambda_j \geq 0; \quad (j = 1, 2, \ldots, N); \quad \varphi_k \text{ free.}$$

From the optimal solution of (8.18), construct the efficient input–output combination (x_*^k, y_*^k) where $y_*^k = \varphi_k^* y_k$ and x_*^k is the slack-adjusted input bundle. Note that x_*^k lies on the efficient subset of the isoquant for the output level y_*^k.

Step 2: Construct the average input bundle

$$\bar{x} = \frac{1}{K} \sum_{k=1}^{K} x_*^k$$

and the average output level

$$\bar{y} = \frac{1}{K} \sum_{k=1}^{K} y_*^k.$$

Step 3: Solve the BCC DEA problem

$$\max \varphi^{\mathrm{H}}$$

$$\text{s.t.} \sum_{j=1}^{N} \lambda_j y^j \geq \varphi^{\mathrm{H}} \bar{y};$$

$$\sum_{j=1}^{N} \lambda_j x^j \geq \bar{x}; \qquad (8.19)$$

$$\sum_{j=1}^{N} \lambda_j x^j = 1;$$

$$\lambda_j \geq 0; \quad (j = 1, 2, \ldots, N); \quad \varphi^{\mathrm{H}} \text{ free.}$$

Step 4: Define the total (slack-adjusted) input bundle of the K firms,

$$x^{\mathrm{T}} = K\bar{x}, \qquad (8.20a)$$

and the total output

$$y_{\mathrm{T}} = K\bar{y}. \qquad (8.20b)$$

Step 5: Solve the BCC DEA problem

$$\max \varphi^{\mathrm{T}}$$

$$\text{subject to} \sum_{j=1}^{N} \lambda_j y^j \geq \varphi^{\mathrm{T}} y_T;$$

$$\sum_{j=1}^{N} \lambda_j x^j \leq x^{\mathrm{T}}; \qquad (8.21)$$

$$\sum_{j=1}^{N} \lambda_j x^j = 1;$$

$$\lambda_j \geq 0; \quad (j = 1, 2, \ldots, N); \quad \varphi^{\mathrm{T}} \text{ free.}$$

Step 6: Compute the merger efficiency as

$$ME = \varphi_*^{\mathrm{T}}. \qquad (8.22a)$$

The harmony and scale components are computed as

$$H = \varphi_*^{\mathrm{H}} \qquad (8.22b)$$

and

$$S = \frac{\varphi_*^T}{\varphi_*^H}.$$ (8.22c)

A value of ME greater than unity implies that gains from merger will be positive whereas a value less than unity shows that it would be more efficient to leave the firms as separate entities. As noted before, for a convex production possibility set, H will be greater than unity. Finally, when S exceeds unity, the merged firm produces more output than what two firms each using the average input bundle would produce collectively. In this case, the returns-to-scale effect favors a merger of the individual firms. It is possible that even though S is less than unity, the harmony effect H dominates and overall M is greater than unity. Several points need to be noted here. First, as emphasized by Bogetoft and Wang, unless both bundles lie on the same isoquant, output of the average bundle will incorporate some scale effect along with the harmony effect.[3] Second, one needs to adjust the observed input–output quantities of the firms under consideration for merger for any technical inefficiency in the output and for slacks in the inputs. In the multiple-output case, we need also to adjust the optimal output bundles for slacks. However, even when output slacks are present in the optimal solution of (8.20), no adjustment should be made in the definition of $\bar{y}$ for the DEA problem in (8.21). Otherwise, φ^T and φ^H would not refer to radial expansion of the same output vector and, therefore, the scale factor measure in (8.22c) will not be meaningful.

8.4 An Empirical Example of Evaluating Gain from Mergers

For this example, we consider Christensen–Greene's electrical utilities data set used in the earlier chapters. Specifically, we evaluate the potential gain from the merger of utilities #43 and #53 (arbitrarily selected) from Table 6.3. Table 8.1 shows the actual input–output quantities of the two firms considered for merger.

Output-oriented BCC DEA models were run for each firm to eliminate technical inefficiencies and relevant input slacks. The revised input–output bundles, along with the aggregate and the average bundles, are shown in Table 8.2.

---

[3] In the differential decomposition shown in (8.9), the two output levels need not be equal. However, when the two output bundles are far apart, the second-order approximation at the mean output bundle will have a large approximation error.

Table 8.1. *Actual output and input quantities for U.S.*
electrical utilities

	Firm #43	Firm #53
Output	4148	6770
Labor	27.2748	50.4825
Fuel	48273	72407
Capital	4805.4	14797

The DEA problem (8.19) was solved for the average output and input quantity data shown in the last column of Table 2. The optimal solution was $\varphi_*^H = 1.0152$, implying the efficient output level 7252.9405 producible from the average input bundle. Subsequently, the DEA problem (8.21) was solved for the total input–output bundle shown in Table 8.2. The optimal solution was $\varphi_*^T = 0.981942$ and the implied maximum output level of 14031.285 from the merger of the two firms. Note that a value of φ_*^T less than unity implies that the firm formed by the merger of the two separate firms being considered would produce lower output than the combined output of the firms from their separate input bundles. The merger efficiency is $ME = 0.9819$, a value less than unity. This implies that it is more efficient to leave the two firms as separate entities rather than to merge them into a single production unit. The harmony effect $H = \varphi_*^H = 1.0152$ shows that two firms, each using the average input bundle, can together produce 1.52% more output than what they would produce collectively when using their different input bundles. But the scale effect

$$S = \frac{\varphi_*^T}{\varphi_*^H} = \frac{0.98194}{1.0151} = 0.96728$$

implies that a single firm using twice the average input bundle would produce 3.2718% lower output than what two firms could produce together if each used the average input bundle. In this case, the negative scale effect overwhelms the positive harmony effect.

Table 8.2. *Efficient output and input quantities for U.S. electrical utilities*

	Firm #43	Firm #53	Total	Average
Output	5314.1425	8975.1805	14289.32	7144.662
Labor	27.2748	50.4825	77.7609	38.88045
Fuel	48273	72407	120680	60340
Capital	4805.4	12341.901	17148.3	8574.151

8.5 Economies of Scope and Gains from Diversification

In some cases, it is technically more efficient if an output bundle is produced by a single diversified firm than if each individual output is produced by a separate specialized firm. Such gains from a merger of several specialized firms to form a diversified firm derive from what is known as *economies of scope*. This section describes how one can use DEA to determine whether a merger between two firms results in economies of scope.

For simplicity, consider the case of two outputs and n inputs. Further suppose that the observed input–output data come from three groups of firms: A, B, and C. Firms in group A produce only output 1, firms in group B produce output 2 only, and firms in group C produce both outputs. The output "bundles" of the specialized firms can be expressed as $y^A = (y_{1j}^A, 0)$ and $y^B = (0, y_{2j}^B)$; the output bundle of a diversified firm is $y^C = (y_{1j}^C, y_{2j}^C)$. Assume that firms from all groups use all the inputs so that their input bundles are not specialized. Next, consider two firms – one of type A and another of type B. Suppose that their input and output bundles are

$$x_0^A = \left(x_{10}^A, x_{20}^A, \ldots, x_{n0}^A\right) \quad \text{and} \quad y_0^A = \left(y_{10}^A, 0\right) \quad \text{for the group } A \text{ firm}$$

and

$$x_0^B = \left(x_{10}^B, x_{20}^B, \ldots, x_{n0}^B\right) \quad \text{and} \quad y_0^B = \left(0, y_{20}^B\right) \quad \text{for the group } B \text{ firm.}$$

Let

$$\theta_0^{*A} = \min \theta : \theta x_0^A \in V\left(y_0^A\right)$$

and

$$\theta_0^{*B} = \min \theta : \theta x_0^B \in V\left(y_0^B\right).$$

Define

$$x_0^{*A} = \theta_0^{*A} x_0^A - s_0^{*A}, \quad x_0^{*B} = \theta_0^{*B} x_0^B - s_0^{*B}, \quad x_*^{AB} = x_0^{*A} + x_0^{*B}, \quad \text{and}$$
$$y_0^{AB} = y_0^A + y_0^B.$$

Here, the vectors s_0^{*A} and s_0^{*B} are the input slacks at the efficient radial projections of the input bundles of the specialized firms.

The input set for the diversified output bundle y_0^{AB} can be specified as follows:

$$V\left(y_0^{AB}\right) = \left\{ x : \sum_{j \in A} \lambda_j^A x_j^A + \sum_{j \in B} \lambda_j^B x_j^B + \sum_{j \in C} \lambda_j^C x_j^C \leq x; \right.$$

$$\sum_{j \in A} \lambda_j^A y_j^A + \sum_{j \in B} \lambda_j^B y_j^B + \sum_{j \in C} \lambda_j^C y_j^C \geq y_0^{AB}; \quad (8.23)$$

$$\left. \sum_{j \in A} \lambda_j^A + \sum_{j \in B} \lambda_j^B + \sum_{j \in C} \lambda_j^C = 1; \lambda_j^A, \lambda_j^B, \lambda_j^C \geq 0 \right\}.$$

There are positive economies of scope if there is any $x \in V(y_0^{AB}) : x \leq x_*^{AB}$.

The efficient input bundles x_0^{*A} and x_0^{*B} can be obtained directly from the optimal solution of the relevant input-oriented BCC models as follows:

$$\theta_0^{*A} = \min \theta$$

$$\text{s.t. } \sum_{j \in A} \lambda_j^A y_{1j}^A + \sum_{j \in C} \lambda_j^C y_{1j}^C \geq y_{10}^A;$$

$$\sum_{j \in A} \lambda_j^A x_j^A + \sum_{j \in C} \lambda_j^C x_j^C - s_0^A = \theta x_0^A; \quad (8.24)$$

$$\sum_{j \in A} \lambda_j^A + \sum_{j \in C} \lambda_j^C = 1;$$

$$s_0^A \geq 0; \quad \lambda_j^A, \lambda_j^C \geq 0.$$

and

$$\theta_0^{*B} = \min \theta$$

$$\text{s.t. } \sum_{j \in A} \lambda_j^B y_{2j}^B + \sum_{j \in C} \lambda_j^C y_{2j}^C \geq y_{20}^B;$$

$$\sum_{j \in A} \lambda_j^B x_j^B + \sum_{j \in C} \lambda_j^C x_j^C - s_0^B = \theta x_0^B; \quad (8.25)$$

$$\sum_{j \in A} \lambda_j^B + \sum_{j \in C} \lambda_j^C = 1;$$

$$s_0^B \geq 0; \quad \lambda_j^B, \lambda_j^C \geq 0.$$

For the diversified model, we solve the following DEA problem:

$$\max \iota' z$$

$$\text{s.t.} \quad \sum_{j \in A} \lambda_j^A y_{1j}^A + \sum_{j \in C} \lambda_j^C y_{1j}^C \geq y_{10}^A;$$

$$\sum_{j \in A} \lambda_j^B y_{2j}^B + \sum_{j \in C} \lambda_j^C y_{2j}^C \geq y_{20}^B; \tag{8.26}$$

$$\sum_{j \in A} \lambda_j^A x_j^A + \sum_{j \in A} \lambda_j^B x_j^B + \sum_{j \in C} \lambda_j^C x_j^C - z = x_*^{AB};$$

$$z \geq 0; \quad \lambda_j^A, \lambda_j^B, \lambda_j^C \geq 0.$$

In this problem, ι is a column vector with each element equal to 1, and z is a vector of nonnegative input slacks. If the optimal value of the objective function in this problem is greater than 0, then there is room for reducing at least one input and positive economies of scope exist.

It is important to note that the DEA problem (8.26) may not have a feasible solution, even though feasible solutions do exist for the problems for the specialized firms.

8.6 Breakup of a Large Firm

In this section, we describe a method introduced by Maindiratta (1990) to determine whether it is technically more efficient to break up a large firm with a specific input bundle into a number of smaller firms than to let it operate as a single production unit. Again, consider the single-output, multiple-input case. Clearly, when the production function is subadditive at the input bundle x^0, there exist K smaller input bundles x^k $(k = 1, 2, \ldots, K)$ such that $\sum_1^K x^k = x^0$ and $\sum_1^K f(x^k) > f(x^0)$. In this case, it is technically more efficient to break up a single firm using the input bundle x^0 into K smaller firms using the bundles $x^k (k = 1, 2, \ldots, K)$. In that sense, a single firm using input x^0 is too large. Specifically, suppose that (x^0, y_0) is the observed input–output combination of the firm. Further, let $f(x^0) = \varphi_0^* y_0$ be the maximum output producible from x^0. Similarly, let $y_*^k = \varphi_*^k y_0 = f(x^k)$ be the maximum output producible from the input bundle x^k. Then, the K smaller bundles would collectively produce the output $\sum_{k=1}^K y_*^k = (\sum_{k=1}^K \varphi_k^*) y_0$ from the input bundle x^0. Thus, the single firm using the input bundle x^0 is too large if $\sum_{k=1}^K \varphi_k^* > \varphi_0^*$.

We need to address two questions before we can proceed any further. First, how do we decide the number of smaller firms that the existing firm should be broken up into, if it is to be broken up at all? In other words, how do we determine K? Second, how do we determine the size of each constituent input bundle after the breakup? We address the second question first. To do this, set K to some positive integer value tentatively. Our objective initially is to determine the composition of the K individual input bundles that will maximize the collective output producible from them. Let x^j be the jth input bundle and y_j the maximum output producible from x^j. Clearly, under the usual assumptions of DEA, (x^j, y_j) would be a feasible input–output combination as long as there exists some $\lambda^j = (\lambda_{1j}, \lambda_{2j}, \ldots, \lambda_{Nj})$ such that $\sum_{s=1}^{N} \lambda_{sj} x^s \leq x^j$, $\sum_{s=1}^{N} \lambda_{sj} y_s \geq y_j$, $\sum_{s=1}^{N} \lambda_{sj} = 1$, and $\lambda_{sj} \geq 0$ $(s = 1, 2, \ldots, N)$. The collective output from the K individual input bundles would be $\sum_{j=1}^{K} y_j$. The problem is to select the vectors $\lambda^j (j = 1, 2, \ldots, K)$ so as to maximize φ where $\sum_{j=1}^{K} y_j \geq \varphi y_0$. For this, we solve the following DEA problem:

$$\max \varphi$$

$$\text{s.t.} \quad \sum_{s=1}^{N} \lambda_{sj} x^s = x^j; \quad (j = 1, 2, \ldots, K)$$

$$\sum_{s=1}^{N} \lambda_{sj} y_s = y_j; \quad (j = 1, 2, \ldots, K)$$

$$\sum_{j=1}^{K} x^j \leq x^0; \qquad\qquad\qquad (8.27)$$

$$\sum_{j=1}^{K} y_j \geq \varphi y_0;$$

$$\sum_{s=1}^{N} \lambda_{sj} = 1; \quad (j = 1, 2, \ldots, K);$$

$$\lambda_{sj} \geq 0; \quad (s = 1, 2, \ldots, N; j = 1, 2, \ldots, N).$$

Suppose that the optimal solution yields the vectors $\lambda_*^j (j = 1, 2, \ldots, K)$. Define the bundles $x_*^j = \sum_{s=1}^{N} \lambda_{sj}^* x^s$. Then, $\sum_{j=1}^{K} x_*^j = \sum_{j=1}^{K} (\sum_{s=1}^{N} \lambda_{sj}^* x^s) \leq x^0$. Now, for each s $(s = 1, 2, \ldots, N)$, define $\bar{\lambda}_s = \frac{1}{K} \sum_{j=1}^{K} \lambda_{sj}$ and construct an input bundle $\bar{x} = \sum_{s=1}^{N} \bar{\lambda}_s x^s$. Then,

$$\bar{x} = \frac{1}{K} \sum_{j=1}^{K} \sum_{s=1}^{N} \lambda_{sj} x^s.$$

Similarly, define

$$\bar{y} = \sum_{s=1}^{N} \bar{\lambda}_s y^s = \frac{1}{K} \sum_{j=1}^{K} \sum_{s=1}^{N} \lambda_{sj} y_s.$$

Set each $x^j = \bar{x}$ and $y_j = \bar{y}$. Then,

$$\sum_{j=1}^{K} x^j = K\bar{x} = \sum_{j=1}^{K} \sum_{s=1}^{N} \lambda_{sj} x^s \le x^0$$

and

$$\sum_{j=1}^{K} y_j = K\bar{y} = \sum_{j=1}^{K} \sum_{s=1}^{N} \lambda_{sj} y_s \ge \varphi^* y_0.$$

Hence, an alternative solution is one in which each smaller input bundle equals $\bar{x}$ and the corresponding output is $\bar{y}$, where the same optimal value of the objective function φ^* is attained. This alternative problem can be set up as

$$\max \varphi$$

$$\text{s.t.} \quad K \left(\sum_{s=1}^{N} \bar{\lambda}_s x^s \right) \le x^0;$$

$$K \left(\sum_{s=1}^{N} \bar{\lambda}_s y_s \right) \ge \varphi y_0;$$

$$\sum_{s=1}^{N} \bar{\lambda}_s = 1; \quad \bar{\lambda}_s \ge 0 \, (s = 1, 2, \ldots N).$$

(8.28)

Of course, we still need to determine K. At this point, all we know is that K is some positive integer. Now, define $\alpha_s = K\bar{\lambda}_s (s = 1, 2, \ldots, N)$. Then, the

DEA problem (8.28) becomes

$$\max \varphi$$

$$\text{s.t. } \sum_{s=1}^{N} \alpha_s x^s \leq x^0;$$

$$\sum_{s=1}^{N} \alpha_s y_s \geq \varphi y_0; \tag{8.29}$$

$$\sum_{s=1}^{N} \alpha_s = K;$$

$$\alpha_s \geq 0 \ (s = 1, 2, \ldots, N); \quad K \in \{1, 2, \ldots\}.$$

At the optimal solution of this problem, K^* represents the desired number of smaller units into which the single firm should be broken up. Note that this is a mixed-integer programming problem in which one variable (K) is constrained to be a positive integer whereas the other variables can take any nonnegative value. An interesting feature of this problem is that if K is preset to 1, it reduces to the familiar BCC problem for a VRS technology. On the other hand, if K is allowed to take any positive value (not necessarily an integer), the problem in (8.29) reduces to the output-oriented CCR problem for a CRS technology. Suppose that the maximum value of the objective function in problem (8.29) is φ^K and those in the corresponding BCC and CCR problems are φ^V and φ^C, respectively. Then, by virtue of the hierarchy of the feasible sets of the problems,

$$\varphi^V \leq \varphi^K \leq \varphi^C. \tag{8.30}$$

As is well known, the scale efficiency of the input bundle x^0 is measured as

$$SE = \frac{\varphi^V}{\varphi^C} \leq 1.$$

Maindiratta defines the *size efficiency* of the firm as

$$\sigma = \frac{\varphi^V}{\varphi^K} \leq 1. \tag{8.31}$$

It is clear from (8.31) that

$$SE \leq \sigma \leq 1. \tag{8.32}$$

If $\sigma = 1$, there is no size inefficiency and even when we are allowed to select *any integer value* for K in problem (8.29), the optimal solution selects $K^* = 1$.

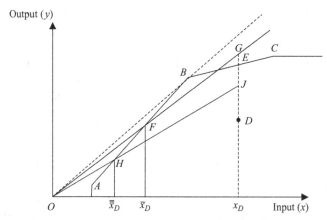

Figure 8.2 An example of size inefficiency: break up of firm leads to higher output.

If, on the other hand, $K^* > 1$, the firm is size inefficient. Deviation of the measure σ from unity shows the shortfall in output from a single-firm production relative to a multifirm production using the same input bundle x^0.

It needs to be emphasized that locally diminishing returns to scale at x^0 is a necessary but not a sufficient condition for size inefficiency. Thus, a firm that is smaller than the MPSS for its input mix is never a candidate for breakup into a number of smaller firms. But a firm that is larger than its MPSS is not automatically a candidate for breakup simply because it is operating in the region of diminishing returns to scale.

The concept of size efficiency and its difference from scale efficiency is best explained by making use of a diagram. In Figure 8.2, the VRS production possibility set is shown by the free disposal convex hull of the points A, B, C, and D representing the observed input–output bundles of 4 firms. Consider point D, where the firm produces output Dx_D using x_D units of the input. If technical inefficiency is eliminated, the firm moves to the point E on the frontier and produces output Ex_D from the same input quantity x_D. Now, suppose the input x_D is split equally and allocated to two firms. Each of the two firms uses input $\bar{x}_D = \frac{1}{2}x_D$ and at full efficiency produces output $F\bar{x}_D$. Together, the two firms produce the output level $Gx_D = 2F\bar{x}_D$ from x_D units of the input. This is greater than the maximum output Ex_D that a single firm can produce using input x_D. It is, therefore, technically more efficient to break up the firm D into two smaller identical firms. A measure of its size efficiency is

$$\sigma(D) = \frac{Ex_D}{Gx_D}.$$

What would happen if we broke the firm D into 3 rather than 2 smaller units? In that case, each subunit would be using the input level $\bar{\bar{x}}_D = \frac{1}{3}x_D$ and (at full efficiency) would produce the output level $H\bar{\bar{x}}_D$. Collectively, the smaller firms would produce the output Jx_D from the input x_D as shown in Figure 8.3. This output is not only lower than Gx_D (what we get from a breakup of D into two smaller firms) but even less than what a single efficient firm would produce from x_D. Thus, the optimal value of K (the number of units that the firm D should be broken up into) is 2.

Note that size efficiency of the firm D is the ratio of the average productivities at E (the output-oriented efficient projection of D) and F (the efficient output for the input $\bar{x}_D$). Scale efficiency, on the other hand, is the ratio of the average productivities at E and at B (the point on the frontier that corresponds to the MPSS, x^*). Even though x_D exceeds x^*, the ratio $\frac{x_D}{x^*}$ is usually not an integer. Unless we assume CRS, the point L is not attainable by any replication of the input–output bundle observed at the MPSS. Suppose that we decided to create one firm with input x^* producing output Bx^* and another firm using the residual input $x^R = x^D - x^*$ producing output Mx^R, the collective output from these two firms will not be equal to Lx^D.

Figure 8.3 shows the case where even though the firm D operates in the region of diminishing returns to scale, breaking it up into two or more firms would not be technically more efficient that allowing it to operate as a single firm. In this example, if the firm is broken up into two smaller firms, each using input $\bar{x}_D$ and producing output $F\bar{x}_D$, their combined output is Gx_D, which is less than what a single firm could efficiently produce from input x_D. Breaking it up into 3 or more smaller firms is not efficient either. Thus, even though the

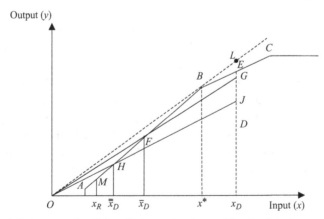

Figure 8.3 An example of size efficiency: break up of firm leads to lower output.

Table 8.3. *Input–output data for testing size efficiency*

Firm	A	B	C	D	E
Input (x)	4	6	10	12	14
Output (y)	6	11	12	9	17

firm operates under diminishing returns to scale, it is not size inefficient and, in that sense, not "too large."

Although the DEA problem in (8.25) is a mixed-integer programming problem, given that the integer constraint applies to only one variable, one can solve the problem easily using the "branch and bound" algorithm. The steps are as follows:

Step 1: Solve the CCR problem (i.e., without any restriction on the sum of the λ_j's).

Compute $K^* = \sum_{j=1}^{N} \lambda_j^*$. If K^* is an integer, stop; otherwise, go to step 2.

Step 2: Define $K_-^* = [K^*]$ = largest integer no greater than K^*.
Solve the problem (8.26) with the restriction $K = K_-^*$.
Denote the optimal value of the objective function as φ_-^*.

Step 3: Define $K_+^* = [K^*] + 1$.
Solve the problem (8.26) with the restriction $K = K_+^*$.
Denote the optimal value of the objective function as φ_+^*.

Step 4: $\varphi^{**} = \max\{\varphi_-^*, \varphi_+^*\}$. The optimal K is correspondingly determined.

We now consider a simple example of measuring size efficiency. The input–output quantities of five hypothetical firms are shown in Table 8.3.

We measure the size efficiency of firm C. For this, we first solve the output-oriented CCR problem. The optimal solution was $\varphi_E^* = 1.52777$, $\lambda_B^* = 1.667$, $\lambda_j^* = 0 (j = A, C, D, E)$, $K^* = 1.667$. We next set up the following LP problem:

$$\max \varphi$$

$$\text{s.t. } 6\lambda_A + 11\lambda_B + 12\lambda_C + 9\lambda_D + 17\lambda_E \geq 12\varphi;$$

$$4\lambda_A + 6\lambda_B + 10\lambda_C + 12\lambda_D + 14\lambda_E \leq 10; \tag{8.33}$$

$$\lambda_A + \lambda_B + \lambda_C + \lambda_D + \lambda_E = K;$$

$$\lambda_j \geq 0 \ (j = A, B, C, D, E), \varphi \text{ unrestricted.}$$

This problem is solved twice – once for $K = 1$ and again for $K = 2$. For $K = 1$, $\varphi^* = 1.1667$ and for $K = 2$, $\varphi^* = 1.4167$. Hence, the optimal value of K is 2. Note that for $K = 1$, (8.29) becomes the output-oriented BCC DEA problem. Hence, the size efficiency of this firm is

$$\sigma(C) = \frac{1.1667}{1.4167} = 0.8235.$$

A single firm using 10 units of the input can produce, at most, 14 units of the output, whereas two smaller firms each using 5 units of the input can each produce 8.5 units of output. Thus, the total output from two firms would be 17 units, thereby exceeding what can be produced by a single firm using the same input quantity. Hence, this firm is too large and is a candidate for breakup.

We conclude this section with an empirical application. In this application, we again use the Christensen–Greene data set for U.S. electrical utilities and examine whether one of the larger firms in the sample (#93) should be broken up into several smaller firms and, if so, what is its size efficiency. The firm under consideration produces 27,708 units of the output using 144.754 units of labor, 286,748 units of fuel, and 30,910 units of capital. At the optimal solution of the output-oriented CCR DEA problem, $\varphi^* = 1.15156$ and $K^* = \sum_1^N \lambda_j^* = 2.78793$. Hence, the potential values of optimal K are 2 and 3. Recall that for $K = 1$, we merely get the BCC DEA problem for which $\varphi^* = 1.07269$. For the other models, we merely replace the right-hand side of the constraint $\sum_1^N \lambda_j = 1$ in the BCC model by the 2 and 3, respectively. For $K = 2$, we obtain $\varphi^* = 1.12523$, and for $K = 3$, $\varphi^* = 1.15099$. Hence, the optimal value of K is 3. The size efficiency of firm #93 is

$$\sigma = \frac{1.07269}{1.15099} = 0.9351.$$

This implies that a single firm using the input bundle of firm #93 would produce only 93.51% of what 3 identical firms would collectively produce from the same input bundle.

8.7 Summary

Merger and breakup of firms can be justified on a variety of economic grounds. In this chapter, we consider whether a merger of a number of specific firms can be justified on grounds of technical efficiency alone. It should be understood that there could be other reasons why such mergers may not be recommended even when technical gains from merger might be positive. For example, merging two schools from two different parts of the state would not be meaningful even when the DEA models show that the local superadditivity of the technology would justify such mergers. Similarly, breakup of firms is technically justified when the technology is locally subadditive. But, even when that is not the case, breaking up a monopoly in the interest of increased competition would be valid grounds for breakup.

Guide to the Literature

The concept of sub/superadditivity of technology was introduced by Baumol, Panzar, and Willig (1982) in the context of contestable markets and natural monopoly. They also defined *economies of scope* as a special case of subadditivity of the cost function. In the nonparametric literature, Färe (1986) examined the relation between additivity and efficiency. The DEA formulation of merger efficiency and its decomposition is due to Bogetoft and Wang (1996). The concept of size efficiency was introduced by Maindiratta (1990). Ray and Hu (1997) use the size efficiency concept to determine the technically optimal number of firms in the U.S. airline industry. Ray and Mukherjee (1998a) applied the size efficiency model in the case of a cost function using public schools data from Connecticut. Ray and Mukherjee (1998b) used data from U.S. banking to identify banks that are too large and are candidates for breakup into two or more smaller banks.

9

Efficiency Analysis with Market Prices

9.1 Introduction

In DEA models for measuring input-oriented technical efficiency, the objective was to contract *all inputs at the same rate* to the extent possible without reducing any output. In practice, however, some inputs are more valuable than other inputs and conserving such inputs would be more efficient than saving other inputs. When market prices of inputs are available, the firm would seek to minimize the *total input cost* for a given level of output. This would mean not only that inputs are changed by different proportions but also that some inputs may actually be *increased* while others are reduced when that is necessary for cost minimization. Our discussion of DEA, so far, has made no use whatsoever of prices of inputs and/or outputs. Even in our discussion of nonradial measures of efficiency, although disproportionate changes in inputs and outputs were allowed, we did not consider the possibility that some inputs could actually be increased or that some outputs could be reduced. This is principally due to the fact that DEA was originally developed for use in a nonmarket environment where prices are either not available at all or are not reliable, even if they are available. This may give the impression that when accurate price data do exist, it would be more appropriate to measure efficiency using econometric methods with explicitly specified cost or profit functions and not to use DEA. This, however, is not the case. DEA provides a nonparametric alternative to standard econometric modeling even when prices exist; its objective is to analyze the data in order to assess to what extent a firm has achieved the specified objective of cost minimization or profit maximization.

In this chapter, we develop DEA models for cost minimization and profit maximization by a firm that takes input and output prices as given. Section 9.2 begins with a brief review of the cost-minimization problem of a firm facing a competitive input market and presents Farrell's decomposition of cost efficiency into two separate factors measuring technical and allocative efficiency, respectively. Section 9.3 presents the DEA models for cost minimization in the long run when all inputs are variable. The concept of economic scale efficiency is introduced in Section 9.4. The problem of cost minimization in the short run in the presence of quasi-fixed inputs is described in Section 9.5. Section 9.6 provides an empirical example of DEA for cost minimization. In Section 9.7, the output quantities are also treated as choice variables with output prices treated as given and the cost-minimization problem is generalized to a profit-maximization problem. The relevant DEA model is presented in Section 9.8. An additive decomposition of profit efficiency that parallels Farrell's multiplicative decomposition of cost efficiency is shown in Section 9.9. Section 9.10 includes an empirical application of DEA to a profit-maximization problem. The main points of this chapter are summarized in Section 9.11.

9.2 Cost Efficiency and its Decomposition

Consider the cost-minimization problem of a firm that is a price-taker in the input markets and produces a prespecified output level. Many not-for-profit organizations like hospitals, schools, and so forth fit this description. A hospital, for example, does not select the number of patients treated. The output level is exogenously determined. It still has to select the inputs so as to provide this level of care at the minimum cost. For simplicity, we consider a single-output, two-input production technology. Suppose that an observed firm uses the input bundle $x^0 = (x_1^0, x_2^0)$ and produces the scalar output level y_0. The prices of the two inputs are w_1 and w_2, respectively. Thus, the cost incurred by the firm is $C_0 = w_1 x_1^0 + w_2 x_2^0$. The firm is cost efficient if and only if there is no other input bundle that can produce the output level y_0 at a lower cost.

Define the production possibility set

$$T = \{(x_1, x_2; y) : (x_1, x_2) \text{ can produce } y\} \qquad (9.1a)$$

and the corresponding input requirement set for output y_0

$$V(y_0) = \{(x_1, x_2) : (x_1, x_2) \text{ can produce } y_0\} \qquad (9.1b)$$

Then, the cost minimization problem of the firm can be specified as

$$\min w_1 x_1 + w_2 x_2$$
$$\text{s.t.} \quad (x_1, x_2) \in V(y_0). \qquad (9.2)$$

Suppose that an optimal solution of this problem is $x^* = (x_1^*, x_2^*)$. Then, the minimum cost is

$$C^* \equiv C(w_1, w_2; y_0) = w_1 x_1^* + w_2 x_2^*.$$

Note that, by assumption, $x^0 \in V(y_0)$ and is, therefore, a feasible solution for the minimization problem (9.2). Hence, by the definition of a minimum, $C(w_1, w_2; y_0) = w_1 x_1^* + w_2 x_2^* \leq C_0 = w_1 x_1^0 + w_2 x_2^0$. The firm is cost efficient if and only if $C^0 = C^*$. Following Farrell (1957), the cost efficiency of the firm can be measured as

$$\gamma = \frac{C^*}{C_0} \leq 1. \tag{9.3}$$

Now consider, as an aside, the input bundle $x^T = \beta x^0$, which is the efficient radial projection of the input bundle x^0 for the output level y_0. The cost of this technically efficient bundle $x^T = (\beta x_1, \beta x_2)$ is

$$C^T = \beta^*(w_1 x_1 + w_2 x_2) = \beta^* C_0. \tag{9.4}$$

Because $\beta \leq 1$, $C^T \leq C_0$. Again, because $x^T \in V(y_0)$, $C^* \leq C^T$.

Farrell introduced the decomposition of cost efficiency

$$\frac{C^*}{C_0} = \left(\frac{C^T}{C_0}\right)\left(\frac{C^*}{C^T}\right). \tag{9.5}$$

The two components of cost efficiency (γ) are (i) (input-oriented) technical efficiency β, and (ii) allocative efficiency α, where

$$\alpha = \frac{\gamma}{\beta}. \tag{9.6}$$

Note that both factors, α and β, lie in the (0, 1) interval. The overall cost efficiency (γ) measures the factor by which the cost can be scaled down if the firm selects the optimal input bundle x^* and performs at full technical efficiency. When technical efficiency is eliminated, both inputs are scaled down by the factor β, and that by itself would lower the cost by this factor. The allocative efficiency factor (α) shows how much the cost of the firm can be further scaled down when it selects the input mix that is most appropriate for the input price ratio faced by the firm in a given situation. The two distinct sources of cost inefficiency are (a) technical inefficiency in the form of wasteful use of inputs, and (b) allocative inefficiency due to selection of an inappropriate input mix.

Cost efficiency and its decomposition are illustrated diagrammatically in Figure 9.1. The point A represents the observed input bundle x^0 of a firm and

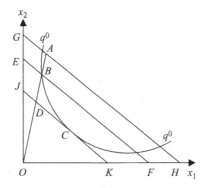

Figure 9.1 Technical, allocative, and overall cost efficiency.

the curve q^0q^0 is the isoquant for the output level y_0 produced by the firm. Thus, all points on and above this line represent bundles in the input requirement set $V(y_0)$. The point B where the line OA intersects the isoquant q^0q^0 is the efficient radial projection of x^0. It represents the bundle $x^T = (\beta x_1^0, \beta x_2^0)$. The expenditure line GH through the point A is the isocost line

$$w_1x_1 + w_2x_2 = C_0 = w_1x_1^0 + w_2x_2^0.$$

Similarly, the line through B shows the cost (C^T) of the technically efficient bundle x^T at these prices. Finally, the point C where the expenditure line JK is tangent to the isoquant q^0q^0 shows the bundle that produces output y_0 at the lowest cost. The line JK is the isocost line

$$w_1x_1 + w_2x_2 = C^* = w_1x_1^* + w_2x_2^*.$$

Therefore, the cost of the bundle represented by the point D on the line OA is also C^*.

Hence, the cost efficiency of the firm using input x^0 to produce output y_0 is

$$\gamma = \frac{C^*}{C_0} = \frac{OJ}{OG} = \frac{OD}{OA}.$$

This is decomposed into the two factors

$$\frac{OE}{OG} = \frac{OB}{OA} = \beta \quad \text{representing technical efficiency, and}$$

$$\frac{OJ}{OE} = \frac{OD}{OB} = \alpha \quad \text{representing allocative efficiency.}$$

To minimize cost, the firm would have to move from point A to point C, switching from the input bundle x^0 to the optimal bundle x^*. This can be visualized as a two-step move. First, it moves to the point B by eliminating technical inefficiency. This lowers the cost from C_0 to C^T. But, even though all points on the line $q^0 q^0$ are technically efficient, they are not equally expensive. At the input prices considered in this example, C^* is the least-cost bundle. Compared to C^T, the firm can lower cost even further by substituting input 1 for input 2 till it reaches the point C^*. Of course, when the input price ratio is such that point B itself is the tangency point with the correspondingly sloped expenditure line, B itself is the optimal point. In that case, there is no need to alter the input mix, and allocative efficiency equals unity.

We now consider a numerical example of measurement and decomposition of cost efficiency. Suppose that the production function is

$$f(x_1, x_2) = \sqrt{x_1} + 2\sqrt{x_2}. \tag{9.7}$$

A firm uses the input bundle ($x_1^0 = 4$, $x_2^0 = 9$) to produce output $y_0 = 6$. The input prices are ($w_1 = 3$, $w_2 = 2$). Thus, its actual cost is $C_0 = 30$. We want to find out what is the least cost of producing the output y_0 at these input prices when the technology is represented by the production function specified in (9.7).

We first solve the cost-minimization problem of the firm for arbitrary values of the parameters (w_1, w_2, y). Minimization of $w_1 x_1 + w_2 x_2$ s.t. (9.7) yields the optimal input bundles

$$x_1^* = \left(\frac{w_2}{4w_1 + w_2} \right)^2 y^2 \tag{9.8}$$

and

$$x_2^* = \left(\frac{4w_1}{4w_1 + w_2} \right)^2 y^2 \tag{9.9}$$

and the minimum cost

$$C^* = w_1 x_1^* + w_2 x_2^* = \left(\frac{w_1 w_2}{4w_1 + w_2} \right) y^2 \tag{9.10}$$

Thus, for $y_0 = 6$ and ($w_1 = 3$, $w_2 = 2$), $C^* = \frac{108}{7}$. A measure of the cost efficiency of the firm is

$$\gamma = \frac{C^*}{C_0} = \frac{18}{35}.$$

That is, the firm can reduce its cost to nearly half of what it is spending on the bundle x^0 by selecting instead the input bundle $(x_1 = \frac{36}{49}, x_2 = \frac{81}{49})$.

To obtain the measure of technical efficiency, we solve for the value of β that satisfies

$$\sqrt{\beta x_1^0} + 2\sqrt{\beta x_2^0} = y_0. \tag{9.11}$$

In the present example,

$$\sqrt{\beta} = \frac{6}{\sqrt{4} + 2\sqrt{9}} = \frac{3}{4} \quad \text{and} \quad \beta = \frac{9}{16}.$$

Therefore, a measure of the firm's allocative efficiency is

$$\alpha = \frac{\dfrac{18}{35}}{\dfrac{9}{16}} = \frac{32}{35}.$$

The measures of technical and allocative efficiency imply that firm can reduce its cost by more than 43% of its actual expenses by eliminating technical efficiency and further by about 10% of this lower cost by appropriately changing its input mix.

9.3 DEA for Cost Minimization

In the previous numerical example, the technology was represented by an explicit production function. It is possible, however, to leave the functional form of the technology unspecified and yet to obtain a nonparametric measure of the cost efficiency of a firm using DEA. For this, we define the production possibility set as the free disposal convex hull of the observed input–output bundles, if VRS is assumed. In the case of CRS, we use, instead, the free disposal conical hull of the data points.

As in the previous chapters, we start with the observed input–output data from N firms. Let $y^j = (y_{1j}, y_{2j}, \ldots, y_{mj})$ be the m-element output vector of firm j while $x^j = (x_{1j}, x_{2j}, \ldots, x_{nj})$ is the corresponding n-element input vector. Recall that the empirically constructed production possibility set under VRS is

$$T^V = \left\{ (x, y) : x \geq \sum_{j=1}^N \lambda_j x^j; \ y \leq \sum_{j=1}^N \lambda_j y^j; \ \sum_{j=1}^N \lambda_j = 1; \right.$$

$$\left. \lambda_j \geq 0 \ (j = 1, 2, \ldots, N) \right\} \tag{9.12a}$$

and the corresponding input requirement set for any output vector y is

$$V(y) = \left\{ (x) : x \geq \sum_{j=1}^{N} \lambda_j x^j; \; y \leq \sum_{j=1}^{N} \lambda_j y^j; \; \sum_{j=1}^{N} \lambda_j = 1; \right.$$

$$\left. \lambda_j \geq 0 \; (j = 1, 2, \ldots, N) \right\}. \qquad (9.12b)$$

Then, for a target output bundle y^0 and at a given input price vector w^0, the minimum cost under the assumption of VRS is

$$C^* = \min \; w^{0'} x : x \in V(y^0). \qquad (9.13)$$

The minimum cost is obtained by solving the DEA LP problem:

$$\min \sum_{i=1}^{n} w_i^0 x_i$$

$$\text{s.t.} \sum_{i=1}^{n} \lambda_j x_{ij} \leq x_i \; (i = 1, 2, \ldots, n);$$

$$\sum_{i=1}^{n} \lambda_j y_{rj} \geq y_{r0} \; (r = 1, 2, \ldots, m); \qquad (9.14)$$

$$\sum_{i=1}^{n} \lambda_j = 1;$$

$$\lambda_j \geq 0 \; (j = 1, 2, \ldots, N).$$

The optimal solution of this problem yields the cost-minimizing input bundle $x^* = (x_1^*, x_2^*, \ldots, x_n^*)$ and the objective function value shows the minimum cost. It should be noted that at the optimal solution, all the inequality constraints involving the inputs are binding. That is, there cannot be any input slacks at the optimal bundle. This is intuitively obvious. When any slack is present in any input, it is possible to reduce the relevant input by the amount of the slack without reducing any output. Because all inputs have strictly positive prices, this would lower the cost without affecting outputs. That, of course, would imply that the input bundle unadjusted for slacks could not have been cost minimizing. Thus, the optimal input bundle will necessarily lie in the efficient subset of the isoquant for the target output bundle. Unlike the input constraints, the output constraints need not be binding. The dual variable associated with the constraint for any individual output is the marginal cost of that output. When the constraint is nonbinding, the relevant marginal cost is zero.

Table 9.1. *Output and input quantity data for cost minimization*

Firm	1	2	3	4	5	6	7
Output (y)	12	8	17	5	14	11	9
Input 1 (x_1)	8	6	12	4	11	8	7
Input 2 (x_2)	7	5	8	6	9	7	10

We now consider a simple example of cost minimization for the one-output, two-input case. Table 9.1 shows the output and input data from 7 hypothetical firms.

Suppose that we want to evaluate the cost efficiency of firm #5 that faces input prices $w_1 = 10$ and $w_2 = 5$. The actual cost of firm #5 is $C^0 = 155$. The DEA problem to be solved is

$$\min 10x_1 + 5x_2$$

$$\text{s.t.} \quad 8\lambda_1 + 6\lambda_2 + 12\lambda_3 + 4\lambda_4 + 11\lambda_5 + 8\lambda_6 + 7\lambda_7 \le x_1;$$

$$7\lambda_1 + 5\lambda_2 + 8\lambda_3 + 6\lambda_4 + 9\lambda_5 + 7\lambda_6 + 10\lambda_7 \le x_2; \quad (9.15)$$

$$12\lambda_1 + 8\lambda_2 + 17\lambda_3 + 5\lambda_4 + 14\lambda_5 + 11\lambda_6 + 9\lambda_7 \ge 14;$$

$$\lambda_1 + \lambda_2 + \lambda_3 + \lambda_4 + \lambda_5 + \lambda_6 + \lambda_7 = 1;$$

$$\lambda_j \ge 0; \ (j = 1, 2, \ldots, 7).$$

The optimal solution of (9.15) is

$$x_1^* = 9.6, \ x_2^* = 7.4, \ \lambda_1^* = 0.6, \ \lambda_3^* = 0.4, \ \lambda_j^* = 0 \ (j \ne 1, 3), \ C^* = 133.$$

Thus, the cost efficiency of this firm is

$$\gamma = \frac{133}{155} = 0.85806.$$

The input-oriented BCC DEA for firm #5 yields a measure of technical efficiency

$$\beta = 0.87273.$$

Hence, the allocative efficiency is

$$\alpha = \frac{0.85806}{0.87273} = 0.9832.$$

9.4 Economic Scale Efficiency

Consider the average cost of a single-output firm

$$\mathrm{AC}\,(w, y) = \frac{C(w, y)}{y}. \tag{9.16}$$

Economies of scale are present at any given output level if $\mathrm{AC}(w, y)$ falls as y increases. Similarly, when $\mathrm{AC}(w, y)$ rises with y, diseconomies of scale are present. In the multi-output case, average cost is not defined in the usual sense. We may, however, define the ray average cost for a given output bundle y^0 as

$$\mathrm{RAC}\,(w, t; y^0) = \frac{C(w, ty^0)}{t}. \tag{9.17}$$

As in the single-output case, scale economies (diseconomies) are present when the ray average cost declines (increases) with an increase in the output scale. In production economics, the output level (scale) where the average cost (ray average cost) reaches a minimum is called the *efficient scale of production*. The dual or economic scale efficiency of a firm is measured by the ratio of the minimum (ray) average cost attained at this efficient scale and the average cost at its actual production scale. This measure shows by what factor a firm can reduce its average cost (ray average cost) by altering its output scale to fully exploit economies of scale.

The minimum average cost can be obtained by exploiting the following two useful propositions:

(P1) Locally constant returns to scale holds at the output where the average cost (ray average cost) is minimized.

(P2) When CRS holds everywhere, the average cost (ray average cost) remains constant.

Consider, first, the MPSS of a given input mix (x) in the single-output case. Recall that a feasible input–output combination (x^0, y_0) is an MPSS for the specific input and output mix if *for every feasible input–output combination* (x, y) *satisfying* $x = \tau x^0$ *and* $y = \mu y_0$, $\frac{\mu}{\tau} \leq 1$. Further, locally CRS holds at (x^0, y_0) if it is an MPSS (Banker [1984], proposition 1).

Next, note that if the input bundle x^* minimizes the average cost at the output level y^*, then (x^*, y^*) is an MPSS. Suppose this were not true. Then, by the definition of an MPSS, there exist nonnegative scalars (τ, μ) such that

$(\tau x^*, \mu y^*)$ is a feasible input–output combination satisfying $\frac{\mu}{\tau} > 1$. Define $x^{**} = \tau x^*$ and $C^{**} = w' x^{**}$. Then, at input price w, the minimum cost of producing the output bundle (μy^*) cannot be any greater than C^{**}. This implies that

$$\text{AC}(w, \mu y^*) = \frac{C(w, \mu y^*)}{\mu y^*} \leq \frac{C^{**}}{\mu y^*} = \frac{\tau w' x^*}{\mu y^*} = \frac{\tau}{\mu} \text{AC}(w, y^*).$$

But, by assumption, $\frac{\tau}{\mu} < 1$. Thus,

$$\text{AC}(w, \mu y^*) < \text{AC}(w, y^*).$$

Hence, y^* cannot be the output level where average cost reaches a minimum. This shows that the average cost-minimizing input–output combination must be an MPSS and, therefore, exhibit locally CRS. The proof of this proposition in the multiple-output case is quite analogous.

Now, consider (P2). For this, we need to show that, under globally CRS, the dual cost function $C^* = C(w, y)$ is homogeneous of degree 1 in y. Again, consider the single-output case. Suppose that the input bundle x_0^* minimizes the cost of producing the output level y_0. Now, consider the output level $y_1 = t y_0$ and the input bundle $x_1^* = t x_0^*$. We need to show that x_1^* minimizes the cost of the output y_1. Suppose that this were not true. Then, there must exist some other input bundle x_1^{**} that produces the output y_1 at a lower cost. Hence, $w' x_1^{**} < w' x_1^* = t\, w' x_0^*$. Now, define $x_0^{**} = \frac{1}{t} x_1^{**}$. Then $w' x_1^{**} < w' x_0^*$. But, by virtue of globally CRS, the input $x_0^{**} = \frac{1}{t} x_1^{**}$ can produce the output $y_0 = \frac{1}{t} y_1$. That means that x_0^* does not minimize the cost of the output y_0. This results in a contradiction. Therefore, if x_0^* minimizes the cost of the output y_0, then $t x_0^*$ must minimize the cost of output $t y_0$. This proves that the dual cost function is homogeneous of degree 1 in y and the average cost remains constant.

Figure 9.2 illustrates the relation between the average cost curves under the alternative assumptions of VRS and CRS, respectively. The U-shaped curve AC_A shows the average cost curve under the VRS assumption. The horizontal line AC_B, on the other hand, shows the constant average cost under CRS. The two curves are tangent to one another at output y^*. The average cost at this output level is ρ. This will also be the average cost *at any output level* when CRS is assumed.

Suppose that C^{**} is the minimum cost of producing the output level y_0 relative to a CRS production possibility set. Then, a measure of the minimum

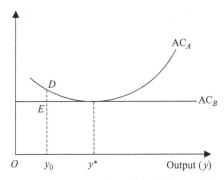

Figure 9.2 Locally constant returns to scale at the minimum of the average cost curve.

average cost under VRS is

$$\rho = \frac{C^{**}}{y_0}. \tag{9.18}$$

The average cost at output y_0 is shown in Figure 9.2 by the point D on the AC_A curve and is

$$Dy_0 = \frac{C^*}{y_0}$$

and the minimum average cost is

$$Ey_0 = \frac{C^{**}}{y_0} = \rho.$$

Thus, the economic scale efficiency of the firm is

$$ESE = \frac{C^{**}}{C^*} = \frac{Ey_0}{Dy_0}.$$

At the most productive scale size, the ray average productivity for a given input mix reaches a maximum. It is not clear, however, why one would like to change all inputs proportionately altering only the scale of the input bundle but not the input mix. When input prices are available, the total cost of an input bundle can be regarded as an input quantity index. Then, minimizing average cost is the same as maximizing the average productivity of this composite input. This is also equivalent to maximizing the "return for the dollar."

To obtain the minimum average cost in the single-output case, one solves the following DEA problem for the unit output level under the CRS assumption:

$$c^{**} = \min \sum_{i=1}^{n} w_i^0 x_i$$

$$\text{s.t.} \sum_{i=1}^{n} \lambda_j x_{ij} \leq x_i \ (i = 1, 2, \ldots, n);$$

$$\sum_{i=1}^{n} \lambda_j y_j \geq 1; \tag{9.19}$$

$$\lambda_j \geq 0 \ (j = 1, 2, \ldots, N).$$

Note that the optimal value of the objective function in (9.19) yields the minimum cost of producing one unit of the output and is the constant average cost for all output levels under CRS. But, as shown previously, this will also be the minimum average cost under VRS. Thus, the economic scale efficiency of the firm under investigation is

$$\text{ESE} = \frac{c^{**} y_0}{C^*}. \tag{9.20}$$

But, under CRS, the minimum cost of producing output y_0 is

$$C^{**} = c^{**} y_0.$$

Hence,

$$\text{ESE} = \frac{C^{**}}{C^*}. \tag{9.21}$$

This means that the economic scale efficiency of the output level y_0 can be measured simply by the ratio of its minimum cost under the assumption of CRS and the minimum cost under the assumption of VRS, respectively.

9.5 Quasi-Fixed Inputs and Short-Run Cost Minimization

In the discussion of the cost-minimization problem of a firm, we have so far treated all inputs as choice variables. By implication, all inputs are variable inputs. In reality, however, some inputs may be quasi-fixed in the short run. For example, a firm may not alter the plant size even though the output level has changed because the adjustment cost entailed by the desired change in the capital input may overweigh the cost savings that might be derived from such change. In such situations, the quasi-fixed input will be treated as an exogenously determined parameter (like the level of output) rather than as a choice variable.

For simplicity, we consider the case of a single quasi-fixed input, K, and partition the input vector as $x = (x^v, K)$, where $x^v = (x_1, x_2, \ldots, x_{n-1})$ is the vector of the $(n-1)$ variable inputs and K is the only quasi-fixed input. Let $w^v = (w_1, w_2, \ldots, w_{n-1})$ be the corresponding vector of variable input prices and r be the price of the quasi-fixed input.

From the previous definition of an input requirement set, we may define the conditional input requirement set for a given level of the quasi-fixed input K_0 and a specific output level y_0 as

$$V(y_0|K_0) = \{x^v : (x^v, K_0) \in V(y_0)\}. \tag{9.22}$$

The short-run cost-minimization problem of the firm is to minimize $w^{v\prime}x^v + rK_0$ subject to the restriction that $x^v \in V(y_0|K_0)$. But rK_0 is a fixed cost that plays no role in the minimization process. Hence, the firm needs to minimize the cost only of its variable inputs.

The DEA problem for variable cost minimization under VRS is

$$\min \sum_{i=1}^{n-1} w_i x_i$$

$$\text{s.t.} \quad \sum_{j=1}^{N} \lambda_j x_{ij} \leq x_i \ (i = 1, 2, \ldots, n-1);$$

$$\sum_{j=1}^{N} \lambda_j K_j \leq K_0;$$

$$\sum_{j=1}^{N} \lambda_j y_{rj} \geq y_0 \tag{9.23}$$

$$\sum_{j=1}^{N} \lambda_j = 1;$$

$$\lambda_j \geq 0 \ (j = 1, 2, \ldots, N).$$

The dual variable associated with the output constraint is nonnegative. It shows the *short-run* marginal cost of the output. On the other hand, the dual variable for the quasi-fixed input constraint is nonpositive. It shows by how much the total variable cost would decline with a marginal increase in the quantity of the quasi-fixed input. The negative of this dual variable is the *shadow price* of the quasi-fixed input. When this shadow price exceeds the market price (r), the firm is using too little of the quasi-fixed input for the output it is producing. On the other hand, if the market price exceeds the shadow price, it is using too much of the fixed input.

9.6 An Empirical Application: Cost Efficiency in U.S. Manufacturing

In this example, we use data on input and output quantities per establishment from the 1992 Census of Manufacturers in the United States. There are 51 observations – one each for the 50 states and one for Washington, D.C. Output (Q) in total manufacturing is measured by the gross value of production. The inputs included are (a) production workers (L), (b) nonproduction workers or employees (EM), (c) building and structures (BS), (d) machinery and equipment (ME), (e) materials consumed (MC), and (e) energy (ENER). The output and input quantities along with input prices are shown in Table 9.2. Prices of materials consumed (MC) and machinery and equipment (ME) are assumed to be constant across states. The SAS program for the cost-minimization LP problem for California (State #5) under the assumption of VRS is shown in Exhibit 9.1. Note that the variables $X1$ through $X6$ are decision variables that represent the optimal quantities of the inputs. In the constraint for the output, the actual output quantity of State #5 appears on the right-hand side of the inequality. The objective function coefficients for the $X1$–$X6$ columns are the corresponding (actual) input prices in State #5 and the _TYPE_ for this row is specified as MIN, indicating that it is a minimization problem.

Exhibit 9.2 shows the relevant sections of the SAS output for this program. The objective function value shows that the minimum cost (3.80177) and the optimal input bundle is

$$X_1^*(L) = 0.01762; \quad X_2^*(EM) = 0.01978; \quad X_3^*(BS) = 0.00055;$$

$$X_4^*(ME) = 0.13325; \quad X_5^*(MC) = 1.80707; \quad X_6^*(E) = 0.00655.$$

The cost of the observed bundle for State #5 was 4.5143. Thus, the cost efficiency is

$$CE = \frac{3.8018}{4.5143} = 0.8421.$$

Comparison of the actual and the optimal input bundles shows that the average firm in California uses more than the optimal quantities of L, ME, MC, and E but less than the optimal quantities of EM and BS.

Table 9.2. *Output and input quantities from U.S. Census of Manufacturers 1992*

			STATE LEVEL DATA			
OBS	V	L	EM	BS	ME	MC	ENER
1	8.2572	0.044045	0.014848	.0014270	0.25796	4.1684	0.03118
2	7.1181	0.023669	0.007101	.0005064	0.20237	4.0830	0.03286
3	5.3844	0.021087	0.016471	.0005407	0.15661	2.1395	0.00718
4	8.7708	0.045719	0.012190	.0009661	0.22014	4.7153	0.02010
5	5.9327	0.022092	0.016479	.0005150	0.16738	2.5902	0.00686
6	5.5128	0.019770	0.014464	.0005793	0.13482	2.4787	0.00800
7	6.3889	0.027221	0.023846	.0005381	0.17822	2.2152	0.00635
8	17.7167	0.042334	0.048168	.0007485	0.35834	10.4651	0.02789
9	4.4072	0.008297	0.020087	.0004932	0.09563	0.9293	0.00121
10	3.9262	0.017605	0.011232	.0003930	0.10792	1.7552	0.00720
11	9.2876	0.040340	0.016513	.0007278	0.23170	4.7781	0.01976
12	3.7374	0.012647	0.007549	.0003712	0.07814	1.9261	0.00284
13	5.8745	0.024932	0.011184	.0008848	0.18020	3.1690	0.02067
14	8.4058	0.031226	0.020374	.0007339	0.21677	4.0254	0.01463
15	11.3526	0.046810	0.020047	.0012852	0.33154	5.5030	0.03144
16	11.8150	0.040276	0.017812	.0010513	0.24163	6.0035	0.02718
17	10.4075	0.036487	0.017825	.0010862	0.20940	5.6884	0.01876
18	13.8676	0.046924	0.017181	.0010407	0.28718	7.0584	0.04122
19	15.1141	0.031077	0.013068	.0011361	0.43197	9.2702	0.10789
20	5.3115	0.030318	0.011091	.0011113	0.21364	2.3552	0.01828
21	7.1500	0.026391	0.018379	.0006293	0.19245	3.1956	0.01510
22	6.4034	0.026999	0.020363	.0008557	0.17705	2.5310	0.00579
23	9.6275	0.034741	0.020719	.0008788	0.24166	5.0341	0.01350
24	7.2206	0.028344	0.020994	.0005960	0.18535	3.4894	0.01097
25	8.7361	0.049867	0.013417	.0011271	0.23175	4.5963	0.02217
26	9.2734	0.033049	0.019100	.0007464	0.15388	4.7200	0.01333
27	3.0190	0.011410	0.004288	.0003503	0.06526	1.7887	0.02228
28	10.7881	0.035422	0.013962	.0007106	0.14460	6.2015	0.01554
29	2.6890	0.014171	0.007846	.0003186	0.10184	1.1323	0.00602
30	4.8364	0.025912	0.014200	.0005300	0.16890	1.8446	0.00481
31	6.5414	0.022855	0.020534	.0005148	0.15037	2.7226	0.00981
32	5.3512	0.016928	0.007712	.0008420	0.10940	2.7275	0.01050
33	5.7122	0.022230	0.017085	.0006359	0.16363	2.2301	0.00731
34	10.8546	0.051310	0.018716	.0010185	0.25026	4.9404	0.01831
35	5.2859	0.018891	0.008696	.0005183	0.14123	3.1663	0.01635
36	10.0225	0.037233	0.019894	.0010454	0.23080	4.8511	0.02604
37	7.4102	0.026747	0.011614	.0007084	0.16284	3.7284	0.02129
38	4.7141	0.021040	0.009835	.0005035	0.13538	2.3499	0.01536
39	7.6928	0.033601	0.018907	.0007585	0.18576	3.4622	0.01474
40	3.5574	0.022131	0.011065	.0004225	0.09209	1.4362	0.00571
41	10.8181	0.056375	0.019446	.0011567	0.34648	5.0809	0.03657
42	6.7800	0.028459	0.011136	.0009940	0.10990	4.0206	0.00822
43	10.0773	0.048212	0.017390	.0009848	0.28077	4.8329	0.01991
44	9.8220	0.026881	0.017154	.0008011	0.28424	5.3972	0.04413
45	6.1665	0.026337	0.014772	.0008359	0.16238	2.9833	0.01630
46	4.7367	0.022057	0.011103	.0004603	0.24948	1.8513	0.00598
47	10.1611	0.043470	0.018945	.0007116	0.23755	4.2401	0.02136
48	8.5364	0.023504	0.016322	.0007443	0.16075	4.9492	0.03010
49	7.4723	0.031352	0.012675	.0008429	0.22872	3.3199	0.04817
50	8.7849	0.036621	0.017508	.0009759	0.20659	4.2414	0.01719
51	4.1237	0.011073	0.004498	.0003655	0.16799	2.4042	0.02559

(continued)

Table 9.2. *(continued)*

		INPUT PRICE DATA			
OBS	PL	PEM	PBS	PME	PMC	PENER
1	20.9181	58.7455	52.045	1	1	7.8745
2	25.55	57.2222	122.683	1	1	7.4601
3	22.9045	56.651	97.368	1	1	12.7827
4	18.7602	58.7966	53.488	1	1	9.05
5	24.0879	63.8647	151.622	1	1	13.7183
6	25.4766	57.4295	84.186	1	1	7.9193
7	27.8053	67.8758	124.39	1	1	15.8455
8	27.2436	67.138	94.444	1	1	9.1559
9	30.6842	58.9674	129.706	1	1	16.4462
10	20.0558	55.038	103.077	1	1	9.0456
11	20.7316	58.0602	78.182	1	1	9.227
12	22.4884	49.8182	161.892	1	1	19.6685
13	22.3961	53.639	59.318	1	1	6.0062
14	25.4314	62.3123	87.857	1	1	9.7544
15	26.848	69.3505	66.136	1	1	6.9283
16	24.408	62.6686	56.739	1	1	7.0938
17	24.1202	61.1812	63.333	1	1	7.6703
18	23.139	64.8892	58.14	1	1	6.994
19	26.3959	67.1134	61.905	1	1	5.4851
20	23.8261	63.3074	85.238	1	1	13.2558
21	26.2966	60.7399	105.111	1	1	11.8719
22	26.	63.2228	92.	1	1	16.7225
23	32.1999	72.9258	79.767	1	1	10.8921
24	23.9791	58.3015	96.	1	1	8.8392
25	17.9185	56.8238	48.864	1	1	8.3507
26	23.2535	58.2437	65.581	1	1	8.6638
27	23.2038	57.2034	57.045	1	1	6.1162
28	21.656	54.3922	61.304	1	1	7.3294
29	21.7401	54.5204	117.105	1	1	11.043
30	24.3808	60.9154	114.048	1	1	18.978
31	25.3903	61.7404	130.25	1	1	11.9889
32	20.8296	52.0488	76.098	1	1	8.3613
33	24.2428	61.2633	112.632	1	1	12.6816
34	19.4408	58.6925	64.545	1	1	10.1348
35	20.4206	50.4655	60.455	1	1	5.2167
36	28.3533	68.3305	67.273	1	1	8.3725
37	23.9503	59.947	60.233	1	1	6.4092
38	23.9114	59.36	81.905	1	1	6.6651
39	24.26	61.8184	74.884	1	1	11.5317
40	20.8085	59.7593	101.463	1	1	11.317
41	20.8563	62.4463	62.727	1	1	8.4472
42	17.8379	48.2626	55.	1	1	7.9414
43	21.145	61.226	63.488	1	1	9.9394
44	24.3591	60.2699	82.	1	1	5.5978
45	21.5895	53.9732	68.182	1	1	6.4299
46	22.2399	64.0537	87.907	1	1	15.8117
47	22.5561	61.0526	91.333	1	1	7.7345
48	27.5966	66.1366	93.415	1	1	5.1643
49	26.4562	69.6283	48.043	1	1	6.471
50	24.8468	60.8194	60.182	1	1	7.7693
51	22.8594	52.5769	58.696	1	1	6.3005

Exhibit: 9.1. *The SAS program for measuring the cost efficiency of State #5*
(California)

```
DATA QUAN9292;
INPUT OBS V L EM BS ME MC ENER ;
*RV=V*102.6/117.4;
*RME=ME*110.4/123.4;
*RMC=MC*105.3/117.9;
c=1;d=0;
DROP OBS;
CARDS;
  1  8.2572 0.044045 0.014848 .0014270 0.25796 4.1684 0.03118
  2  7.1181 0.023669 0.007101 .0005064 0.20237 4.0830 0.03286
  3  5.3844 0.021087 0.016471 .0005407 0.15661 2.1395 0.00718
  4  8.7708 0.045719 0.012190 .0009661 0.22014 4.7153 0.02010
  5  5.9327 0.022092 0.016479 .0005150 0.16738 2.5902 0.00686
  .  ...      ...      ...      ...      ...     ...    ...
  .  ...      ...      ...      ...      ...     ...    ...
 46  4.7367 0.022057 0.011103 .0004603 0.24948 1.8513 0.00598
 47 10.1611 0.043470 0.018945 .0007116 0.23755 4.2401 0.02136
 48  8.5364 0.023504 0.016322 .0007443 0.16075 4.9492 0.03010
 49  7.4723 0.031352 0.012675 .0008429 0.22872 3.3199 0.04817
 50  8.7849 0.036621 0.017508 .0009759 0.20659 4.2414 0.01719
 51  4.1237 0.011073 0.004498 .0003655 0.16799 2.4042 0.02559
;
PROC transpose out=next;
dATA MORE; INPUT OBS X1 X2 X3 X4 X5 X6 _TYPE_ $ _RHS_;
CARDS;
1  0    0    0    0    0    0 >= 5.9327
2 -1    0    0    0    0    0 <= 0
3  0   -1    0    0    0    0 <= 0
4  0    0   -1    0    0    0 <= 0
5  0    0    0   -1    0    0 <= 0
6  0    0    0    0   -1    0 <= 0
7  0    0    0    0    0   -1 <= 0
8  0    0    0    0    0    0 = 1
9 24.0879   63.8647    151.622 1  1 13.7183  MIN .
;
DATA LAST; MERGE NEXT MORE;
;
DROP OBS;
PROC PRINT;
PROC LP;
```

Exhibit: 9.2. *The SAS output of the cost minimization DEA problem for State #5 (California)*

				Solution Summary		
	Objective Value				3.8017721	

			Variable Summary			
Col	Variable Name	Status	Type	Price	Activity	Reduced Cost
1	COL1		NON-NEG	0	0	1.4451897
2	COL2		NON-NEG	0	0	1.1001931
3	COL3		NON-NEG	0	0	0.6669724
4	COL4		NON-NEG	0	0	1.1980196
5	COL5		NON-NEG	0	0	0.712577
6	COL6		NON-NEG	0	0	0.740349
7	COL7		NON-NEG	0	0	0.5792778
8	COL8		NON-NEG	0	0	2.3228306
9	COL9	BASIC	NON-NEG	0	0.7348755	0
10	COL10		NON-NEG	0	0	0.9430949
11	COL11		NON-NEG	0	0	0.9706397
12	COL12		NON-NEG	0	0	0.8153125
13	COL13		NON-NEG	0	0	1.3258494
14	COL14		NON-NEG	0	0	0.855845
15	COL15		NON-NEG	0	0	0.7935547
16	COL16		NON-NEG	0	0	0.4455407
17	COL17		NON-NEG	0	0	1.0072757
18	COL18		NON-NEG	0	0	0.2384873
19	COL19		NON-NEG	0	0	1.8969621
20	COL20		NON-NEG	0	0	1.1147312
21	COL21		NON-NEG	0	0	0.7385528
22	COL22		NON-NEG	0	0	0.6951602
23	COL23		NON-NEG	0	0	1.0393762
24	COL24		NON-NEG	0	0	1.1219336
25	COL25		NON-NEG	0	0	1.3490749
26	COL26		NON-NEG	0	0	0.75012
27	COL27		NON-NEG	0	0	1.2568986
28	COL28		NON-NEG	0	0	0.7820128
29	COL29		NON-NEG	0	0	0.963133
30	COL30		NON-NEG	0	0	0.7534767
31	COL31		NON-NEG	0	0	0.6658366
32	COL32		NON-NEG	0	0	0.6655944
33	COL33		NON-NEG	0	0	0.5891071
34	COL34		NON-NEG	0	0	0.3451474
35	COL35		NON-NEG	0	0	1.3290086
36	COL36		NON-NEG	0	0	0.7387113
37	COL37		NON-NEG	0	0	0.7100325
38	COL38		NON-NEG	0	0	1.0662666
39	COL39		NON-NEG	0	0	0.7925463
40	COL40		NON-NEG	0	0	0.9814283

(continued)

Exhibit: 9.2. *(continued)*

Solution Summary

Objective Value	3.8017721

Variable Summary

Col	Variable Name	Status	Type	Price	Activity	Reduced Cost
41	COL41		NON-NEG	0	0	1.050722
42	COL42		NON-NEG	0	0	1.3208796
43	COL43		NON-NEG	0	0	0.7385375
44	COL44		NON-NEG	0	0	1.2831078
45	COL45		NON-NEG	0	0	1.0877336
46	COL46		NON-NEG	0	0	0.6341981
47	COL47	BASIC	NON-NEG	0	0.2651245	0
48	COL48		NON-NEG	0	0	1.389668
49	COL49		NON-NEG	0	0	0.8862771
50	COL50		NON-NEG	0	0	0.7814991
51	COL51		NON-NEG	0	0	1.1571522
52	X1	BASIC	NON-NEG	24.0879	0.0176222	0
53	X2	BASIC	NON-NEG	63.8647	0.0197842	0
54	X3	BASIC	NON-NEG	151.622	0.0005511	0
55	X4	BASIC	NON-NEG	1	0.1332565	0
56	X5	BASIC	NON-NEG	1	1.8070743	0
57	X6	BASIC	NON-NEG	13.7183	0.0065523	0
58	_OBS1_		SURPLUS	0	0	0.7884336
59	_OBS2_		SLACK	0	0	24.0879
60	_OBS3_		SLACK	0	0	63.8647
61	_OBS4_		SLACK	0	0	151.622
62	_OBS5_		SLACK	0	0	1
63	_OBS6_		SLACK	0	0	1
64	_OBS7_		SLACK	0	0	13.7183

Constraint Summary

Row	Constraint Name	Type	S/S Col	Rhs	Activity	Dual Activity
1	_OBS1_	GE	58	5.9327	5.9327	0.7884336
2	_OBS2_	LE	59	0	0	−24.0879
3	_OBS3_	LE	60	0	0	−63.8647
4	_OBS4_	LE	61	0	0	−151.622
5	_OBS5_	LE	62	0	0	−1
6	_OBS6_	LE	63	0	0	−1
7	_OBS7_	LE	64	0	0	−13.7183
8	_OBS8_	EQ	.	1	1	−0.875768
9	_OBS9_	OBJECTVE	.	0	3.8017721	.

The input-oriented BCC DEA solution shows a value of technical efficiency (β) equal to 0.9731. Hence, the level of allocative efficiency (α) is 0.8654. This means that there is little room for cost reduction through elimination of technical inefficiency (only by 2.7%) without changing the input mix. The average firm in State #5 operates at close to full technical efficiency. There is, however, considerable room for cost reduction through a change in the input proportions (about 13.5%). In fact, most of the observed cost inefficiency in this case derives from allocative inefficiency.

For an analysis of cost efficiency in the short run, the two capital inputs, BS and ME, can be treated as quasi-fixed. The optimal solution of the variable cost minimization problem yields an objective function value of 3.6801. The actual cost of the bundle of variable inputs used was 4.2689. This shows that in the short run, when the machinery and equipment (ME) and building and structures (BS) are treated as quasi-fixed, the firm can lower its variable cost by about 13.8%. It is interesting to note that when the two types of capital inputs are treated as given, the optimal solution shows that the firm should reduce its consumption of materials while increasing the other variable inputs in order to minimize total cost in the short run.

9.7 Profit Maximization and Efficiency

In the discussion of cost efficiency, the output quantities of a firm are treated as parameters and the focus is on the choice of variable inputs in the short run and all inputs in the long run. This is not an inappropriate analytical framework for nonprofit organizations like hospitals, schools, and so forth. But an overwhelming proportion of the economic activities in a developed economy (and also of most developing economies) is carried out by commercial firms operating for profit. For such firms, quantities of output to be produced are also choice variables like the input quantities. The objective of the firm is to select the input–output combination that results in the maximum profit at the applicable market prices of outputs and inputs. The only constraint is that the input–output combination selected must constitute a feasible production plan.

The profit-maximization problem of a competitive firm is

$$\max \Pi = p'y - w'x$$

$$\text{subject to } (x, y) \in T, \tag{9.24}$$

where $p = (p_1, p_2, \ldots, p_m)$ is the vector of output prices and $w = (w_1, w_2, \ldots, w_n)$ is the vector of input prices.

Consider, first, the single-input, single-output case. Let the production function be

$$y^* = f(x). \tag{9.25a}$$

Define the production possibility set

$$T = \{(x, y) : y \le f(x)\} \tag{9.25b}$$

The firm maximizes the profit by selecting the optimal pair (x, y) within T.

The Lagrangian for this constrained optimization problem is

$$L(x, y, \lambda) = py - wx - \lambda(y - f(x)) \tag{9.26}$$

and the first-order conditions for a maximum are

$$\frac{\partial L}{\partial y} = p - \lambda = 0; \tag{9.27a}$$

$$\frac{\partial L}{\partial x} = -w + \lambda f'(x) = 0; \tag{9.27b}$$

$$\text{and} \quad \frac{\partial L}{\partial \lambda} = y - f(x) = 0. \tag{9.27c}$$

From (9.27a–b), we obtain

$$f'(x) = \frac{w}{p}. \tag{9.28a}$$

This can be inverted to derive the input demand function

$$x^* = x\left(\frac{w}{p}\right). \tag{9.28b}$$

The output supply function is

$$y^* = f(x^*) = f\left(x\left(\frac{w}{p}\right)\right) = y\left(\frac{w}{p}\right) \tag{9.28c}$$

and the profit function is

$$\Pi^* = py^* - wx^* = py\left(\frac{w}{p}\right) - wx\left(\frac{w}{p}\right) = \Pi(w, p). \tag{9.28d}$$

This is the dual-profit function showing the maximum profit that a firm facing the production function defined in (9.25a) earns at prices p for the output and w for the input.

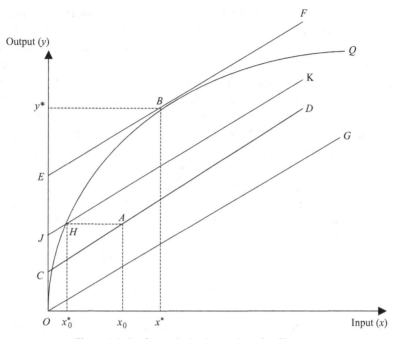

Figure 9.3 Profit maximization and profit efficiency.

Define the normalized variables $\pi = \frac{\Pi}{p}$ and $\omega = \frac{w}{p}$. Consider, now, all input–output combinations (not all of which need to be feasible) that yield the same normalized profit (say $\bar{\pi}$) at a given pair of prices (w, p). The equation of this normalized isoprofit line would be

$$\bar{\pi} = y - \omega x \qquad (9.29a)$$

that can be alternatively expressed as

$$y = \bar{\pi} + \omega x. \qquad (9.29b)$$

Given that both input prices and the output price will be strictly positive, $\omega > 0$. The intercept in (9.29b) represents the level of normalized profit for any isoprofit line.

In Figure 9.3, the curve OQ shows the production function. The actual input–output combination of the firm is (x_0, y_0) shown by the point A. The profit earned here is $\Pi_0 = py_0 - wx_0$ with the normalized profit $\pi_0 = \frac{\Pi_0}{p}$. The line CD through the point A shows input–output bundles, all of which yield the normalized profit π_0. The slope of this line measures the normalized input price (ω) and its intercept OC equals π_0. The firm's objective is to reach the highest isoprofit line parallel to the line CD that can be attained at any point on or below the curve OQ. The highest such isoprofit line is reached at the point B representing the tangency of the isoprofit line EF with the production function. The optimal input–output bundle is (x^*, y^*). The intercept of this line OE equals the maximum normalized profit $\pi^* = y^* - \omega x^*$. The line OG is a ray through the origin with slope equal to ω. It represents the zero profit line $y - \omega x = 0$. At any input level x, the vertical distance between the production function and the point on the OG line shows the normalized profit earned if the firm produced the maximum output from the given input. At the actual input–output bundle (x_0, y_0), the firm does exhibit considerable technical inefficiency. The efficient input-oriented projection of the point A onto the production function OQ is the point H where the same output quantity y_0 is produced from input x_0^*. The intercept of the isoprofit line JK through this technically efficient point measures the normalized profit

$$\pi_T = y_0 - \omega x_0^* = y_0 - \beta(\omega x_0) \qquad (9.30)$$

where $\beta = \frac{x_0^*}{x_0}$ is the measure of the input-oriented technical efficiency of the firm. The firm earns the normalized profit π_T if it eliminates technical inefficiency from its observed input use. Note that all points on the production function OQ represent input–output combinations that are technically efficient. There is no reason to choose one over another on grounds of technical efficiency alone. Given the normalized input price (ω) equal to the slope of the line OG, the firm can increase its profit, however, by moving from the point H to the point B along OQ. This increase in profit is due to an improvement in the allocative efficiency of the firm. The firm maximizes profit by moving from point A to point B. This can be visualized as a two-step process. First, it eliminates technical inefficiency to move to the point H. As a result, the normalized profit increases from π_0 to π_T. In the second step, the firm moves from H to B. As a result, its normalized profit rises further from π_T to π^*.

Next, consider a single-output, two-input example. Recall the production function (9.7) and the input prices ($w_1 = 3$, $w_2 = 2$). Assume further that the output price is $p = 8$. Then, the profit earned by a firm producing output $y_0 = 6$ from the input bundle ($x_1^0 = 4$, $x_2^0 = 9$) is $\Pi_0 = 18$. For the parametrically given input and output prices (w_1, w_2, p), the profit maximization problem is:

$$\max \Pi = py - w_1 x_1 - w_2 x_2$$

subject to

$$\sqrt{x_1} + 2\sqrt{x_2} \geq y. \tag{9.31}$$

For the optimal solution of this constrained optimization problem, we get the input demand functions

$$x_1^* = x_1(w_1, w_2, p) = \frac{p^2}{4w_1^2} \tag{9.32a}$$

and

$$x_2^* = x_2(w_1, w_2, p) = \frac{p^2}{w_2^2}, \tag{9.32b}$$

the output supply function

$$y^* = y(w_1, w_2, p) = p\left(\frac{1}{2w_1} + \frac{2}{w_2}\right), \tag{9.33}$$

and the profit function

$$\Pi^* = \Pi(w_1, w_2, p) = p^2\left(\frac{4w_1 + w_2}{4w_1 w_2}\right). \tag{9.34}$$

Evaluated at the output and input prices specified herein,

$$x_1^* = \frac{16}{3}, \quad x_2^* = 16, \quad y^* = \frac{11}{3}, \quad \text{and} \quad \Pi^* = \frac{112}{3}.$$

Thus, the unrealized or lost profit is

$$\Delta = \Pi^* - \Pi_0 = \frac{112}{3} - 18 = \frac{58}{3}.$$

Alternatively, the firm's profit efficiency is

$$\gamma_\Pi = \frac{\Pi_0}{\Pi^*} = \frac{18}{112/3} = \frac{27}{56}.$$

Thus, the firm has an unrealized potential profit of $19\frac{1}{3}$. Alternatively, its actual profit is a little under 50% of the maximum profit it can earn at these prices.

9.8 DEA for Profit Maximization

The profit-maximization problem of a multiple-output, multiple-input firm facing input and output prices w and p, respectively, can be formulated as the following DEA problem:

$$\max \sum_{r=1}^{m} p_r y_r - \sum_{i=1}^{n} w_i x_i$$

$$\text{subject to} \quad \sum_{j=1}^{N} \lambda_j y_{rj} \geq y_r \quad (r = 1, 2, \ldots, m);$$

$$\sum_{j=1}^{N} \lambda_j x_{ij} \leq x_i \quad (i = 1, 2, \ldots, n); \qquad (9.35)$$

$$\sum_{j=1}^{N} \lambda_j = 1;$$

$$\lambda_j \geq 0; \quad (j = 1, 2, \ldots, N).$$

The profit-maximizing input and output quantities $x_i^* (I = 1, 2, \ldots, n)$ and $y_r^* (r = 1, 2, \ldots, m)$ are obtained along with the other decision variables $\lambda_j^* (j = 1, 2, \ldots, N)$ at the optimal solution of this problem. The optimal value of the objective function $\Pi^* = p'y^* - w'x^*$ is the maximum profit that the firm can earn. An important point needs to be noted in this context. For a bounded solution of the LP problem in (9.35), we *must* allow VRS. Without the restriction $\sum_{1}^{N} \lambda_j = 1$, if (λ^*, x^*, y^*) is a feasible solution, then, for any arbitrary $t > 0$, $(t\lambda^*, tx^*, ty^*)$ is also a feasible solution. But, in that case, Π^* also gets multiplied by t. Therefore, by making t arbitrarily large, we can increase the maximum profit indefinitely. Hence, for a finite (nonzero) profit, we must assume VRS.

9.9 Decomposition of Profit Efficiency

Banker and Maindiratta (1988) proposed a multiplicative decomposition of profit efficiency that parallels Farrell's decomposition of cost efficiency. They decompose the ratio measure of profit efficiency as

$$\gamma_\Pi = \frac{\Pi_0}{\Pi^*} = \left(\frac{\Pi_0}{\Pi_T} \right) \left(\frac{\Pi_T}{\Pi^*} \right). \qquad (9.36)$$

The first factor is the ratio of the actual profit to what the firm would earn if it eliminated (input-oriented) technical inefficiency and moved to the point H

on the curve OQ. They define technical efficiency as

$$\beta_\Pi = \left(\frac{\Pi_0}{\Pi_T}\right) = \frac{p'y^0 - w'x^0}{p'y^0 - \beta w'x^0}. \tag{9.37}$$

In Figure 9.3, this technical-efficiency factor is measured by the ratio $\frac{OC}{OJ}$. The other factor

$$\alpha_\Pi = \left(\frac{\Pi_T}{\Pi^*}\right) = \frac{p'y^0 - \beta w'x^0}{p'y^* - w'x^*} \tag{9.38}$$

is defined by Banker and Maindiratta as allocative efficiency. In Figure 9.3, this component of profit efficiency is measured by the ratio $\frac{OJ}{OE}$.

A potential problem with the ratio measure of profit efficiency is that if the actual profit is negative when the maximum profit is positive, the ratio becomes negative. On the other hand, if both actual and maximum profits are negative, the ratio exceeds unity. In the long run, when all inputs and outputs are treated as choice variables, with free entry and exit, zero profit is always possible. Thus, the maximum profit of a firm that has stayed in business should not be negative. But negative actual profit is still possible due to inefficiency.

A more serious problem with this decomposition by Banker and Maindiratta, however, is that their technical-efficiency measure is not independent of prices. This is a serious limitation because the technical efficiency of any firm should be determined by the technology only and should not depend on prices. To overcome this problem, Färe et al. (2000) offer an additive decomposition of the difference measure of profit efficiency (Δ) that circumvents the problem of price dependence of the technical-efficiency component. One can exploit the identity

$$\Delta = \Pi^* - \Pi_0 = (\Pi_T - \Pi_0) + (\Pi^* - \Pi_T)$$

to get

$$\delta \equiv \frac{\Delta}{C_0} = \left(\frac{(\Pi_T - \Pi_0)}{C_0}\right) + \left(\frac{(\Pi^* - \Pi_T)}{C_0}\right). \tag{9.39}$$

Here, δ represents the lost or unrealized part of the maximum return on outlay. The first of the two individual components of δ is

$$\delta_T = \frac{(p'y^0 - \beta w'x^0) - (p'y^0 - w'x^0)}{w'x^0} = (1 - \beta). \tag{9.40}$$

It is the measure of technical *inefficiency*. The other component

$$\delta_A = \frac{p'(y^* - y^0) - w'(x^* - \beta x^0)}{w'x^0} \tag{9.41}$$

denotes the return on outlay lost due to allocative *inefficiency*.

Note that because the input-oriented technical efficiency lies between 0 and 1, so does δ_T. But δ_A, which is nonnegative by construction, can actually exceed unity. As a result, the normalized difference measure of profit inefficiency can also exceed unity.

9.10 An Empirical Application to U.S. Banking

This section presents an example of using SAS to solve the DEA model for profit maximization using data relating to the operations of 50 large banks in the United States during the year 1996. The five outputs considered are (i) commercial and industrial loans (y_1), (ii) consumer loans (y_2), (iii) real estate loans (y_3), (iv) investments, and (v) other income. All outputs are measured in millions of current dollars. The inputs included are (i) transaction deposits, (ii) nontransaction deposits, (iii) labor, and (iv) capital. Labor is measured in full-time equivalent employees. Other inputs are measured in dollars. Following the usual practice in the banking literature, output prices are measured by dividing the revenue by the dollar value of the appropriate output. Similarly, prices of nonlabor items are measured by dividing the relevant item of expenditure by the dollar value of the input. For price of labor, we divide the total wages and salaries by the number of employees. The output and input quantity and price data for the banks included in this example are reported in Table 9.3.

Exhibit 9.3 shows the SAS program for the profit maximization problem for Bank #1. The variables A_1 through A_5 are the quantities of the output and B_1 through B_4 are the input quantities that the firm chooses in order to maximize profit. Note that in the objective function row, the actual output prices faced by Bank #1 appear in the columns for the variables A_1–A_5. At the same time, the input prices appear in the objective function row with a negative sign in the columns for the variables B_1–B_4. To solve the problem for other banks, one needs only to replace the output and (negatives of the) input prices in the objective function row.

Exhibit 9.4 shows the relevant sections of the SAS output for the profit maximization problem. The objective function value 49.12418 shows the maximum

Table 9.3. Data for 50 large U.S. banks (1996)

	BANK OUTPUT QUANTITY DATA				
Obs	Y1	Y2	Y3	Y4	Y5
1	42.654	281.660	141.454	75.657	14.688
2	32.985	70.183	109.357	191.057	4.318
3	75.474	8.832	290.180	155.438	0.944
4	57.935	74.259	196.960	98.871	2.433
5	39.382	49.084	316.682	48.674	3.138
6	41.054	33.290	247.589	148.686	3.751
7	50.278	75.520	286.727	53.148	3.015
8	87.693	52.779	165.261	56.463	9.432
9	28.026	55.779	239.118	208.537	6.249
10	58.602	31.585	278.365	128.449	4.912
11	35.884	44.263	174.700	256.871	4.111
12	44.125	48.241	210.124	158.738	3.225
13	55.637	64.486	150.870	185.250	4.470
14	31.702	105.386	200.102	85.255	6.652
15	34.788	50.011	246.324	159.393	3.236
16	56.553	6.625	222.897	157.066	6.156
17	18.520	222.234	165.645	66.920	3.985
18	44.031	29.020	243.223	171.917	5.783
19	52.169	36.165	119.370	205.256	1.862
20	120.032	87.585	208.670	87.041	6.371
21	19.113	28.154	262.832	162.963	6.074
22	45.141	14.585	225.703	169.499	4.402
23	61.691	101.368	180.709	90.164	6.773
24	65.723	86.496	249.611	52.840	11.689
25	44.266	88.868	235.361	116.791	4.256
26	38.908	75.033	229.876	111.597	2.511
27	109.580	33.155	184.179	176.744	5.741
28	159.743	35.745	156.233	107.137	3.785
29	72.329	53.262	137.252	140.817	7.591
30	106.340	23.693	226.540	161.803	5.431
31	54.868	69.261	168.534	166.432	3.497
32	32.195	35.251	209.341	143.877	4.257
33	78.170	118.097	209.424	103.907	11.349
34	84.317	54.948	229.375	99.756	6.116
35	81.401	55.116	180.483	149.994	5.789
36	40.884	10.652	233.734	186.361	4.739
37	61.556	73.014	263.974	103.391	8.075
38	112.470	105.948	239.786	139.941	3.848
39	14.875	109.965	62.685	131.780	6.642
40	59.532	78.519	187.906	59.538	9.140
41	85.824	73.366	191.824	207.116	5.657
42	79.859	100.083	230.688	88.693	4.363
43	48.902	4.890	333.867	56.814	7.527
44	30.466	42.900	289.771	156.866	3.087
45	40.999	5.203	304.792	114.665	4.191
46	279.037	0.428	28.666	27.217	9.760
47	40.818	30.847	191.266	206.572	9.231
48	63.333	86.147	167.996	280.677	16.237
49	51.656	107.739	228.967	57.192	77.482
50	17.836	6.684	204.330	321.243	4.704

(continued)

Table 9.3. *(continued)*

	BANK INPUT QUANTITY DATA			
Obs	X1	X2	X3	X4
1	111.805	434.194	0.411	19.356
2	154.721	311.423	0.203	8.266
3	76.975	396.428	0.083	5.795
4	77.369	361.009	0.205	7.576
5	33.051	424.549	0.189	9.207
6	130.316	363.854	0.178	5.670
7	95.421	369.313	0.185	11.238
8	141.980	284.723	0.248	8.822
9	84.012	422.808	0.192	7.861
10	79.081	354.272	0.256	6.988
11	36.780	382.783	0.142	10.189
12	94.138	284.341	0.218	10.237
13	64.621	316.446	0.144	3.070
14	101.855	338.586	0.210	11.547
15	99.539	316.927	0.270	20.199
16	181.594	304.163	0.205	8.888
17	79.715	382.693	0.255	7.698
18	171.637	297.141	0.191	8.668
19	108.916	287.656	0.184	6.237
20	215.757	279.379	0.195	8.010
21	116.651	340.618	0.214	5.253
22	78.890	351.791	0.212	9.458
23	171.298	285.875	0.251	5.186
24	131.046	282.000	0.229	5.471
25	129.676	316.831	0.226	10.430
26	136.549	310.071	0.275	9.483
27	168.394	301.344	0.261	18.676
28	174.401	274.875	0.207	9.586
29	174.940	302.552	0.247	5.857
30	231.463	330.746	0.209	12.092
31	108.419	327.439	0.251	11.223
32	144.217	336.406	0.273	15.439
33	221.628	294.729	0.259	10.933
34	85.677	354.134	0.180	7.776
35	139.870	337.857	0.280	3.926
36	187.583	294.983	0.241	8.219
37	118.168	369.407	30.273	9.955
38	3155.287	430.204	0.299	8.993
39	223.944	283.096	0.186	38.244
40	154.830	3280.436	0.263	9.201
41	131.127	365.442	0.320	16.014
42	94.432	368.091	0.229	8.505
43	222.651	282.545	0.299	15.718
44	116.617	326.074	0.231	8.274
45	193.806	236.212	0.175	5.151
46	73.233	486.438	0.220	3.460
47	151.344	349.154	0.359	8.551
48	161.773	549.270	0.257	6.580
49	179.098	354.372	1.313	12.878
50	95.447	321.750	0.264	11.692

(continued)

Table 9.3. *(continued)*

		BANK OUTPUT PRICE DATA		
Obs	P1	P2	P3	P4	P5
1	0.21967	0.13250	0.05154	0.063770	1
2	0.07849	0.10477	0.06728	0.024000	1
3	0.09960	0.07892	0.07404	0.060260	1
4	0.09431	0.09999	0.07976	0.055500	1
5	0.12155	0.12601	0.06853	0.068110	1
6	0.08245	0.08567	0.08244	0.054700	1
7	0.09453	0.07766	0.09412	0.069330	1
8	0.09712	0.13740	0.05984	0.063564	1
9	0.09591	0.09400	0.08016	0.057088	1
10	0.29330	0.15533	0.03119	0.054917	1
11	0.09380	0.09191	0.08498	0.051870	1
12	0.10701	0.09200	0.08069	0.052900	1
13	0.07427	0.14135	0.07607	0.064092	1
14	0.09170	0.09085	0.08456	0.062401	1
15	0.10423	0.07970	0.08195	0.055000	1
16	0.10938	0.19668	0.07467	0.052700	1
17	0.11134	0.08149	0.08404	0.076100	1
18	0.12314	0.08218	0.06223	0.066590	1
19	0.08449	0.08199	0.06468	0.055570	1
20	0.08048	0.07669	0.08122	0.078040	1
21	0.08743	0.12531	0.08745	0.065150	1
22	0.10492	0.09640	0.07889	0.063493	1
23	0.25077	0.07519	0.03253	0.056985	1
24	0.08810	0.09345	0.07759	0.066976	1
25	0.09987	0.10655	0.07983	0.069517	1
26	0.12327	0.08522	0.07660	0.068174	1
27	0.06890	0.11045	0.08624	0.068421	1
28	0.08646	0.08351	0.08051	0.058400	1
29	0.09664	0.11355	0.10683	0.073620	1
30	0.10021	0.10328	0.08419	0.053299	1
31	0.11752	0.09523	0.07430	0.060139	1
32	0.07625	0.10590	0.08361	0.062129	1
33	0.09687	0.11053	0.08966	0.059920	1
34	0.08989	0.09938	0.07628	0.067625	1
35	0.08437	0.09975	0.07544	0.054800	1
36	0.08568	0.08271	0.09283	0.061853	1
37	0.10053	0.10191	0.08727	0.046300	1
38	0.09438	0.06856	0.08076	0.057238	1
39	0.08760	0.13264	0.07739	0.060426	1
40	0.10070	0.08664	0.07836	0.069367	1
41	0.20274	0.08764	0.03422	0.061444	1
42	0.09003	0.09947	0.07976	0.055920	1
43	0.09431	0.20716	0.08438	0.077740	1
44	0.09607	0.10193	0.08328	0.062289	1
45	0.08456	0.12839	0.08187	0.066167	1
46	0.10653	0.09346	0.03436	0.055150	1
47	0.16385	0.18400	0.05278	0.057956	1
48	0.09663	0.11140	0.07650	0.069500	1
49	0.07426	0.09884	0.07540	0.067107	1
50	0.07053	0.07346	0.08183	0.064001	1

(continued)

Table 9.3. *(continued)*

	BANK	INPUT PRICE	DATA	
Obs	W1	W2	W3	W4
1	0.006905	0.054842	34.8856	0.22928
2	0.010044	0.029718	32.3448	0.46443
3	0.008522	0.049931	55.8070	0.12045
4	0.013326	0.052387	29.3659	0.18598
5	0.010741	0.046960	32.3120	0.23297
6	0.001727	0.046073	28.3483	0.21746
7	0.009547	0.058695	30.2270	0.11799
8	0.008776	0.052089	37.4435	0.38540
9	0.008606	0.043124	38.1719	0.24539
10	0.013315	0.040720	31.3477	0.32055
11	0.023355	0.045605	37.9507	0.14516
12	0.007383	0.048108	28.8119	0.21520
13	0.005184	0.044077	28.6736	0.20651
14	0.002278	0.034839	30.4857	0.22517
15	0.006148	0.041928	31.5185	0.15149
16	0.010061	0.032657	50.4537	0.28904
17	0.010299	0.035185	27.9412	0.20512
18	0.015632	0.046608	40.7853	0.20558
19	0.024422	0.051249	29.9565	0.24964
20	0.013436	0.052527	32.8510	0.26841
21	0.012207	0.049539	31.0280	0.45764
22	0.006515	0.046061	34.9434	0.26390
23	0.007875	0.042718	35.6892	0.61955
24	0.005555	0.039862	35.3974	0.26595
25	0.017027	0.045340	29.2080	0.21055
26	0.008297	0.041249	34.3200	0.24096
27	0.006633	0.049667	43.5402	0.18082
28	0.000872	0.038396	42.7633	0.26966
29	0.009243	0.046518	34.0810	0.45433
30	0.006558	0.039988	43.5789	0.27464
31	0.013881	0.047810	27.8486	0.18337
32	0.008515	0.046685	29.3956	0.15804
33	0.019831	0.047260	37.9380	0.16811
34	0.010003	0.052525	30.1222	0.19792
35	0.009652	0.048334	29.0357	0.68161
36	0.012618	0.043379	48.0747	0.31099
37	0.007904	0.043545	35.8901	0.25364
38	0.012158	0.048689	31.0970	0.35316
39	0.014352	0.046807	50.6290	0.29415
40	0.004741	0.043525	35.4791	0.35811
41	0.006627	0.048002	29.9063	0.18446
42	0.009700	0.052302	34.5109	0.31193
43	0.004905	0.034143	38.7590	0.29648
44	0.009741	0.046244	29.1515	0.29236
45	0.018446	0.044308	43.6743	0.56688
46	0.007032	0.049080	49.7050	0.82601
47	0.015567	0.024725	34.1309	0.42042
48	0.004179	0.042660	35.5681	0.49635
49	0.010257	0.047176	36.8104	0.81760
50	0.008832	0.045887	36.4924	0.17918

Exhibit: 9.3. *SAS program for the DEA-LP for profit maximization by Bank #1*

```
data qout;
input obs y1-y5;
drop obs;
cards;
    1     42.654    281.660    141.454     75.657    14.688
    2     32.985     70.183    109.357    191.057     4.318
    3     75.474      8.832    290.180    155.438     0.944
    4     57.935     74.259    196.960     98.871     2.433
    5     39.382     49.084    316.682     48.674     3.138
    .       ...        ...        ...        ...       ...
    .       ...        ...        ...        ...       ...
   45     40.999      5.203    304.792    114.665     4.191
   46    279.037      0.428     28.666     27.217     9.760
   47     40.818     30.847    191.266    206.572     9.231
   48     63.333     86.147    167.996    280.677    16.237
   49     51.656    107.739    228.967     57.192    77.482
   50     17.836      6.684    204.330    321.243     4.704
;
DATA QIN; INPUT OBS X1-X4;
drop obs;c=1;d=0;
    1    111.805    434.194      0.411     19.356
    2    154.721    311.423      0.203      8.266
    3     76.975    396.428      0.083      5.795
    4     77.369    361.009      0.205      7.576
    5     33.051    424.549      0.189      9.207
    .       ...        ...        ...        ...
    .       ...        ...        ...        ...
   45    193.806    236.212      0.175      5.151
   46     73.233    486.438      0.220      3.460
   47    151.344    349.154      0.359      8.551
   48    161.773    549.270      0.257      6.580
   49    179.098    354.372      1.313     12.878
   50     95.447    321.750      0.264     11.692
;
data qty; merge qout qin;
proc transpose out=next;
data more1;
input a1-a5;
cards;
```

(continued)

Exhibit: 9.3 *(continued)*

```
-1 0  0  0  0
 0 -1 0  0  0
 0  0 -1 0  0
 0  0  0 -1 0
 0  0  0  0 -1
 0  0  0  0  0
 0  0  0  0  0
 0  0  0  0  0
 0  0  0  0  0
 0  0  0  0  0
0.21967    0.13250 0.05154 0.063770 1
;
data more2;
input b1-b4 _type_ $ _rhs_;
cards;
  0  0  0  0 >= 0
  0  0  0  0 >= 0
  0  0  0  0 >= 0
  0  0  0  0 >= 0
  0  0  0  0 >= 0
 -1  0  0  0 <= 0
  0 -1  0  0 <= 0
  0  0 -1  0 <= 0
  0  0  0 -1 <= 0
  0  0  0  0  = 1
 -0.006905       -0.054842 -34.8856 -0.22928 max .
;
data last; merge next more1 more2;
proc print;
proc lp;
run;
```

profit that a bank can earn at the output and input prices faced by Bank #1. In this particular example, λ_{49}^* equals unity while all other λ_j's are equal to 0. This means that the firm should merely select the actual input–output quantities of Bank #49 in order to earn this level of profit. The actual amounts of revenue earned and cost incurred by the bank under examination are 73.4929 and 43.3600, respectively. Thus, the amount of actual profit earned is 30.1329. The actual (gross) return on outlay is 1.6949. The amount of unrealized profit is

Exhibit: 9.4. *The SAS output for the profit-maximization problem for Bank #1*

		Solution Summary				

Objective Value					49.124182	

		Variable Summary				

Col	Variable Name	Status	Type	Price	Activity	Reduced Cost
1	COL1		NON-NEG	0	0	−18.99125
2	COL2		NON-NEG	0	0	−37.56557
3	COL3		NON-NEG	0	0	−32.05901
4	COL4		NON-NEG	0	0	−36.89022
5	COL5		NON-NEG	0	0	−43.62147
6	COL6		NON-NEG	0	0	−38.06545
7	COL7		NON-NEG	0	0	−36.83429
8	COL8		NON-NEG	0	0	−28.58673
9	COL9		NON-NEG	0	0	−35.97359
10	COL10		NON-NEG	0	0	−35.12391
11	COL11		NON-NEG	0	0	−34.41744
12	COL12		NON-NEG	0	0	−35.05785
13	COL13		NON-NEG	0	0	−27.82693
14	COL14		NON-NEG	0	0	−35.04011
15	COL15		NON-NEG	0	0	−40.87838
16	COL16		NON-NEG	0	0	−35.28736
17	COL17		NON-NEG	0	0	−31.01896
18	COL18		NON-NEG	0	0	−32.45639
19	COL19		NON-NEG	0	0	−36.14552
20	COL20		NON-NEG	0	0	−13.92601
21	COL21		NON-NEG	0	0	−39.33829
22	COL22		NON-NEG	0	0	−39.8338
23	COL23		NON-NEG	0	0	−27.11086
24	COL24		NON-NEG	0	0	−20.91604
25	COL25		NON-NEG	0	0	−32.33759
26	COL26		NON-NEG	0	0	−38.87563
27	COL27		NON-NEG	0	0	−25.2314
28	COL28		NON-NEG	0	0	−16.32598
29	COL29		NON-NEG	0	0	−30.29374
30	COL30		NON-NEG	0	0	−25.00067
31	COL31		NON-NEG	0	0	−35.13317
32	COL32		NON-NEG	0	0	−45.6683
33	COL33		NON-NEG	0	0	−16.77182
34	COL34		NON-NEG	0	0	−27.09754

(continued)

Exhibit: 9.4 *(continued)*

Solution Summary

Objective Value						49.124182

Variable Summary

Col	Variable Name	Status	Type	Price	Activity	Reduced Cost
35	COL35		NON-NEG	0	0	−29.44642
36	COL36		NON-NEG	0	0	−37.82651
37	COL37		NON-NEG	0	0	−30.53558
38	COL38		NON-NEG	0	0	−22.40739
39	COL39		NON-NEG	0	0	−38.46062
40	COL40		NON-NEG	0	0	−30.7549
41	COL41		NON-NEG	0	0	−27.58092
42	COL42		NON-NEG	0	0	−27.18967
43	COL43		NON-NEG	0	0	−40.44378
44	COL44		NON-NEG	0	0	−37.36575
45	COL45		NON-NEG	0	0	−33.79494
46	COL46		NON-NEG	0	0	−10.44939
47	COL47		NON-NEG	0	0	−38.48636
48	COL48		NON-NEG	0	0	−22.71743
49	COL49	BASIC	NON-NEG	0	1	0
50	COL50		NON-NEG	0	0	−38.7947
51	A1	BASIC	NON-NEG	0.21967	51.656	0
52	A2	BASIC	NON-NEG	0.1325	107.739	0
53	A3	BASIC	NON-NEG	0.05154	228.967	0
54	A4	BASIC	NON-NEG	0.06377	57.192	0
55	A5	BASIC	NON-NEG	1	77.482	0
56	b1	BASIC	NON-NEG	−0.006905	179.098	0
57	b2	BASIC	NON-NEG	−0.054842	354.372	0
58	b3	BASIC	NON-NEG	−34.8856	1.313	0
59	b4	BASIC	NON-NEG	−0.22928	12.878	0
60	OBS1		SURPLUS	0	0	−0.21967
61	OBS2		SURPLUS	0	0	−0.1325
62	OBS3		SURPLUS	0	0	−0.05154
63	OBS4		SURPLUS	0	0	−0.06377
64	OBS5		SURPLUS	0	0	−1
65	OBS6		SLACK	0	0	−.006905
66	OBS7		SLACK	0	0	−.054842
67	OBS8		SLACK	0	0	−4.8856
68	OBS9		SLACK	0	0	−.22928

(continued)

Exhibit: 9.4 *(continued)*

Constraint Summary

Row	Constraint Name	Type	S/S Col	Rhs	Activity	Dual Activity
1	OBS1	GE	60	0	0	-0.21967
2	OBS2	GE	61	0	0	-0.1325
3	OBS3	GE	62	0	0	-0.05154
4	OBS4	GE	63	0	0	-0.06377
5	OBS5	GE	64	0	0	-1
6	OBS6	LE	65	0	0	0.006905
7	OBS7	LE	66	0	0	0.054842
8	OBS8	LE	67	0	0	34.8856
9	OBS9	LE	68	0	0	0.22928
10	OBS10	EQ	.	1	1	49.124182
11	OBS11	OBJECTVE	.	0	49.124182	.

18.9913, implying

$$\delta = \frac{49.1242 - 30.1329}{43.3600} = 0.4380.$$

It should be noted that the input-oriented technical efficiency (β) equals unity. Hence, δ_T equals zero. No part of the unrealized profit is due to technical inefficiency. By implication, all of the profit inefficiency is allocative.

9.11 Summary

When market prices of inputs and outputs are available, one can use DEA to measure the level of *economic efficiency* of a firm. The minimum cost of producing the observed output level of a firm can be obtained from the optimal solution of the relevant cost-minimization problem. The ratio of this minimum cost and the actual cost of the firm measures its *cost efficiency*, which can be decomposed into two separate factors representing its *technical* and *allocative efficiency*, respectively. When outputs as well as inputs are choice variables, the appropriate format for efficiency analysis is the DEA model for profit maximization. The difference between the maximum and the actual profit normalized by the actual cost of a firm measures the *return on outlay* lost due to inefficiency. It is possible to separately identify the contribution of technical and allocative inefficiency in a differential decomposition of the lost *return on outlay*.

Guide to the Literature

A dual representation of the technology through an indirect aggregator function like the cost or the profit function is at the core of neoclassical production economics. Building on the earlier work of Hotelling (1932) and Shephard (1953), researchers have introduced various innovative specifications (e.g., the Translog and the Generalized Leontief form) of the dual cost and profit functions to analyze the characteristics of the technology. Decomposition of cost efficiency into the technical and allocative efficiency components is due to Farrell (1957). Banker and Maindiratta (1988) carried out a parallel decomposition of profit efficiency. The additive decomposition of profit inefficiency (measured as the lost return on outlay) is due to Färe, Grosskopf, Ray, Miller, and Mukherjee (2000).

10

Nonparametric Approaches in Production Economics

10.1 Introduction

There are two distinct strands in the literature on nonparametric analysis of productivity and efficiency. One, identifiable as the *Charnes–Cooper school*, builds on the DEA models with primary focus on observed input and output quantity data. In a sense, it is a continuation of the mathematical programming approach to optimization developed by Charnes and Cooper in various papers prior to the introduction of DEA and forms a part of the overall operational research/management science methodology. The other, often identified as the *Afriat school*, uses both quantity and price information and makes use of the neoclassical theory of duality between direct and indirect aggregator functions like the production, cost, and profit functions. Building on earlier work by Debreu, Shephard, and Farrell and developed by Afriat (1972), Hanoch and Rothschild (1972), Diewert and Parkan (1983), and Varian (1984), among others, the nonparametric approach to production analysis fits right into the standard neoclassical tradition while, at the same time, providing a nonparametric alternative to the ubiquitous econometric methodology. An implication of the duality theorems is that the important characteristics of the technological relationship between inputs and outputs (e.g., the elasticity of substitution between a pair of inputs, returns to scale, homotheticity of the technology) can be analyzed through the cost function instead of the production function. For duality theory to be valid, however, one must assume optimizing behavior of producers.

Researchers in the *Afriat school* (e.g., Varian [1984]) address the following questions using behavioral data on input and output prices and quantities of firms:

- Are the data consistent with profit maximization (cost minimization) by price-taking firms for any regular production technology satisfying the assumptions of free disposability of inputs and outputs (with or without convexity)?

- How can we recover the underlying technological constraints faced by the firm from the observed data?
- How can we test restrictions on the underlying technology (e.g., separability or homogeneity)?
- Can we make extrapolations for out-of-sample data?

Varian developed the Weak Axiom of Cost Minimization (WACM) and the Weak Axiom of Profit Maximization (WAPM) to test the consistency of the data with cost minimization and profit maximization, respectively. He also showed how one can utilize the data to construct an outer and an inner approximation of the underlying production possibility set faced by firms in an industry. These may, in turn, be used to define upper and lower bounds on the production efficiency of a firm. This chapter explores the links between Varian's axioms of optimizing behavior and other nonparametric models of efficiency analysis. Section 10.2 provides the rationale behind the WACM and examines how it relates to FDH analysis on the one hand and the standard cost-minimization DEA model on the other.

In econometric analysis, the neoclassical dual cost function can be estimated from total expenditure, input price, and output quantity data. One does not need information on input quantities. To apply the WACM, however, one must have input quantity data along with input price and output quantity data. Section 10.3 presents a nonparametric test due to Diewert and Parkan (1983) that can be applied even when input quantity data are not available. Section 10.4 describes the Weak Axiom of Cost Dominance (WACD) developed by Ray (1997). The relation among WACD, WACM, and an FDH-type dominance analysis is examined in Section 10.5. Section 10.6 presents Varian's WAPM and defines an outer approximation of the production possibility set. In Section 10.7, the inner and outer approximations are employed to define upper and lower bounds on the technical efficiency of a firm. Section 10.8 summarizes the main points of the chapter.

10.2 Weak Axiom of Cost Minimization

Consider a data set relating to N firms from an industry. For any individual firm $i (i = 1, 2, \ldots, N)$, let y_i denote its scalar output, x^i its actual input vector, and w^i the vector of input prices paid by this firm. Thus, its actual cost is

$C_i = w^{i\prime} x^i$. The question is whether the firm is producing its output using the least-cost input bundle. To answer this question, one needs to define the input requirement set

$$V(y_i) = \{x : x \text{ can produce } y_i\}. \tag{10.1}$$

It is possible, of course, to derive $V(y_i)$ from the free disposal convex hull of the observed input–output bundles. One would, then, solve the relevant LP problem to determine the minimum cost $C(w^i, y_i)$ and compare it with the actual cost C_i. Varian (1984) proposes a simple alternative to this LP procedure. Suppose that the observations are rearranged in ascending order of the output quantities produced. Thus, $j \geq i$ implies $y_j \geq y_i$. Now, if there is some firm $j \geq i$ such that $w^{i\prime} x^j < w^{i\prime} x^i$, then firm i cannot be minimizing cost. The intuition behind this test is quite straightforward. Note that x^j actually produces y_j. Hence, by free disposability of output, x^j can also produce y_i. That is, $x^j \in V(y_i)$. Hence, if $w^{i\prime} x^j < w^{i\prime} x^i$, obviously x^i is not the least-cost bundle in the input requirement set of output y_i. That is, firm i is not minimizing cost. This is a remarkably powerful test that can be carried out with the very little computation.

Varian formalized this test as the Weak Axiom of Cost Minimization (WACM) that can be stated as follows:

For an observed data set to be consistent with competitive cost minimizing hypothesis, we must have $w^{i\prime} x^i \leq w^{i\prime} x^j$ for all $i = 1, 2, \ldots, N$, and $j \geq i$.

Figure 10.1 illustrates the WACM for the two-input, one-output case. The points P_1 through P_5 show the observed input bundles of five firms that have been arranged in ascending order of the output levels. That is, $y_5 \geq y_4 \geq \cdots \geq y_1$. Focus on firm 3 and its input bundle $x^3 = (x_1^3, x_2^3)$ shown by the point P_3. The line AB is the expenditure line $w^{3\prime} x = C_3 = w^{3\prime} x^3$. All input bundles shown by points to the left of this line would cost less than C_3. In this diagram, point P_4 showing the input bundle x^4 (used by firm 4) that produces output $y_4 \geq y_3$ lies to the left of AB and is, therefore, less expensive than x^3 at price w^3. Thus, firm 3 violates WACM and cannot be minimizing cost.

It may be noted that in deriving WACM it was not necessary to assume convexity of the input requirement set. The relation between WACM and the standard DEA model for cost minimization under VRS can be best understood

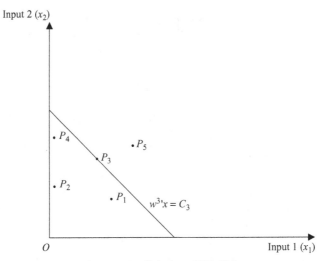

Figure 10.1 Violation of WACM.

by considering the following mixed-integer programming problem:

$$\min w^{i\prime} x$$

$$\text{s.t.} \sum_{j=1}^{N} \lambda_j x^j \leq x;$$

$$\sum_{j=1}^{N} \lambda_j y_j \geq y_i; \tag{10.2}$$

$$\sum_{j=1}^{N} \lambda_j = 1;$$

$$x \geq 0; \quad \lambda_j \in \{0, 1\} \ (j = 1, 2, \ldots, N).$$

Note that the constraints on the λ_j's ensure that only one λ_j will take the value 1 whereas all others will be 0 at the optimal solution. Further, the output constraint requires $j \geq i$. Clearly, there will not be any input slack in the optimal bundle x^*. That means that x^* will be the observed input bundle of some firm j satisfying $j \geq i$. In other words, applying WACM to test for cost-minimizing behavior on the part of firm i is equivalent to solving the mixed integer programming problem (10.2). This is a restricted version of the standard DEA LP model for cost minimization under the VRS assumption, where the λ_j's are allowed to take *any nonnegative value* as long as they add up to unity.

It can be easily shown that using WACM is equivalent to applying FDH analysis with aggregated inputs. Suppose that one uses the input price vector w^i to define the aggregate input bundles

$$X_j = w^{i'} x^j \quad (j = 1, 2, \ldots, N).$$

Then, the input–output combination (x^j, y_j) can be expressed as the single-input, single-output pair (X_j, y_j). Now, consider the input-oriented FDH efficiency of firm i. For this, we only consider firms with output at least as large as y_i. Firm i is evaluated as 100% FDH efficient if and only if $X_j \geq X_i$ for all $j \geq i$. This is equivalent to the condition $w^{i'} x^j \geq w^{i'} x^i$ for $j \geq i$. But that is exactly the WACM.

Consider again the optimization problem (10.2) and the constraints

$$\sum_{j=1}^{N} \lambda_j x^j \leq x.$$

Now, premultiply multiply both sides by w^i to get

$$\sum_{j=1}^{N} \lambda_j (w^{i'} x^j) \leq w^{i'} x.$$

This can be expressed as $\sum_{j=1}^{N} \lambda_j X_j \leq X$.
Define

$$\theta = \frac{w^{i'} x}{w^{i'} x^i} = \frac{X}{X_i}.$$

Then, the objective function in (10.2) is θX_i. Because $X_i = w^{i'} x^i$ is a constant, minimizing $w^{i'} x$ is equivalent to minimizing θ. Thus, the optimization problem in (10.2) can be expressed as

$$\min \theta$$

$$\text{s.t.} \sum_{j=1}^{N} \lambda_j X_j \leq \theta X_i;$$

$$\sum_{j=1}^{N} \lambda_j y_j \geq y_i; \qquad \qquad (10.2a)$$

$$\sum_{j=1}^{N} \lambda_j = 1;$$

$$x \geq 0; \quad \lambda_j \in \{0, 1\}(j = 1, 2, \ldots, N); \quad \theta \text{ free.}$$

This is, clearly, the FDH problem in the aggregated input.

10.3 Testing Cost-Minimizing Behavior without Input Quantity Data

An advantage of estimating the dual cost function parametrically is that one does not need information on input quantities. By contrast, one needs the input quantity data to apply WACM as a test for cost-minimizing behavior. Diewert and Parkan (1983) proposed the following nonparametric test of consistency of the observed output, expenditure, and input price data with cost-minimizing behavior when input quantities are not known.

Suppose that observations are arranged in ascending order of the output quantities produced. Focus on firm i producing output y_i and consider all firms k with output $y_k \leq y_i$. Now, consider the LP problem

$$\tilde{C}_i = \min w^{i'} x$$

$$\text{s.t.} \quad w^{k'} x \leq C_k (k \leq i); \qquad \qquad (10.3)$$

$$x \geq 0.$$

Diewert and Parkan show that if $\tilde{C}_i > C_i$ for any observation i, then the data cannot be consistent with cost minimization for any regular technology. The underlying logic is easily explained by means of a diagram. Suppose that there

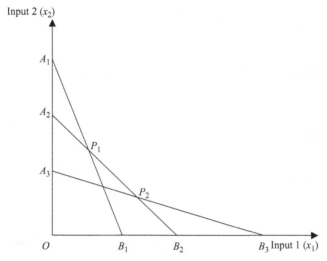

Figure 10.2 An application of the Diewert-Parkan test of cost minimization.

are only three firms and consider the LP problem for $i = 3$:

$$\tilde{C}_3 = \min w^{3\prime} x$$

$$\text{s.t. } w^{1\prime} x \geq C_1;$$

$$w^{2\prime} x \geq C_2; \tag{10.4}$$

$$w^{3\prime} x \geq C_3;$$

$$x \geq 0.$$

For the two-input case, the constraints are shown in Figure 10.2. The line $A_1 B_1$ shows the expenditure line of firm 1 ($w^{1\prime} x = C_1$). Similarly, the lines $A_2 B_2$ and $A_3 B_3$ correspond to the expenditure lines of firms 2 and 3, respectively. If the optimal solution x^* lies on the line $A_3 B_3$, then $\tilde{C}_3 = C_3$. By construction, $\tilde{C}_3 \geq C_3$. But if $\tilde{C}_3 > C_3$, then the entire feasible set lies strictly above the line $A_3 B_3$. This implies that at least one of the other two lines $A_1 B_1$ and $A_2 B_2$ lies entirely above the line $A_3 B_3$. In Figure 10.3, $A_2 B_2$ lies above $A_3 B_3$. Now, the unobserved input bundles of firms 2 and 3 lie somewhere on the expenditure lines $A_2 B_2$ and $A_3 B_3$, respectively. But all input bundles below the line $A_2 B_2$ cost less than C_2 at the input price vector w^2. This means that the input bundle of firm 3 costs less than the input bundle of firm 2. Thus, the input bundle of firm 2 violates WACM with respect to the input bundle of firm 3. Hence, a necessary condition for the data to be consistent with WACM is that $\tilde{C}_i = C_i$

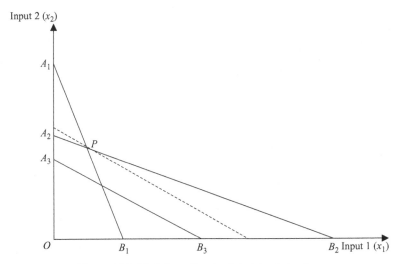

Figure 10.3 Violation of cost-minimizing behavior.

for each observation i. Diewert and Parkan have shown that this is also a sufficient condition for the data to be consistent with cost minimization for a regular technology characterized by the family of input requirement sets:

$$\tilde{V}(y_i) = \{x : w^{k\prime} x \geq C_k : k \leq i\}. \tag{10.5}$$

Although this test provides a check of consistency of the data with cost-minimizing behavior by the relevant firms, if any violation is detected, it fails to provide a measure of the degree of inefficiency of any individual firm. Diewert and Parkan (1983) suggest the ratio

$$\tilde{\beta}_i = \frac{\tilde{C}_i}{C_i} \tag{10.6}$$

to measure the degree of violation of cost minimization. This ratio has no natural efficiency interpretation, however. Clearly, $\tilde{\beta}_i \geq 1$ by construction. Hence, it cannot be a measure of efficiency of firm i. Nor can it be a measure of the level of efficiency of any other firm $k < i$. In fact, even when $C_i < \tilde{C}_i = C_k$ for some firm k, this does not indicate that firm k has violated the assumption of cost-minimizing behavior. This is illustrated in Figure 10.3. In this example, the feasible area is the set of points on or above the broken line A_1PB_2. The minimum of $w^{3\prime} x$ is attained at the point P representing the input bundle z. Thus, $\tilde{C}_3 = w^{3\prime} z > C_3$. But the point P also lies on both the lines A_1B_1 and A_2B_2. Hence, $\tilde{C}_3 = C_1 = C_2$. When we look at the diagram, however, we find that a segment of the line $A_1 B_1$ lies below both the lines $A_2 B_2$ and $A_3 B_3$ and the unobserved input bundle of firm 1 could be located in this segment of its expenditure line. In that case, there is no violation of cost-minimizing behavior by firm 1. On the other hand, the line $A_2 B_2$ lies entirely above the line $A_3 B_3$. Hence, firm 2 is definitely cost inefficient. But the optimal solution of the LP problem fails to distinguish between firm 1 and firm 2. In any case, $\tilde{\beta}_3$ does not measure the degree of violation of WACM by firm 2.

10.4 Weak Axiom of Cost Dominance

Consider any firm j producing the output y_j. It faces the input price vector w^j and incurs the cost C_j. Now, consider the set of input bundles

$$E(j) = \{x : w^{j'}x = C_j; x \geq 0\}. \tag{10.7}$$

This is the set of all input bundles that lie on the expenditure line of firm j. Now, consider the input price vector w^i faced by the firm i producing output $y_i \leq y_j$ and define

$$C_{ij}^* = \max w^{i'}x$$

$$\text{s.t. } x \in E(j). \tag{10.8}$$

Clearly, the true but unobserved input bundle of firm $j(z_j)$ is in $E(j)$. Hence, $w^{i'}z^j \leq C_{ij}^*$. But $z^j \in V(y_i)$. Thus, by free disposability of output, $z^j \in V(y_i)$. Next, consider the minimum cost of firm output y_i at input price w^i:

$$C_i^* = \min w^{i'}x$$

$$\text{s.t. } x \in V(y_i). \tag{10.9}$$

We know that $z^j \in V(y_i)$. Hence, $C_i^* \leq w^{i'}z^j$. But $w^{i'}z^j \leq C_{ij}^*$. Thus, C_{ij}^* is an upper bound on C_i^*. For each $j \geq i$, we can compute C_{ij}^*. Of course, for $j = i$, $C_{ij}^* = C_i$. We can find the lowest upper bound

$$C_i^{**} = \min [C_i; C_{ij}^* (j > i)]. \tag{10.10}$$

Consider the one-output, n-input case. Let $i = 1$ and $j = 2$. In this case,

$$C_{12}^* = \sum_{i=1}^{n} w_i^1 x_i$$

$$\text{s.t.} \sum_{i=1}^{n} w_i^2 x_i = C_2. \qquad (10.11)$$

$$x_i \geq 0 \ (i = 1, 2, \ldots, n).$$

The dual of this problem is

$$\min \alpha C_2$$

$$\text{s.t.} \ \alpha w_i^2 \geq w_i^1 (i = 1, 2, \ldots, n); \qquad (10.12)$$

$$\alpha \text{ unrestricted.}$$

Clearly,

$$\alpha^* = \max \left\{ \frac{w_1^1}{w_1^2}, \frac{w_2^1}{w_2^2}, \ldots, \frac{w_n^1}{w_n^2} \right\}. \qquad (10.13)$$

By duality,

$$C_{12}^* = \alpha^* C_2 = \max \left\{ \frac{w_1^1 C_2}{w_1^2}, \frac{w_2^1 C_2}{w_2^2}, \ldots, \frac{w_n^1 C_2}{w_n^2} \right\}. \qquad (10.14)$$

For any observation k, define the normalized input prices

$$v_r^k = \frac{w_r^k}{C_k} \quad (r = 1, 2, \ldots, n). \qquad (10.15)$$

Then,

$$C_{12}^* = \max \left\{ \frac{v_1^1}{v_1^2}, \frac{v_2^1}{v_2^2}, \ldots, \frac{v_n^1}{v_n^2} \right\} \cdot C_1. \qquad (10.16)$$

When only firms 1 and 2 are considered,

$$C_1^* = \min \{C_1, C_{12}^*\}. \qquad (10.17)$$

Hence, an upper bound on the cost efficiency of firm 1 is

$$\frac{C_1^*}{C_1} = \min \left\{ 1, \frac{C_{12}^*}{C_1} \right\}. \qquad (10.18)$$

Clearly, if $v_r^1 < v_r^2$ for every input r, then the cost efficiency of firm 1 must be less than 1.

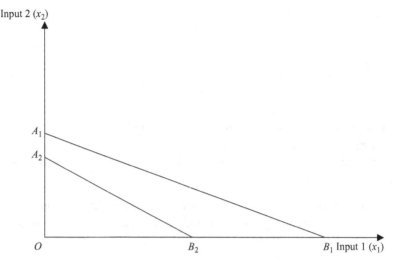

Figure 10.4 An application of WACD.

Here, we have looked at only two firms. In the general case for any firm i, its minimum cost is bounded from above by

$$C_i^{**} = \min \{C_{ij}^*; j \geq i\} \qquad (10.19a)$$

where

$$C_{ij}^* = \max \left\{ \frac{v_1^i}{v_1^j}, \frac{v_2^i}{v_2^j}, \ldots, \frac{v_n^i}{v_n^j} \right\} \cdot C_i. \qquad (10.19b)$$

We have now derived the following WACD:

If, for any firm i producing output y_i, there is any other firm j producing output $y_j \geq y_i$ such that for every input $r(r = 1, 2, \ldots, n)$

$$\frac{w_r^i}{C_i} < \frac{w_r^j}{C_j},$$

then firm i cannot be cost minimizing.

For the two-input case, this result is quite obvious and is illustrated in Figure 10.4. Assume that $\frac{w_1^1}{C_1} < \frac{w_1^2}{C_2}$ and $\frac{w_2^1}{C_1} < \frac{w_2^2}{C_2}$. Let the expenditure line of firm 1 be $A_1 B_1$. Similarly, $A_2 B_2$ shows the expenditure line of firm 2. Hence,

$$OB_1 = \frac{C_1}{w_1^1}; \quad OB_2 = \frac{C_2}{w_1^2}.$$

Thus,

$$OB_2 < OB_1.$$

Similarly,

$$OA_2 = \frac{C_2}{w_2^2} < OA_1 = \frac{C_1}{w_2^1}.$$

This implies that the line $A_2 B_2$ lies entirely to the left of the line $A_1 B_1$. Thus, firm 1 cannot be cost minimizing.

A practical application of the proposed test of consistency would involve the following steps:

1. For any firm i, delete all observations with lower levels of output.
2. For each remaining firm k (including firm i), compute the normalized input prices

$$v_r^k = \frac{w_r^k}{C_k} \quad (r = 1, 2, \ldots, n).$$

3. Obtain the ratios

$$f_1^{ki} = \frac{v_1^k}{v_1^i}; \quad f_2^{ki} = \frac{v_2^k}{v_2^i}, \ldots, v_m^{ki} = \frac{v_m^k}{v_m^i}. \tag{10.20}$$

4. If for any $k \neq i$, $f_r^{ki} > 1$ for all $r (r = 1, 2, \ldots, n)$, then firm i is not cost efficient.

If firm i is found to be inefficient, its cost efficiency can be obtained as

$$\theta_i = \min \left\{ f_r^{ki}; r = 1, 2, \ldots, n; k \geq i \right\} \tag{10.21}$$

10.5 Relation among WACM, WACD, and Dominance Analysis

Consistency with WACM requires that for $j \geq i$, that is, for $y_j \geq y_i$,

$$w^{i\prime} x^i \leq w^{i\prime} x^j. \tag{10.22}$$

Dividing both sides of this inequality by C_i, we get

$$\frac{w^{i\prime} x^i}{C_i} \leq \frac{w^{i\prime} x^j}{C_i}. \tag{10.23}$$

But

$$\frac{w^{i\prime} x^i}{C_i} = 1 = \frac{w^{j\prime} x^j}{C_j}. \tag{10.24}$$

Thus, WACM implies

$$\frac{w^{j\prime} x^j}{C_j} - \frac{w^{i\prime} x^j}{C_i} \leq 0. \tag{10.25}$$

This is the same as

$$\sum_{r=1}^{m} \left(v_r^j - v_r^i \right) x_r^j \leq 0. \tag{10.26}$$

Of course, when WACD is violated, $v_r^i < v_r^j$ for all r. In that case, this last inequality cannot hold for any semipositive input vector x^j. Thus, violation of WACD is sufficient for violation of WACM. With quantity information, however, we can detect violation of WACM even when WACD has not been violated.

We now show that in implementing WACD, we essentially apply the dominance criterion and our approach is similar to the method of FDH analysis but is applied in the context of the cost-indirect technology defined by Shephard (1974).

Consider an output vector[1] y and its input requirement set $V(y)$ consisting of all input vectors x that can produce y. Now, consider some input price vector w and a specified expenditure level C. As before, let $v = \frac{w}{C}$ be the resulting normalized input price vector. Define the budget set

$$B(v) = \{x : v'x \leq 1\}. \tag{10.27}$$

Now, consider the intersection of $V(y)$ and $B(v)$. If, for a given pair of y and v, $V(y) \cap B(v) \neq \emptyset$, then there is at least one input bundle x that can produce the output bundle y and costs no more than C at input price w. If this is the case, we may say that y is affordable at normalized input prices v. The cost-indirect technology can be characterized by the input price requirement set

$$\text{IV}(y) = \{v : V(y) \cap B(v) \neq \emptyset\}. \tag{10.28}$$

It is easy to show that input price requirement sets are monotonic in the normalized input price vector: If $v^0 \in \text{IV}(y_0)$ and $v^1 \leq v^0$, then $v^1 \in \text{IV}(y_0)$. It should be emphasized here that we do not need to assume free disposability of inputs for this monotonicity property. Suppose that $x^0 \in V(y_0)$ satisfies $v^0 x^0 \leq 1 \Leftrightarrow w^0 x^0 \leq C$. Now, suppose that $w^1 \leq w^0$. Then clearly,

---

[1] Varian considered the single-output case. But, generalization to multiple outputs is quite straightforward.

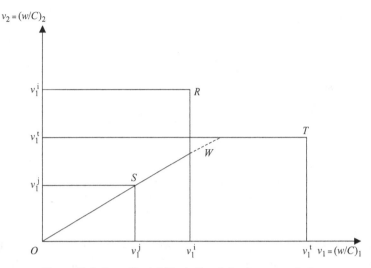

Figure 10.5 Free affordability hull and dominance analysis.

$w^{1'}x^0 \leq w^{0'}x \leq C$. Thus, $v^{1'}x^0 \leq 1 \Rightarrow x^0 \in B(v^1)$. Hence, $v^1 \in \mathrm{IV}(y_0)$. Because the same input bundle x^0 is considered for the production of y_0 under two different input price situations, the question of free disposability of inputs is irrelevant here. We do continue to assume free disposability of outputs, however. This assumption ensures that input price requirement sets are nested. That is, if $v \in \mathrm{IP}(y)$ and $\tilde{y} \leq y$, then $v \in \mathrm{IP}(\tilde{y})$.

Suppose that firm j faces the input price w^j and produces output y_j at cost C_j. The actual input bundle of firm $j (x^j)$ is not observed. We know, however, that $v^j = \frac{w^j}{C_j} \in \mathrm{IV}(y_j)$. Now, define the free affordability hull (FAH) of v^j:

$$\mathrm{FAH}(v^j) = \{v : v \leq v^j\}. \tag{10.29}$$

We may say that firm i facing input price w^i and producing output y_i at cost C_i dominates firm j if $y^i \geq y^j$ and $v^j = \frac{w^j}{C_j} \in \mathrm{FAH}(v^i)$.

An example of cost dominance[2] in the two-input case is given is Figure 10.5. The normalized input prices faced by firm i (v_1^i, v_2^i) are represented by the point R. Similarly, points S and T represent (v_1^j, v_2^j) and (v_1^t, v_2^t), the normalized input prices of firm j and firm t, respectively. Assume that both

---

[2] The concept of cost-dominance was first introduced by Van den Eeckaut, Tulkens, and Jamar (1993). However, they did not formally construct a model of cost-dominance when input prices vary across firms.

output levels y_i and y_t are at least as large as the output y_j because v^j is in the FAH of both v^i and v^t, the firms i and t cost dominate firm j. Now, consider the point W, showing the maximum radial expansion of v^j within the FAH of v^i. Let the scale of expansion be $\kappa_1 = \frac{OW}{OS}$. Thus, the point W represents the normalized input price vector $v^W = (\kappa_1 v_1^j, \kappa_1 v_2^j)$. Because W is in the FAH of R, there exists at least one input bundle x satisfying $v^{W\prime} x \leq 1 \Rightarrow \kappa_1(\frac{w^{j\prime}}{C}x) \leq 1$ such that $x \in V(y^i)$. But, by free disposability of outputs $v^W \in$ IP (y^j). Therefore, there exists some input bundle $x \in V(y^j)$ satisfying $w^j x \leq \frac{C_j}{\kappa_1}$. Hence, the minimum cost of producing y^j at input price w^j cannot be any more than $\frac{C_j}{\kappa_1}$. In other words, $\frac{1}{\kappa_1}$ is an upper bound of the cost efficiency of firm j.

In the two-input case illustrated in Figure 10.5,

$$\kappa_1 = \min \left\{ \frac{v_1^i}{v_1^j}, \frac{v_2^i}{v_2^j} \right\}. \tag{10.30}$$

In a perfectly analogous manner,

$$\kappa_2 = \min \left\{ \frac{v_1^t}{v_1^j}, \frac{v_2^t}{v_2^j} \right\} \tag{10.31}$$

is also an upper bound of the cost efficiency of firm j. In this example, an estimate of the cost efficiency of firm j is $\min\{\kappa_1, \kappa_2\}$. Generalization of this criterion to multiple comparisons and to the n-input case is quite straightforward. Let the set D consist of firms that cost dominate the firm j. Thus,

$$D = \left\{ i : y^i \geq y^j, \frac{w^j}{C_j} \leq \frac{w^i}{C_i} \right\}. \tag{10.32}$$

Then, an upper bound of the cost efficiency of firm j is

$$\min_{i \in D} \left[\max \left\{ \frac{v_1^i}{v_1^j}, \frac{v_2^i}{v_2^j}, \dots, \frac{v_m^i}{v_m^j} \right\} \right] \tag{10.33}$$

This is clearly equivalent to the measure obtained earlier using WACD.

It should be noted here that efficiency based on FDH analysis is a primal measure because it uses output and input quantities. On the other hand, WACD (or, equivalently, FAH analysis) yields a dual efficiency measure because output, input price, and cost data are utilized but input quantities are not required. Moreover, this dual approach does not require free disposability of inputs and is, therefore, even less restrictive about the admissible technology.

10.6 Weak Axiom of Profit Maximization

We now add output price information to the input price, input quantity, and output quantity data. The objective is to test whether the observed input–output choices of the firms are consistent with competitive profit-maximizing behavior by these firms. A profit-maximizing firm can choose *any input–output combination* (x, y) as long as it lies in the production possibility set and is a feasible production plan. Because all observed input–output bundles are feasible by assumption, any firm in the sample could choose the actual input–output bundle of any other firm if it found it more profitable to do so. Consider firm i and its actual input–output bundle (x^i, y_i). It faces the output price p_i and the input price vector w^i. Thus, the actual profit earned by this firm is

$$\Pi_i = p_i y_i - w^{i\prime} x^i. \tag{10.34}$$

If this firm selected some other input–output combination (x^j, y_j), at prices (p_i, w^i), it would earn the profit

$$\Pi_{ij} = p_i y_j - w^{i\prime} x^j. \tag{10.35}$$

Clearly, if $\Pi_i < \Pi_{ij}$ for any $j \neq i$, then firm i is not maximizing profit. Varian (1984) formalized this simple but extremely powerful result as the WAPM:

If $p_i y_i - w^{i\prime} x^i \geq p_i y_j - w^{i\prime} x^j$ for $i, j = 1, 2, \ldots, N$, then there exists a production possibility set that rationalizes the data.

Here, rationalization implies that the input–output bundles are consistent with competitive profit-maximizing behavior at the relevant input–output prices. Despite its computational simplicity, WAPM is by far the most powerful nonparametric test of optimizing behavior. As has been shown herein, consistency with WAPM is a necessary condition for profit maximization by the observed firms *over any production possibility set containing the observed input–output bundles*. At the same time, if the data are indeed consistent with WAPM, then there exists a convex production possibility set containing the data points, for which the actual input–output combinations of the individual firms are profit maximizing at the applicable prices. In fact, the free disposal convex hull of the observed input–output bundles is one such production possibility set. In other words, if firm j satisfies WAPM, then its actual profit is what one would obtain at the optimal solution of the DEA LP problem for profit maximization specified previously in Chapter 9.

The proof is quite straightforward. Suppose that

$$p_i y_i - w^{i'} x^i \geq p_i y_j - w^{i'} x^j \quad (j = 1, 2, \ldots, N). \quad (10.36)$$

Then, for any $\lambda_j > 0$,

$$\lambda_j(p_i y_i - w^{i'} x^i) \geq p^{i'}(\lambda_j y_j) - w^{i'}(\lambda_j x^j) \quad (j = 1, 2, \ldots, N). \quad (10.37)$$

Now, suppose $\sum_{j=1}^{N} \lambda_j = 1$. Define $\sum_{j=1}^{N} \lambda_j y_j = \bar{y}$ and $\sum_{j=1}^{N} \lambda_j x^j = \bar{x}$. Then,

$$p_i y_i - w^{i'} x^i \geq p_i \bar{y} - w^{i'} \bar{x} \quad (10.38)$$

for any $\bar{x} = \sum_{j=1}^{N} \lambda_j x^j$ and $\bar{y} = \sum_{j=1}^{N} \lambda_j y_j$ satisfying $\sum_{j=1}^{N} \lambda_j = 1$. Hence, by free disposability of inputs and output, $p_i y_i - w^{i'} x^i \geq p_i y - w^{i'} x$ for all (x, y) satisfying $x \geq \bar{x}$ and $y \leq \bar{y}$. This proves that the actual input–output bundle of firm i maximizes profit for prices (p_i, w^i) over the free disposal convex hull of the observed bundles.

What is more interesting is that even when a firm fails to satisfy WAPM, one can get a measure of the maximum profit without having to solve the DEA LP. This is because the free disposal convex hull is a finite polytope and the optimal solution will be one of the extreme points of the set. But each extreme point represents some actually observed input–output bundle. Hence, the optimal solution is merely the input–output combination (x^j, y_j) for which $\Pi_{ij} = p_i y_j - w^{i'} x^j$ is the maximum for all $j(j = 1, 2, \ldots, N)$.

It should be noted that one does not get the optimal value of the DEA LP problem for cost minimization by merely applying WACM. In particular, if firm k does satisfy WACM, its actual cost need not be what one would get at the optimal solution of the DEA problem. This is because in the application of WACM, all firms producing strictly smaller quantities of output than y_k are deleted. This reduces the set of feasible bundles for cost minimization.

Apart from providing a direct way to measure the maximum profit $\Pi(p_i, w^i)$, WAPM helps to define a unique "outer approximation" of the production possibility set that serves as a complement to the "inner approximation" defined by the free disposal convex hull of the input–output data points. As is shown in the following section, the alternative approximations of the production possibility set can be used to define upper and lower bounds on the efficiency of a firm.

10.7 Upper and Lower Bounds on Efficiency

Efficiency of a firm is measured with reference to a specific production possibility set. In nonparametric analysis, we assume only free disposability of inputs and outputs along with convexity of the production possibility set. In this section, we show how to construct two different production possibility sets from observed input–output data that satisfy these assumptions.

Consider, first, the following one-input, one-output production function, $y = f(x)$. Assume that $f(x)$ is concave and nondecreasing in x. Then, the production possibility set

$$A = \{(x, y) : y \le f(x)\} \text{ is convex.}$$

Now, suppose that (x_0, y_0) satisfies $f(x_0) = y_0$ and thus lies on the production function. Then, convexity of the production possibility set ensures that there exists a tangent line

$$y = \alpha_0 + \beta_0 x; \quad \beta_0 \ge 0$$

such that

$$y_0 = \alpha_0 + \beta_0 x_0,$$

and for any (x, y) satisfying $y = f(x)$,

$$y \le \alpha_0 + \beta_0 x.$$

Clearly, this tangent line $y = \alpha_0 + \beta_0 x$ is a linear approximation of the production function and the half-space

$$B_0 = \{(x, y) : y \le \alpha_0 + \beta_0 x\}$$

is one such production possibility set that satisfies all the regularity assumptions. It should be noted further that the production possibility set A is a subset of B_0. Of course, (x_0, y_0) is only one point on the production function. Suppose that we have k different points (x_j, y_j) $(j = 1, 2, \ldots, k)$ all lying on the production function. Then, for each such point (x_j, y_j), there exists a tangent line

$$y = \alpha_j + \beta_j x$$

such that

$$y_j = \alpha_j + \beta_j x_j,$$

and for any (x, y) satisfying $y = f(x)$,

$$y \leq \alpha_j + \beta_j x.$$

Each associated half-space

$$B_j = \{(x, y) : y \leq \alpha_j + \beta_j x\} \quad (j = 1, 2, \ldots, k) \quad (10.39)$$

is a valid estimate of the underlying production possibility set. Thus, an outer approximation to the true production possibility set A is the set

$$L = \cap_{j=1}^{k} B_j. \quad (10.40)$$

Correspondingly, an outer approximation to the true production function is

$$f^+(x) = \min \{\alpha_j + \beta_j x; (j = 1, 2, \ldots, k)\}. \quad (10.41)$$

Diewert and Parkan (1983) and Varian (1984) call this the *overproduction function* because $f^+(x) \geq f(x)$ for all values of x. If one uses the overproduction function to measure the efficiency of an actual input–output pair $(\hat{x}, \hat{y})$, then the measured efficiency

$$\text{TE}^+ = \frac{\hat{y}}{f^+(\hat{x})} \quad (10.42)$$

underestimates the true efficiency

$$\text{TE} = \frac{\hat{y}}{f(\hat{x})}. \quad (10.43)$$

In this sense, it is a lower bound of the efficiency of the firm. This is best explained with the help of a numerical example and an accompanying diagram. Consider the production function

$$f(x) = 2\sqrt{x} - 1; \quad x \geq \frac{1}{4}. \quad (10.44)$$

This is shown by the curve AQ in Figure 10.6. The corresponding production possibility set is

$$A = \left\{ (x, y) : x \geq \frac{1}{4}; \ y \leq 2\sqrt{x} - 1 \right\}. \quad (10.45)$$

Suppose that we observe the following input–output quantities of six firms:

Firm 1: $(x = 1, y = 1)$; Firm 2: $(x = 4, y = 3)$; Firm 3: $(x = 9, y = 5)$;

Firm 4: $(x = 16, y = 7)$; Firm 5: $(x = 2.25, y = 1.5)$; Firm 6: $(6.25, y = 3.6)$.

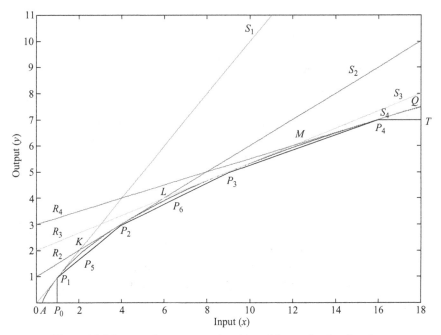

Figure 10.6 Inner and outer approximations of the production function.

These input–output bundles are shown by the points P_1 through P_6. Of these, firms 1 through 4 are fully efficient and the corresponding points all lie on the production frontier. By contrast, firms 5 and 6 are inefficient and points P_5 and P_6 both lie below the frontier. The tangents to the production possibility set are

$$y = x \quad \text{at point } P_1 \text{ shown by the line } OS_1,$$

$$y = 1 + \frac{1}{2}x \quad \text{at point } P_2 \text{ shown by the line } R_2S_2,$$

$$y = 2 + \frac{1}{3}x \quad \text{at point } P_3 \text{ shown by the line } R_3S_3, \text{ and}$$

$$y = 3 + \frac{1}{4}x \quad \text{at point } P_4 \text{ shown by the line } R_4S_4.$$

Thus, the outer approximation of the true production possibility set A is the area lying on or below all four tangent lines. The overproduction function is the broken line segment $OKLMS_4$. In this case, is the function

$$f^+(x) = x, \qquad 0 \le x \le 2;$$

$$f^+(x) = 1 + \frac{1}{2}x, \quad 2 \le x \le 6; \qquad (10.46)$$

$$f^+(x) = 2 + \frac{1}{3}x, \quad 6 \le x \le 12;$$

$$f^+(x) = 3 + \frac{1}{4}x, \quad 12 \le x.$$

Note that $f^+(x)$ equals $f(x)$ at the tangency points and exceeds $f(x)$ at all other levels of x. Thus, for firms 1 through 4, $TE^+ = TE = 1$. On the other hand, for firm 5, $f(x) = 2$ and $f^+(x) = 2.125$. Hence,

$$TE^+(P_5) = \frac{1.5}{2.125} = 0.70588 \quad \text{and} \quad TE(P_5) = \frac{1.5}{2} = 0.75.$$

Similarly, for firm 6, $f^+(x) = 4.125$ and $f(x) = 4$. Thus,

$$TE^+(P_6) = \frac{3.6}{4.125} = 0.87273 \quad \text{and} \quad TE(P_6) = \frac{3.6}{4} = 0.9.$$

Next, consider the familiar free disposable convex hull of the observed points P_1 through P_6 shown by the area under the broken line $P_0 P_1 P_2 P_3 P_4 T$ in Figure 10.6. Obviously, it is a subset of the true production possibility set.

However, when the number of observed points lying on the frontier increases, the free disposal convex hull converges to the true production possibility set A. In this sense, it provides an inner approximation. The boundary points of this set constitute the underproduction function:

$$f^-(x) = \max y : y \le \sum_{j=1}^{6} \lambda_j y_j; \quad x \ge \sum_{j=1}^{6} \lambda_j x_j; \quad \sum_{j=1}^{6} \lambda_j = 1;$$

$$\lambda \ge 0 \, (j = 1, 2, \ldots, 6).$$

It is called the underproduction function because $f^-(x) \le f(x)$ for all values of x. One gets an upper bound of technical efficinency of any firm producing output y from input x as

$$TE^- = \frac{y}{f^-(x)}. \qquad (10.47)$$

In the present example,

$$f^-(x) \leq 1 \qquad\qquad \text{for } x = 1;$$

$$f^-(x) = \frac{1}{3} + \frac{2}{3}x \qquad \text{for } 1 \leq x \leq 4;$$

$$f^-(x) = \frac{7}{5} + \frac{2}{5}x \qquad \text{for } 4 \leq x \leq 9; \qquad\qquad (10.48)$$

$$f^-(x) = \frac{17}{7} + \frac{2}{7}x \qquad \text{for } 9 \leq x \leq 16;$$

$$f^-(x) = 7 \qquad\qquad \text{for } x \geq 16.$$

It may be noted that for the efficient points P_1 through P_4, $f^-(x) = f(x) = f^+(x)$. But for the inefficient points, $f^-(x) < f(x) < f^+(x)$. For firm 5, $f^-(x) = 1.67$ and $\text{TE}^- = \frac{1.5}{1.67} = \frac{9}{10}$. Similarly, for firm 6, $f^-(x) = 3.9$ and $\text{TE}^- = \frac{3.6}{3.9} = \frac{12}{13}$.

Of course, when, as in this example, the true production function is known, an exact measure of the technical efficiency of a firm is directly available and there is no need to bother about any upper or lower bound. In any empirical application, the true production technology is unknown and has to be estimated from the data. Consider a sample of input–output bundles shown in Figure 10.7 as isolated data points without the production function. We do not need to know the production function to obtain the free disposal convex hull of these points. Hence, a unique inner approximation of the production possibility set along with the underproduction function $f^-(x)$ is obtained from this sample. But the outer approximation now becomes problematic. Without specific knowledge of the production function, it is not possible to precisely draw a tangent to the production possibility set at any given point. We do know, however, that no feasible point from the production possibility set lies above the tangent. Hence, any straight line $y = \alpha + \beta x$ satisfying $\beta \geq 0$ and $\alpha + \beta x_j \geq y_j$ for all input–output bundles (x_j, y_j) $(j = 1, 2, \ldots, N)$ in the data set could potentially be a tangent to the production possibility set. To be a tangent to the unknown production possibility set at the point (x_k, y_k), it would have to actually pass through this point. If (x_k, y_k) is not an efficient input–output bundle, it would be an interior point of the production possibility set and no straight line through this point can be a tangent to the production possibility set. It is not known beforehand whether any point is on or below the frontier. Hence, an appropriate strategy is to draw the line $y = \alpha + \beta x$ as close as possible to the point ensuring at the same time that no observed point lies above it. For each observed input–output bundle (x_j, y_j), we will draw the specific line $y = \alpha_j + \beta_j x$ that lies

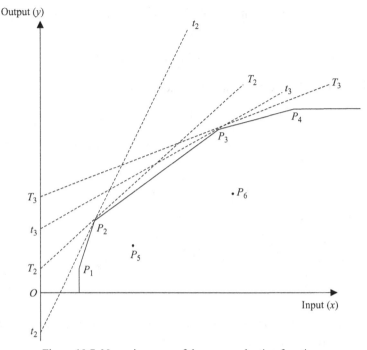

Figure 10.7 Nonuniqueness of the overproduction function.

above all of the data points. The half-space $B_j = \{(x, y) : \alpha_j + \beta_j x \geq y\}$ is a valid estimate of the production possibility set with the regularity properties assumed previously. The intersection of these half-spaces is an outer approximation of the unobserved true production possibility set. It is easy to see that, unlike the inner approximation, the outer approximation is not unique. As is shown in Figure 10.7, there are multiple tangent lines going through the efficient points like P_2 and P_3 resulting in alternative estimates of the overproduction function and the outer approximation of the production possibility set. It is precisely in this context that WAPM helps to construct an outer approximation that is also economically meaningful.

When firm k satisfies WAPM, $p_k y_k - w_k x_k \geq p_k y_j - w_k x_j$ for all firms j $(j = 1, 2, \ldots, N)$. Define $\Pi_k = p_k y_k - w_k x_k$, $\alpha_k = \frac{\Pi_k}{p_k}$, $\beta_k = \frac{w_k}{p_k}$. Then, $\alpha_k + \beta_k x_k = y_k$ and $\alpha_k + \beta_k x_j \geq y_j$ for all (x_j, y_j) in the data set. Hence, as shown before, $\alpha_k + \beta_k x \geq y$ for all (x, y) in the free disposal convex hull of the observed input bundles. Thus, $y = \alpha_k + \beta_k x$ is a tangent hyperplane to the production possibility set. Define the index set $E = \{j : \text{observation } j \text{ is consistent}$

with WAPM}. Then, an outer approximation to the production possibility set is

$$L = \{(x, y) : y \le \alpha_j + \beta_j x; \; j \in E\}. \tag{10.49}$$

Correspondingly, the overproduction function is

$$f^+(x) = \min(\alpha_k + \beta_k x) : k \in E\}. \tag{10.50}$$

Similarly, the outer approximation to the input requirement set for a specific output level y_0 is

$$\text{VO}(y_0) = \{x : (x, y_0) \in L\}. \tag{10.51}$$

The inner approximation, on the other hand, is

$$\text{VI}(y_0) = \left\{ x : \sum_{j=1}^{N} \lambda_j x_j \le x; \; \sum_{j=1}^{N} \lambda_j y_j \ge y_0; \; \sum_{j=1}^{N} \lambda_j = 1; \; \lambda_j \ge 0 \right\}. \tag{10.52}$$

The outer approximation to the input requirement set defined here is based on WAPM and is derived from the underlying outer approximation of the production possibility set. Varian, on the other hand, uses input prices of observations satisfying WACM to define the outer approximation of the input requirement set directly. The two definitions do not lead to the same set of input bundles for any given output level.

We conclude this section with an example using input and output quantity and price data for 21 U.S. airlines for the year 1984. The data form a part of a much larger data set constructed by Caves, Christensen, and Tretheway (1984). The output is a quantity index (QYI) constructed from (a) revenue passenger miles flow on scheduled flights, (b) revenue passenger miles flown on chartered flights, (c) revenue ton-miles of mail carried, and (d) revenue ton-miles of other cargo flown. The inputs included are quantity indexes of (a) labor (QLI), (b) fuel (QFI), (c) materials (QMI), (d) flight capital (QFLI), and (e) ground capital (QGRI). The corresponding price indexes are PYI (output price), PLI (labor price), PFI (fuel price), PMI (materials price), PFLI (flight capital price), and PGRI (ground capital price). One can use the IML procedure in SAS to check the consistency of the input–output data of the firms with WAPM. This is shown in Exhibit 10.1. The SAS data sets QTY84 and PRICE84 contain the input–output quantity and price data, respectively. For computational convenience, the input prices are entered with negative signs attached to them

Exhibit: 10.1. *Profitability study for 21 U.S. airlines (1984)*

```
OPTIONS NOCENTER;
DATA QTY84;
INPUT YI      QLI       QFI       QMI       QFLI      QGRI;
CARDS;
0.0816    1.2518    0.0702    1.2631    1.2579    0.0784
1.9365    0.3344    1.3036    0.3931    0.3273    2.1644
0.5455    0.2778    0.3906    0.3431    0.3012    0.4303
1.3897    0.6984    1.1230    0.6272    0.6006    1.7945
1.5157    1.1117    1.1765    1.1327    0.9668    1.4440
0.2133    0.1210    0.1524    0.1095    0.0859    0.1961
0.0370    0.1164    0.0456    0.1275    0.0791    0.0233
0.0439    0.1128    0.0395    0.0893    0.0774    0.0323
1.2485    0.1291    0.7906    0.1674    0.1071    0.6194
0.0458    0.0833    0.0459    0.0766    0.0672    0.0339
0.1387    1.2552    0.1236    1.5153    1.1490    0.1266
1.5685    0.1045    0.9764    0.0690    0.0670    1.2589
0.3277    0.0632    0.2154    0.0645    0.0545    0.2064
0.3040    0.0813    0.3004    0.0778    0.0611    0.2591
0.1550    1.4780    0.1168    1.5579    1.2602    0.2274
0.4332    1.6912    0.4369    1.5600    1.7614    0.3107
0.1997    0.1703    0.1806    0.1770    0.1387    0.1587
1.5134    0.2983    0.9349    0.3558    0.3177    1.5457
2.4424    1.2481    1.5965    1.2830    1.2726    2.7084
0.4214    0.3209    0.3740    0.3812    0.2898    0.4883
0.4933    0.2892    0.3547    0.3677    0.3239    0.3141
;
DATA PRICE84;
INPUT OBS PY PL PF PM PFL PGR;
DROP OBS;
CARDS;
 1 3564205 -383249.19 -894019.31 -283203.25 -194992.50 -86208.00
 2 2419225 -344729.88 -823391.00 -283819.63 -199609.44 -86158.31
 3 2098122 -353894.00 -843951.31 -283779.50 -175142.38 -86153.19
 4 3173110 -345456.00 -821327.56 -283797.00 -186283.00 -86154.19
 5 2781221 -338026.19 -814236.88 -283207.38 -169123.56 -86154.06
 6 2698588 -336276.88 -844862.81 -284970.81 -137560.88 -86159.31
 7 3851513 -348559.56 -855663.06 -284983.56 -131301.75 -86121.06
 8 2281389 -348071.38 -790689.50 -284858.56 -129331.38 -86281.44
 9 1952129 -366434.63 -860378.25 -283768.25 -196795.69 -86149.94
10 3820698 -333140.38 -824780.75 -285004.19 -128801.19 -86168.56
11 3302877 -359895.31 -819571.50 -283820.19 -204325.88 -86178.56
12 2072299 -308360.19 -867325.31 -285030.94 -136297.88 -86154.19
13 1782716 -308486.31 -825227.81 -284879.56 -128931.38 -86165.94
14 3697954 -338440.06 -819421.06 -284863.75 -129227.50 -86157.63
15 3202013 -331526.75 -834531.06 -283208.06 -202811.94 -86145.75
```

(continued)

Exhibit: 10.1. *(continued)*

```
16 3482475  -391499.38  -828228.88  -283208.63  -194647.19  -86161.00
17 2675433  -351176.75  -808326.44  -284839.56  -129386.50  -86165.50
18 2212803  -346849.44  -835999.50  -283792.69  -198661.88  -86155.25
19 2364884  -414678.69  -831375.13  -296689.00  -184200.56  -86155.88
20 3781303  -355947.38  -831339.50  -297321.81  -186006.19  -86151.44
21 2290557  -382666.00  -844183.69  -297305.56  -172419.88  -86144.31
;
PROC IML;
USE QTY84; READ ALL VAR _NUM_ INTO X;
USE PRICE84; READ ALL VAR _NUM_ INTO Y;
PRINT X;
PRINT Y;
PI=X*T(Y);
PI1=PI[1:21,1:5];
PRINT PI1;
MPI1=PI1[<:>,];
PRINT MPI1;
PI2=PI[1:21,6:10];
PRINT PI2;
MPI2=PI2[<:>,];
PRINT MPI2;
PI3=PI[1:21,11:16];
PRINT PI3;
MPI3=PI3[<:>,];
PRINT MPI3;
PI4=PI[1:21,17:21];
PRINT PI4;
MPI4=PI4[<:>,];
PRINT MPI4;
```

---

already. Once we call the matrix procedure through PROC IML, the matrices X and Y are created from the quantity and price data sets. Each row of the X matrix contains the output and input quantity data of one airline. The corresponding row of the Y matrix has the relevant price information. The Y matrix is transposed so that the prices faced by each firm are now contained in a column (rather than a row). This is premultiplied by the X matrix. The resulting matrix has been called the PI matrix. It is a square matrix with 21 rows and columns. The diagonal elements of the PI matrix show the actual profit earned by any airline. The element in the ith row and the jth column shows the profit that firm j would earn if it selected the input–output bundle of firm i. The input–output combination chosen by airline j is found to be consistent with WAPM if and only if the jth diagonal element is the maximum element of column j. For this we need only to identify the row containing the maximum element in each column. This is done by the command following the relevant comment in the program. In the present case, for all columns except column 13, the maximum element was in row 19. For column 13, however, the maximum element was in row 2. This means that only airline 19 satisfies WAPM. Thus, the overproduction function is defined by the actual profit and input–put prices of firm 19 alone. The actual profit earned by airline 19 was 3,082,731. The output and input prices were

$$PY = 2364884; \quad PL = -414678.69; \quad PF = 831375.13;$$

$$PM = 296689.00; \quad PFL = 184200.56; \quad PGR = 86155.88.$$

Deflating the profit by the output price to get the intercept and using similarly deflated input prices as the slope coefficients, we get the overproduction function

$$YI^+ = 1.30354 + 0.17534 \, QLI + 0.35155 \, QFI + 0.12546 \, QMI$$

$$+ \, 0.07789 \, QFLI + 0.036431 \, QGRI.$$

One can use the ratio

$$TE^- = \frac{YI}{YI^+}$$

as the lower bound of the technical efficiency of an individual airline.

Exhibit 10.2 reports the actual output, along with the value of the overproduction function and the resulting lower bound of technical efficiency. Also reported alongside are the values of the underproduction function and the upper bound of technical efficiency obtained from the output-oriented BCC DEA models. The upper and lower bounds of technical efficiency differ considerably. Interestingly, the smaller airlines with YI less than unity have the lowest values of TE^- but are much closer to full efficiency when we consider TE^+.

10.8 Summary

The nonparametric approach in production economics was introduced much earlier than DEA and is a quite well-developed strand in the literature. Although

Exhibit: 10.2. *Lower and upper bounds on efficient output and technical efficiencies of U.S. airlines, 1984*

Obs	YI	Y*−	Y*+	TE−	TE+
1	0.0816	0.09407	1.80702	0.04516	0.86741
2	1.9365	1.93650	1.97412	0.98094	1.00000
3	0.5455	0.61254	1.57175	0.34707	0.89055
4	1.3897	1.77680	2.01164	0.69083	0.78213
5	1.5157	1.71977	2.18209	0.69461	0.88134
6	0.2133	0.22810	1.40591	0.15172	0.93510
7	0.0370	0.03700	1.36299	0.02715	1.00000
8	0.0439	0.04390	1.35561	0.03238	1.00000
9	1.2485	1.24850	1.65602	0.75391	1.00000
10	0.0458	0.04580	1.35036	0.03392	1.00000
11	0.1387	0.18007	1.85131	0.07492	0.77026
12	1.5685	1.56850	1.72486	0.90935	1.00000
13	0.3277	0.32770	1.41020	0.23238	1.00000
14	0.3040	0.44418	1.44736	0.21004	0.68441
15	0.1550	0.17076	1.90566	0.08134	0.90770
16	0.4332	0.62111	2.09792	0.20649	0.69747
17	0.1997	0.27094	1.43568	0.13910	0.73707
18	1.5134	1.51340	1.81021	0.83604	1.00000
19	2.4424	2.44240	2.44240	1.00000	1.00000
20	0.4214	0.58888	1.57948	0.26680	0.71559
21	0.4933	0.55104	1.56175	0.31586	0.89522

the DEA methodology has greatly facilitated the viability of the nonparametric approach in empirical applications, there are other models like the WACM and WAPM that provide computationally simple tests of optimizing behavior by firms. Even when input quantity data are unavailable, one may use the WACD to test whether the behavior of an individual firm in the sample is consistent with cost minimization. The WAPM not only provides a test of profit-maximizing behavior but also provides a lower bound on technical efficiency of a firm using an overproduction function for a benchmark.

Guide to the Literature

Nonparametric analysis of optimizing behavior on the part of an economic agent was introduced by Samuelson (1948) in his Weak Axiom of Revealed Preference in the context of consumer's choice. Afriat (1967) extended this approach to construct a utility function from observed price and consumption data. Subsequently, a set of tests of consistency of production data with various regularity properties of an underlying production technology was introduced by Afriat (1972) and Hanoch and Rothschild (1972). Diewert and Parkan (1983) introduced additional tests along the same lines. Varian (1984) formalized many of these tests as axioms of optimizing behavior and developed new ones. Banker and Maindiratta (1988) used Varian's nonparametric framework to define upper and lower bounds on technical and allocative efficiency of a firm. Although in the initial phase, the objective of the tests was to screen out observations inconsistent with optimizing behavior prior to any statistical analysis, many of the nonparametric tests also yield measures of efficiency as well. For more recent contributions to the literature, one should refer to Färe, Grosskopf, and Lovell (1994), and Färe and Primont (1995).

11

Measuring Total Productivity Change over Time

11.1 Introduction

Back in Chapter 2, quite early in this book, we distinguished between productivity and efficiency as two different measures of performance of a firm – the former descriptive and the latter normative. In all of the chapters in this book, we have so far dealt only with efficiency. Yet, in the macroeconomics literature as well as in the business economic press, there is a keen interest in variation in productivity across countries and over time. Unfortunately, increase in output per hour (or labor productivity), the most widely used measure, ignores differences in other inputs used and fails to measure *Total Factor Productivity Growth* (TFPG). To address this problem, one needs to construct measures of input and output changes that incorporate changes in all individual outputs and inputs. Two of the popular measures of total factor productivity (TFP) are the Tornqvist and the Fisher productivity indexes. Both use price information along with quantity data to construct quantity indexes of output and input. The ratio of the output and input quantity indexes is the TFP index. Both Tornqvist and Fisher indexes are descriptive measures of productivity change. Neither of the two measures requires any knowledge of the underlying production technology faced by the firm. By contrast, the Malmquist productivity index introduced by Caves, Christensen, and Diewert (CCD) (1982) is a normative measure that constructs a production frontier representing the technology and uses the corresponding distance functions evaluated at different input–output combinations for productivity comparison. In this chapter, we focus primarily on the measurement and decomposition of the Malmquist productivity index using DEA followed by a similar decomposition of the Fisher productivity index. It should be emphasized, however, that although virtually all empirical applications of the Malmquist productivity index have used the nonparametric DEA methodology, there is no reason why one cannot use instead a parametrically specified frontier production function and estimate it by the maximum likelihood procedure.

The concept of multifactor productivity growth is introduced and the Tornqvist and Fisher indexes are described in Section 11.2. This is followed by a more detailed description of the Malmquist productivity index and its decomposition into several factors measuring the contributions of technical change, technical efficiency change, and scale change in Section 11.3. The relevant DEA models for measurement and decomposition of the Malmquist productivity index are described in Section 11.4. A comparable nonparametric decomposition of the Fisher productivity index is shown in Section 11.5. An empirical application using data from Indian manufacturing is presented in Section 11.6. Section 11.7 summarizes the main points from this chapter.

11.2 Multifactor Productivity Indexes

Productivity of a firm is measured by the quantity of output produced per unit of input. In the single-output, single-input case, it is merely the ratio of the firm's output and input quantities. Thus, if in period 0 a firm produces output y_0 from input x_0, its productivity is

$$\Pi_0 = \frac{y_0}{x_0}. \tag{11.1a}$$

Similarly, in period 1, when output y_1 is produced from input x_1, the productivity is

$$\Pi_1 = \frac{y_1}{x_1}. \tag{11.1b}$$

Moreover, the productivity index in period 1, with period 0 as the base, is

$$\pi_1 = \frac{\Pi_1}{\Pi_0} = \frac{y_1/x_1}{y_0/x_0} = \frac{y_1/y_0}{x_1/x_0}. \tag{11.2}$$

This productivity index shows how productivity of the firm has changed from the base period. The rate of productivity growth is the difference in the growth rates of the output and input quantities, respectively.

When multiple inputs and/or multiple outputs are involved, one must replace the simple ratios of the output and input quantities in (11.2) by a ratio of quantity indexes of output and input. In this case, the index of *multifactor productivity* (MFP) is

$$\pi_1 = \frac{\Pi_1}{\Pi_0} = \frac{Q_y}{Q_x}, \tag{11.3}$$

where Q_y and Q_x are, respectively, output and input quantity indexes of the firm in period 1 with period 0 as the base. Different measures of the multifactor productivity index are obtained, however, when one uses alternative quantity index numbers available in the literature.

The Tornqvist Productivity Index

By far, the most popular quantity index number is the Tornqvist index measured by a weighted geometric mean of the relative quantities from the two periods. Consider the output quantity index first. Suppose that m outputs are involved. The output vectors produced in periods 0 and 1 are, respectively, $y^0 = (y_1^0, y_2^0, \ldots, y_m^0)$ and $y^1 = (y_1^1, y_2^1, \ldots, y_m^1)$. The corresponding output price vectors are $p^0 = (p_1^0, p_2^0, \ldots, p_m^0)$ and $p^1 = (p_1^1, p_2^1, \ldots, p_m^1)$, respectively.

Then, the Tornqvist output quantity index is

$$TQ_y = \left(\frac{y_1^1}{y_1^0}\right)^{v_1} \left(\frac{y_2^1}{y_2^0}\right)^{v_2} \cdots \left(\frac{y_m^1}{y_m^0}\right)^{v_m} ; \quad \sum_{j=1}^{m} v_j = 1. \qquad (11.4)$$

Here,

$$v_j = \frac{p_j y_j}{\sum\limits_{k=1}^{m} p_k y_k}$$

is the share of output j in the total value of the output bundle. Of course, the value shares of the individual outputs are, in general, different in the two periods. In practical applications, for v_j one uses the arithmetic mean of v_j^0 and v_j^1, where

$$v_j^0 = \frac{p_j^0 y_j^0}{\sum\limits_{k=1}^{m} p_k^0 y_k^0} \quad \text{and} \quad v_j^1 = \frac{p_j^1 y_j^1}{\sum\limits_{k=1}^{m} p_k^1 y_k^1}.$$

It may be noted that in the single-output case, the Tornqvist output quantity index trivially reduces to the ratio of output quantities in the numerator of (11.2). This is also true when the quantity ratio remains unchanged across all outputs.

Similarly, let the input vectors in the two periods be $x^0 = (x_1^0, x_2^0, \ldots, x_n^0)$ and $x^1 = (x_1^1, x_2^1, \ldots, x_n^1)$. The corresponding input price vectors are $w^0 = (w_1^0, w_2^0, \ldots, w_n^0)$ and $w^1 = (w_1^1, w_2^1, \ldots, w_n^1)$. Then, the Tornqvist input quantity index is

$$TQ_x = \left(\frac{x_1^1}{x_1^0}\right)^{s_1} \left(\frac{x_2^1}{x_2^0}\right)^{s_2} \cdots \left(\frac{x_n^1}{x_n^0}\right)^{s_n} ; \quad \sum_{j=1}^{n} s_j = 1. \qquad (11.5)$$

Here,

$$s_j = \frac{w_j x_j}{\sum_{k=1}^{n} w_k x_k}$$

is the share of input j in the total cost of the input bundle. Again, in practice, one uses the average of the cost share of any input in the two periods.

The Tornqvist productivity index is the ratio of the Tornqvist output and input quantity indexes. Thus,

$$\pi_{TQ} = \frac{TQ_y}{TQ_x}. \qquad (11.6)$$

When $TQ_y > TQ_x$, output in period 1 has grown faster (or declined slower) than input as a result of which productivity has increased in period 1 compared to what it was in period 0.

It may be noted that the Tornqvist productivity index can be measured without any knowledge of the underlying technology as long as data are available for the input and output quantities as well as the shares of the individual inputs and outputs in the total cost and total revenue, respectively.

The Fisher Productivity Index

An alternative to the Tornqvist index of productivity is the Fisher index, where one uses Fisher indexes of output and input quantity in the multifactor productivity index measure. It may be noted that the Fisher quantity (or price) index is itself the geometric mean of the relevant Laspeyres and Paasche indexes.

The Laspeyres output quantity index is the value ratio of the two output vectors at base period prices and is measured as

$$LQ_y = \frac{\sum_{j=1}^{m} p_j^0 y_j^1}{\sum_{j=1}^{m} p_j^0 y_j^0}. \qquad (11.7)$$

It is easy to see that $\mathrm{LQ}_y = \sum_{j=1}^{m} \lambda_j^0 \left(\frac{y_j^1}{y_j^0} \right)$

where $\lambda_j^0 = \frac{p_j^0 y_j^0}{\sum_{k=1}^{m} p_k^0 y_k^0}$ is the same as v_j^0 defined previously.

Thus, while the Tornqvist quantity index is a weighted geometric mean of the quantity relatives, the corresponding Laspeyres index is a similarly weighted arithmetic mean.

The Paasche output quantity index, for which we evaluate the current and base period output bundles at current period prices, is measured as

$$\mathrm{PQ}_y = \frac{\sum_{1}^{m} p_j^1 y_j^1}{\sum_{j=1}^{m} p_j^1 y_j^0}. \tag{11.8}$$

Thus, $\mathrm{PQ}_y = \sum_{j=1}^{m} \mu_j^1 \left(\frac{y_j^1}{y_j^0} \right)$, where $\mu_j^1 = \frac{p_j^1 y_j^0}{\sum_{k=1}^{m} p_k^1 y_k^0}$.

The Fisher output quantity index is the geometric mean of the Laspeyres and Paasche output quantity indexes. Hence,

$$\mathrm{FQ}_y = \sqrt{\mathrm{LQ}_y \cdot \mathrm{PQ}_y}.$$

In an analogous manner, the Laspeyres, Paasche, and Fisher input quantity indexes are obtained as

$$\mathrm{LQ}_x = \frac{\sum_{j=1}^{n} w_j^0 x_j^1}{\sum_{j=1}^{n} w_j^0 x_j^0}, \tag{11.10a}$$

$$\mathrm{PQ}_x = \frac{\sum_{j=1}^{n} w_j^1 x_j^1}{\sum_{j=1}^{n} w_j^1 x_j^0}, \tag{11.10b}$$

and

$$\mathrm{FQ}_x = \sqrt{\mathrm{LQ}_x \cdot \mathrm{PQ}_x}, \tag{11.10c}$$

respectively. The resulting Fisher productivity index is

$$\pi_\mathrm{F} = \frac{\mathrm{FQ}_y}{\mathrm{FQ}_x}. \tag{11.11}$$

It may be noted that because the Tornqvist and Fisher indexes are derived from the geometric and arithmetic means of ratios of the output and input quantities, in practical applications, their numerical values are generally quite close.

11.3 The Production Technology and the Malmquist Productivity Index: One-Output, One-Input Case

Now, suppose that the production function is $y^* = f^0(x)$ in period 0 and $f^1(x)$ in period 1. Because each observed input–output bundle is by definition feasible in the relevant period, we know that $f^0(x_0) \geq y_0$ and $f^1(x_1) \geq y_1$. But y_1 may not be producible from x_1 in period 0. Similarly, the output y_0 may not be feasible from input x_0 in period 1. Now, in the absence of constant returns to scale (CRS), the average productivity varies with the input level as one moves along the production function. Frisch (1965) defined the technically optimal scale (TOPS) of input as one where average productivity reaches a maximum. Recall that along a production function $y = f(x)$, the average productivity at any input level x is

$$AP(x) = \frac{f(x)}{x}.$$

From the first-order condition for a maximum, at the TOPS x^*,

$$x^* f'(x^*) = f(x^*).$$

Thus, at the TOPS, the tangent to the production function is also a ray through the origin. The slope of this ray is merely the marginal productivity of x at x^*. Define $w^* \equiv f'(x^*)$ and $R(x) = w^* x$. Then, the ray $y = R(x)$ is a tangent to production function at $x = x^*$. This is the TOPS ray defined in Chapter 3. If we assume that the production possibility set is convex, then

$R(x) \geq f(x)$ over the entire domain of the production function and

$R(x) = f(x)$ at $x = x^*$.

As noted before, for the production possibility set

$$T = \{(x, y) : y \leq f(x)\},$$

the (output-oriented) Shephard distance function evaluated at any input–output pair (x, y) is

$$D(x, y) = \min \delta : \left(x, \frac{y}{\delta}\right) \in T. \tag{11.12}$$

Thus,

$$\delta = \frac{y}{f(x)}. \tag{11.13}$$

Clearly, when $y < f(x)$, $D(x, y) < 1$. But, in this case, the actual output y is less than the maximum producible output $f(x)$. Hence, the input–output pair (x, y) is technically inefficient. For an efficient pair, $y = f(x)$ and $D(x, y) = 1$. The distance function exceeds unity when $y > f(x)$. But, by definition, $f(x)$ is the maximum output quantity producible from input x. Thus, if $D(x, y) > 1$, (x, y) is an infeasible input–output pair. Therefore, an equivalent characterization of the production possibility set is

$$T = \{(x, y) : D(x, y) \leq 1\}. \tag{11.14}$$

Recall that the output-oriented technical efficiency is

$$\text{TE}(x, y) = \frac{1}{\phi^*}$$

where

$$\phi^* = \max \phi : (x, \phi y) \in T.$$

Thus, the output-oriented Shephard distance function $D(x, y)$ coincides with the Farrell measure of technical efficiency, $\text{TE}(x, y)$.

We may use the TOPS ray to define the pseudo production possibility set

$$T^C = \{(x, y) : y \leq R(x)\}. \tag{11.15}$$

The set T^C is the smallest convex cone that contains the true production possibility set T. The function $y = R(x)$ is the pseudo production function that corresponds to the true production function $y = f(x)$. Note that the pseudo production function exhibits CRS globally. Further, when CRS holds everywhere along the true production function, $T^C = T$ and $R(x) = f(x)$ for all admissible values of x. We may use T^C to define the pseudo distance function

$$D^C(x, y) = \min \delta : \left(x, \frac{y}{\delta}\right) \in T^C. \tag{11.16}$$

The corresponding technical efficiency would then be $\text{TE}^C(x, y)$. Obviously,

$$D^C(x, y) = \text{TE}^C(x, y) = \frac{y}{R(x)}. \tag{11.17}$$

The productivity index can also be written as

$$\pi_1 = \frac{\dfrac{y_1}{R(x_1)}}{\dfrac{y_0}{R(x_0)}} \cdot \frac{\dfrac{R(x_1)}{x_1}}{\dfrac{R(x_0)}{x_0}}. \tag{11.18}$$

But, because $y = R(x)$ is a ray through the origin,

$$\frac{R(x_1)}{x_1} = \frac{R(x_0)}{x_0}. \tag{11.19}$$

Hence,

$$\pi_1 = \frac{\dfrac{y_1}{R(x_1)}}{\dfrac{y_0}{R(x_0)}}. \tag{11.20}$$

Alternatively,

$$\pi_1 = \frac{D^C(x_1, y_1)}{D^C(x_0, y_0)} = \frac{\text{TE}^C(x_1, y_1)}{\text{TE}^C(x_0, y_0)}. \tag{11.21}$$

This ratio of pseudo distance functions (or, equivalently, of pseudo technical efficiencies) is the Malmquist productivity index. In the single-output, single-input case, it is computationally equivalent to the ratio of average productivities in the two periods. But the essential characteristic of the Malmquist index is that it is a normative measure and uses a pseudo production function as a benchmark to compute efficiency or distance function. It will be shown later how the Malmquist index can be measured even in the multiple-input case, where average productivity cannot be measured in the usual sense. We will also consider how the Malmquist index can be geometrically interpreted.

Whenever $\text{TE}(x, y) = 1$, we know that (x, y) is a point on the production function. However, the average productivity at this point need not be the maximum average productivity attainable along the production function. We can measure the scale efficiency of the input level x by comparing the average productivity at x with the maximum average productivity attainable at the TOPS x^*.

Thus,

$$\text{SE}(x) = \frac{f(x)/x}{f(x^*)/x^*}. \tag{11.22}$$

But, as explained earlier,

$$f(x^*) = R(x^*) = w^*x^* \quad \text{and} \quad \frac{f(x^*)}{x^*} = f'(x^*) = w^*.$$

Thus,

$$\text{SE}(x) = \frac{f(x)}{w^*x}. \tag{11.23a}$$

Further, from the definition of the TOPS ray, $w^*x = R(x)$. Hence,

$$\text{SE}(x) = \frac{f(x)}{R(x)}. \tag{11.23b}$$

Alternatively,

$$\text{SE}(x) = \frac{\dfrac{y}{R(x)}}{\dfrac{y}{f(x)}} = \frac{D^C(x, y)}{D(x, y)} \tag{11.23c}$$

We now focus on the period 0 production function $y = f^0(x)$. The TOPS corresponding to this production function is x_0^* satisfying

$$x_0^* f^{0\prime}(x_0^*) = f^0(x_0^*).$$

The corresponding TOPS ray is

$$y = R^0(x) = w_0^*x,$$

where $w_0^* = f^{0\prime}(x_0^*)$.

We may now express the productivity index π_1 as

$$\pi_0 = \frac{\dfrac{y_1}{x_1}}{\dfrac{y_0}{x_0}} = \frac{\dfrac{y_1}{f^0(x_1)} \dfrac{f^0(x_1)}{x_1}}{\dfrac{y_0}{f^0(x_0)} \dfrac{f^0(x_0)}{x_0}}. \tag{11.24}$$

But,

$$\frac{f^0(x_1)}{x_1} = \frac{f^0(x_1)}{R^0(x_1)} \cdot \frac{R^0(x_1)}{x_1} = \frac{f^0(x_1)}{R^0(x_1)} \cdot w_0^*. \tag{11.25a}$$

Similarly,

$$\frac{f^0(x_0)}{x_0} = \frac{f^0(x_0)}{R^0(x_0)} \cdot \frac{R^0(x_0)}{x_0} = \frac{f^0(x_0)}{R^0(x_0)} \cdot w_0^*. \tag{11.25b}$$

Therefore, the productivity index is

$$\pi_0 = \frac{\dfrac{y_1}{f^0(x_1)} \cdot \dfrac{f^0(x_1)}{R^0(x_1)}}{\dfrac{y_0}{f^0(x_0)} \cdot \dfrac{f^0(x_0)}{R^0(x_0)}}. \qquad (11.26a)$$

Hence,

$$\pi_0 = \frac{TE^0(x_1, y_1)}{TE^0(x_0, y_0)} \cdot \frac{SE^0(x_1)}{SE^0(x_0)}. \qquad (11.26b)$$

Similarly, we can use the period 1 production function $y = f^1(x)$ as the reference technology to obtain the TOPS x_1^* and, correspondingly, $w_1^* = f^{1\prime}(x_1^*)$. The TOPS ray would then be $R^1(x) = w_1^* x$. Hence, an alternative decomposition of the productivity index is

$$\pi_1 = \frac{\dfrac{y_1}{f^1(x_1)} \cdot \dfrac{f^1(x_1)}{R^1(x_1)}}{\dfrac{y_0}{f^1(x_0)} \cdot \dfrac{f^1(x_0)}{R^1(x_0)}}. \qquad (11.27)$$

Using the geometric mean of the alternative expressions,

$$\pi = \left[\frac{\dfrac{y_1}{f^0(x_1)} \dfrac{y_1}{f^1(x_1)} \cdot \dfrac{f^0(x_1)}{R^0(x_1)} \dfrac{f^1(x_1)}{R^1(x_1)}}{\dfrac{y_0}{f^0(x_0)} \dfrac{y_0}{f^1(x_0)} \cdot \dfrac{f^0(x_0)}{R^0(x_0)} \dfrac{f^1(x_0)}{R^1(x_0)}} \right]^{\frac{1}{2}}. \qquad (11.28)$$

This can be expressed as

$$\pi = \left[\frac{f^1(x_1)}{f^0(x_1)} \frac{f^1(x_0)}{f^0(x_0)} \right]^{\frac{1}{2}} \cdot \left[\frac{\dfrac{y_1}{f^1(x_1)}}{\dfrac{y_0}{f^0(x_0)}} \right] \cdot \left[\frac{\dfrac{f^0(x_1)}{R^0(x_1)} \dfrac{f^1(x_1)}{R^1(x_1)}}{\dfrac{f^0(x_0)}{R^0(x_0)} \dfrac{f^1(x_0)}{R^1(x_0)}} \right]^{\frac{1}{2}}. \qquad (11.29)$$

Define

$$TC = \left[\frac{f^1(x_1)}{f^0(x_1)}\frac{f^1(x_0)}{f^0(x_0)}\right]^{\frac{1}{2}} = \left[\frac{D^0(x_1, y_1)}{D^1(x_1, y_1)}\frac{D^0(x_0, y_0)}{D^1(x_0, y_0)}\right]^{\frac{1}{2}}, \quad (11.30a)$$

$$TEC = \left[\frac{\dfrac{y_1}{f^1(x_1)}}{\dfrac{y_0}{f^0(x_0)}}\right] = \frac{D^1(x_1, y_1)}{D^0(x_0, y_0)}, \quad (11.30b)$$

and

$$SCF = \left[\frac{\dfrac{f^0(x_1)}{R^0(x_1)}\dfrac{f^1(x_1)}{R^1(x_1)}}{\dfrac{f^0(x_0)}{R^0(x_0)}\dfrac{f^1(x_0)}{R^1(x_0)}}\right]^{\frac{1}{2}} = \left[\frac{\dfrac{D_C^0(x_1, y_1)}{D^0(x_1, y_1)}}{\dfrac{D_C^0(x_0, y_0)}{D^0(x_0, y_0)}} \cdot \frac{\dfrac{D_C^1(x_1, y_1)}{D^1(x_1, y_1)}}{\dfrac{D_C^1(x_0, y_0)}{D^1(x_0, y_0)}}\right]^{\frac{1}{2}}. \quad (11.30c)$$

Then, the productivity index becomes

$$\pi_1 = TC \cdot TEC \cdot SCF. \quad (11.31)$$

Ray and Desli (RD) (1997) proposed this decomposition of the Malmquist productivity index. In the first factor, TC, the ratio $\frac{f^1(x_0)}{f^0(x_0)}$ shows how the maximum producible output from input x_0 changes between periods 0 and 1. Because the input level remains unchanged, the ratio captures the autonomous shift in the production function due to technical change. Similarly, $\frac{f^1(x_1)}{f^0(x_1)}$ measures the proportionate shift at input level x_1. TC is the geometric mean of these two terms and represents the contribution of technical change. The second term, TEC, is merely the ratio of the technical efficiencies of the observed input–output pairs in the two periods. Clearly, it shows the contribution of technical efficiency change. The last term, SCF, is less easy to interpret. Each component under the square-root sign shows the scale efficiency of input x_1 relative to x_0 – one for period 0 technology and the other for the period 1 technology. This can be called the scale (efficiency) change factor. Before we examine this component of the Malmquist productivity index in further detail, let us consider two earlier decompositions: one due to Färe, Grosskopf, Lindgren, and Roos (FGLR) (1992) and the other due to Färe, Grosskopf, Norris, and Zhang (FGNZ) (1994).

FGLR (1992) assumed that the true production technology was characterized by CRS. Therefore, for their case, the pseudo production function was the same as the true production function. They started with the geometric mean

$$\pi = \left[\frac{\dfrac{y_1}{R^0(x_1)}}{\dfrac{y_0}{R^0(x_0)}} \cdot \frac{\dfrac{y_1}{R^1(x_1)}}{\dfrac{y_0}{R^1(x_0)}} \right]^{\frac{1}{2}} \tag{11.32a}$$

This easily reduces to

$$\pi = \left[\frac{R^1(x_0)}{R^0(x_0)} \cdot \frac{R^1(x_1)}{R^0(x_1)} \right]^{\frac{1}{2}} \cdot \frac{\dfrac{y_1}{R^1(x_1)}}{\dfrac{y_0}{R^0(x_0)}}. \tag{11.32b}$$

The first factor shows technical change measured by the geometric mean of the shift in the true (CRS) production function at input levels x_0 and x_1. The other component is the technical efficiency change – again using the true (CRS) production function as the benchmark. Note, further, that when CRS holds, the last component in the RD decomposition disappears whereas the other two factors are identical with the corresponding factor in this FGLR decomposition.

Of course, globally CRS is a restrictive assumption about the underlying technology and when CRS does not hold everywhere, the FGLR decomposition is not particularly meaningful. For example, neither the numerator nor the denominator in their second factor represents the technical efficiency of the observed input–output bundle in any period. In an effort to accommodate variable returns to scale (VRS), FGNZ proposed the extended decomposition

$$\pi = \left[\frac{R^1(x_0)}{R^0(x_0)} \cdot \frac{R^1(x_1)}{R^0(x_1)} \right]^{\frac{1}{2}} \cdot \frac{\dfrac{y_1}{f^1(x_1)}}{\dfrac{y_0}{f^0(x_0)}} \cdot \frac{\dfrac{f^1(x_1)}{R^1(x_1)}}{\dfrac{f^0(x_0)}{R^0(x_0)}}. \tag{11.33}$$

In the FGNZ decomposition, the measure of technical efficiency change (TEC) is the same as that in RD. But the technical change measure

$$\text{TC}_{\text{FGNZ}} = \left[\frac{R^1(x_0)}{R^0(x_0)} \cdot \frac{R^1(x_1)}{R_0(x_1)} \right]^{\frac{1}{2}} \tag{11.34a}$$

corresponds to the shift in the CRS pseudo production function. As argued by RD, this is not an appropriate measure of technical change when the technology does not exhibit globally CRS. On the other hand, their scale efficiency change measure

$$\mathrm{SEC}_{\mathrm{FGNZ}} = \frac{\dfrac{f^1(x_1)}{R^1(x_1)}}{\dfrac{f^0(x_0)}{R^0(x_0)}} \tag{11.34b}$$

is, indeed, the ratio of actual levels of scale efficiency experienced by the firm in the two periods.

By contrast, the SCF component of the Malmquist productivity index in the Ray–Desli decomposition has a different interpretation. One can compare the levels of scale efficiency of *any* two different input quantities with reference to a production function irrespective of whether the input levels were actually selected by a firm.

The two ratios

$$\frac{\dfrac{f^0(x_1)}{R^0(x_1)}}{\dfrac{f^0(x_0)}{R^0(x_0)}} \quad \text{and} \quad \frac{\dfrac{f^1(x_1)}{R^1(x_1)}}{\dfrac{f^1(x_0)}{R^1(x_0)}}$$

measure the scale efficiency of input x_1 relative to the scale efficiency of input x_0 using, respectively, the period 0 and the period 1 production functions. The geometric mean of the two ratios is SCF. As Lovell (2001) points out, it pertains to the difference in the scale efficiency of the input levels rather than a change in the scale efficiency of the firm.

The following example shows how one can measure the Malmquist productivity index and perform the Ray–Desli decomposition. Assume that the production function is

$$f^0(x) = 2\sqrt{x} - 4; \quad x \geq 4 \quad \text{in period 0} \tag{11.35}$$

and changes to

$$f^1(x) = 2\sqrt{x} - 3, \quad x \geq \tfrac{9}{4} \quad \text{in period 1.} \tag{11.36}$$

Note that this is merely a parallel shift and there is no change in the curvature of the production function. The corresponding production possibility sets are

$$T_V^0 = \{(x, y) : x \geq 4, \ y \leq 2\sqrt{x} - 4\} \quad \text{in period 0,} \tag{11.37}$$

and

$$T_V^1 = \left\{(x, y) : x \geq \tfrac{9}{4}, \ y \leq 2\sqrt{x} - 3\right\} \quad \text{in period 1.} \tag{11.38}$$

The functions $y = f^0(x)$ and $y = f^1(x)$ are the production frontiers in periods 0 and 1, respectively. It can be seen that average productivity varies with the input level along the production frontier, implying VRS in each period. Following Frisch (1965), one could define the input scale where average productivity reaches a maximum, as the TOPS. Note that at the TOPS, average and marginal productivities are equal. Hence, in period 0, the TOPS is x_0^*, satisfying

$$f^0(x_0^*) = x_0^* \frac{df^0(x_0^*)}{dx}.$$

Thus, $x_0^* = 16$. The marginal productivity at this input level is $\frac{1}{4}$. Consider the straight line

$$y = R^0(x) = \frac{1}{4}x. \tag{11.39}$$

This ray through the origin is the tangent to the period 0 production frontier at the TOPS and the set

$$T_C^0 = \left\{ (x, y) : x \geq 0, y \leq \tfrac{1}{4}x \right\} \tag{11.40}$$

is the smallest convex cone containing T_V^0. The upper boundary of T_C^0 is $y = R^0(x)$. We may regard it as the *pseudo production frontier* in period 0 and, in the same spirit, T_C^0 is the *pseudo production possibility set*. Note that unlike the *true* frontier $f^0(x)$ and T_V^0, which corresponds to it, $R^0(x)$ and T_C^0 are characterized by CRS.

Recall that the output-oriented distance function is defined as

$$D(x, y) = \min \delta : \left(x, \tfrac{1}{\delta}y \right) \in T$$

where T is the relevant production possibility set. Hence, with reference to T_V^0, the distance function is

$$D^0(x, y) = \min \delta : \tfrac{1}{\delta}y \leq f^0(x) = 2\sqrt{x} - 4. \tag{11.41}$$

Thus,

$$D^0(x, y) = \frac{y}{f^0(x)} = \frac{y}{2\sqrt{x} - 4}. \tag{11.42}$$

If, instead, one used T_C^0 as the reference, we would get the pseudo distance function

$$D_C^0(x, y) = \frac{y}{R^0(x)} = \frac{4y}{x}. \tag{11.43}$$

Using the condition

$$f^1(x_1^*) = x_1^* \frac{df^1(x_1^*)}{dx}$$

we get $x_1^* = 9$ as the TOPS in period 1. The marginal productivity at this input level in period 1 is

$$\frac{df^1(x_1^*)}{dx} = \frac{1}{\sqrt{x_1^*}} = \frac{1}{3}.$$

Hence, the ray

$$y = R^1(x) = \frac{1}{3}x \qquad (11.44)$$

is the tangent to the period 1 frontier at the TOPS. Thus,

$$y = R^1(x)$$

is the *pseudo production function* and

$$T_C^1(x, y) = \left\{ (x, y) : x \geq \tfrac{9}{4}; y \leq \tfrac{1}{3}x \right\} \qquad (11.45)$$

is the pseudo production possibility set in period 1.

The corresponding distance and pseudo distance functions in period 1 are

$$D^1(x, y) = \frac{y}{2\sqrt{x} - 3} \qquad (11.46a)$$

and

$$D_C^1(x, y) = \frac{3y}{x}. \qquad (11.46b)$$

Note that in this example,

$$\frac{D^0(x, y)}{D_C^0(x, y)} = \frac{x}{8\sqrt{x} - 16}$$

and

$$\frac{D^1(x, y)}{D_C^1(x, y)} = \frac{x}{6\sqrt{x} - 9}.$$

In the single-output case, neither of the two ratios depends upon y.

Suppose that the observed input–output bundles are $(x_0 = 6.25, y_0 = 0.75)$ in period 0 and $(x_1 = 25, y_1 = 4)$ in period 1. Then, in this example,

$$\text{AP}_0 = \frac{y_0}{x_0} = \frac{0.75}{6.25} = \frac{3}{25} \quad \text{and} \quad \text{AP}_1 = \frac{y_1}{x_1} = \frac{4}{25}.$$

The productivity index is

$$\pi = \frac{\text{AP}_1}{\text{AP}_0} = \frac{4}{3}.$$

Further,

$$f^0(x_0) = 1, \quad f^0(x_1) = 6, \quad f^1(x_0) = 2, \quad f^1(x_1) = 7, \quad R^0(x_0) = \frac{25}{16},$$

$$R^0(x_1) = \frac{25}{4}, \quad R^1(x_0) = \frac{25}{12}, \quad \text{and} \quad R^1(x_1) = \frac{25}{3}.$$

Thus,

$$\text{TC} = \left[\frac{f^1(x_1) f^1(x_0)}{f^0(x_1) f^0(x_0)} \right]^{\frac{1}{2}} = \left[\left(\frac{7}{6} \right) \left(\frac{2}{1} \right) \right]^{\frac{1}{2}} = \sqrt{\frac{7}{3}},$$

$$\text{TEC} = \left[\frac{\dfrac{y_1}{f^1(x_1)}}{\dfrac{y_0}{f^0(x_0)}} \right] = \left[\frac{\dfrac{4}{7}}{\dfrac{0.75}{1}} \right] = \frac{16}{21},$$

$$\text{SCF} = \left[\frac{\dfrac{f^0(x_1)}{R^0(x_1)} \dfrac{f^1(x_1)}{R^1(x_1)}}{\dfrac{f^0(x_0)}{R^0(x_0)} \dfrac{f^1(x_0)}{R^1(x_0)}} \right]^{\frac{1}{2}} = \left[\frac{24}{25} \cdot \frac{21}{25} \cdot \frac{1}{\frac{16}{25} \cdot \frac{24}{25}} \right]^{\frac{1}{2}} = \sqrt{\frac{21}{16}}.$$

In this example, the input–output bundle (x_1, y_1), shows a 33% increase in productivity over the bundle (x_0, y_0). The detailed decomposition reveals that technical change (resulting in an outward shift in the production function) by itself would have led to a 52.75% increase whereas the effect of a decline in technical efficiency alone would be a 23.81% decrease in productivity. Finally, the scale change factor would cause a 14.56% increase in productivity. The combined effect of all these three factors is the 33% rise in productivity.

In this example, we used an explicit parametric specification of the production function to measure and decompose the Malmquist productivity index. Alternatively, one can evaluate the various distance functions using DEA to

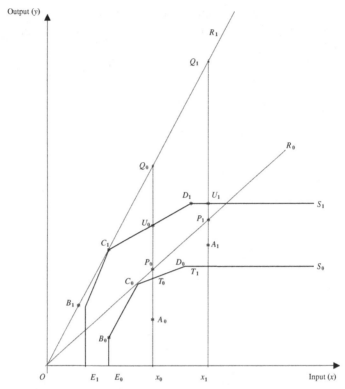

Figure 11.1 Geometry of the Malmquist productivity index and its decomposition.

measure and decompose the Malmquist productivity index nonparametrically. This is illustrated geometrically in Figure 11.1. Suppose that the points A_0, B_0, C_0, and D_0 show the input–output combinations of four firms in period 0. Similarly, input–output combinations of these firms in period 1 are shown by the points A_1, B_1, C_1, and D_1. The broken line segment $E_0 B_0 C_0 D_0 S_0$ is the boundary of the free disposal convex hull of the observed bundles in period 0 and is the production frontier in period 0. Similarly, $E_1 B_1 C_1 D_1 S_1$ is the production frontier in period 1. The ray OR_0 passing through the point C_0 is the *pseudo* production frontier in period 0 and the ray OR_1 through C_1 is the *pseudo* production function in period 1. Consider the points A_0 and A_1 showing the input–output quantities of firm A in the two periods. The firm produces output y_A^0 from input x_0 in period 0 and output y_A^1 from input x_1 in period 1.

Note that the point T_0 is the output-oriented projection of the point A_0 onto the (VRS) frontier in period 0. Similarly, P_0 is the output-oriented projection on to the *pseudo* (CRS) frontier. Thus,

$$D_V^0\left(x_0, y_A^0\right) = \frac{A_0 x_0}{T_0 x_0} \quad \text{and} \quad D_C^0\left(x_0, y_A^0\right) = \frac{A_0 x_0}{P_0 x_0}.$$

In an analogous manner,

$$D_V^0\left(x_1, y_A^1\right) = \frac{A_1 x_1}{T_1 x_1} \quad \text{and} \quad D_C^0\left(x_1, y_A^1\right) = \frac{A_1 x_1}{P_1 x_1}.$$

The average productivity levels of the firm are

$$AP_A^0 = \frac{A_0 x_0}{O x_0} \quad \text{in period 0 and}$$

$$AP_A^1 = \frac{A_1 x_1}{O x_1} \quad \text{in period 1.}$$

Thus, the productivity index of firm A is

$$\pi_A = \frac{AP_A^1}{AP_A^0} = \frac{\dfrac{A_1 x_1}{O x_1}}{\dfrac{A_0 x_0}{O x_0}} = \frac{\dfrac{A_1 x_1}{P_1 x_1}}{\dfrac{A_0 x_0}{P_0 x_0}} \cdot \frac{\dfrac{P_1 x_1}{O x_1}}{\dfrac{P_0 x_0}{O x_0}} = \frac{\dfrac{A_1 x_1}{P_1 x_1}}{\dfrac{A_0 x_0}{P_0 x_0}} = \frac{D_C^0\left(x_1, y_A^1\right)}{D_C^0\left(x_0, y_A^0\right)} \qquad (11.47)$$

Two alternative ways to factorize this productivity index are

$$\pi_A = \frac{\dfrac{A_1 x_1}{T_1 x_1}}{\dfrac{A_0 x_0}{T_0 x_0}} \cdot \frac{\dfrac{T_1 x_1}{P_1 x_1}}{\dfrac{T_0 x_0}{P_0 x_0}} = \frac{\dfrac{A_1 x_1}{U_1 x_1} \cdot \dfrac{U_1 x_1}{T_1 x_1} \cdot \dfrac{T_1 x_1}{P_1 x_1}}{\dfrac{A_0 x_0}{T_0 x_0} \cdot \dfrac{T_0 x_0}{P_0 x_0}} \qquad (11.47a)$$

and

$$\pi_A = \frac{\dfrac{A_1 x_1}{U_1 x_1} \cdot \dfrac{U_1 x_1}{Q_1 x_1}}{\dfrac{A_0 x_0}{U_0 x_0} \cdot \dfrac{U_0 x_0}{Q_0 x_0}} = \frac{\dfrac{A_1 x_1}{U_1 x_1} \cdot \dfrac{U_1 x_1}{Q_1 x_1}}{\dfrac{A_0 x_0}{T_0 x_0} \cdot \dfrac{T_0 x_0}{U_0 x_0} \cdot \dfrac{U_0 x_0}{Q_0 x_0}}. \qquad (11.48b)$$

Taking the geometric mean of the two, we get

$$\pi_A = \left[\frac{\dfrac{A_1 x_1}{U_1 x_1}}{\dfrac{A_0 x_0}{T_0 x_0}} \right] \cdot \left[\frac{U_1 x_1}{T_1 x_1} \cdot \frac{U_0 x_0}{T_0 x_0} \right]^{\frac{1}{2}} \left[\frac{\dfrac{T_1 x_1}{P_1 x_1} \cdot \dfrac{U_1 x_1}{Q_1 x_1}}{\dfrac{T_0 x_0}{P_0 x_0} \cdot \dfrac{U_0 x_0}{Q_0 x_0}} \right]^{\frac{1}{2}}. \qquad (11.49)$$

The first term on the right-hand side

$$\frac{\dfrac{A_1 x_1}{U_1 x_1}}{\dfrac{A_0 x_0}{T_0 x_0}} = \frac{D^1\left(x_1, y_A^1\right)}{D^0\left(x_0, y_A^0\right)} \qquad (11.50a)$$

measures the ratio of technical efficiencies of the firm in the two periods and is the TEC factor.

The ratio

$$\frac{U_0 x_0}{T_0 x_0} = \frac{D^0\left(x_0, y_A^0\right)}{D^1\left(x_0, y_A^0\right)} \qquad (11.50b)$$

measures the shift in the production function between the two periods evaluated at the input level x_0.

Similarly,

$$\frac{U_1 x_1}{T_1 x_1} = \frac{D^0\left(x_1, y_A^1\right)}{D^1\left(x_1, y_A^1\right)} \qquad (11.51)$$

shows the production function shift at input x_1. The geometric mean of the two is the second factor on the right-hand side and represents the technical change (TC) factor.

Finally,

$$\left[\frac{\dfrac{T_1 x_1}{P_1 x_1} \dfrac{U_1 x_1}{Q_1 x_1}}{\dfrac{T_0 x_0}{P_0 x_0} \dfrac{U_0 x_0}{Q_0 x_0}}\right]^{\frac{1}{2}} = \left[\frac{\dfrac{D_C^0\left(x_1, y_A^1\right)}{D^0\left(x_1, y_A^1\right)}}{\dfrac{D_C^0\left(x_0, y_A^0\right)}{D^0\left(x_0, y_A^0\right)}} \cdot \frac{\dfrac{D_C^1\left(x_1, y_A^1\right)}{D^1\left(x_1, y_A^1\right)}}{\dfrac{D_C^1\left(x_0, y_A^0\right)}{D^1\left(x_0, y_A^0\right)}}\right]^{\frac{1}{2}} \qquad (11.52)$$

is the scale change factor (SCF). As was explained before, distance functions can be evaluated using the CCR and BCC DEA models without specifying any production function.

11.4 Measurement and Decomposition of the Malmquist Productivity Index: One-Output, Multiple-Input Case

Although the one-input, one-output example was quite useful as an illustration of the *decomposition* of the Malmquist productivity index, actual *measurement* of the productivity index is a trivial arithmetic job. This is not the case when multiple inputs are involved and the input proportions differ across bundles.

One has to construct aggregate quantities of inputs in order to make any productivity comparison. Of course, for the multiple-output, multiple-input case, output aggregation will also be necessary. Earlier, in Section 11.2, we have seen how one constructs output and input quantity indexes for productivity measurement using the Tornqvist and Fisher indexes. This section extends the Malmquist methodology introduced herein and shows how one can use the underlying production technology to construct aggregate input quantities for productivity measurement. For this, we consider the one-output (y), two-input (x_1, x_2) case. Suppose that the production functions in the two periods are

$$y = f^0(x_1, x_2) = 2\sqrt{x_1} + \sqrt{x_2} - 2; \quad x_1 \geq \tfrac{1}{4}, \quad x_2 \geq 1 \quad \text{in period 0}$$

(11.53a)

and

$$y = f^1(x_1, x_2) = 2\sqrt{x_1} + \sqrt{x_2} - 1; \quad x_1 \geq \tfrac{1}{4}, \quad x_2 \geq 1 \quad \text{in period 1.}$$

(11.53b)

Assume further that the observed input bundles are $x^A = (x_1^A, x_2^A) = (9, 16)$ in period 0 and $x^B = (x_1^B, x_2^B) = (16, 9)$ in period 1. The corresponding output levels are $y_A = 5$ and $y_B = 6$. It is important to realize that there will be a different TOPS ray for each input mix and also for each production function. Consider the bundle x^A and the period 0 production function. The optimal scale is attained at bundle $x_*^0 = (x_{*1}^0, x_{*2}^0)$ that satisfies the conditions

$$\frac{\partial f^0(x_*^0)}{\partial x_1} x_{*1}^0 + \frac{\partial f^0(x_*^0)}{\partial x_2} x_{*2}^0 = f^0(x_*^0) \quad \text{and}$$

$$\frac{x_{*1}^0}{x_{*2}^0} = \frac{x_1^0}{x_2^0}.$$

In this example,

$$\frac{\partial f^0(x)}{\partial x_1} \equiv f_1^0 = \frac{1}{\sqrt{x_1}}, \quad \frac{\partial f^0(x)}{\partial x_2} \equiv f_2^0 = \frac{1}{2\sqrt{x_2}}, \quad \text{and} \quad \frac{x_1^0}{x_2^0} = \frac{9}{16}.$$

Hence, the scale efficient input bundle is

$$x_*^0 = \left(\frac{36}{25}, \frac{64}{25} \right).$$

Further,

$$f_1^0(x_*^0) = \frac{5}{6} \quad \text{and} \quad f_2^0(x_*^0) = \frac{5}{16}.$$

Hence, the relevant TOPS ray or the pseudo production function is

$$R_*^0(x_1, x_2) = \frac{5}{6}x_1 + \frac{5}{16}x_2. \qquad (11.55a)$$

Thus,

$$\frac{y_A}{R_*^0(x^A)} = D_C^0(x^A, y_A) = \frac{5}{12.5}. \qquad (11.54b)$$

Consider next the input bundle x^B and the period 0 production function. In this case, the scale efficient input bundle is $x_{**}^0 = (x_{**1}^0, x_{**2}^0)$, satisfying

$$\frac{\partial f^0(x_{**}^0)}{\partial x_1}x_{**1}^0 + \frac{\partial f^0(x_{**}^0)}{\partial x_2}x_{**2}^0 = f^0(x_{**}^0) \quad \text{and}$$

$$\frac{x_{**1}^0}{x_{**2}^0} = \frac{x_1^B}{x_2^B} = \frac{16}{9}.$$

Using the relevant information, we obtain the scale efficient input bundle $x_{**}^0 = (\frac{256}{121} \cdot \frac{144}{121})$. The relevant TOPS ray or the pseudo production function is

$$R_{**}^0(x_1, x_2) = \frac{11}{16}x_1 + \frac{11}{24}x_2. \qquad (11.54c)$$

Thus,

$$\frac{y_B}{R_{**}^0(x^B)} = D_C^0(x^B, y_B) = \frac{6}{15.125}. \qquad (11.54d)$$

Next, we use the period 1 production function and the input bundle x^B. This time, the scale efficient input bundle is $x_{**}^1 = (x_{**1}^1, x_{**2}^1)$, satisfying

$$\frac{\partial f^1(x_{**}^1)}{\partial x_1}x_{**1}^1 + \frac{\partial f^1(x_{**}^1)}{\partial x_2}x_{**2}^1 = f^1(x_{**}^1) \quad \text{and}$$

$$\frac{x_{**1}^1}{x_{**2}^1} = \frac{x_1^B}{x_2^B} = \frac{16}{9}.$$

For the input bundle x^B, the efficient scale in period 1 is attained at the bundle $x_{**}^1 = (\frac{64}{121}, \frac{256}{121})$ and the relevant TOPS ray is

$$R_{**}^0(x_1, x_2) = \frac{11}{8}x_1 + \frac{11}{12}x_2. \qquad (11.55a)$$

Thus,

$$\frac{y_B}{R_{**}^1(x^B)} = D_C^1(x^B, y_B) = \frac{6}{30.25}. \qquad (11.55b)$$

Finally, consider the input bundle x^A and the production function from period 1. This time, the scale efficient bundle is $x_*^1 = (\frac{9}{25}, \frac{16}{25})$ and the relevant TOPS ray is

$$R_*^1(x) = \frac{5}{3}x_1 + \frac{5}{8}x_2. \tag{11.56a}$$

Thus,

$$\frac{y_A}{R_*^1(x^A)} = D_C^1(x^A, y_A) = \frac{5}{25}. \tag{11.56b}$$

Hence, the Malmquist productivity index is

$$\pi = \left[\frac{\frac{6}{30.25}}{\frac{5}{25}} \frac{\frac{6}{15.25}}{\frac{5}{12.5}} \right]^{\frac{1}{2}} = 0.99173. \tag{11.57}$$

This shows a 0.827% decline in total factor productivity in period 1 compared to period 0. The Malmquist productivity index can be decomposed as

$$\mathrm{TEC} = \frac{D^1(x_1, y_A^1)}{D^0(x_0, y_A^0)} = \frac{\frac{6}{10}}{\frac{5}{8}} = 0.96; \tag{11.58a}$$

$$\mathrm{TC} = \left[\frac{D^0(x^A, y_A)}{D^1(x^A, y_A)} \cdot \frac{D^0(x^B, y_B)}{D^1(x^B, y_B)} \right]^{\frac{1}{2}} = \sqrt{\frac{9}{8} \cdot \frac{10}{9}} = 1.11803; \tag{11.58b}$$

and

$$\mathrm{SCF} = \left[\frac{\frac{D_C^0(x_1, y_A^1)}{D^0(x_1, y_A^1)}}{\frac{D_C^0(x_0, y_A^0)}{D^0(x_0, y_A^0)}} \cdot \frac{\frac{D_C^1(x_1, y_A^1)}{D^1(x_1, y_A^1)}}{\frac{D_C^1(x_0, y_A^0)}{D^0(x_0, y_A^0)}} \right]^{\frac{1}{2}} = \left[\frac{\frac{9}{15.25}}{\frac{8}{12.25}} \cdot \frac{\frac{10}{30.25}}{\frac{9}{25}} \right]^{\frac{1}{2}} = 0.92399. \tag{11.58c}$$

The TC factor shows technical progress at the rate of 11.8% in period 1 relative to period 0. TEC shows a 4% decline in technical efficiency. The contribution of SCF is a 7.601% decline in productivity. The total outcome is the 0.827% productivity decline.

11.5 DEA Methodology for Measuring the
Malmquist Productivity Index

Consider a multiple-output, multiple-input technology. Suppose that we have the input–output data for N firms observed over two different time periods. Let $y_j^t = (y_{1j}^t, y_{2j}^t, \ldots, y_{mj}^t)$ be the output bundle and $x_j^t = (x_{1j}^t, x_{2j}^t, \ldots, x_{nj}^t)$ the input bundle for firm j $(j = 1, 2, \ldots, N)$ in period t $(t = 0, 1)$. As explained before, the free disposal convex hull of the input–output vectors observed in that period approximates the production possibility set exhibiting VRS in period $t(T_t)$. Correspondingly, the *pseudo* production possibility set (T_C^t) showing globally CRS is the free disposal conical hull of these points. In principle, one can evaluate the distance function at a specific input–output bundle (x, y) with reference to any arbitrary production possibility set. We may describe the distance function as the *same-period distance function,* if one uses the T_t (or T_C^t) to evaluate the distance function at an input–output combination observed in period t. On the other hand, if the distance function based on the technology from one period is evaluated at an input–output bundle from another period, it can be described as a *cross-period distance function.*

As noted before, the (Shephard) distance function is the same as the Farrell measure of technical efficiency and can, therefore, be obtained straightaway from the optimal solution of the appropriate BCC or CCR DEA problem. In particular, the *same-period (VRS)* distance function is

$$D^t\left(x_k^t, y_k^t\right) = \frac{1}{\phi_k^*},$$

where $\phi_k^* = \max \phi$

$$\text{s.t.} \quad \sum_{j=1}^{N} \lambda_j y_j^t \geq \phi y_k^t;$$

$$\sum_{j=1}^{N} \lambda_j x_j^t \leq x_k^t; \qquad (11.59)$$

$$\sum_{j=1}^{N} \lambda_j = 1;$$

$$\lambda_j \geq 0; \quad (j = 1, 2, \ldots, N).$$

This, obviously, is the standard BCC model.

For the *cross-period (VRS)* distance function $D^s(x_k^t, y_k^t)$, one needs to solve the BCC problem

$$\max \delta$$

$$\text{s.t.} \sum_{j=1}^{N} \lambda_j y_j^s \geq \phi y_k^t;$$

$$\sum_{j=1}^{N} \lambda_j x_j^s \leq x_k^t; \qquad (11.60)$$

$$\sum_{j=1}^{N} \lambda_j = 1;$$

$$\lambda_j \geq 0; \quad (j = 1, 2, \ldots, N).$$

This, it may be noted, is quite different from the usual BCC model. Although the input–output quantities of firm k observed in period t appear on the right-hand sides of the inequality constraints, they *do not* appear on the left-hand sides of these constraints. An implication of this feature of the problem is that, unlike the BCC problem, it may not have a feasible solution. This will be true if the quantity of any individual input of firm k in period t is smaller than the smallest quantity of the corresponding input across all firms in period s.

For the *cross-period (CRS)* distance function $D_C^s(x_k^t, y_k^t)$, one solves the previous problem without the constraint that the λ_j's have to add up to unity. Note that in the case of CRS, the DEA problem will always have a feasible solution.

11.6 Nonparametric Decomposition of the Fisher Productivty Index

We now consider an analogous decomposition of the Fisher productivity index introduced by Ray and Mukherjee (1996). As was recognized before, the Fisher productivity index is a descriptive rather than a normative measure. It is, nonetheless, possible to use the dual representation of an empirically constructed best practice technology to decompose the Fisher productivity index into a number of economically meaningful factors.

As explained before, the Fisher productivity index is the geometric mean of Laspeyres and Paasche productivity indexes. Consider the Laspeyres index first. For simplicity, assume that the firm produces a single output from multiple inputs. Suppose that we are measuring the productivity index for firm k. The output quantities produced by the firm are y_k^0 in period 0 (the base period) and

y_k^1 in period 1 (the current period). The observed input bundles are x_k^0 and x_k^1 in the two periods. The corresponding input price vectors are w_k^0 and w_k^1. Then, the Laspeyres productivity index becomes

$$L = \frac{\dfrac{y_k^1}{y_k^0}}{\dfrac{w_k^{0\prime} x_k^1}{w_k^{0\prime} x_k^0}} \qquad (11.61)$$

At this point, recall the dual cost function for period t:

$$C^t(w, y) = \min w'x : (x, y) \in T^t, \qquad (11.62)$$

where T^t is the production possibility set in period t. In the present context, we can use the free disposal convex hull of the observed input–output quantities in any period to construct the production possibility set for that period. Then, the Laspeyres productivity index can be expressed as

$$L = \frac{\dfrac{y_k^1}{C^1\left(w_k^0, y_k^1\right)} \dfrac{C^1\left(w_k^0, y_k^1\right)}{w_k^{0\prime} x_k^1}}{\dfrac{y_k^0}{C^0\left(w_k^0, y_k^0\right)} \dfrac{C^0\left(w_k^0, y_k^0\right)}{w_k^{0\prime} x_k^0}}. \qquad (11.63)$$

But, following the Farrell decomposition of the cost efficiency, we can write

$$\frac{C^1\left(w_k^0, y_k^1\right)}{w_k^{0\prime} x_k^1} = \mathrm{TE}^1\left(x_k^1, y_k^1\right) \cdot AE^1\left(x_k^1, y_k^1; \; w_k^0\right), \qquad (11.64a)$$

where $\mathrm{TE}^1(x_k^1, y_k^1)$ is the technical efficiency of the input–output pair (x_k^1, y_k^1) in period 1 and $AE^1(x_k^1, y_k^1; \; w_k^0)$ is the allocative efficiency of the input mix of the bundle x_k^1 at input price w_k^0 in period 1. In an analogous manner,

$$\frac{C^0\left(w_k^0, y_k^0\right)}{w_k^{0\prime} x_k^0} = \mathrm{TE}^0\left(x_k^0, y_k^0\right) \cdot AE^0\left(x_k^0, y_k^0; \; w_k^0\right). \qquad (11.64b)$$

Thus,

$$L = \frac{\mathrm{TE}^1\left(x_k^1, y_k^1\right) \cdot AE^1\left(x_k^1, y_k^1; \; w_k^0\right) \cdot \dfrac{C^0\left(w_k^0, y_k^0\right)}{y_k^0}}{\mathrm{TE}^0\left(x_k^0, y_k^0\right) \cdot AE^0\left(x_k^0, y_k^0; \; w_k^0\right) \cdot \dfrac{C^1\left(w_k^0, y_k^1\right)}{y_k^1}}. \qquad (11.65)$$

This can be further manipulated to get

$$L = \left[\frac{\mathrm{TE}^1\left(x_k^1, y_k^1\right)}{\mathrm{TE}^0\left(x_k^0, y_k^0\right)}\right]\left[\frac{AE^1\left(x_k^1, y_k^1;\ w_k^0\right)}{AE^0\left(x_k^0, y_k^0;\ w_k^0\right)}\right]\left[\frac{C^0\left(w_k^0, y_k^0\right)}{C^1\left(w_k^0, y_k^0\right)}\right]\left[\frac{\dfrac{C^1\left(w_k^0, y_k^0\right)}{y_k^0}}{\dfrac{C^1\left(w_k^0, y_k^1\right)}{y_k^1}}\right].$$

(11.66)

Similar manipulations of the Paasche productivity index

$$P = \frac{\dfrac{y_k^1}{y_k^0}}{\dfrac{w_k^{1\prime} x_k^1}{w_k^{1\prime} x_k^0}}$$

(11.67)

lead to the decomposition

$$P = \left[\frac{\mathrm{TE}^1\left(x_k^1, y_k^1\right)}{\mathrm{TE}^0\left(x_k^0, y_k^0\right)}\right]\left[\frac{AE^1\left(x_k^1, y_k^1;\ w_k^1\right)}{AE^0\left(x_k^0, y_k^0;\ w_k^1\right)}\right]\left[\frac{C^0\left(w_k^1, y_k^0\right)}{C^1\left(w_k^1, y_k^1\right)}\right]\left[\frac{\dfrac{C^0\left(w_k^1, y_k^0\right)}{y_k^0}}{\dfrac{C^0\left(w_k, y_k^1\right)}{y_k^1}}\right].$$

(11.68)

Now, define

$$\mathrm{TEI} = \frac{\mathrm{TE}^1\left(x_k^1, y_k^1\right)}{\mathrm{TE}^0\left(x_k^0, y_k^0\right)};$$

(11.69)

$$\mathrm{AEI} = \left[\frac{AE^1\left(x_k^1, y_k^1;\ w_k^0\right)}{AE^0\left(x_k^0, y_k^0;\ w_k^0\right)} \cdot \frac{AE^1\left(x_k^1, y_k^1;\ w_k^1\right)}{AE^0\left(x_k^0, y_k^0;\ w_k^1\right)}\right]^{\frac{1}{2}};$$

(11.70)

$$\mathrm{TCI} = \left[\frac{C^0\left(w_k^0, y_k^0\right)}{C^1\left(w_k^0, y_k^0\right)} \cdot \frac{C^0\left(w_k^1, y_k^1\right)}{C^1\left(w_k^1, y_k^1\right)}\right]^{\frac{1}{2}};$$

(11.71)

and

$$\text{ACI} = \left[\frac{\dfrac{C^1\left(w_k^0, y_k^0\right)}{y_k^0}}{\dfrac{C^1\left(w_k^0, y_k^1\right)}{y_k^1}} \cdot \frac{\dfrac{C^0\left(w_k^1, y_k^0\right)}{y_k^0}}{\dfrac{C^0\left(w_k^1, y_k^1\right)}{y_k^1}} \right]^{\frac{1}{2}} . \tag{11.72}$$

Then,

$$F = \sqrt{L \cdot P} = (\text{TEI}) \cdot (\text{AEI}) \cdot (\text{TCI}) \cdot (\text{ACI}). \tag{11.73}$$

In this factorization, the four terms on the right-hand side relate to (a) technical efficiency change, (b) allocative efficiency change, (c) technical change, and (d) change in scale economies, respectively. The first, TEI, obviously shows the increase (decrease) in technical efficiency in period 1 relative to what it was in period 0. The factor AEI is itself the geometric mean of two ratios, each of which shows the relative allocative efficiency of the input bundle from period 1 compared to the bundle from period 0. The allocative efficiencies are measured using the same technology and input prices for both bundles. TCI is a dual measure of technical change. It shows the autonomous shift of the cost function between the two periods evaluated alternatively at the input price and output quantity levels from the two periods. Finally, the factor ACI shows the relative (dual) scale efficiencies of the output levels from the two periods. When any one of the two ratios under the square-root sign in this factor is greater than unity, it implies that along the dual cost curve for the technology and input prices specified, the average cost is lower at the output level in the current period than at the output level from the base period. That is, the current period output is relatively more scale efficient. This contributes positively to productivity growth.

A note of caution is in order here. As with all nonparametric models based on *cross-period* DEA, some components of this decomposition of the Fisher productivity index may be unavailable. This will be the case when the output level from one period is larger than the maximum output observed in the other period. In that case, the input requirement set relevant for the *cross-period* cost minimization problem would be empty.

11.7 Productivity Growth in Indian Manufacturing: An Application
of the Malmquist Index

In this example, (per establishment) input–output data from 22 states (and union territories) constructed from the *Annual Survey of Indian Industries* for the years 1987–88 and 1993–94 have been used to measure and decompose the Malmquist productivity index for the state of West Bengal (WB). Output was measured by the gross value of production at constant prices. The inputs included were (a) production workers (*Labor*), (b) nonproduction workers (*Employees*), (c) capital used (*Capital*), (d) fuel and power (*Fuel*), and (e) raw materials consumed (*Materials*). Labor inputs are measured by numbers of workers. Capital is measured by the sum of expenses on depreciation, interest, and rent deflated by the price index of capital equipment. Fuel and material inputs are measured by the expenditure on these two inputs deflated by appropriate price indexes. The data for the 22 states included in this example are reported for the years 1987–88 and 1993–94 in Table 11.1. To measure the *same-period* VRS and CRS distance functions for any one year, we solve the (output-oriented) BCC and CCR DEA problems for WB using the data for the particular year.

The SAS program for a *cross-period* DEA is shown in Exhibit 11.1. Note that there are 44 rows of data. The first 22 are for the individual states in the year 1987–88 and the other 22 are for the same states in 1993–94. The 1987–88 data for WB are in row 17 and the 1993–94 data for the same states are in row 34. Once we transpose the data, the rows become columns. Thus, the input–output data for WB are now contained in COL17 and COL34 in the new data set called NEXT. After the data sets NEXT and MORE have been merged into the new data set LAST, the input data from COL17 (i.e., the 1987–88 data for WB) are moved to the right-hand sides of the relevant constraints and the output value from COL17 appears with a negative sign attached in the column for PHI. Finally, we delete COL1 through COL22 from this data set. Thus, only COL23 through COL44 (the 1993–94) input–output data are used to define the production possibility set. Programs for other *cross-period* DEA problems can be written with appropriate changes.

The various distance functions evaluated at the input–output quantities of WB from 1987–88 and 1993–94 were

$$D^{87}(x^{87}, y_{87}) = 0.86352; \quad D^{93}(x^{93}, y_{93}) = 1.0; \quad D_C^{87}(x^{87}, y_{87}) = 0.862313;$$

$$D_C^{93}(x^{93}, y_{93}) = 0.972720;$$

$$D^{87}(x^{93}, y_{93}) = 1.16808; \quad D^{93}(x^{87}, y_{87}) = 0.98449;$$

$$D_C^{87}(x^{93}, y_{93}) = 0.991609; \quad D_C^{93}(x^{87}, y_{87}) = 0.984489.$$

Table 11.1. *Manufacturing output and input quantity data for selected Indian states (1987–88 and 1993–94)*

OBS	NAME	YEAR	Y	K	L	EM	F	M
1	AP	8788	46.614	24.254	42.784	7.770	4.0769	29.920
2	AS	8788	86.794	29.856	53.139	11.143	5.0706	53.499
3	BI	8788	167.179	129.631	86.371	24.508	18.0124	87.173
4	GU	8788	110.697	54.941	49.793	13.246	12.5116	64.629
5	HA	8788	139.545	63.827	64.209	21.094	11.6412	90.793
6	HP	8788	204.535	313.583	134.520	61.956	10.9886	112.843
7	JK	8788	87.880	81.027	94.108	24.186	3.1358	56.658
8	KA	8788	82.362	40.753	50.878	16.785	6.5360	47.433
9	KE	8788	98.234	45.126	66.378	14.170	5.0056	61.369
10	MP	8788	168.560	153.145	77.630	32.229	21.6828	84.330
11	MH	8788	155.768	60.845	58.626	21.918	12.4070	93.010
12	OR	8788	132.912	181.199	78.216	23.839	15.5687	72.518
13	PU	8788	90.793	48.095	49.707	12.792	7.7376	60.323
14	RA	8788	106.959	83.136	62.058	17.929	11.0055	63.136
15	TN	8788	89.155	37.459	53.910	13.234	8.0536	53.586
16	UP	8788	113.911	75.359	69.421	17.781	10.0384	68.193
17	WB	8788	149.677	72.141	108.084	29.772	12.6083	86.244
18	AN	8788	46.956	13.462	105.481	16.019	1.8424	22.956
19	CH	8788	45.112	7.326	33.876	9.736	1.3390	30.449
20	DE	8788	73.077	13.091	30.332	11.745	6.4656	44.771
21	GO	8788	175.185	59.511	50.686	18.292	9.8116	116.737
22	PO	8788	86.090	43.685	84.170	20.733	6.2500	49.623
23	AP	9394	76.687	50.724	47.413	9.919	8.3907	53.170
24	AS	9394	105.616	36.756	66.085	13.052	5.1927	75.890
25	BI	9394	214.200	105.728	69.892	20.713	19.9078	111.976
26	GU	9394	163.286	70.369	48.094	16.235	10.8751	116.073
27	HA	9394	180.607	59.434	59.164	22.689	10.5558	146.136
28	HP	9394	236.891	189.549	112.953	62.117	12.7376	122.290
29	JK	9394	119.287	11.675	44.079	12.540	2.5349	91.492
30	KA	9394	126.697	42.263	54.983	18.837	7.5110	85.712
31	KE	9394	89.892	33.036	61.666	13.232	3.6991	68.200
32	MP	9394	252.038	139.716	77.599	35.033	25.7707	161.420
33	MH	9394	202.865	72.287	50.422	19.903	11.3195	138.533
34	OR	9394	212.668	189.112	85.886	28.530	28.9937	125.945
35	PU	9394	129.839	55.903	54.061	17.673	11.6865	99.027
36	RA	9394	137.258	50.861	44.461	15.917	14.2284	96.014
37	TN	9394	101.391	37.198	47.868	11.944	8.3237	66.075
38	UP	9394	160.067	79.411	58.159	17.098	9.7695	115.728
39	WB	9394	160.145	116.611	97.336	28.246	12.5743	104.580
40	AN	9394	92.351	59.181	155.265	38.470	3.3229	65.816
41	CH	9394	71.982	6.641	19.267	7.958	0.9910	64.063
42	DE	9394	81.735	9.259	25.375	10.587	3.2155	58.160
43	GO	9394	279.303	65.184	46.304	18.688	12.8889	219.392
44	PO	9394	190.522	88.118	77.753	22.366	11.7984	135.438

Exhibit: 11.1. *SAS program for measuring cross-period CRS efficiency*

```
OPTIONS NOCENTER;
DATA INDIA;
INPUT NAME $ YEAR Y K L EM F M;
C=1;OBJ=0;
*IF YEAR NE 8788 THEN DELETE;
DROP YEAR;
CARDS;
AP  8788   46.614   24.254    42.784    7.770    4.0769    29.920
AS  8788   86.794   29.856    53.139   11.143    5.0706    53.499
BI  8788  167.179  129.631    86.371   24.508   18.0124    87.173
GU  8788  110.697   54.941    49.793   13.246   12.5116    64.629
HA  8788  139.545   63.827    64.209   21.094   11.6412    90.793
HP  8788  204.535  313.583   134.520   61.956   10.9886   112.843
.    ..       ..        ..        ..       ..        ..        ..
.    ..       ..        ..        ..       ..        ..        ..
.    ..       ..        ..        ..       ..        ..        ..
TN  8788   89.155   37.459    53.910   13.234    8.0536    53.586
UP  8788  113.911   75.359    69.421   17.781   10.0384    68.193
WB  8788  149.677   72.141   108.084   29.772   12.6083    86.244
AN  8788   46.956   13.462   105.481   16.019    1.8424    22.956
CH  8788   45.112    7.326    33.876    9.736    1.3390    30.449
DE  8788   73.077   13.091    30.332   11.745    6.4656    44.771
GO  8788  175.185   59.511    50.686   18.292    9.8116   116.737
PO  8788   86.090   43.685    84.170   20.733    6.2500    49.623
AP  9394   76.687   50.724    47.413    9.919    8.3907    53.170
AS  9394  105.616   36.756    66.085   13.052    5.1927    75.890
BI  9394  214.200  105.728    69.892   20.713   19.9078   111.976
GU  9394  163.286   70.369    48.094   16.235   10.8751   116.073
HA  9394  180.607   59.434    59.164   22.689   10.5558   146.136
HP  9394  236.891  189.549   112.953   62.117   12.7376   122.290
.    ..       ..        ..        ..       ..        ..        ..
.    ..       ..        ..        ..       ..        ..        ..
.    ..       ..        ..        ..       ..        ..        ..
TN  8788   89.155   37.459    53.910   13.234    8.0536    53.586
TN  9394  101.391   37.198    47.868   11.944    8.3237    66.075
UP  9394  160.067   79.411    58.159   17.098    9.7695   115.728
WB  9394  160.145  116.611    97.336   28.246   12.5743   104.580
AN  9394   92.351   59.181   155.265   38.470    3.3229    65.816
CH  9394   71.982    6.641    19.267    7.958    0.9910    64.063
DE  9394   81.735    9.259    25.375   10.587    3.2155    58.160
GO  9394  279.303   65.184    46.304   18.688   12.8889   219.392
PO  9394  190.522   88.118    77.753   22.366   11.7984   135.438
```

(continued)

Exhibit: 11.1. *(continued)*

```
PROC TRANSPOSE OUT=NEXT;
DATA MORE;
INPUT PHI _TYPE_ $ _RHS_;
CARDS;
0    >=    0
0    <=    0
0    <=    0
0    <=    0
0    <=    0
0    <=    0
0    =     1
1    MAX   .
DATA LAST; MERGE NEXT MORE;
IF _N_ =1 THEN PHI = - COL17;
IF _N_ >= 2 AND _N_ <= 6 THEN _RHS_ = COL17;
IF _N_ = 7 THEN DELETE;
DROP COL1 - COL22;
PROC PRINT;
PROC LP;
```

Using these figures, we obtain

$$\pi = \sqrt{\frac{0.9916088}{0.862313}\frac{0.9727195}{0.9583383}} = 1.080369.$$

This implies a productivity increase of 8.0369% over the seven-year period. The individual components of the Malmquist productivity index are

$$\text{TEC} = \frac{1}{0.8635813} = 1.158053;$$

$$\text{TC} = \sqrt{\frac{0.8635183}{0.9844894}\frac{1.1680771}{1}} = 1.0121998;$$

and

$$\text{SCF} = \sqrt{\frac{\dfrac{0.9916088}{1.1680771}\dfrac{0.9727195}{1}}{\dfrac{0.862313}{0.8635183}\dfrac{0.9583383}{0.9844894}}} = 0.9216746.$$

This shows that

(a) technical efficiency in 1993–94 was 15.8% higher than what it was in 1987–88;
(b) there was technical progress of 1.22% over this period; and
(c) the scale change factor resulted in a 7.83% decline in productivity.

The total effect was the 8.039% productivity increase measured by the Malmquist productivity index.

11.8 Summary

A multifactor index of productivity change involves aggregation of the individual components of output and input bundles into composite measures of total output and total input. Both the Tornqvist and Fisher indexes are measured as the ratio of the quantity indexes of output and input. These are essentially descriptive measures and use only accounting information relating to input and output quantities and prices. No information about the technology is necessary. By contrast, the Malmquist productivity index is a normative measure in the sense that it is measured by the ratio of distance functions pertaining to some benchmark technology. The Malmquist productivity index can be decomposed to isolate the specific contributions of technical efficiency change, technical change, and scale efficiency change towards the overall productivity change. The relevant distance functions for measuring the Malmquist productivity index can be evaluated by DEA. Even though the Fisher index is descriptive in nature, one can perform a similar decomposition of the Fisher productivity index using DEA in order to separate the different components of the overall productivity index.

Guide to the Literature

In the parametric literature, the practice is to measure *rates* rather than *indexes* of productivity change. Denney, Fuss, and Waverman (1981) offer a decomposition of the rate of productivity change into two separate components measuring the rate of technical change and a returns to scale factor.[1] Nishimizu and Page (1982) identified technical change and change in technical efficiency as

---

[1] See also Nadiri and Schankerman (1981) in the same volume. Orea (2002) offers a decomposition of the total factor productivity growth along the lines of Denney, Fuss, and Waverman (1981) using a distance function.

two distinct components of productivity change. The Malmquist productivity index was defined in terms of the distance functions by Caves, Christensen, and Diewert (1982) and later operationalized in the DEA framework by Färe, Grosskopf, Lindgren, and Roos (1992) using a CRS production technology for a benchmark. Subsequently, Färe, Grosskopf, Norris, and Zhang (1994) extended the decomposition to a VRS technology. Ray and Desli (1997) pointed out an inherent contradiction in the FGNZ decomposition and offered an alternative. In an earlier paper, Griffel-Tatje and Lovell (1995) had considered the decomposition of the Malmquist productivity index for the VRS technology. See, in this regard, Färe, Grosskopf, and Norris (1997) for their response to Ray and Desli. Lovell (2001) argues in favor of the Ray–Desli decomposition. An extended decomposition of the scale efficiency change factor of RD was proposed by Wheelock and Wilson (1997). The same decomposition was proposed independently but interpreted differently by Zofio and Lovell (1997). Balk (2001) proposes a different decomposition that separately identifies the contribution of change in the output or input mix. For an example of what Diewert (1992a) calls a Hicks–Moorsteen approach, see Bjurek (1996), where the Malmquist productivity index is measured by the ratio of a (Malmquist) output quantity index and a (Malmquist) input quantity index. Diewert (1992b) describes in detail a number of desirable properties of the Fisher productivity index. Färe and Grosskopf (1992) and Balk (1993) consider the conditions for equivalence between the Malmquist and the Fisher productivity indexes. The decomposition of the Fisher productivity index considered in this chapter is due to Ray and Mukherjee (1996). For an excellent survey of the Malmquist productivity index, see Färe, Grosskopf, and Roos (1998).

12

Stochastic Approaches to Data Envelopment Analysis

12.1 Introduction

The most important impediment to a more widespread acceptance of DEA as analytical methodology for productivity and efficiency analysis is that it is viewed as lacking any statistical foundation. After all, the measured value of the maximum (or frontier) output (y_0^*) producible from a given input bundle (x^0) obtained by DEA will depend on the *particular set of input–output bundles* that define the production technology. A different sample with the same input bundles producing a different set of output quantities would lead to a different measure of the maximum output producible from that particular input bundle. Given this sampling variation, a specific value of y_0^* obtained from a single sample is of limited use. One would prefer a confidence interval instead. For this, of course, one would need the sampling distribution of the frontier output. In contrast to the case of econometric models of the stochastic frontier production function, in the case of mathematical programming models the statistical properties of the estimators are not well developed.

In this chapter, we consider a number of different approaches to stochastic DEA. Section 12.2 considers Banker's interpretation of DEA as the maximum likelihood estimation procedure for a deterministic frontier and the parametric F tests proposed by him. Next, in Section 12.3, we describe the chance-constrained DEA, an approach based on the chance-constrained programming (CCP) models developed by Charnes and Cooper (1963) as introduced by Land, Lovell, and Thore (1993). A statistical test of WACM for cost-minimizing behavior proposed by Varian (1985) is described in Section 12.4. Finally, the resampling and bootstrap approach popularized by Simar (1992) and Simar and Wilson (1998a, 1998b, 2000) is presented in Section 12.5. The main points of the chapter are summarized in Section 12.6.

12.2 DEA as the Maximum Likelihood Estimator of a Deterministic Frontier Production Function

We start with N observed input–output bundles. The pair (x^j, y_j) represents the input bundle x^j used by firm j to produce the scalar output y_j. Next, following Banker (1993), consider the production function mapping from the n-element input bundle $x^0 \in X \subseteq R_+^n$ onto the nonnegative scalar output y_0:

$$y_0 = g(x^0). \tag{12.1}$$

We assume that the production function satisfies the following postulates:

(P1) $g(x)$ is monotonic in x. That is, if $x'' \geq x'$, then $g(x'') \geq g(x')$.

(P2) $g(x)$ is concave. Hence, if $x^1, x^2 \in X$ and $x^* = \lambda x^1 + (1 - \lambda)x^2, 0 < \lambda < 1$, then $g(x^*) \geq \lambda g(x^1) + (1 - \lambda)g(x^2)$.

(P3) For each observation $(x^j, y_j), g(x^j) \geq y_j; (j = 1, 2, \ldots, N)$.

(P4) For *any* other function $\tilde{g}(x)$ also satisfying (P1–P3), $\tilde{g}(x) \geq g(x)$ for all $x \in X$.

Now, consider the set $X^* = \left\{ x : x \geq \sum_{j=1}^N \lambda_j x^j; \ \sum_{j=1}^N \lambda_j = 1; \ \lambda_j \geq 0 \right\} \subseteq X$. Clearly, X^* is the free disposal convex hull of the observed input bundles. Banker has shown that the unique function $y = g(x)$ determined for $x \in X^*$ by the postulates (P1–P4) corresponds to that estimated by DEA.

We first note that if the function $y = \hat{g}(x)$ satisfies properties (P1–P4) and if $\hat{y}_0 = \hat{g}(x^0)$ for $x^0 \in X^*$, then $\hat{y}_0 = g^*(x^0)$, where

$$g^*(x^0) = y_0^* = \max \sum_{j=1}^N \lambda_j y_j$$

$$\text{s.t.} \quad \sum_{j=1}^N \lambda_j x^j \leq x^0;$$

$$\sum_{j=1}^N \lambda_j = 1; \tag{12.2}$$

$$\lambda_j \geq 0.$$

It is easy to see that $g^*(.)$ satisfies (P1–P3). First, consider the input bundle $\tilde{x} \geq x^0$. Clearly, the optimal solution for the DEA problem for x^0 is a feasible solution of the DEA problem for $\tilde{x}$. Thus, $g^*(\tilde{x}) \geq y_0^* = g^*(x^0)$. Next, we show that $g^*(x)$ is concave. Suppose that $\lambda' = (\lambda_1', \lambda_2', \ldots, \lambda_N')$ and $g^*(x')$ is the optimal solution of the DEA LP problem for the input bundle $x \in X^*$. Similarly, $\lambda'' = (\lambda_1'', \lambda_2'', \ldots, \lambda_N'')$ and $g^*(x'')$ is the optimal solution for $x'' \in X^*$. For any arbitrary $\theta \in [0, 1]$, define $\bar{\lambda} = \theta \lambda' + (1 - \theta)\lambda''$ and $\bar{x} = \theta x' + (1 - \theta)x''$. Clearly, $\bar{\lambda}$ is a feasible solution for the DEA LP for $\bar{x}$ leading to the objective function value $\theta g^*(x') + (1 - \theta)g^*(x'')$. Obviously, the optimal solution $g^*(\bar{x})$ satisfies $g^*(\bar{x}) \geq \theta g^*(x') + (1 - \theta)g^*(x'')$. This verifies that $g^*(x)$ is a concave function.

Let $y_0^* = g^*(x^0) = \sum_{j=1}^{N} \lambda_j^* y_j$ be the optimal solution of the DEA LP for x^0. Next, suppose that some other function $\hat{g}(x)$ satisfies the postulates (P1–P3). Then,

$$\hat{g}\left(\sum_{j=1}^{N} \lambda_j^* x^j\right) \geq \sum_{j=1}^{N} \lambda_j^* \hat{g}(x^j) \geq \sum_{j=1}^{N} \lambda_j^* y_j = g^*(x^0).$$

Further, because $x^0 \geq \sum_{j=1}^{N} \lambda_j^* x^j$, $\hat{g}(x^0) \geq \hat{g}\left(\sum_{j=1}^{N} \lambda_j^* x^j\right) \geq g^*(x^0)$. Thus, the function $g^*(x) \leq \tilde{g}(x)$ over the set X^* for any function $\tilde{g}(x)$ satisfying (P1–P3). This implies that the deviation $\epsilon_j = \tilde{g}(x^j) - y_j$ is minimized for each observation j by the function $g^*(x)$.

Now, consider the frontier production function

$$y = g(x) - \epsilon; \quad \epsilon \geq 0. \tag{12.3}$$

Here, the nonnegative deviation of the observed output y from the frontier $g(x)$ has some one-sided probability distribution $f(\epsilon)$. Then, the likelihood maximization problem can be specified as

$$\max L = \prod_{j=1}^{N} f(\epsilon_j = g(x^j) - y_j)$$

$$f(.), g(.)$$

subject to $g(x^j) - y_j \geq 0;$ \tag{12.4}

$g(.)$ is a monotonically increasing and concave function.

It may be noted that the DEA efficiency residuals ϵ_j are obtained independently of each other. This is in contrast with the frontier production function model proposed by Aigner and Chu (1968). In their case, a single parametric function is fitted to the entire data set and the efficiency residuals are jointly derived and, therefore, are not independent of one another. Now, suppose that we choose a probability density function $f(.)$ such that $f(\epsilon_j)$ is monotonically decreasing in the efficiency residuals. In that case, because the DEA estimate of the production function minimizes each ϵ_j, it thereby maximizes each $f(\epsilon_j)$. Hence, the DEA frontier $g^*(x)$ maximizes the likelihood function subject to the constraints specified herein.

It should be noted, however, that the DEA estimator of the frontier production function is biased. Suppose that the *true* frontier production function is $g(x)$. Thus, the maximum output producible from some observed input bundle is $g(x^0)$ and the DEA estimator is $g^*(x^0)$. As shown previously, $g(x^0) \geq g^*(x^0) = y_0^*$. Define $\delta_0 = g(x^0) - g^*(x^0) \geq 0$. We have assumed that the inefficiency residuals are identically distributed. Then, for any $\Delta > 0$, the probability that for any observation j,

$$\Pr(\epsilon_j < \Delta) = \int_0^\Delta f(\epsilon) \, d\epsilon = F(\Delta). \tag{12.5}$$

Thus, the probability that any realized ϵ_j is at least as large as Δ is $1 - F(\Delta)$.

Next, let $\epsilon_{\min} = \min_j\{\epsilon_j; j = 1, 2, \ldots, N\}$. If $\epsilon_{\min} > \Delta$, then each $\epsilon_j > \Delta$. The probability that each $\epsilon_j > \Delta$ simultaneously is $[1 - F(\Delta)]^N$. Consider the DEA solution for the input bundle x^0,

$$y_0^* = \sum_{j=1}^N \lambda_j^* y_j = \sum_{j=1}^N \lambda_j^* [g(x^j) - \epsilon_j]. \tag{12.6}$$

But $g(x)$ is a monotonically increasing and concave function. Hence, $\sum_{j=1}^N \lambda_j^* g(x^j) \leq g(\sum_{j=1}^N \lambda_j^* x^j)$.

Further, $\sum_{j=1}^N \lambda_j^* x^j \leq x^0$. Also, $\sum_{j=1}^N \lambda_j^* \epsilon_j \geq \sum_{j=1}^N \lambda_j^* \epsilon_{\min} = \epsilon_{\min}$. Hence,

$$\delta_0 = g(x^0) - g^*(x^0) \geq \epsilon_{\min} \tag{12.7a}$$

and

$$\Pr\{\delta_0 > \Delta\} \geq \Pr\{\epsilon_{\min} > \Delta\} = [1 - F(\Delta)]^N. \tag{12.7b}$$

An implication of this inequality is that if $F(\Delta) < 1$ for $\Delta = 0$, then the DEA estimator is biased.

It can be shown, however, that the DEA estimator is weakly consistent. Consider the relation $y = g(x) - \epsilon$ for $x \in X$, where X is a compact subset of R_+^n. Assume that the input bundle x and the inefficiency component ϵ are independently distributed. The input vector x has the multivariate probability density function $h(x) > 0$ for all $x \in X$. Also, the density function of ϵ satisfies

$$f(\epsilon) = 0 \quad \text{for } \epsilon < 0 \quad \text{and} \quad F(\epsilon) = \int_{-\infty}^{\epsilon} f(t)\,dt > 0 \quad \text{for all } \epsilon > 0.$$

Initially, consider the single-input case. Because the function $g(x)$ is continuous, for any value of x, say x_0, in the interior of the domain of the function, for any arbitrary $\Delta > 0$ there exists a $\delta > 0$ such that for all $x \in (x_0 - \delta, x_0 + \delta)$, $g(x) \in (g(x_0) - \Delta, g(x_0) + \Delta)$. Hence, for all values of x in the interval $(x_0 - \delta, x_0 + \delta)$, $g(x) > g(x_0) - \Delta$. Now, consider a randomly drawn observation (x, y) where $y = g(x) - \epsilon$. As already assumed, x is distributed independently of ϵ and has some density function $h(.)$. The probability that x lies in the interval $(x_0 - \delta, x_0)$ is

$$\Pr\{x \in (x_0 - \delta, x_0)\} = \int_{x_0-\delta}^{x_0} h(x) \quad dx > 0. \tag{12.8}$$

Moreover, because $g(x) > g(x_0) - \Delta$ for $x \in (x_0 - \delta, x_0)$ and $F(\epsilon) > 0$ for all $\epsilon > 0$, it follows that

$$\Pr\{\epsilon < g(x) - g(x_0) + \Delta\} > 0. \tag{12.9}$$

Define the event $A_1 = \{x \in (x_0 - \delta, x_0) \text{ and } \epsilon < g(x) - g(x_0) + \Delta\}$. Because x and ϵ are independently distributed, the joint probability that $x \in (x_0 - \delta, x_0)$ and, at the same time, $\epsilon < g(x) - g(x_0) + \Delta$ is the product of the probabilities of these two independent events. Call this joint probability p_1. Clearly, $p_1 > 0$. Now, define the event, $A_2 = \{x \in (x_0, x_0 + \delta) \text{ and } \epsilon < g(x) - g(x_0) + \Delta\}$. By similar reasoning, the probability of the event A_2 is $\Pr(A_2) = \Pr\{x \in (x_0, x_{0+\delta})\} \cdot \Pr\{\epsilon < g(x) - g(x_0) + \Delta\} = p_2 > 0$. Next, consider a sample of N independent observations. Clearly, the probability that event A_1 does not occur for any observation is $(1 - p_1)^N$. Similarly, the probability that event A_2 does not occur for any observation in the sample is $(1 - p_2)^N$. Now suppose that both of the events A_1 and A_2 occur for at least one observation each in the sample. In particular, there are two observations (x_1, y_1) and (x_2, y_2), such that $x_1 \in (x_0 - \delta, x_0)$ and $x_2 \in (x_0, x_0 + \delta)$ while both y_1 and y_2 are greater than $g(x_0) - \Delta$. In this case, the DEA estimator $g_N^*(x_0)$ based on the specific sample of size N must be at least as large as min $\{y_1, y_2\}$. This implies that $g_N^*(x_0) > \min\{y_1, y_2\} > g(x_0) - \Delta$. Hence, $g(x_0) - g_N^*(x_0) < \Delta$. Thus, the probability that $g(x_0) - g_N^*(x_0) < \Delta$ is the probability that the events A_1 and A_2 occur for less than all of the N observations in the sample. Hence, $\Pr\{g(x_0) - g_N^*(x_0) < \Delta\} \leq (1 - p_1)^N + (1 - p_2)^N$. Clearly, this probability goes to 0 as N goes to ∞. This can be formally expressed as

$$\lim_{N \to \infty} \Pr\{|g(x_0) - g_N^*(x_0)| > \Delta\} = 0. \tag{12.10}$$

In other words, the DEA estimator $g_N^*(x_0)$ is weakly consistent. It is important to note at this point that we need not impose any special restrictions on the probability density function $f(\epsilon)$. In particular, we do not need to assume that $f(\epsilon)$ is monotonically decreasing in ϵ. Extension of this consistency result to the multiple-input case is quite straightforward. Now, we need to consider an open ball with radius δ such that $g(x) > g(x_0) - \Delta$ for all input bundles x satisfying $\|x - x^0\| < \Delta$ and note that there is a positive probability that an observation (x, y) will be such that x is in a specific orthant (relative to x^0) of the open ball with $y > g(x^0) - \Delta$. An implication of the consistency of the DEA estimator $g_N^*(x)$ is that for any given $\Delta > 0$ and any realized pair (x^j, y_j),

$$\lim_{N \to \infty} \Pr\left\{\epsilon_j - \epsilon_j^{*(N)} > \Delta\right\} = 0. \tag{12.11}$$

Thus, the DEA residual ϵ_j^* based on a sample of size N is asymptotically distributed as the true ϵ_j itself. In particular, if the ϵ_j's have the exponential or the half-normal distribution, the DEA residual $\epsilon_j^{*(N)}$ will also be so distributed in large samples.

Banker has proposed a number of statistical tests for comparing two groups of firms to assess whether one group is more efficient than the other. Assume that there are N firms in the sample of which m_1 are in group 1 and m_2 are in group 2. Firms in group 1 have the exponential distribution of (in)efficiency ϵ_j with parameter σ_1 and those in group 2 also have the exponential distribution but with parameter σ_2. Designate the first group of firms as M_1 and the second group as M_2. Consider the DEA residuals $\epsilon_j^*(j = 1, \ldots, N)$. Under the maintained hypothesis,

$$\sum_{j \in M_i} \frac{\epsilon_j^*}{\sigma_i}$$

has the χ^2 distribution with $2m_i$ $(i = 1, 2)$ degrees of freedom.

Under the null hypothesis $\sigma_1 = \sigma_2$, the test statistic

$$F = \frac{\sum\limits_{j \in M_1} \epsilon_j^* \Big/ m_1}{\sum\limits_{j \in M_2} \epsilon_j^* \Big/ m_2} \tag{12.12}$$

has the F distribution with $(2m_1, 2m_2)$ degrees of freedom.

On the other hand, if the ϵ_j's have the half-normal distribution, $\sum_{j \in M_1} \left(\frac{\epsilon_j^*}{\sigma_1} \right)^2$ has the χ^2 distribution with m_1 degrees of freedom. Similarly, $\sum_{j \in M_2} \left(\frac{\epsilon_j^*}{\sigma_2} \right)^2$ has the χ^2 distribution with m_2 degrees of freedom. Hence, in this case, under the null hypothesis $\sigma_1 = \sigma_2$, the statistic

$$F = \frac{\sum\limits_{j \in M_1} (\epsilon_j^*)^2 \Big/ m_1}{\sum\limits_{j \in M_2} (\epsilon_j^*)^2 \Big/ m_2} \qquad (12.13)$$

has the F distribution with (m_1, m_2) degrees of freedom.

12.3 Chance-Constrained DEA

The production function estimated by DEA is a deterministic frontier. For any input bundle x^0, the value of the DEA estimate $g^*(x^0)$ defines the maximum output producible from x^0 under all circumstances. In this sense, it is comparable to the parametric frontier with one-sided deviations estimated using mathematical programming methods by Aigner and Chu (1968). In econometric analysis also, Richmond (1974) specified a log gamma distribution of the stochastic component of the output to formulate a deterministic production frontier. Any deviation of the observed output from this frontier output is, by implication, ascribed to inefficiency. It is common knowledge, however, that shortfalls in actual output from the benchmark can be due to a variety of random factors beyond the control of and unrelated to the efficiency of the firm. For example, poor rainfall in farming or unexpected machine breakdown in manufacturing may result in low output. In fact, the stochastic frontier production function introduced independently by Aigner, Lovell, and Schmidt (1977) and Meeusen and van den Broeck (1977) allows the frontier to move up or down because of random influences that may be either favorable or detrimental. This is achieved through a composite stochastic term that is the sum of a two-sided and a one-sided disturbance term. The two-sided term captures random shifts in the frontier either up or down. The one-sided term, on the other hand, corresponds to the level of technical efficiency of the firm. Note that the actual output must always lie below the frontier that is relevant for the firm given the realized value of the random shock. It is, nonetheless, possible that the actual output, in spite of inefficiency, would lie above the *average frontier* that corresponds to a zero realized value of the random shock. Thus, the *average frontier* does not necessarily envelop all of the observed points in the sample.

Land, Lovell, and Thore (1993) modified the standard DEA model to measure technical efficiency in the presence of random variation in the output produced from a given input bundle. Their chance-constrained DEA model builds on the method of chance-constrained programming (CCP) developed by Charnes and Cooper (1963). The essence of a CCP model is that it allows a positive (although low) probability that one or more inequality restrictions will be violated at the optimal solution of the problem.

Consider, as usual, the input–output observation $(x^j, y_j)(j = 1, 2, \ldots, N)$. As in econometric analysis, assume that the inputs are deterministic while the output is random. This implies that a convex combination of the output quantities associated with the corresponding convex combination of the input bundles will also be randomly variable. As a result, the boundary of the free disposal convex hull of the observed input–output bundles will define a random frontier. Hence, the restriction involving the output quantities in the DEA model will be a random inequality that may at times be violated. Because an inequality involving a number of random variables can never be imposed with certainty, the strategy in CCP is to ensure that the probability that the inequality holds for a random sample of these variables does not fall below a certain level.

The chance-constrained output-oriented BCC DEA model for firm k can be specified as follows:

$$\max \phi$$

$$\text{s.t. } \Pr\left\{\sum_{j=1}^{N}\lambda_j y_j \geq \phi y_k\right\} \geq (1 - \alpha);$$

$$\sum_{j=1}^{N}\lambda_j x^j \leq x^k; \tag{12.14}$$

$$\sum_{j=1}^{N}\lambda_j = 1; \quad \lambda_j \geq 0 \, (j = 1, 2, \ldots, N).$$

At this point, assume that each output y_j is normally distributed with mean μ_j and variance σ_j^2. Further assume that $\text{Cov}(y_i, y_j) = 0$. Now, define the random variable

$$u = \sum_{j=1}^{N}\lambda_j y_j - \phi y_k. \tag{12.15}$$

Then,

$$E(u) = \sum_{j=1}^{N} \lambda_j \mu_j - \phi \mu_k \equiv \mu_u \tag{12.16a}$$

and

$$\mathrm{Var}(u) = \sum_{j=1,j\neq k}^{N} \lambda_j^2 \sigma_j^2 + (\lambda_k - \phi)^2 \sigma_k^2 \equiv \sigma_u^2. \tag{12.16b}$$

Because the y_j's have the normal distribution, so does the variable u. Therefore, the variable

$$z = \frac{u - \mu_u}{\sigma_u}$$

has the standard normal distribution. Hence,

$$\Pr\left\{ \sum_{j=1}^{N} \lambda_j y_j \geq \phi y_k \right\} = \Pr\{u \geq 0\} = \Pr\left\{ z \geq \frac{-\mu_u}{\sigma_u} \right\}. \tag{12.17}$$

But, because of the symmetry property of the normal distribution,

$$\Pr\left\{ z \geq \frac{-\mu_u}{\sigma_u} \right\} = \Pr\left\{ z \leq \frac{\mu_u}{\sigma_u} \right\} = \Phi\left(\frac{\mu_u}{\sigma_u} \right), \tag{12.18}$$

where $\Phi(.)$ is the cumulative standard normal distribution function. Thus, the random inequality restriction in the chance-constrained DEA problem can be replaced by the equivalent restriction

$$\Phi\left(\frac{\mu_u}{\sigma_u} \right) \geq (1 - \alpha). \tag{12.19}$$

Suppose that we set α at the conventional level of 0.05. That is, we require the inequality restriction involving the outputs to hold with probability 95% or higher. The critical value of the standard normal distribution at the 5% level of significance is 1.96. Thus, the previous inequality becomes

$$\mu_u \geq 1.96 \sigma_u. \tag{12.20}$$

That is,

$$\sum_{j=1}^{N} \lambda_j \mu_j - \phi \mu_k \geq 1.96 \sqrt{ \sum_{j=1,j\neq k}^{N} \lambda_j^2 \sigma_j^2 + (\lambda_k - \phi)^2 \sigma_k^2 }. \tag{12.21}$$

The revised DEA problem can be specified as

$$\max \phi$$

$$\text{s.t.} \sum_{j=1}^{N} \lambda_j \mu_j \geq \phi \mu_k + 1.96 \sqrt{\sum_{j=1, j \neq 1}^{N} \lambda_j^2 \sigma_j^2 + (\lambda_k - \phi)^2 \sigma_k^2};$$

$$\sum_{j=1}^{N} \lambda_j x^j \leq x^k; \tag{12.22}$$

$$\sum_{j=1}^{N} \lambda_j = 1; \quad \lambda_j \geq 0 \ (j = 1, 2, \ldots, N).$$

This, of course, is a nonlinear programming problem and one needs to apply an appropriate solution algorithm. We do not attempt that in this chapter. Several features of this problem may be highlighted, however. First, instead of the observed output quantities of the firms, one uses the expected values of the output levels. Additionally, we need information about the variances of the random output levels. Further, we have assumed $\text{Cov}(y_i, y_j) = \sigma_{ij} = 0$. If that is not the case, the variance of u would have to be suitably modified to include the σ_{ij}'s. On the other hand, if we assume that $\sigma_{ij} = 0$ and also that $\sigma_j^2 = \sigma^2$ for all j, the output restriction becomes

$$\sum_{j=1}^{N} \lambda_j \mu_j \geq \phi \mu_k + 1.96\sigma \sqrt{\sum_{j=1, j \neq k}^{N} \lambda_j^2 + (\lambda_k - \phi)^2} \tag{12.23}$$

and the value of only one additional parameter (namely σ) will be needed. In fact, the assumption of constant variance and absence of covariance is quite standard in the econometric production frontier literature and may quite reasonably be made in the present context as well. In practical applications, ideally one would like to collect repeated data for each firm over a short period of time (e.g., over several months within a quarter) so that the input bundle of the firm remains (more or less) unchanged and variation in the observed output is due to random factors. One may use the sample mean of the output data of a firm j as a measure of μ_j. Deviations of the observed outputs of firms from the firm means can be utilized to estimate a pooled variance as a measure of σ^2.

Another interesting point may be noted. Suppose that the outputs of all of the firms were observed at their mean values so that $y_j = \mu_j$ for each observation j. But, it is known that $\sigma_j^2 = \sigma^2 \neq 0$. In that case, the output inequality restriction in the chance-constrained DEA problem becomes

$$\sum_{j=1}^{N}\lambda_j y_j - 1.96\sigma \sqrt{\sum_{j=1,j\neq k}^{N} \lambda_j^2 + (\lambda_k - \phi)^2} \geq \phi y_k. \quad (12.24)$$

Note that the presence of the negative term on the left-hand side of the inequality implies that compared to the basic BCC DEA model, the chance-constrained DEA effectively uses a production frontier that is shifted inwards and, therefore, results in a lower optimal value of ϕ.

12.4 Varian's Statistical Test of Consistency with the WACM

It was shown in Chapter 10 that unless the observed economic behavior of a firm is consistent with the WACM, the firm under consideration cannot have been minimizing cost. Varian (1985) proposed a statistical test of consistency of the data with WACM when the observed input quantities in the data set are random. Such random elements in the input data may be introduced, for example, by measurement errors. The randomness may also arise from the fact that the firm may not have complete control over the input quantities chosen. As a result, the actual input quantities may differ from the desired quantities. When the observed input quantities are random, the proper test of WACM should involve the *true* (or *desired*) input quantities. The problem, of course, is that the *true* quantities are not known and one must use the observed input quantities. Varian proposed a χ^2 type test of WACM for this case.

Suppose that the observed input bundle of firm j is $x^j = (x_{1j}, x_{2j}, \ldots, x_{nj})$ and its true but unobserved input bundle is $z^j = (z_{1j}, z_{2j}, \ldots, z_{nj})$. The output produced by the firm is y_j and the vector of input prices paid by the firm is $w^j = (w_{1j}, w_{2j}, \ldots, w_{nj})$. Similarly, the true input bundle of firm i is z^i and the output produced is y_i. Then, the behavior of firm j is consistent with WACM only when $w^{j'}z^j \leq w^{j'}z^i$ whenever $y_j \leq y_i$. Now, suppose that

$$x_{kj} = z_{kj} + \epsilon_{kj}, \quad (12.25)$$

where the random error ϵ_{kj} has the normal distribution with mean 0 and variance σ^2 for each input k ($k = 1, 2, \ldots, n$) and all firms j ($j = 1, 2, \ldots, N$). Now, consider the test statistic

$$T = \sum_{j=1}^{N}\sum_{k=1}^{n} \frac{(x_{kj} - z_{kj})^2}{\sigma^2}. \quad (12.26)$$

If the true input quantities were observable, then under the null hypothesis, this statistic would have the χ^2 distribution with $m \cdot n$ degrees of freedom. Suppose that the critical value of the χ^2 distribution at the significant level α for the relevant degrees of freedom is C_α. Then, the null hypothesis would be rejected if the test statistic T exceeded C_α. Of course, T is not observable. We do not know either the *true* input quantities (z_{kj}'s) or the variance σ^2. There is, nevertheless, a way to define a *lower bound* on T for a test of cost-minimizing behavior through WACM.

Consider the following quadratic programming (QP) problem:

$$\min S = \sum_{j=1}^{N} \sum_{k=1}^{n} (x_{kj} - z_{kj})^2$$

$$\text{s.t.} \quad \sum_{k=1}^{n} w_{kj} z_{kj} \leq \sum_{k=1}^{n} w_{kj} z_{ki} \quad (\text{for } y_j \leq y_i) \qquad (12.27)$$

$$z_{kj} \geq 0 \, (k = 1, 2, \ldots, n; j = 1, 2, \ldots, N).$$

Note that because

$$T = \frac{S}{\sigma^2}, \quad \text{if } S < \sigma^2 C_\alpha, \quad \text{then} \quad T < C_\alpha.$$

Of course, without *a priori* knowledge of σ^2, this test cannot be applied in practice. But it is possible to perform this test conditionally on some assumed value of σ^2. Suppose that for some specific data set the optimal value of S is S_0^*. Then, the data would be consistent with WACM for a given value of the variance σ_0^2 if $S_0^* < \sigma_0^2 C_\alpha$. Alternatively, the minimum value of σ^2, for which the data would be consistent with WACM, is $\sigma_*^2 = \frac{S_0^*}{C_\alpha}$. Note that a low value of the variance σ^2 implies lower noise in the data so that violation of WACM is less likely to be due to random variation in the observed input quantities. On the other hand, if the variance is large, the probability that violation of WACM is due to random noise in the observed input data will be higher. In any empirical application, if any prior measure of σ^2 is available, one would compare that with the critical value σ_*^2. Otherwise, one needs to decide whether the degree of possible noise in the data would be consistent with a value of the variance greater than σ_*^2.

The fact that a value of the variance parameter has to be specified *a priori* in order to perform this test does not make it any more demanding in terms of data requirement than chance-constrained DEA. After all, a value of the variance of the output quantities also must be specified. But the assumption that the random components in all of the inputs have the same variance is rather strong. In most cases, some inputs are more controllable and/or are better measured than other inputs. This argues for differences in the variance across inputs. At the computational level, the problem quickly becomes quite unwieldy with even a moderate sample size and a limited number of inputs. For example, with 50 firms and only 5 inputs, there are 250 decision variables in the QP problem. Finally, it is a test of consistency of *the entire data set* with WACM and says nothing about individual firm behavior.

12.5 Bootstrap

The idea of the bootstrap[1] was first introduced by Efron (1979), who proposed the use of computer-based simulations to obtain the sampling properties of random variables. The starting point of any bootstrap procedure is a sample of observed data $X = \{x_1, x_2, \dots, x_n\}$ drawn randomly from some population with an unknown probability distribution f. The basic assumption behind the bootstrap method is that the random sample actually drawn "mimics" its parent population.

Suppose that a sample of observed data $X = \{x_1, x_2, \dots, x_n\}$ is drawn randomly from some population with an unknown probability distribution f. The sample statistic $\hat{\theta} = \theta(X)$ computed from this state of observed values is merely an estimate of the corresponding population parameter $\theta = \theta(f)$. When it is not possible to analytically derive the sampling distribution of that statistic, one examines its empirical density function. Unfortunately, however, the researcher has access to only one sample rather than multiple samples drawn from the same population. As noted before, the basic assumption behind the bootstrap method is that the random sample actually drawn "mimics" its parent population. Therefore, if one draws a random sample with replacement from the observed values in the original sample, it can be treated like a sample drawn from the underlying population itself. Repeated samples with replacement yield different values of the sample statistic under investigation and the associated empirical distribution (over these samples) can provide the sampling distribution of this statistic. For reasons explained later, this is known as a *naïve bootstrap*.

The bootstrap sample $X^* = \{x_1^*, x_2^*, \dots, x_n^*\}$ is an unordered collection of n items drawn randomly from the original sample X with replacement, so that any $x_i^*(i = 1, 2, \dots, n)$ has $1/n$ probability of being equal to any $x_j(j = 1, 2, \dots, n)$. Some observations from the original sample X may not appear

[1] Materials in this and the next section are based on Desli (1999).

in the bootstrap sample, while other observations may drawn repeatedly. Let $\hat{f}$ denote the empirical density function of the observed sample X from which X^* was drawn. Then, it can take the form

$$\hat{f}(t) = \begin{cases} 1/n & \text{if } t = x_i^*, \ i = 1, 2, \ldots, n \\ 0 & \text{otherwise} \end{cases}. \tag{12.28}$$

If $\hat{f}$ is a consistent estimator of f, then the bootstrap distributions will mimic the original unknown sampling distributions of the estimators that we are interested in. Let $\hat{\theta}^* = \theta(X^*)$ be the estimated parameter from the bootstrap sample X^*. Then, the distribution of $\hat{\theta}^*$ around $\hat{\theta}$ in $\hat{f}$ is the same as that of $\hat{\theta}$ around θ in f. That is,

$$(\hat{\theta}^* - \hat{\theta}) \,|\, \hat{f} \sim (\hat{\theta} - \theta) \,|\, f. \tag{12.29}$$

Because every time that we replicate the bootstrap sample we get a different sample X^*, we will also get a different estimate of $\hat{\theta}^* = \theta(X^*)$. Thus, we need to select a large number of bootstrap samples, B, in order to extract as many combinations of $x_j \, (j = 1, 2, \ldots, n)$ as possible. The bootstrap algorithm has the following steps:

i) Compute the statistic $\hat{\theta} = \theta(X)$ from the observed sample X.
ii) Select bth $(b = 1, 2, \ldots, B)$ independent bootstrap sample X_b^*, which consists of n data values drawn with replacement from the observed sample X.
iii) Compute the statistic $\hat{\theta}^* = \theta(X_b^*)$ from the bth bootstrap sample X_b^*.
iv) Repeat steps (ii)–(iii) a large number of times (say, B times).
v) Calculate the average of the bootstrap estimates of θ as the arithmetic mean

$$\hat{\theta}^*(\cdot) = \frac{1}{B} \sum_{b=1}^{B} \hat{\theta}_b^*. \tag{12.30}$$

A measure of the accuracy of an estimator $\hat{\theta}$ of the parameter θ is the bias measure

$$\text{bias}_f = \text{bias}_f(\hat{\theta}, \theta) = E_f(\hat{\theta}) - \theta. \tag{12.31}$$

The bias-corrected estimator is

$$\hat{\theta}_{\text{bc}} = \hat{\theta} - \text{bias}_f. \tag{12.32}$$

The bias of the bootstrap estimator $\hat{\theta}_b^* \ (b = 1, 2, \ldots, B)$ as an estimate of $\hat{\theta}$ can be measured as $\text{bias}_{\hat{f}} = E_{\hat{f}}(\hat{\theta}_b^*) - \hat{\theta}$, where we use the average of the bootstrap estimators $\hat{\theta}^*(\cdot)$ for the expectation of each bootstrap estimator $\hat{\theta}_b^*$. The estimated bias of the bootstrap estimator based on B replications is

$$\text{bias}_B = \hat{\theta}^*(\cdot) - \hat{\theta}. \tag{12.33}$$

Taking bias$_B$ as an estimate for the unknown bias$_f$, the bias-corrected estimator of θ is

$$\hat{\theta}_{\text{bc}} = \hat{\theta} - \text{bias}_B = 2\hat{\theta} - \hat{\theta}^*(\cdot). \tag{12.34}$$

The intuition behind this is quite simple. It is believed that if $\hat{\theta}^*(.)$ overestimates (underestimates) the statistic $\hat{\theta}$ from the original sample, then $\hat{\theta}$ itself also overestimates (underestimates) the true population parameter θ. Thus, if $\hat{\theta}^*(\cdot)$ is greater than $\hat{\theta}$, then the bias-corrected estimate $\hat{\theta}_{\text{bc}}$ should be less than the sample statistic $\hat{\theta}$.

Efron and Tibshirani (1993) point out that bias correction can be problematic in some situations. Even if $\hat{\theta}_{\text{bc}}^*$ is less biased than $\hat{\theta}$, it might have substantially greater standard error due to high variability in bias$_B$. The standard error of $\hat{\theta}^*(\cdot)$ is measured as

$$\text{se}_B = \text{se}(\hat{\theta}^*) = \sqrt{\frac{1}{B-1} \sum_{b=1}^{B} (\hat{\theta}_b^* - \hat{\theta}^*(\cdot))^2}. \tag{12.35}$$

Correcting for the bias may result in a larger root-mean-squared error. If bias$_B$ is small compared to the estimated standard error of $\hat{\theta}^*(\cdot)$, then it is safer to use $\hat{\theta}$ than $\hat{\theta}_{\text{bc}}$. As a rule of thumb, Efron and Tibshirani (1993) suggest the computation of the ratio of the estimated bootstrap bias to standard error, bias$_B$/se$_B$. If the ratio does not exceed 0.25, bias correction may not be recommended.

The corrected empirical density function of $\hat{\theta}_b^*$, $(b = 1, 2, \ldots, B)$ should be centered around $\hat{\theta}_{\text{bc}}$, the bias-corrected estimate of θ, that is $E(\hat{\theta}_{b,\text{bc}}^*) = \hat{\theta}_{\text{bc}}$ $(b = 1, 2, \ldots, B)$, where the bias-corrected estimate from each bootstrap is

$$\hat{\theta}_{b,\text{bc}}^* = \hat{\theta}_b^* - 2\,\text{bias}_B, \quad (b = 1, 2, \ldots, B). \tag{12.36}$$

Once we have the bias-corrected estimates, we can use the percentile method to construct the $(1 - 2a)\%$ confidence intervals for θ as

$$\left(\hat{\theta}_{\text{bc}}^{*(a)}, \hat{\theta}_{\text{bc}}^{*(1-a)}\right), \quad (b = 1, 2, \ldots, B), \tag{12.37}$$

where $\hat{\theta}_{\text{bc}}^{*(a)}$ is the (100^*ath) percentile of the empirical density of $\hat{\theta}_{b,\text{bc}}^*$ $(b = 1, 2, \ldots, B)$.

One major drawback of the bootstrap procedure outlined is that even when sampling with replacement, a bootstrap sample will not include observations from the parent population that were not drawn in the initial sample. The empirical distribution $\hat{f}$ is effectively a histogram that looks like a collection of boxes of width h, a small number, centered at the observations and zero anywhere else. Thus, the bootstrap samples are effectively drawn from a discrete population and they fail to reflect the fact that the underlying population density function f is continuous. Hence, the empirical distribution from the bootstrap samples as they were drawn in this section is an inconsistent estimator of the population density function. This is why it is known as a naïve bootstrap.

12.5.1 Smooth Bootstrap Methodology
One way to overcome this problem is to use kernel estimators as weight functions. The empirical distribution $\hat{f}$ will take the form

$$\hat{f}(t) = \frac{1}{nh} \sum_{i=1}^{n} K\left(\frac{t - x_i}{h}\right), \qquad (12.38)$$

where h is the window width or smoothing parameter for the density function. $K(.)$ is a kernel function, which satisfies the condition

$$\int_{-\infty}^{\infty} K(x)\,dx = 1. \qquad (12.39)$$

Usually, K is a symmetric probability density function like the normal density function. If we use the standard normal density function as the kernel density function, then the smoothing is called *Gaussian smoothing*. The empirical density function then can be written as

$$\hat{f}(t) = \frac{1}{nh} \sum_{i=1}^{n} \phi\left(\frac{t - x_i}{h}\right). \qquad (12.40)$$

Here, $\phi(.)$ is the standard density function.

By virtue of the convolution theorem (Efron and Tibshirani, 1993), we can generate the smoothed bootstrap sample $X^{**} = \{x_1^{**}, x_2^{**}, \ldots, x_n^{**}\}$ as

$$x_i^{**} = x_i^{*} + h\,\epsilon_i \sim f; \quad i = 1, 2, \ldots, n, \qquad (12.41)$$

where x_i^{*} is from the naïve bootstrap sample in the previous section.

Sometimes it is the case that the natural domain of the definition of the density function to be estimated is not the whole real line but an interval bounded on one side or both sides. For example, we might be interested in obtaining density estimates $\hat{f}$ for which $\hat{f}(x)$ is zero for all negative x. One possible way to solve this problem is to calculate $\hat{f}(x)$ ignoring the boundary restrictions and then to set the empirical density function equal to zero for values of x that are out of the boundary domain. A drawback of this approach is that the estimates of the empirical density function will no longer integrate to unity.

Silverman (1986) suggests the use of the negative reflection technique to handle such problems. Suppose that we are interested in values of x such that $x \geq \alpha$. If the resulting value from the bootstrap is $x_i^{**} < \alpha$, then we will reflect the x_i^{**}, such that $2\alpha - x_i^{**} \geq \alpha$. The empirical density function will be

$$\hat{f}(t) = \frac{1}{nh} \sum_{i=1}^{n} \left[\phi \left(\frac{t - x_i}{h} \right) + \phi \left(\frac{t - 2\alpha + x_i}{h} \right) \right]. \tag{12.42}$$

Again, by the convolution theorem, we can generate the smoothed bootstrap sample $X^{**} = \{x_1^{**}, x_2^{**}, \ldots, x_n^{**}\}$ as

$$x_i^{**} = \begin{cases} x_i^* + h\epsilon_i \quad \sim \frac{1}{nh} \sum_{i=1}^{n} \phi \left(\frac{t - x_i}{h} \right) & \text{if } x_i^* + h\epsilon_i \geq \alpha \\ \\ 2\alpha - (x_i^* + h\epsilon_i) \quad \sim \frac{1}{nh} \sum_{i=1}^{n} \phi \left(\frac{t - 2\alpha + x_i}{h} \right) & \text{otherwise,} \end{cases}$$

$$\tag{12.43}$$

where x_i^* is from the naïve bootstrap sample in the previous section.

Choice of the smoothing parameter (h) is crucial to the estimated empirical density function. Following Silverman (1986), we can select the value of the window width that minimizes the approximate mean integrated square error. This leads to

$$h = 0.9An^{-1/5}, \tag{12.44}$$

where $A = \min$ (standard deviation of X, interquartile range of $X/1.34$).

The bootstrap algorithm can be rewritten as follows:

i) Compute the statistic $\hat{\theta} = \theta(X)$ from the observed sample X.
ii) Select bth $(b = 1, 2, \ldots, B)$ independent naive bootstrap sample $X_b^* = \{x_{1,b}^*, x_{2,b}^*, \ldots, x_{n,b}^*\}$, which consists of n data values drawn with replacement from the observed sample X.
iii) Construct the smoothed bootstrap sample $X_b^{**} = \{x_{1,b}^{**}, x_{2,b}^{**}, \ldots, x_{n,b}^{**}\}$, from the naïve bootstrap sample.
vi) Compute the statistic $\hat{\theta}^* = \theta(X_b^*)$ from the bth bootstrap sample X_b^*.

v) Repeat steps (ii)–(iii) a large number of times (say, B times).
vi) Calculate the average of the bootstrap estimates of θ as the arithmetic mean

$$\hat{\theta}^*(\cdot) = \frac{1}{B} \sum_{b=1}^{B} \hat{\theta}_b^*. \tag{12.45}$$

We can now calculate the bias and bias-corrected estimates and construct confidence intervals following the same steps described in Section 12.5.

12.6 DEA and Bootstrap

Simar (1992) and Simar and Wilson (1998a, 1998b) set the foundation for the consistent use of bootstrap techniques to generate empirical distributions of efficiency scores and have developed tests of hypotheses relating to returns to scale of bootstrapping. Following Simar and Wilson (1997a), we can describe the existing bootstrap techniques for the output-oriented technical efficiency measure given in (1.32) with the following algorithm:

i) Solve the DEA problem to obtain $\hat{\phi}_j$ for each DMU $j = 1, 2, \ldots, n$.
ii) Select the bth ($b = 1, 2, \ldots, B$) independent naïve bootstrap sample $\{\phi_{1,b}^*, \phi_{2,b}^*, \ldots, \phi_{n,b}^*\}$, which consists of n data values drawn with replacement from the estimated values $\hat{\phi}_j$s.
iii) Construct the smoothed bootstrap sample $\{\phi_{1,b}^{**}, \phi_{2,b}^{**}, \ldots, \phi_{nb}^{**}\}$ from the naïve bootstrap sample. Notice that all the ϕ_js are greater than or equal to 1. Therefore, the smoothed bootstrap sample should be appropriately bounded. It will be computed according to

$$\phi_{j,b}^{**} = \begin{cases} \phi_j^* + h\epsilon_j & \text{if } \phi_j^* + h\epsilon_j \geq 1; \quad \text{for } j = 1, 2, \ldots, n. \\ 2 - (\phi_j^* + h\epsilon_j) & \text{otherwise} \end{cases}$$

$$\tag{12.46}$$

As before, h is the optimal width that minimizes the approximate mean integrated square error of $\hat{\phi}_j$'s distribution, given by $h = 0.9An^{-1/5}$, where $A = \min$ (standard deviation of ϕ, interquartile range of $\phi/1.34$).
iv) Create the bth pseudo-data set as $\{(x^{j*}, y_j^* = y_j\hat{\phi}_j/\phi_j^{**}); j = 1, 2, \ldots, n\}$.
v) Use the pseudo-data set to compute new $\hat{\phi}_j^*$s.
vi) Repeat steps (ii)–(iv) B times to obtain $\{\hat{\phi}_{j,b}^*; b = 1, 2, \ldots, B\}$ for each DMU j, $j = 1, 2, \ldots, n$.
vii) Calculate the average of the bootstrap estimates of ϕ's, the bias, and the confidence intervals as they are described in the previous section.

It should be noted here that an interpretation of the results obtained from the bootstrap procedure is not always clear. For example, in the bth replication using the pseudo-data consisting of the actual input bundles coupled with the fictitious output levels of firms, the optimal solution φ^* shows that the scalar expansion factor for the fictitious output quantity and its inverse *is not a measure of the efficiency of the actual input–output bundle.* It is possible that the actual input–output bundle may lie above the production frontier constructed from the pseudo-data obtained in any one bootstrap sample. One may, of course, use the optimal solutions from the (bootstrap) DEA problems to construct measures of the *frontier output level* producible from the fixed input bundle of a firm. Thus, it is more meaningful to construct a 95% confidence interval of the maximum output with lower and upper bounds $[y_L^*, y_U^*]$. In principle, the upper bound (y_U^*) may be used to derive a probabilistic measure of the technical efficiency of an observed input–output bundle. It should be noted that the actually observed output from a given input bundle may exceed its corresponding upper bound.

12.7 Summary

When a deterministic frontier is conceptualized, all deviation of any observed input–output bundle from the output-oriented projection onto the frontier is treated as inefficiency. As shown by Banker, the DEA efficiency scores yield consistent measures of inefficiency relative to a deterministic frontier and one may employ F tests for hypothesis testing. The chance-constrained programming approach to DEA considers a two-sided normal distribution for the random component in the output and replaces the probabilistic inequality constraint on the output in a DEA model by its certainty equivalent. Varian's approach provides a statistical test of WACM conditional on a specified value of the variance of the random error in the inputs. The bootstrap approach generates an empirical density function for the DEA efficiency score of any firm, constructing a confidence interval of desired width for its efficiency. This approach has gained wide acceptance in the literature and has virtually become the new orthodoxy. As noted previously, the bootstrap efficiency measures should be interpreted carefully.

Guide to the Literature

In the parametric literature, Aigner and Chu (1968) formulated the mathematical programming models for a nonstatistical production frontier. Building on

Afriat (1972), Richmond (1974) specified the one-sided (log) gamma distribution of the disturbance term in the linear-regression model for a frontier production function. In the nonparametric literature, Timmer (1971) extended Farrell's original model and tried to accommodate random noise in the output data by excluding a number of efficient observations and recomputing the Farrell efficiency of the remaining firms. Banker's F tests parallel Richmond's deterministic frontier analysis.

Aigner, Lovell, and Schmidt (1977) and Meeusen and van den Broeck (1977) proposed the stochastic production frontier. For an excellent survey of this parametric strand of production-efficiency literature, see Greene (1993). The recent book on stochastic frontier models by Kumbhakar and Lovell (2000) is an excellent reference and a required reading for understanding the voluminous and rich literature in this area. Banker and Maindiratta (1992) proposed a maximum-likelihood procedure for pointwise estimation of a concave and montone stochastic production frontier using mathematical programming.

Chance-constrained LP was introduced by Charnes and Cooper (1963). Land, Lovell, and Thore (1993) applied chance-constrained programming to DEA. Further extensions of this approach can be found in Olesen and Petersen (1995) and Cooper, Huang, Li, and Olesen (1998).

The bootstrap approach was introduced by Simar (1992) and further developed by Simar and Wilson (1998a). For a survey of the DEA bootstrap literature, see Simar and Wilson (2000).

The various two-stage DEA regression models provide yet another method of handling the presence of random factors along with nondiscretionary factors where relevant. Gstach (1998) and Banker, Janakiraman, and Natarajan (2002) impose restrictions on the probability distribution of the random disturbance. Fried, Lovell, Schmidt, and Yaiswarng (2002) propose a three-stage procedure that uses input–output variables to perform DEA in the first stage, performs a stochastic frontier analysis on the total (radial plus nonradial) slacks in the individual inputs in the second stage, and utilizes an adjusted set of input quantities that are purged of the effects of variation in nondiscretionary inputs for another DEA in the third stage.

Triantis and Girod (1998) combine DEA and fuzzy parametric programming to handle random measurement errors in input and output data. Sengupta (1987) uses the nonparametric Kolmogrov–Smirnov tests for hypothesis testing in the context of DEA. For a selective survey of various stochastic approaches to DEA, see Grosskopf (1996).

13

Looking Ahead

Over the past quarter of a century since its inception, Data Envelopment Analysis has burgeoned into a rich and luxuriant field of research within the broad area of productivity and efficiency analysis. Valuable contributions in the form of new models, creative extensions of existing models, and innovative empirical applications to new areas continuously add to the voluminous literature. In such a vibrant and dynamic context, no book on the subject of DEA can remain current or up to date very long.

As stated at the outset, the objective of this book was to familiarize the reader with the economic foundations of the various DEA models that are currently available and widely used in the literature which, in turn, should make the technical details of the relevant mathematical programming models more easily understandable. With the background provided in this book, the interested reader should be able to follow the new contributions appearing in various journals without much difficulty.

The major outlets for research in DEA include, among others, *Management Science*, *European Journal of Operational Research*, *Journal of Productivity Analysis*, and *Socio-Economic Planning Sciences*. In particular, *Journal of Productivity Analysis* (under the editorship of Knox Lovell) has played a significant role in bridging the gap between the economics and OR/MS strands on the one hand and the stochastic frontier and DEA practitioners on the other. The North American and European Productivity Workshops held in alternate years on the two sides of the Atlantic provide an important forum for intellectual exchange between researchers in the field of productivity and efficiency analysis. Indeed, many of the most influential papers in the field were first articulated in preliminary form in these meetings.

We conclude this book with the following short list of open questions in DEA that remain unfinished business before the researchers.

- Despite the growing popularity of the bootstrap procedure, DEA in the presence of random errors in inputs or outputs is not by any measure as well developed as the alternative parametric approach of stochastic frontier analysis. Even in the DEA literature, there is no major application of the bootstrap procedure in the context of cost minimization.
- Presence of input and/or output slacks at the optimal solution of a BCC or CCR DEA model undermines the economic validity of a radial measure of technical efficiency. Moreover, the need to choose an input- or an output-orientation is an added constraint. The directional distance function and other graph efficiency measures do eliminate the orientation problem. But slacks may still remain at the optimal projection.
- Standard DEA models are essentially one-period problems and efficiency is computed from current inputs and outputs only. In reality, however, inputs often contribute to outputs over multiple production periods. In the parametric literature, intertemporal models are quite common. Comparable models are not yet well developed in the DEA literature.
- Input and output data for efficiency evaluation are often reported as aggregates at the regional level. For example, in many studies, states or even countries are treated as individual firms. Similarly, outputs may be aggregated over individual goods or inputs aggregated over individual factors. Lastly, the data may be reported as aggregates over several production periods. Effects of such different types of aggregation on measured efficiency remain to be carefully analyzed.

It is only to be expected that future research in DEA will address these and other unresolved questions.

References

Afriat, S. N. (1967) "The Construction of Utility Functions from Expenditure Data," *International Economic Review* 8:1 (February) 67–77.

Afriat, S. N. (1972) "Efficiency Estimation of Production Functions," *International Economic Review* 13:3 (October) 568–98.

Aigner, D. J., and S. F. Chu (1968) "On Estimating the Industry Production Function," *American Economic Review* 58:4 (September) 826–39.

Aigner, D. J., C. A. K. Lovell, and P. Schmidt (1977) "Formulation and Estimation of Stochastic Frontier Production Function Models," *Journal of Econometrics* 6:1, 21–37.

Ali, A. I. "Computational Aspects of DEA," in A. Charnes, W. W. Cooper, A. Lewin, and L. Seiford (1994), eds., *Data Envelopment Analysis: Theory, Methodology, and Application.* Boston: Kluwer Academic Publishers, 63–88.

Ali, A. I., and L. M. Seiford (1990) "Translation Invariance in Data Envelopment Analysis," *Operations Research Letters* 9, 403–5.

Andersen, P., and N. C. Petersen (1993) "A Procedure for Ranking Efficient Units in Data Envelopment Analysis," *Management Science* 39, 1261–64.

Balk, B. (1993) "Malmquist Productivity Indexes and Fisher Productivity Indexes: Comment," *Economic Journal* 103, 680–2.

Balk, B. (2001) "Scale Efficiency and Productivity Change," *Journal of Productivity Analysis* 15:3 (May) 159–83.

Banker, R. D. (1984) "Estimating the Most Productive Scale Size Using Data Envelopment Analysis," *European Journal of Operational Research* 17: 1 (July) 35–44.

Banker, R. D. (1993) "Maximum Likelihood, Consistency, and Data Envelopment Analysis: A Statistical Foundation," *Management Science* 39, 1265–73.

Banker, R. D., H. Chang, and W. W. Cooper (1996) "Equivalence and Implementation of Alternative Methods of Determining Returns to Scale in Data Envelopment Analysis," *European Journal of Operational Research* 89, 583–5.

Banker, R. D., and A. Maindiratta (1988) "Nonparametric Analysis of Technical and Allocative Efficiencies in Production," *Econometrica* 56:5 (November) 1315–32.

Banker, R. D., and A. Maindiratta (1992) "Maximum Likelihood Estimation of Monotone Convex Production Frontiers," *Journal of Productivity Analysis* 3, 401–15.

Banker, R. D., A. Charnes, and W. W. Cooper (1984) "Some Models for Estimating Technical and Scale Inefficiencies in Data Envelopment Analysis," *Management Science* 30:9 (September) 1078–92.

Banker, R. D., and R. C. Morey (1986a) "Efficiency Analysis for Exogenously Fixed Inputs and Outputs," *Operations Research* 34:4 (July–August) 513–21.

Banker, R. D., and R. C. Morey (1986b) "The Use of Categorical Variables in Data Envelopment Analysis," *Management Science* 32:12 (December) 1613–27.

Banker, R. D., S. Janakiraman, and R. Natarajan (2002) "Evaluating the Adequacy of Parametric Functional Forms in Estimating Monotonic and Concave Production Functions," *Journal of Productivity Analysis* 17:1/2, 111–32.

Banker, R. D., and R. M. Thrall (1992) "Estimating Most Productive Scale Size Using Data Envelopment Analysis," *European Journal of Operational Research* 62, 74–84.

Baumol, W. J., J. C. Panzar, and R. D. Willig (1982) *Contestable Markets and the Theory of Industry Structure.* New York: Harcourt Brace Jovanovich.

Bjurek, H. (1996) "The Malmquist Total Factor Productivity Index," *Scandinavian Journal of Economics* 98, 303–13.

Bogetoft, P., and D. Wang (1996) "Estimating the Potential Gains from Mergers," Paper Presented at the Third Georgia Productivity Workshop held in Athens, GA.

Boles, J. N. (1967) "Efficiency Squared – Efficient Computation of Efficiency Indexes," *Western Farm Economic Association, Proceedings* 1966, Pullman, Washington, pp. 137–42.

Bressler, R. G. (1967) "The Measurement of Productive Efficiency," *Western Farm Economic Association, Proceedings* 1966, Pullman, Washington, pp. 129–36.

Brockett, P. L., W. W. Cooper, Y. Wang, and H. C. Shin. (1998) "Congestion and Inefficiency in Chinese Production Before and After the 1978 Economic Reforms," *Socio-Economic Planning Sciences* 32, 1–20.

Brown, W. G. (1967) Discussion of Papers presented on "Production Functions and Productive Efficiency: The Farrell Approach," *Western Farm Economic Association, Proceedings* 1966, Pullman, Washington, pp. 159–61.

Byrnes, P., R. Färe, and S. Grosskopf (1984) "Measuring Productive Efficiency: An Application to Illinois Strip Mines," *Management Science* 30:6 (June) 671–81.

Caves, D. W., L. R. Christensen, and E. Diewert (1982) "The Economic Theory of Index Numbers of the Measurement of Input, Output, and Productivity," *Econometrica* 50:6 (November) 1393–414.

Caves, D. W., L. R. Christensen, and M. W. Trethaway (1984) "Economies of Density versus Economies of Scale: Why Trunk and Local Service Airline Costs Differ," *The RAND Journal of Economics,* Vol. 15, Issue 4, 471–89.

Chambers, R. G., Y. Chung, and R. Färe (1996) "Benefit and Distance Functions," *Journal of Economic Theory* 70 (August 1996) 407–19.

Charnes, A., and W. W. Cooper (1963) "Deterministic Equivalents for Optimizing and Satisficing under Chance Constraints," *Operations Research* 11, 18–39.

Charnes, A., and W. W. Cooper (1962) "Programming with Linear Fractional Functionals," *Naval Research Logistics Quarterly* 9, 181–186.

Charnes, A., W. W. Cooper, B. Golany, L. M. Seiford, and J. Steetz (1985) "Foundations of Data Envelopment Analysis for Pareto–Koopmans Efficient Empirical Production Functions," *Journal of Econometrics*, 30 (1/2), 91–107.

Charnes, A., W. W. Cooper, Z. M. Huang, and D. B. Sun (1990) "Polyhedral Cone Ratio DEA Models with an Illustrative Application to Large Commercial Banks," *Journal of Econometrics* 46(1–2), 73–91.

Charnes, A., W. W. Cooper, A. Lewin, and L. Seiford (1994), eds., *Data Envelopment Analysis: Theory, Methodology, and Application*. Boston: Kluwer Academic Publishers.

Charnes, A., W. W. Cooper, and E. Rhodes (1978) "Measuring the Efficiency of Decision Making Units," *European Journal of Operational Research* 2:6 (November) 429–44.

Charnes, A., W. W. Cooper, and E. Rhodes (1979) "Short Communication: Measuring the Efficiency of Decision Making Units," *European Journal of Operational Research* 3:4, 339.

Charnes, A., W. W. Cooper, and E. Rhodes (1981) "Evaluating Program and Managerial Efficiency: An Application of Data Envelopment Analysis to Program Follow Through," *Management Science,* 27(6): 668–97.

Charnes, A. C., W. W. Cooper, and T. Sueyoshi (1988) "A Goal Programming/ Constrained Regression Review of the Bell System Breakup," *Management Science* 34, 1–26.

Charnes, A., W. W. Cooper, Q. L. Wei, and Z. M. Huang (1989) "Cone Ratio Data Envelopment Analysis and Multi-Objective Programming," *International Journal of Systems Science* 20:7, 1099–118.

Chavas, J. P., and T. L. Cox (1999) "A Generalized Distance Function and the Analysis of Production Efficiency," *Southern Economic Journal* 66:2, 294–318.

Cherchye, L., T. Kuosomanen, and T. Post (2000) "What Is the Economic Meaning of FDH? A Reply to Thrall," *Journal of Productivity Analysis* 13, 263–7.

Christensen, L. R., and W. H. Greene (1976) "Economies of Scale in U.S. Electric Power Generation," *Journal of Political Economy* 84:4, 655–76.

Coelli, T. (1998) "A Multi-Stage Methodology for the Solution of Orientated DEA Models," *CEPA Working Paper* No. 1/98, Department of Econometrics, University of New England, Arimdale, Australia.

Coelli, T., E. Griffel-Tatje, and S. Perelman (2002) "Capacity Utilization and Profitability: A Decomposition of Short-Run Profit Efficiency," *International Journal of Production Economics* 79, 261–78.

Coelli, T., D. S. P. Rao, and G. Battese (1998) *An Introduction to Efficiency and Productivity Analysis*. Boston: Kluwer Academic Publishers.

Cooper, W. W., Z. Huang, S. X. Li, and O. Olesen (1998) "Chance Constrained Programming Formulations for Stochastic Characterizations of Efficiency and Dominance in DEA," *Journal of Productivity Analysis* 9, 53–79.

Cooper, W. W., K. S. Park, and J. T. Pastor (1999) "RAM: A Range Adjusted Measure of Inefficiency for Use with Additive Models and Relation to Other Models and Measure in DEA," *Journal of Productivity Analysis* 11, 5–42.

References

Cooper, W. W., and J. T. Pastor (1995) "Global Efficiency Measurement in DEA," *Working Paper, Depto Estee Inv. Oper.*, Universidad Alicante, Alicante, Spain.

Cooper, W. W., L. Seiford, and K. Tone (2000) *Data Envelopment Analysis: A Comprehensive Text with Uses, Example Applications, References and DEA-Solver Software* (Norwell, Mass.: Kluwer Academic Publishers).

Debreu, G. (1951) "The Coefficient of Resource Utilization," *Econometrica* 19:3 (July) 273–92.

Denney, M., M. A. Fuss, and L. Waverman (1981) "The Measurement and Interpretation of Total Factor Productivity in Regulated Industries with Applications in Canadian Telecommunications," in T. Cowing and R. Stevenson, eds., *Productivity Measurement in Regulated Industries* (New York: Academic Press).

Deprins, D., L. Simar, and H. Tulkens (1984) "Labor–Efficiency in Post Offices," in M. Marchand, P. Pestieau, and H. Tulkens, eds., *The Performance of Public Enterprises: Concepts and Measurement*. North Holland: Elsevier Science Publications B. V., 243–67.

Desli, E. (1999) "Estimation of Technical Efficiency in Parametric and Nonparametric Production Frontiers," Ph.D. Thesis, University of Connecticut, Storrs, CT 06269.

Diewert, W. E. (1992a) "Fisher Ideal Output, Input, and Productivity Indexes Revisited," *Journal of Productivity Analysis* 3, 211–48.

Diewert, W. E. (1992b) "The Measurement of Productivity," *Bulletin of Economic Research* 44, 163–98.

Diewert, W. E., and C. Parkan (1983) "Linear Programming Tests of Regularity Conditions for Production Frontiers," in W. Eichorn, R. Henn, K. Neumann, and R. W. Shephard, eds., *Quantitative Studies in Production and Prices* (Würzburg: Physica-Verlag).

Dorfman, R. P., A. Samuelson, and R. Solow (1958) *Linear Programming and Economic Analysis*. New York: McGraw–Hill.

Dulá, J. H., and B. L. Hickman (1997) "Effects of Excluding the Column Being Scored from the DEA Envelopment LP Technology Matrix," *Journal of the Operational Research Society* 48, 1001–12.

Dyson, R. G., and E. Thanassoulis (1988) "Reducing Weight Flexibility in Data Envelopment Analysis," *Journal of the Operational Research Society* 39:6, 563–76.

Efron, Bradley, and Robert J. Tibshirani. (1993) *An Introduction to the Bootstrap.* New York: Chapman Hall, Inc.

Evans, D. S., and J. J. Heckman (1983) "Multiproduct Cost Function Estimates and Natural Monopoly Tests for the Bell System," in D. S. Evans, ed., *Breaking Up Bell* (Amsterdam: Elsevier Science Publishers).

Färe, R. (1986) "Addition and Efficiency," *Quarterly Journal of Economics* 101:4 (November) 861–66.

Färe, R., and S. Grosskopf (1983) "Measuring Congestion in Production," *Zietschrift für Nationalökonomie;* 43, 253–71.

Färe, R., and S. Grosskopf (1992) "Malmquist Productivity Indexes and Fisher Productivity Indexes," *Economic Journal* 102, 158–60.

Färe, R., and S. Grosskopf (2000) "Theory and Application of Directional Distance Functions," *Journal of Productivity Analysis* 13, 93–103.

Färe, R., S. Grosskopf, B. Lindgren, and P. Roos (1992) "Productivity Changes in Swedish Pharmacies 1980–1989: A Nonparametric Malmquist Approach," *Journal of Productivity Analysis* 3:1/2 (June) 85–101.

Färe, R., and C. A. K. Lovell (1978) "Measuring the Technical Efficiency of Production," *Journal of Economic Theory* 19:1 (October) 150–62.

Färe, R., S. Grosskopf, and C. A. K. Lovell (1985) *The Measurement of Efficiency of Production*. Boston: Kluwer–Nijhoff.

Färe, R., S. Grosskopf, and C. A. K. Lovell (1987) "Nonparametric Disposability Tests," *Zeitschrift für Nationalöikonomie* 47:1, 77–85.

Färe, R., S. Grosskopf, and C. A. K. Lovell (1994) *Production Frontiers*. Cambridge: Cambridge University Press.

Färe, R., S. Grosskopf, C. A. K. Lovell, and C. Pasurka (1989) "Multilateral Productivity Comparisons When Some Outputs Are Undesirable: A Non-parametric Approach," *Review of Economics and Statistics* 71:1 (February) 90–8.

Färe, R., S. Grosskopf, C. A. K. Lovell, and S. Yaiswarng (1993) "Derivation of Virtual Prices for Undesirable Outputs: A Distance Function Approach," *Review of Economics and Statistics,* 75(2), 374–80.

Färe, R., S. Grosskopf, M. Norris, and Z. Zhang (1994) "Productivity Growth, Technical Progress, and Efficiency Change in Industrialized Countries," *American Economic Review* 84, 66–83.

Färe, R., S. Grosskopf, and M. Norris (1997) "Productivity Growth, Technical Progress, and Efficiency Change in Industrialized Countries: Reply," *American Economic Review,* 87(5), 1040–4.

Färe, R., and D. Primont (1995) *Multi-Output Production and Duality: Theory and Applications* (Boston: Kluwer Academic Press).

Färe, R., S. Grosskopf, S. C. Ray, S. M. Miller, and K. Mukherjee (2000) "Difference Measures of Profit Inefficiency: An Application to U.S. Banks," Conference on Banking and Finance, Miguel Hernandez University, Elche, Spain (May 2000).

Färe, R., S. Grosskopf, and P. Roos (1998) "Malmquist Productivity Indexes: A Survey of Theory and Practice," in R. Färe, S. Grosskopf, and R. Russell eds., *Index Numbers: Essays in Honor of Sten Malmquist* (Boston: Kluwer Academic Press) 127–90.

Färe, R., and L. Svensson (1980) "Congestion of Production Factors," *Econometrica* 48:7 (November) 1745–53.

Farrell, M. J. (1957) "The Measurement of Technical Efficiency," *Journal of the Royal Statistical Society* Series A, General, 120, Part 3, 253–81.

Farrell, M. J., and M. Fieldhouse (1962) "Estimating Efficient Production Functions Under Increasing Returns to Scale," *Journal of the Royal Statistical Society* Series A, General, 125, Part 2, 252–67.

Førsund, F. R. (1997) "The Malmquist Productivity Index, TFP, and Scale," 5th European Workshop on Productivity and Efficiency Analysis, Copenhagen, Denmark (October).

Førsund, F. R., and L. Hjalmarsson (1979) "Generalized Farrell Measures of Efficiency: An Application to Milk Processing in Swedish Dairy Plants," *Economic Journal* 89 (June) 294–315.

Førsund, F. R., and N. Sarafoglou (2002) "On the Origins of Data Envelopment Analysis," *Journal of Productivity Analysis* 17:1/2, 23–40.

Fried, H., C. A. K. Lovell, S. Schmidt, and S. Yaiswarng (2002) "Accounting for Environmental Effects and Statistical Noise in Data Envelopment Analysis," *Journal of Productivity Analysis*, 17(1/2), 157–74.

Frisch, R. (1965) *Theory of Production*. Chicago: Rand McNally.

Georgescu-Roegen, N. "The Aggregate Linear Production Function and Its Application to von-Neumann's Economic Model," in T. C. Koopmans, ed., *Activity Analysis of Production and Allocation*, Cowles Commission for Research in Economics, Monograph No. 13. New York: Wiley.

Gilbert, R. A., and P. Wilson (1998) "Effects of Deregulation on the Productivity of Korean Banks," *Journal of Economics and Business*, 50:2, 133–55.

Greene, W. (1980) "Maximum Likelihood Estimation of Econometric Frontier Functions," *Journal of Econometrics*, 13, 101–15.

Greene, W. (1993) "Frontier Production Functions" in *The Measurement of Productive Efficiency*, H. Fried, K. Lovell, and S. Schmidt eds., New York: Oxford University Press.

Grifell-Tatjé, E., and C. A. K. Lovell (1995) "A Note on the Malmquist Productivity Index," *Economics Letters*, 47, 169–75.

Grosskopf, S. (1986) "The Role of the Reference Technology in Measuring Productive Efficiency," *Economic Journal* 96 (June) 499–513.

Grosskopf, S. (1996) "Statistical Inference and Nonparametric Efficiency: A Selective Survey," *Journal of Productivity Analysis* 7: 2/3, 139–60.

Gstach, D. (1998) "Another Approach to Data Envelopment Analysis in Noisy Environments: DEA+," *Journal of Productivity Analysis* 9, 161–76.

Hanoch, G., and M. Rothschild (1972) "Testing the Assumption of Production Theory: A Nonparametric Approach," *Journal of Political Economy* 80:2 (March/April), 256–75.

Harker, P. T., and M. Xue (2002) "Note: Ranking DMUs with Infeasible Super-Efficiency DEA Models," *Management Science* 48, 705–10.

Hotelling, H. (1932) "Edgeworth's Paradox and the Nature of Supply and Demand Functions," *Political Economy* 40, 577–616.

Kniep, A., and L. Simar (1996) "A General Framework for Frontier Estimation with Panel Data," *Journal of Productivity Analysis* 7, 187–212.

Koopmans, T. C. (1951) "An Analysis of Production as an Efficient Combination of Activities," in T. C. Koopmans, ed., *Activity Analysis of Production and Allocation*, Cowles Commission for Research in Economics, Monograph No. 13. New York: Wiley.

Kumbhakar, S., and C. A. K. Lovell (2000) *Stochastic Frontier Analysis* (New York: Cambridge University Press).

Land, K. C., C. A. K. Lovell, and S. Thore (1993) "Chance-Constrained Data Envelopment Analysis," *Managerial and Decision Economics*.

Lovell, C. A. K. (1993) "Production Frontiers and Productive Efficiency" in H. Fried, C. A. K. Lovell, and S. Schmidt, eds., *The Measurement of Productive Efficiency: Techniques and Application* (New York: Oxford University Press), 3–67.

Lovell, C. A. K. (1994) "Linear Programming Approaches to the Measurement and Analysis of Production Efficiency," *TOP,* 2:2, 175–224.

Lovell, C. A. K. (2001) "The Decomposition of Malmquist Productivity Indexes," Working Paper, Department of Economics, University of Georgia, Athens, GA, 30206, U.S.A.

Lovell, C. A. K., and J. T. Pastor (1995) "Units Invariant and Translation Invariant DEA Models," *Operations Research Letters* 18, 147–51.

Lovell, C. A. K., and A. P. B. Rouse (2003) "Equivalent Standard DEA Models to Provide Super-Efficiency Scores," *Journal of the Operational Research Society* 54(1) 101–8.

Lovell, C. A. K., L. C. Walters, and L. L. Wood (1994) "Stratified Models of Education Production Using Modified DEA and Regression Analysis," in A. Charnes, W. W. Cooper, A. Lewin, and L. Seiford (1994), eds., *Data Envelopment Analysis: Theory, Methodology, and Application* (Boston: Kluwer Academic Publishers) 329–52.

Luenberger, D. G. (1992) "Benefit Functions and Duality," *Journal of Mathematical Economics* 21, 461–81.

Maindiratta, A. (1990) "Largest Size-Efficient Scale and Size Efficiencies of Decision-Making Units in Data Envelopment Analysis," *Journal of Econometrics* 46, 39–56.

Meeusen, W., and J. van den Broeck (1977) "Efficiency Estimation from Cobb–Douglas Production Functions with Composed Errors," *International Economic Review* 18:2, 435–44.

Nadiri, M. I., and M. A. Schankerman (1981) "The Structure of Production, Technological Change, and Rate of Growth of Total Factor Productivity in the U.S. Bell System," in T. Cowing and R. Stevenson, eds., *Productivity Measurement in Regulated Industries* (New York: Academic Press).

Nishimizu, M., and J. E. Page, Jr. (1982) "Total Factor Productivity Growth, Technological Progress, Technical Efficiency Change: Dimensions of Productivity Change in Yugoslavia 1965–78," *The Economic Journal* 92, 920–36.

Olesen, O., and N. C. Petersen (1995) "Chance Constrained Efficiency Evaluation," *Management Science* 41, 442–57.

Orea, L. (2002) "Parametric Decomposition of a Generalized Malmquist Productivity Index," *Journal of Productivity Analysis* 18(1), 5–22.

Panzar, J. C., and R. D. Willig (1977) "Economies of Scale in Multi-Output Production," *Quarterly Journal of Economics* 91:3, 481–93.

Park, B. U., and L. Simar (1994) "Efficient Semiparametric Estimation in a Stochastic Frontier Model," *Journal of the American Statistical Association* 89, 929–36.

Park, S. U., and J. B. Lesourd (2000) "The Efficiency of Conventional Fuel Power Plants in South Korea: A Comparison of Parametric and Nonparametric Approaches," *International Journal of Production Economics* 63, 59–67.

Pastor, J. T., J. L. Ruiz, and I. Sirvent (1999) "An Enhanced DEA Russell-Graph Efficiency Measure," *European Journal of Operational Research* 115, 596–607.

Ray, S. C. (1988) "Data Envelopment Analysis, Non-Discretionary Inputs and Efficiency: An Alternative Interpretation," *Socio–Economic Planning Sciences* 22:4, 167–76.

Ray, S. C. (1997) "A Weak Axiom of Cost Dominance: Nonparametric Measurement of Cost Efficiency without Input Quantity Data," *Journal of Productivity Analysis* 8, 151–65.

Ray, S. C. (1998) "Measuring Scale Efficiency from a Translog Production Function," *Journal of Productivity Analysis* 11, 183–94.

Ray, S. C. (2000). "Pareto-Koopmans Measures of Efficiency in Management Education: How Well Managed Are America's Top-40 Business Schools?" Paper presented at the North American Productivity Workshop held at Union College, Schenectady, NY.

Ray, S. C., and H. J. Kim (1995) "Cost Efficiency in the U.S. Steel Industry: A Nonparametric Analysis Using DEA," *European Journal of Operational Research* 80:3, 654–71.

Ray, S. C., and D. Bhadra (1993) "Nonparametric Tests of Cost-Minimizing Behavior: A Study of Indian Farms," *American Journal of Agricultural Economics* 73 (November) 990–9.

Ray, S. C., and K. Mukherjee (1996) "Decomposition of the Fisher Ideal Index of Productivity: A Nonparametric Dual Analysis of U.S. Airlines Data," *The Economic Journal* 106:439, 1659–78.

Ray, S. C., and K. Mukherjee (1998a) "Quantity, Quality, and Efficiency from a Partially Super-additive Cost Function: Connecticut Public Schools Revisited," *Journal of Productivity Analysis* 10: 47–62 (July) 1998.

Ray, S. C., and K. Mukherjee (1998b) "A Study of Size Efficiency in U.S. Banking: Identifying Banks That Are Too Large," *International Journal of Systems Science* 29:11, 1281–94.

Ray, S. C., and X. Hu (1997) "On the Technically Efficient Organization of an Industry: A Study of U.S. Airlines," *Journal of Productivity Analysis* 8, 5–18.

Ray, S. C., and E. Desli (1997) "Productivity Growth, Technical Progress, and Efficiency Change in Industrialized Countries: Comment," *American Economic Review* 87:5 (Dec) 1033–9.

Richmond, J. (1974) "Estimating the Efficiency of Production," *International Economic Review* 15, 515–21.

Roll, Y., W. D. Cook, and B. Golany (1991) "Controlling Factor Weights in Data Envelopment Analysis," *IEEE Transactions* 23:1, 2–9.

Roll, Y., and B. Golany (1993) "Alternative Methods of Treating Factor Weights in DEA," *Omega* 21:1, 99–109.

Russell, R. (1985) "Measures of Technical Efficiency," *Journal of Economic Theory* 35, 109–26.

Samuelson, P. A. (1948) "Consumption Theory in Terms of Revealed Preference," *Econometrica* 15, 243–53.

Seiford, L. R. (1994) "A DEA Bibliography 1978–1992," in A. Charnes, W. W. Cooper, A. Lewin, and L. Seiford, eds., *Data Envelopment Analysis: Theory, Methodology, and Application* (Boston: Kluwer Academic Publishers) 437–70.

Seiford, L. R., and J. Zhu (1999) "Infeasibility of Super–Efficiency Data Envelopment Analysis Models," *INFOR* 37:2, 174–87.

Seitz, W. D. (1967) "Efficiency Measurement for Steam-Electric Generating Plants," *Western Farm Economic Association, Proceedings* 1966, Pullman, WA, 143–51.

Seitz, W. D. (1971) "Productive Efficiency in Steam-Electric Generating Industry," *Journal of Political Economy* 79, 879–86.

Sengupta, J. K. (1987) "Data Envelopment Analysis for Efficiency Measurement in the Stochastic Case," *Computers and Operations Research* 14, 117–29.

Shephard, R. W. (1953), *Cost and Production Functions* (Princeton: Princeton University Press).

Shephard, R. W. (1974) *Indirect Production Functions*. Mathematical Systems in Economics, 10, Meisenheim Am Glan: Verlag Anton Hain.

Silverman, B. W. (1986) *Density Estimation for Statistics and Data Analysis*. London: Chapman and Hall.

Simar, L. (1992) "Estimating Efficiencies from Frontier Models with Panel Data: A Comparison of Parametric, Non-Parametric, and Semi-Parametric Methods with Bootstrapping," *Journal of Productivity Analysis* 3:1/2, 167–203.

Simar, L., and P. Wilson (1998a) "Sensitivity Analysis of Efficiency Scores: How to Bootstrap in Nonparametric Frontier Models," *Management Science* 44:11, 49–61.

Simar, L., and P. Wilson (1998b) "Nonparametric Tests of Returns to Scale," Discussion Paper #9814, Institut de Statistic and C. O. R. E. Université Catholique de Louvain, Louvain-la-Neuve, Belgium.

Simar, L., and P. Wilson (2000) "Statistical Inference in Nonparametric Frontier Models: The State of the Art," *Journal of Productivity Analysis* 13, 49–78.

Sitorus, B. L. (1967) "Productive Efficiency and Redundant Factors of Production in Traditional Agriculture of Underdeveloped Countries: A Note on Measurement," *Western Farm Economic Association, Proceedings* 1966, Pullman, WA, 153–58.

Starrett, D. A. (1977) "Measuring Returns to Scale in the Aggregate, and the Scale Effect of Public Goods," *Econometrica* 45:6, 1439–55.

Stigler, G. J. (1976) "The Xistence of X-Efficiency," *American Economic Review* 66:1 (March) 213–16.

Sturrock. (1957) "Discussion on Mr. Farrell's Paper," *Journal of the Royal Statistical Society* Series A, General, 120:3, 285.

Taveres, G. (2002) *A Bibliography of Data Envelopment Analysis (1978–2001)*. RUT-COR Research Report RRR 01-02 (January), Rutgers University, Piscatway, NJ.

Theil, H. (1971) *Principles of Econometrics* (New York: John Wiley and Sons).

Thompson, R. G., L. N. Langemeier, C. Lee, E. Lee, and R. M. Thrall (1990) "The Role of Multiplier Bounds in Efficiency Analysis with Application to Kansas Farming," *Journal of Econometrics*, 46:1,2; 93–108.

Thompson, R. G., F. D. Singleton, Jr., R. M. Thrall, and B. Smith (1986) "Comparative Site Evaluation for Locating a High Energy Physics Lab in Texas," *Interfaces* 16:6, 35–49.

Thrall, R. M. (1999) "What Is the Economic Meaning of FDH?," *Journal of Productivity Analysis* 11, 243–50.

Timmer, C. P. (1971) "Using a Probabilistic Frontier Production Function to Measure Technical Efficiency," *Journal of Political Economy* 79, 776–94.

Torgersen, A. M., F. R. Førsund, and S. A. C. Kittelsen (1996) "Slack-Adjusted Efficiency Measures and Ranking of Efficient Units," *Journal of Productivity Analysis* 7:4, 379–98.

Triantis, K., and O. Girod (1998) "A Mathematical Programming Approach for Measuring Technical Efficiency in a Fuzzy Environment," *Journal of Productivity Analysis* 10, 85–102.

Tulkens, H. (1993) "On FDH Analysis: Some Methodological Issues and Applications to Retail Banking, Courts, and Urban Transit," *Journal of Productivity Analysis* 4, 183–210.

Van den Eeckaut, P., H. Tulkens, and M-A. Jamar (1993) "Cost Efficiency in Belgian Municipalities," in H. O. Fried, C. A. K. Lovell, and S. Schmidt, eds., *The Measurement of Productive Efficiency: Techniques and Applications* (New York: Oxford University Press).

Varian, H. R. (1984) "The Nonparametric Approach to Production Analysis," *Econometrica* 52:3 (May) 579–97.

Varian, H. R. (1985) "Nonparametric Analysis of Optimizing Behavior with Measurement Error," *Journal of Econometrics,* 30, 445–58.

Varian, H. R. (1990) "Goodness-of-Fit in Optimizing Models," *Journal of Econometrics* 46, 125–40.

Wheelock, D. C., and P. Wilson. (1999) "Technical Progress, Inefficiency, and Productivity Change in U.S. Banking, 1984–1993," *Journal of Money, Credit, and Banking* 31:2 (May), 212–34.

Wilson, P. (1993) "Detecting Influential Observations in Data Envelopment Analysis," *Journal of Productivity Analysis* 6, 27–46.

Winsten, C. B. (1957) "Discussion on Mr. Farrell's Paper," *Journal of the Royal Statistical Society* Series A, General, 120:3, 282–4.

Zieschang, K. (1985) "An Extended Farrell Efficiency Measure," *Journal of Economic Theory* 33, 387–96.

Zofio, J. L., and C. A. K. Lovell (1997) "Yet Another Malmquist Productivity Index Decomposition," Sixth European Workshop on Efficiency and Productivity Analysis, Copenhagen, Denmark (October).

Index

Note to Index: (ex) after a page number denotes an exhibit; (fig) after a page number denotes a figure; (tab) after a page number denotes a table.

Printed in the United States
By Bookmasters